W9-DII-942

Gramley Library
Salem Academy and College
Winston-Salem, N.C. 27108

Heroes & States

Heroes & States

On the Ideology of Restoration Tragedy

J. DOUGLAS CANFIELD

Gramley Library
Salem Academy and College
Winston-Salem, N.C. 27108

The University Press of Kentucky

Publication of this volume was made possible in part
by grants from the University of Arizona and the National Endowment
for the Humanities.

Copyright © 2000 by The University Press of Kentucky

Scholarly publisher for the Commonwealth,
serving Bellarmine College, Berea College, Centre
College of Kentucky, Eastern Kentucky University,
The Filson Club Historical Society, Georgetown College,
Kentucky Historical Society, Kentucky State University,
Morehead State University, Murray State University,
Northern Kentucky University, Transylvania University,
University of Kentucky, University of Louisville,
and Western Kentucky University.
All rights reserved

Editorial and Sales Offices: The University Press of Kentucky
663 South Limestone Street, Lexington, Kentucky 40508-4008

04 03 02 01 00 5 4 3 2 1

Frontispiece: Andrea del Castagno's *The Youthful David,* Widener Collection, Photograph © 1999 Board of Trustees, National Gallery of Art, Washington.

Library of Congress Cataloging-in-Publication Data

Canfield, J. Douglas (John Douglas), 1941-
Heroes and states : on the ideology of Restoration tragedy /
J. Douglas Canfield.
p. cm.
Continues: Tricksters & estates.
Includes bibliographical references (p.) and index.
ISBN 0-8131-2125-6
1. English drama—Restoration, 1660-1700—History and criticism.
2. English drama (Tragedy)—History and criticism. 3. Politics and
literature—Great Britain—History—17th century. 4. Political
plays, English—History and criticism. 5. Nationalism in
literature. 6. State, The, in literature. 7. Heroes in literature.
I. Title.
PR698.T7C36 1999
822'.05120904—dc21 99-13693

This book is printed on acid-free recycled paper
meeting the requirements of the American National Standard
for Permanence of Paper for Printed Library Materials.

Manufactured in the United States of America

For Michael McKeon

Contents

Preface vii

Introduction 1

1. Heroes and States: Heroic Romance 6

2. Villains and States: Romantic Tragedy 26

3. Fathers and Sons: Political Tragedy 41

4. States of Mind: Personal Tragedy 60

5. Apocalypse Now: Tragical Satire 78

6. States and Estates: Tragicomic Romance 114

7. Dramatic Shifts: Shifting Tropes of Ideology in Revolutionary Tragedy 145

Conclusion 199

Notes 201

Bibliography 216

Index 228

Index of Characters 239

Preface

This is a book about the ideology of Restoration tragedy, with a glance at ideological shifts in tragedy from late Stuart to early Georgian. Together with *Tricksters and Estates: On the Ideology of Restoration Comedy,* it constitutes a cultural history of English drama from 1660 to 1690 and beyond.

Why study Restoration tragedy? Because, taken together with Restoration comedy, it constitutes a record of the negotiation of ruling-class ideology through a major cultural institution or state apparatus, the theater. The theater during the Restoration was, first of all, restored, allowed to flourish after its closure by the Puritans of the Commonwealth. And flourish it did, fully supported by the restored royal family and its court. As we have learned through theater history, the audience was not just a court coterie. It included gentry visiting or residing in the city, the "middling sort" from haute to petite bourgeoisie, and even members of the servant class, waiting for their masters and mistresses, and members of the lower class, who came to ply their wares from oranges to sex.

Restoration theater was analogous not to our theater but to our movie houses in its cultural impact. And if contemporary audiences could not purchase videocassettes, they could purchase cheap quartos of the plays produced. If gentry could not get up to town to see a play, they could read it in their parlor (thus the trope—in novels and in plays themselves—of the romantic young lady reading a filthy play that might corrupt her morals). The cultural impact of Restoration drama was enormous.

So anyone interested in the cultural history of England during the Restoration, as well as the eighteenth century, as well as the Renaissance, for that matter, must study this central cultural phenomenon of the theater and its drama: the way it embodies values, meanings, power relations; the way witty playwrights can manipulate and even subvert official ideology; the way theater, then, does not just represent but constitutes, along with other cultural institutions, the value and belief systems of an entire culture.

But are any of these tragedies, as opposed to the delightful comedies, worth reading for aesthetic pleasure? Aesthetics is a vexed term, especially in relation to history. Following Matthew Arnold (one of my colleagues at UCLA once protested in a heated sixties discussion of politics and literature, "You either believe Arnold or you don't!"), we have been led to believe that we want works that transcend time and place, politics and petty concerns, and give us universal truths. I have come to Terry Eagleton's position that great works are those that capture precisely the conflicts of their time and place, the larger issues, power struggles, and real concrete relations of their historical moment.

Accordingly, I have generalized about most tragedies and done extensive readings of those that seem to best embody the crucial conflicts of the Restoration: struggles over not just succession but theories of succession; headlong passion that calls into question aristocratic theories of magnanimity and aristocracy's concomitant right to rule; hypocrisy or corruption that calls aristocratic ethos and even Christian ethics into question; pragmatic wisdom that challenges aristocratic idealism.

So this study is intended not just for the historian of culture, politics in its larger sense, ideas in the seventeenth and eighteenth centuries, but also for the literary critic of that period and perhaps others interested in how English dramatists shaped the conflicts of their time in ways we can still find forceful even if we no longer share their aristocratic ideology.

Why study Restoration tragedy? Because it is of major importance to its culture. And occasionally it is as engaging as film epics like *The Birth of a Nation* or *El Cid* (neither of whose ideologies we share any longer) or film love tragedies like *Doctor Zhivago* or film political tragedies like *Nixon* or weird, dark, absurdist films like *Blue Velvet.*

Restoration tragedy becomes especially interesting for our time when it addresses issues of race (Aphra Behn's *Abdelazer,* for example, which I treat under the rubric of romantic tragedy) and colonization (my running epilogues to each chapter featuring tragedies focusing on English colonizing in the West Indies and the Americas, the East Indies, Ireland). We watch emerging the rhetoric of British imperialism, a rhetoric of superiority movingly challenged after the triumph of bourgeois hegemony by such memorable figures as Southerne's Oroonoko or Gay's Polly.

Theoretical interests also enliven the study of Restoration tragedy. Bakhtin's theory of official discourse helps us understand the way subversion works in these tragedies. Girard's theory of the endless reciprocal violence that results from the shattering of difference can help us to understand the historical conflicts in Dryden's romances, for example. Derrida's theory of *différance* can help us understand the threat of language slippage in some of these plays. Lacan's theory of the other in relation to the symbolic order of the Other helps us understand the power, the danger of threats posed by women and blacks. Kristeva's theory of abjection and rituals of defilement illuminates late seventeenth-century incest plays and the threat of desiring mother as other. Perhaps most important, Freud's theory of the Oedipus crisis, as modified by Girard perhaps, has entered into our cultural interpretive lexicon. It has enormous explanatory power for these tragedies, for the death of the father is the way to the throne in monarchy and the temptation of parricide is ubiquitous. Indeed, these plays constantly return to the problem of parricide and the need for keeping one's hands clean of Oedipal blood.

The role of theory in a historical study, then, is to provide a kind of cross-fertilization between the synchronic and the diachronic. Theory, which is synchronic, through its generalizations provides a way for us to explain conflict in something more than just a local, historical explanation where we might get lost in the details. Theory provides pattern. Even a New Historicist attempting to illuminate a very thin slice of the past has a theory that enables his or her discourse, a theory of the juxtaposition of "texts," for example, that applies to more than just the one slice.

The cultural theory of Williams, Eagleton, Jameson, and Foucault has a particularly effective explanatory power for the study of the transition between late feudal and early bourgeois ideologies, for that is the classic case study of modern times. Their very theories of change are conditioned by and help to recondition the way, since Marx, social historians have viewed what in effect marks the origin of how we understand ourselves—the transition to the bourgeois episteme. Restoration tragedy is on the cusp of this historical moment and helps us view it as much as any other contemporary discourse, especially when we compare and contrast Restoration with some examples of the Revolutionary drama that came after it.

This study reprints yet rethinks a good deal of previously published material. Perhaps a review of that rethinking, especially in the light of my engagement with other critics, is in order to explain how I have arrived at my current position.

In the fall of 1979, I published "The Significance of the Restoration Rhymed Heroic Play." I summarized, "In short, the Restoration rhymed heroic play is an attempt to reinscribe across the pages of a disintegrating cultural scripture the chivalric code which had underwritten aristocratic society for centuries" (50). I made some mistakes in that article. I treated the rhymed heroic play as if it were a genre, and I failed to notice ideological changes produced by the Glorious Revolution. Now, adapting Northrop Frye's scheme (*Anatomy of Criticism*), I discriminate between heroic romance, tragicomic romance, romantic tragedy, political tragedy, personal tragedy, and tragical satire, both corrective and absurdist (among other genres, or modes, if you prefer). The Restoration rhymed heroic play falls into all these genres. Now I also pay attention to the shifting tropes of difference in Revolutionary tragedy.

Simultaneously, Susan Staves published *Players' Scepters* (1979), in which she too took the heroic plays seriously as reflecting a crisis in authority. Shortly thereafter, Laura Brown published "The Divided Plot: Tragicomic Form in the Restoration" (1980), arguing that the genre's only coherence was formal and not thematic, and *English Dramatic Form* (1981), arguing that the language of other serious drama quickly became disjunctive. Staves and Brown posited a *terminus a quo* of uncontested aristocratic ideology in early Restoration drama, a *terminus ad quem* of uncontested bourgeois ideology in Revolutionary drama, and a *mediam res* where form was emptied of meaning, where the fictions of authority broke down into incoherence. Staves saw "democratic romances" emerging as early as the political tragedies of the decade 1679-89. Convinced that Staves and Brown, excellent critics both, had nevertheless in their diachronic narratives emplotted teleology, I responded with "The Ideology of Restoration Tragicomedy" in 1984 and "Royalism's Last Dramatic Stand: English Political Tragedy, 1679-89" in 1985. Both articles articulated a synchronic reading that saw aristocratic ideology as holding firm, despite severe strain. Concerning tragicomic romance I summarized, "Restoration tragicomedy is generally a reaffirmation of feudal aristocratic virtues, portrayed as under stress by challenges from bourgeois parvenus, libertine lovers, and ambitious statesmen; from ethical nominalists, political pragmatists, and metaphysical atheists. Against such challenges almost all these plays affirm a hierarchical social order, bonded together by the virtues of loyalty, constancy, fidelity, trust, and ultimately validated by a divine providence; man's word as the fundamental bond of society is portrayed as underwritten by the Divine Word" (448). Concerning political tragedy, 1679-1689, I summarized, "These tragedies rigorously defend the old feudal aristocratic ideals, especially the code that the word—the avowed pledge of fidelity, constancy, loyalty, trust between friends, lovers, subjects and kings, man and God—is the very bond of human society, without which anarchy is indeed loosed upon the world" (235).

In 1989 I published *Word as Bond in English Literature from the Middle Ages to the Restoration,* which incorporated or developed previous readings of Dryden's and Otway's serious plays included or adumbrated in these early articles (and one on *All for Love*). I portrayed the Restoration as the end of the feudal era, in which era word-as-bond functioned as a master trope, founding society on a fiction of human loyalty and constancy underwritten by divine authority.

Subsequently, my interpretations of Restoration tragedy have been contested, explicitly and implicitly. Like Brown, Derek Hughes (in *Dryden's Heroic Plays* [1681] and *English Drama, 1660-1700* [1996]) reads Dryden's language in particular but that of nearly all writers of serious drama after the early 1660s in general as disjunctive between the ideal and the real, incapable of articulating a coherent social or metaphysical order. Like Brown and Staves, Hughes's history posits a pristine beginning in Orrery, where language's logocentricity is unproblematic. Afterwards, a falling off into Hobbist uncertainty. Hughes was especially kind in his recent book not to attack me personally, but I am present throughout as an implied straw man who has interpreted the serious plays of the period as reflections of logocentric ontological reality, when in fact I have always presented the ideology of these plays as socially constructed ("an attempt to reinscribe across the pages of a disintegrating cultural scripture"). I have great respect for Hughes as a virtuoso at close reading. But, alas, I sometimes find his readings too close. Like a New Critic or deconstructionist, he finds ambiguity nearly everywhere. Lamentably, our logocentric verbal constructions inevitably fail to capture a transcendental signified. But if our close readings continually discover only this truth, we become negative theologians, whose totalizing vision is a function of our own lenses as surely as that of logocentric critics. And if the subversive is the normal, then it is no longer subversive. In other words, I find less subversion, more official discourse than Hughes. But I honor him as one of the Peers of Restoration drama critics.

Nancy Klein Maguire's *Regicide and Restoration: English Tragicomedy, 1660-1671* (by which generic term she conflates heroic with tragicomic romance [1992]), even as she echoes many of the points made by both Staves and myself, also employs a devolutionary model that posits an unproblematic myth of early Stuart kingship followed by a problematized Restoration myth troubled by the doubts of the new society that could no longer believe in the myth and recognized its emptiness. And she also attacks—or rather dismisses—me as a logocentric, indeed a religious critic, despite this conclusion to my tragicomedy article, where I comment on the plays' use of religious rhetoric to underwrite their aristocratic ideology: "Does that mean the plays are religious, that they reflect a cosmic 'pattern'? Perhaps, though Derrida might argue that such language never refers directly to transcendent reality but always only to other language, other tragicomedies, other mythic plots. Marx or Foucault might argue that such language serves only a sociopolitical function, reinforcing the ideology of the contemporary power elite. And Girard might argue that it serves the ritualistic function of defusing potentially anarchic rivalry. At any rate, the fiction of Restoration tragicomedy is that the word as bond of society is underwritten by the Logos, which enforces it. If not, the reasoning goes, who would then pledge allegiance or plight troth or fear committing perjury?" (460-61). The real problem with Maguire's book is that she reads politics topically, not tropically, as if each play were *à clef,* and fails, like Mildred Hartsock years ago, to see Hobbist sentiments in the mouths of villains as part of a dialectic of conflict that almost always ends in the dramatic repudiation of such sentiments through action if not specific language. She repeats the same mistakes in her subsequent readings of Exclusion Crisis adaptations of Shakespeare. To read tropically is not to dismiss the topical as totally irrelevant (indeed, I make topical references throughout this study) but to see the topical as part of a much larger pattern of figuration that embodies, constitutes the hegemonic ideology of the ruling class.

Now Susan J. Owen's *Restoration Theatre in Crisis* (1996, foreshadowed in her 1963 article "Interpreting the Politics of Restoration Drama") takes me to task for failing to read the subtle nuances of Exclusion Crisis drama as the plays from 1679 to 1683 shift in response to political developments and as they deploy contradictory Tory and Whig tropes. But "Royalism" did not generalize about all the drama of the Exclusion Crisis, only what Staves and I call "political tragedies." Most important, Owen ignores the salient fact that "Royalism" was intended as a correction of Staves's and Brown's readings of the plays as either empty of ideology or proto-democratic. It (along with the other two early articles) was a reading out of the implications of *ideology,* not topical political issues or party platforms. Nevertheless, by using the term *royalism,* with its implications of party politics and not just tropes, I did open myself to correction by Owen. I hope I have made my position clearer.

Richard Braverman's *Plots and Counterplots* (1993), on the other hand, argues in a more sophisticated fashion than Owen's book the emergence of a counterplot to the royalist emplotment of their history and ideology. Thanks to him (who like Hughes offered me only implicit correction), I see now more clearly what I began to see when, prodded by Michael McKeon's reading of Leonidas in *Marriage A-la-Mode* as an emergent trope for the bourgeois self-made man, I revisited *The Conquest of Granada* for "Shifting Tropes of Ideology in English Serious Drama, Late Stuart to Early Georgian" in 1995: Almanzor is a figure for merit that must be suppressed, sacrificed to the loyalism of regnant aristocratic ideology. From Orrery's *Generall* at the beginning of the Restoration to the loyal generals of the Exclusion Crisis plays, heroes who could lead states better than weak or insecure kings are forced by Stuart ideology into subservient roles, even torture and martyrdom. As Braverman acknowledges, very rarely does a Restoration tragedy portray such a hero succeeding in founding a new, proto-bourgeois state.

So while I still believe the reactionary aristocratic paradigm of Stuart ideology generally holds for Restoration tragedy (1660-90), that the code of word-as-bond is tried and proved in the fires of conflict, I recognize this emergent trope of the suppressed hero, which, like that of the Younger Brother in comedy, prefigures the eventual triumph of the bourgeois concept of success—and succession—through merit. I am grateful to McKeon and Braverman for their prodding in this direction.

Thanks to all my critics, I hope I have offered more cogent arguments. In the following pages I eschew a running negative dialogue with those critics (though I refer to them at critical moments where our ideas converge or conflict creatively). From Staves and Brown to Hughes, Maguire, and Owen our differences will be obvious enough to the attentive reader without my constant carping.

Another genetic stream flows into this book. Trained in New Criticism and the history of ideas, like others of my critical generation I nevertheless felt inadequately trained in the new theory emanating from France. So first at UCLA, then at Arizona, I codirected a study group on critical theory. Our major topics over the years have been structuralism, poststructuralism, the Frankfurt School, and cultural studies. Unabashedly eclectic, using whatever cracks interpretive problems—like the theories of Lacan, Derrida, Kristeva, and Girard that figure from time to time, either explicitly or implicitly, in this book—I have nonetheless moved steadily in the direction of a culturalist criticism, following especially such theorists as Althusser, Eagleton, Raymond Williams, Jameson, and Foucault: criticism which focuses on the presentation through ideological state apparatuses, like the theater, of discursive formations that embody power relations. Hence my attempt to write a cultural history of Restoration drama, focusing on ideology.

Recent reading in postcolonial theory and analysis has led me to consider the importance of a subtext of Restoration tragedy, what I call, appropriating Laura Brown's splendid phrase, the "romance of empire." Postcolonial theory enables us to interpret emerging British colonial power relations, which are increasingly negotiated through theater, as well as other ideological state apparatuses.

Chapter 1 on heroic romance reprints some of "The Significance of the Restoration Rhymed Heroic Play," as well as my fuller reading of *The Conquest of Granada* from *Word as Bond,* but the whole has been rethought, examples of nonrhymed romances have been added, and the reading of *Aureng-Zebe* is new, as is the epilogue. Chapter 2 on romantic tragedy is entirely new. Chapter 3 on political tragedy includes much material from "Royalism's Last Dramatic Stand," but presents a new thesis about the return of the culturally repressed. Chapter 4 on personal tragedy is new except the reading of *All for Love* from *Word as Bond,* which I have also rethought and reinterpreted at the end. Chapter 5 on tragical satire reprints material from "Poetical Injustice in Some Masterpieces of Restoration Drama," as well as from my *Dictionary of Literary Biography* article on Otway, and my reading of his *Venice Preserv'd* from *Word as Bond,* but the section on Shadwell's *Timon* is new. Chapter 6 on tragicomic romance reprints most of "The Ideology of Restoration Tragicomedy," augmented with readings of tragicomedies I had missed and with my extended reading of *Marriage A-la-Mode* from *Word as Bond,* again rethought at the end. Chapter 7 on dramatic shifts after the Revolution reprints most of "Shifting Tropes of Ideology in English Serious Drama, Late Stuart to Early Georgian," also augmented with a good deal of new material, particularly from the 1690s, as well as "*Regulus* and *Cleomenes* and 1688," "Mother as Other: The Eruption of Feminine Desire in Some Late Restoration Incest Plays," and some material from the late Al Hesse's and my *DLB* entry on Nicholas Rowe (Al was responsible for the biographical material in that piece, I for the criticism). My running epilogues on the subtext of imperialism are entirely new. Full citations are given in the secondary bibliography. I am grateful to the editors of all these publications for permission to reprint.

I am also grateful to the following: the National Endowment for the Humanities, the Folger Shakespeare Library, and the William Andrews Clark Memorial Library for early fellowship assistance toward this study. The staffs of those two libraries, plus the staff of the Beinecke Library at Yale, were enormously helpful.

To Maja-Lisa von Sneidern for research assistance as well as prompting in postcolonial theory. To Carla Stoffle, dean of the University of Arizona Library, and her staff for general library assistance and special help accessing materials. To Paul Sypherd, provost of the University of Arizona. To Charles (Chuck) Tatum, dean of the UA College of Humanities, for financial assistance—and especially for moral and intellectual support. To my friends and colleagues L.D. Clark, Meg Lota Brown, Naomi Miller, Lincoln Faller, Pat Gill, Paul Hunter, Stephan Flores, Ellen Pollak, Chris Wheatley, Mita Choudhury, and the late, lamented Bradley Rubidge, for lending ears. To Bob Markley and James Thompson for positive and helpful readings of the manuscript for the University Press of Kentucky. To my students in my graduate drama seminars for engaging in dialogue about these plays. To assistants Karen Wyndham and Paul Burkhardt for lending eyes. To my sons Rob, Bret, and Colin for lending encouragement. To my wife Pamela for lending me space and time.

Finally, I dedicate this book with admiration and deep affection to Michael McKeon, who for over twenty years has been my friend and my constant inspiration. All of us working in this field owe him a debt. I owe him profound gratitude for his sensitivity, wisdom, patience, and generosity.

Introduction

Restoration tragedy in general marks a desperate reactionary attempt after the English Civil War to reinscribe feudal, aristocratic, monarchial ideology. My thesis in general is that Restoration tragedy, like Restoration comedy (as I have argued in *Tricksters and Estates: On the Ideology of Restoration Comedy*), remains essentially conservative, reaffirming aristocratic ideology in the teeth of challenges—until the Glorious Revolution called forth a new bourgeois ideology. No ideology is seamless, however. It must be repeatedly supplemented, and occasionally we can see between the seams. I argue that the conflict in Restoration tragedy features the values of the ruling class brought under attack not so much by oppositional values clearly and fairly expressed but by opposites generated within the system itself as transgressive of established order. Overwhelmingly that transgression is portrayed as disloyalty, inconstancy, ingratitude—because even late European feudal society portrayed itself as linked by an allegiance that was ultimately sanctioned by divine authority. If nobility obliges constancy to one's word, one's pledge of allegiance, one's trothplight, then ignobility frees one from any such restraint. Yet even the nobility itself generates transgressors, class enemies—tyrants, traitors, usurpers, rapists, atheists. In contrast, upon noble heroes states are built. They are culture heroes, at war with external and internal monsters. Even if they do not triumph, their culture's values must prevail or the culture will implode. Or such is the fear inculcated into audiences. Most often villains—Machiavels, ambitious queens—are caricatures, easily defeated/dismissed. But the transgressive forces they represent have been allowed to strut and fret openly, and at their best, they represent formidable, nominalistic threats to established order. It is hard to get some of these genies back into their bottles. But that is how an ideology creates bogeymen.[1]

The real threat, as portrayed especially in political and personal tragedy and in tragical satire, is that the emperor has no clothes: the way to the throne is always bloody, always over the dead body of the father;

the way to personal happiness may be antithetical to the patriarchy's values—and merely an emergent bourgeois trope of the private; the imaging systems we employ to hold the world together inevitably fail.

As in *Tricksters and Estates,* by Restoration I mean the period of the Stuart monarchy's last attempt at absolutism, from the restoration of Charles II to the defeat of James II's forces at the Battle of the Boyne.[2] By tragedy I mean a series of subgenres that includes heroic romance, romantic tragedy, political tragedy, personal tragedy, tragical satire, and tragicomic romance. Rob Hume noted two decades ago, citing French critic François Hédelin, l'abbé d'Aubignac, that "Dryden's contemporaries tend . . . to conceive [tragedy] in terms of subject matter," that is, in the words of d'Aubignac, "the Agitations and sudden turns of the fortune of great people" (Hume, *Development* 151-52). In practice, such a loose and baggy term covers all of these subgenres.

By ideology I mean the set of cultural ideas, values, and especially power relations that social discursive and imaging systems propound as if they were natural even as they are in reality constructed to serve the interests of the hegemonic class. Or to quote Louis Althusser from his famous essay, "Ideology and Ideological State Apparatuses," "Ideology represents the imaginary relationship of individuals to their real conditions of existence." Althusser explains the criticism of ideology: "However, while admitting that they [the world visions of ideology] do not correspond to reality, i.e. that they constitute an illusion, we admit that they do make allusion to reality, and that they need only be 'interpreted' to discover the reality of the world behind their imaginary representation of that world" (162). In his *Criticism and Ideology,* Terry Eagleton further delineates this interpretive act, especially as it relates to what he calls "an ideological production to the second power"—a literary work:

> Indeed in most literary works it is an effect of the productive modes to conceal and 'naturalise' ideological categories, dissolving them into the spontaneity of the 'lived'. In this sense, what ideology does to history the literary work raises to the second power, producing as 'natural' the significations by which history naturalises itself; but the work simultaneously reveals (to criticism, if not to the casually inspecting glance) how that naturalness is the effect of a particular production. If the text displays itself as 'natural', it manifests itself equally as constructed artifice; and it is in this duality that its relation to ideology can be discerned. [85]

Eagleton thus provides an answer to the question why separate out dramatic or even literary discourse for analysis. Literature, especially drama, is a powerful mode of ideological production, for it generally provides quick wish fulfillment that reinscribes what Mikhail Bakhtin calls "official discourse," that is, hegemonic ideology. Challenges to the prevailing system are most often caricatured for easy dismissal. Moreover, Restoration tragedy was produced by two theater companies operating by royal patent. As Deborah Payne has best shown, the patentees were political, not artistic, appointments. So Restoration theaters were indeed state apparatuses.

Why organize a book on ideology by genre? As we move from the reinforcing dénouements of comedy and romance to the more disturbing of tragedy and satire, the seams of social construction seem to spread. Sometimes they are rent asunder. There is a great deal of cultural sense in an ending. How best to divide the study of Restoration drama other than by following the different implications of endings?

My generic categories, while loosely constituting variations on Northrop Frye's scheme in *Anatomy of Criticism,* are heuristic. That is, they are nonessentialist categories that have some traditional resonance, but mostly they constitute critical categories designed to facilitate interpretation. Moreover, though they are traditional categories, they are deployed in any given age at the service, extending Frye's comment about romance, of "the ideology of an ascendant class" (*Secular Scripture* 57). Employing Frye's notion of gradations from one of the four seasonal genres into another, let me propose the following (minimalist) generic distinctions. Heroic romance features great warriors and noble women who endure hardship and who triumph in the end. Romantic tragedy features heroic innocents who suffer at the hands of villains but are vindicated in the end. In the romantic world, the threats are largely external, although heroes often grow in moral stature. In personal tragedy, they are internal, the passions that wrack the great souls of heroes and cost them the world, which may be well lost but loses them as leaders. Political tragedy focuses on the fate of states and on threats to prevailing ideology (or, rarely, on oppositional ideologies). Either form of tragedy portrays loss compensated usually by the restoration of order. Romance concludes with distributive poetical justice, tragedy with retributive. Tragical satire, on the other hand, concludes either with a poetical justice that is draconian and virtually apocalyptic or with no poetical justice at all. The major differences that distinguish heroic from tragicomic romance are that the former almost always includes *intérêts d'état,* the latter almost always comic material. It too generally concludes with a world restored, the heroic supplemented by the comic.

Perhaps because of our institutionalized Elizabethophilia, Restoration tragedy has suffered critical neglect if not critical abuse. What strikes the modern reader as excessive rant has been explained by Eric Rothstein as a triumph of sensationalism over plot (*Restoration Tragedy*) and by Derek

Hughes as a failure of language in a Hobbist universe (*English Drama*). I think that once one inserts different generic lenses into one's glasses, one might have different expectations: heroic romance demands heroes larger than life, often with outsized pride; romantic tragedy demands melodramatic villains; political tragedy demands propagandistic rhetoric (and Oedipal excess); personal tragedy demands great-souled protagonists torn by great passions; tragical satire demands scathing indictments if not incoherent babbling; tragicomic romance demands registers of both the heroic and the comic, coexisting not always peacefully cheek-by-jowl. And once one reads the plays ideologically, their excesses might be seen as signs of the failure of the hegemonic to weave a seamless garment.

By consensus, the glory of Restoration tragedy resides in plays by John Dryden (especially, as they occur in my treatment, *The Conquest of Granada, Aureng-Zebe, Don Sebastian, All for Love, Secret Love, Marriage A-la-Mode*), Nathaniel Lee (especially *Mithridates, Lucius Junius Brutus, Sophonisba, The Rival Queens, The Princess of Cleve*), and Thomas Otway (especially *Don Carlos, The Orphan, Venice Preserv'd*). Yet I value occasional gems by the earl of Orrery (*Mustapha*), Aphra Behn (*Abdelazer*), John Crowne (*Darius*), John Banks (*The Earl of Essex*), John Milton (*Samson Agonistes*), Sir Robert Howard (*The Duke of Lerma*), Thomas Shadwell (*Timon of Athens*), and Sir Charles Sedley (*The Mulberry Garden*). I have given more extended treatment to the jewels in an attempt to share their brilliance. If *tragedy* as we have come to essentialize it—that is, the pseudo-Aristotelian pattern of a hero with a tragic flaw who falls through some *hamartia*—seems rare (I treat only five in the chapter on personal tragedy, although some of the political tragedies contain the same pattern, like *Mithridates* and *The Earl of Essex,* if not *Don Sebastian* and *Lucius Junius Brutus*), perhaps we value them more highly because of their rarity. More probably we value them because of our essentialist view of tragedy and of the human condition: a lingering mid-twentieth-century view that, ironically, grew out of existentialism. But something in us loves a protagonist who learns through losing that for which the world is well lost. An ideological reading of such tragedy, however, allows us to complicate this apparently universal humanist theme.

If I seem to have favored tragical satires with more extensive readings of more examples, it is probably because I find such a concentration of gems there, several relatively unheralded. I also admit to being attracted by their unromantic, unsentimental criticism, skepticism, and even absurdity. In my cursory survey of dramatic shifts in post-Revolutionary tragedy, I have also concentrated on jewels, most of them already treasured, a few undervalued.

The aesthetic theory implied in my use of the metaphor of treasures involves language, characterization, plot, and especially conflict: the ability to embody in a profoundly effective and affective manner conflictual power relations at the heart of a culture. Eagleton writes, "The value of a text, then, is determined by its double mode of insertion into an ideological formation and into the available lineages [genres, for example] of literary discourse. . . . Literary works 'transcend' their contemporary history, not by rising to the 'universal', but by virtue of the character of their concrete relations to it—relations themselves determined by the nature of the historical conditions into which the work is inserted" (185, 178).

This survey will concentrate on new plays in the Restoration, sketching what happens to the subgenres of tragedy after the Glorious Revolution. I begin and end the survey with romance to complete a circle of official discourse. I end with tragicomic romances also because their comic plots link with Restoration comedy in their concern with estates—and with the pragmatic reasons for sustaining that official discourse of aristocratic ideology. And I conclude each chapter with an epilogue in which I examine a major subtext of Restoration tragedy, the romance of empire, a subtext that moves into maintext after the Revolution. It is a romance because it glorifies and naturalizes incipient British imperialism. Ironically, in drama which is essentially conservative, it reveals an emergent bourgeois text or set of tropes that mark the transition from England to Great Britain.

After the Revolution, except for tragicomedy, the genres themselves do not change much. But tropes that were *emergent* during the Restoration become *dominant,* to borrow useful terms from Raymond Williams. By examining signal examples, we can see how the drama helps to constitute the new, bourgeois order—and how its rhetoric too fails to plaster over the fissures in its ideology.

In the conclusion, I have attempted not only to summarize my argument but to place it in a larger context about the historiography of the Long Eighteenth Century. Revisionists have maintained that there is no revolution in England until 1832 and that there is overwhelming political continuity throughout the period. I believe that there is a dramatic shift from aristocratic to bourgeois ideologies *at least in the important ideological state apparatus of the theater.* If other state apparatuses, as the revisionists insist, are more resistant to change, then the drama becomes even more "revolutionary"—conditioning, enabling a more gradual political revolution.

1
Heroes & States
Heroic Romance

The restored king and court had been quite taken with French drama in their exiled sojourn on the continent, particularly the rhymed romances and tragedies of France's greatest dramatist at midcentury, Pierre Corneille. So Charles II invited his courtier playwrights to follow suit. The very formal style of such plays, with their oratorical declamations, can only be appreciated today if we view them as operatic spectacles (indeed, such spectacles developed alongside them). Despite Puritanical strictures against the theater, Sir William Davenant had already staged the first version of the Restoration rhymed heroic play, *The Siege of Rhodes,* in 1656, an operatic romance he expanded into a two-part version for the stage in 1661. Heeding the king's call in addition were Roger Boyle, earl of Orrery, Sir William Killigrew, and Sir Robert Howard. Howard was assisted by a professional playwright, the great John Dryden. In the early sixties, these authors developed the rhymed heroic romance as a celebration of the king's restoration and a reinscribing across the pages of a disintegrating cultural scripture of the chivalric code which had underwritten aristocratic society for centuries. They portrayed the aristocracy as naturally superior, born and bred and divinely appointed (if not anointed) to rule. They portrayed their enemies as self-interested statesmen and unruly mobs, who might mouth the rhetoric of rights but who simply desired power through revolt and usurpation. The villains of these plays critics call Machiavels, so named after the (in)famous Niccolò Machiavelli, who had preached in *The Prince* that it was better for a ruler to be feared than loved, that the end justifies the means, and that might makes right. Machiavelli's theories of de facto as opposed to de jure government had been brought home to England by Thomas Hobbes, who wrote his treatise of de facto absolutism, *The Leviathan,* while in exile with Charles II.

However beleaguered, the heroes and heroines of these romances are always vindicated; right finally makes might. The implication of this poetical justice is that it is underwritten by divine providence. If it were not, then the aristocratic politics of de jure hereditary monarchy and its ethics of obligation and loyalty and virtue would be exposed as the mere rhetoric that the Machiavels claimed it to be.

The Machiavels are as often women as men. The Restoration introduced actresses on the English stage, and the playwrights created great villainess roles for them, from Roxalana in Davenant's *Siege of Rhodes;* to Zempoalla in the Howard-Dryden *Indian-Queen* (1664) and her successors, Lyndaraxa in Dryden's *Conquest of Granada* (1670-71) and Nourmahal in his *Aureng-Zebe* (1675); to the versions of Alexander's scorned Roxana in John Weston's *Amazon Queen* (not acted; publ. 1667), Samuel Pordage's *Siege of Babylon* (1677), and Edward Cooke's *Love's Triumph* (probably not acted; publ. 1678); to the Queen Mother in William Whitaker's *Conspiracy* (1680).[1] Whatever the setting, this uppity-woman type symbolized the rebellious aspects of England, which should be the submissive bride of her king. Her promiscuous sexuality threatened the patrilinearity upon which the succession of property—and the very kingdom itself—depended. Against her was juxtaposed the virtuous woman, constant as lover, wife, queen. This concept of *constancy* or *trust* is central to aristocratic monarchial ideology. God entrusts kings and queens with government. The people owe them allegiance. Thus constancy, loyalty, trust are central to conflict on several levels: between friends, couples, subjects and kings, man and god.

Two of the early playwrights establish the pattern, for the conflicts in Davenant's *Siege* and Orrery's first plays are resolved in terms of trust. In the *Siege,* herself a model of constancy to her doubting lover Alphonso, Ianthe trusts so much to Solyman's honor that, even without safe passage, she goes to him to sue for peace, a design that Villerius says has Heaven's blessing. Thus Christian Rhodes is saved, at least temporarily. In Orrery's *Generall* (first acted as *Altemira* in Dublin, 1662; again as *The Generall* in London, 1664), trust in the ultimate might of the right is vindicated when the rightful king defeats the usurper in a trial by combat. And the code is validated by Altemira's apparent death for her constancy, her resurrection and reunion with her lover (the drug was not fatal), and her conversion of the Herculean Clorimun to virtue and mutual trust. In Orrery's *History of Henry the Fifth* (1664), the entire conflict between England and France is portrayed as one between might and right, the latter carrying the day. Meanwhile, when Henry trusts so much to Katherine that he enters the French camp disguised, she refuses to betray him. Friendship is such a powerful tie that, though he loves her himself, Tudor courts Katherine for his friend Henry, affirming, "Friendship above all tyes does bind the heart; / And faith in Friendship is the noblest part" (IV.288-89). Even enemies, Henry and Chareloys, trust each other. And the play concludes in a treaty between the English and the French, a sign of mutual trust. In what might serve as an epigraph to these heroic romances, Henry concludes, "Trust is the strongest Bond upon the Soul" (V.168).[2]

Rhymed heroic romance as continued by Orrery and Dryden and as created by their followers through the sixties and into the late seventies reinforces this ideology. As with Orrery's Clorimun, sometimes the valorous are diamonds in the rough who must be polished, usually by the power of love; they must be taught the chivalric code. The most obvious examples are Dryden's Montezuma, Almanzor, and Morat. Even Aureng-Zebe must learn to trust absolutely his lover Indamora. Sometimes when lovers or husbands distrust or violate their own vows, virtuous women seek a greater lover, a higher form of constancy—in a nunnery, as in George Cartwright's *Heroick-Lover* (probably not acted; publ. 1661).

The relationship between subjects and kings in these plays is depicted as ideally one of reciprocal trust. Not only must subjects remain loyal, but kings are bound, too. For example, Queen Cleandra in Sir William Killigrew's *Ormasdes* (1664?) says, "'Tis a Prince his chief Businesse to be Just, / The Gods impose on us no higher Trust" (II, 18). Even when faced with rulers who are usurpers or who break their sacred trust with their subjects, in almost all of these plays the heroes refuse to rebel, leaving vengeance to Heaven, as in Cartwright's play or Orrery's *Tryphon* (1668) or Dryden's *Aureng-Zebe* or Elkanah Settle's *Cambyses, King of Persia* (1671).

In every one of these rhymed heroic romances, the wicked antagonists are finally overthrown, the virtuous protagonists triumphant. And as the ultimate inscription of aristocratic ideology, somebody usually explicitly attributes the dénouement to an underwriting Logos, a *verbum dei* that underwrites word-as-bond. To take random examples, in John Caryll's *English Princess* (1667), a Richard III play, Richmond concludes, "Heaven, thou art just, and good! / So Tyrants rise, and so they fall in Blood" (V.vii, 58). The usurper Tryphon overthrown by his own hand, in Orrery's play of that name, the rightful king Aretus declares, "Now let us to the Gods Oblations pay, / For all the Blessings of this Glorious day" (V, 435). Darius concludes Settle's *Cambyses*, "Thus the gods guard those Virtues they inspire" (V, 84). In Settle's *Conquest of China* (1675), the apparently victorious, blasphemous Machiavel Lycungus condemns the hero and the heroine to death, exulting,

> Fate grants the High command
> Of this Great Empire to a Martial Hand.
> And to confirm my Interest with heaven,
> The Gods to my Just Cause success have given. [V, 62]

The pious hero Quitazo responds, "Savage Infidel, can you believe, / That there are Gods, and such a sentence give?" (64). The virtuous attribute their rescue to "th'high Powers" (67). "The Hand of Providence" is manifest in the dénouement of Thomas Rymer's *Edgar* (V.xi, 59; probably not acted; publ. 1678). "The gentle Calm of Peace from Heav'n descends" at the end of Cooke's *Love's Triumph* (V.xv, 62). In Pordage's *Siege of Babylon,* at the moment the heroes appear to have lost the lovers for whom they fought, they are cautioned that "The ways of Providence, do Riddles seem," that they must nevertheless have trust (V.i, 51); indeed, the women are restored by divine agency, the villainess Roxana goes mad, blasphemes, and stabs herself, and the constant Statira concludes, "Thus Gods their Judgment show, / That poor ambitious Mortals, here may know, / They sit above, and see, and govern all below" (V.ii, 61).

Not all Restoration heroic romances are rhymed, and as we shall see in the following chapters, not all rhymed heroic plays are romances. But the unrhymed heroic romances embody the same aristocratic ideology, from Henry Cary, Viscount Faulkland's *Marriage Night* (1663) and the anonymous Irena (unacted; publ. 1664), both of which have providential endings in support of *loyalty;* to John Banks's *Cyrus the Great* (1695, but written earlier) and Edward Ravenscroft's version of the story of Edgar (1677, but also apparently written earlier), both of which have bizarre romance endings; to Nahum Tate's (in)famous adaptation of *King Lear* (late 1680), which ends with Lear alive, Cordelia married to the triumphant Edgar, and the pronouncement, "Then there are Gods, and Vertue is their Care" (V, 65); to Charles Saunders's *Tamerlane the Great* (1681), which ends with the title character recalled to aristocratic virtue, reconciled to his estranged loyal son and his bride, and thanking "Propitious Heav'n" (V, 59); to the anonymous *Romulus and Hersilia* (1682), which concludes with the title couple overcoming treason and distrust.

Thus, as one observes the dates of performance, it is obvious that the heroic romance, whether rhymed or unrhymed, figures prominently at least through the Exclusion Crisis of the early 1680s.[3] It is not just a genre spawned by the restoration of Charles Stuart and petering out quickly as the euphoria waned. In the midst of that crisis comes Whitaker's *Conspiracy; or, The Change of Government* (1680), a retelling in an exotic Turkish setting of the English Civil War with the death of one sultan at the hands of rebels and the restoration of his son. As late as 1683, Thomas Southerne penned an unrhymed heroic romance, *The Loyal Brother*, whose title indicates its ethos. Despite the machinations of the play's Machiavellian statesman, the younger brother's undying loyalty to his sovereign brother—and his mirroring constancy to his beloved—are finally rewarded, and the chastened ruler, Seliman, exhorts, "[M]ay succeeding

Monarchs learn from me, / How far to trust a Statesmans policy" (V.iii.295-96).

The greatest writer of these heroic romances was, hands down, John Dryden. Let us examine in detail his best contribution, with a final glance at his farewell not just to rhyme but to heroic romance on the stage. Dryden's *Conquest of Granada by the Spaniards* (two parts, Dec.-Jan. 1670-71) opens with key imagery from the two games being held to celebrate the Granadan king Boabdelin's imminent marriage to Almahide. The first game is a *juego de cañas* and the second a *juego de toros.* The former is a ritualized form of combat consisting of darting blunted spears or "canes" between mock armies. In this particular game, groups of thirty or more of the two feuding factions in Granada are conducting (offstage) a typical "flying skirmish,"[4] that is, fighting "like *Parthyans*" (158), until Tarifa, a Zegry, breaks the rules of combat, changes "his blunt Cane for a steel-pointed Dart" (162), and wounds Ozmyn, an Abencerrago. The act is characterized as "Treason" (164), because it violates fundamental sociopolitical codes designed to sublimate the very deadly rivalry it now precipitates, a rivalry governed only by rules of revenge.

Instead of ritual, Granada is faced with what René Girard in *Violence and the Sacred* calls a "sacrificial crisis" that threatens to destroy the city from within. The rivalry is imitated everywhere in the play. The old Abencerrago Abenamar is already a deadly rival of the Zegry chief, Selin, and their inveterate hatred causes them to violate the bonds of nature and attempt to kill their children, Ozmyn and Benzayda, who, like Romeo and Juliet, fall in love despite their clans' feud. Prince Abdalla and the Abencerrago chief, Abdelmelech, become deadly rivals for Lyndaraxa's hand. Abdalla also becomes a rival for his brother Boabdelin's throne, violating both the bonds of nature and of society. Lyndaraxa eventually becomes a rival with Almahide for the love of the heroic Almanzor. Almanzor becomes a rival with Boabdelin for the love of Almahide. And, of course, the Moors are deadly rivals with the Christians for the last Islamic stronghold in Western Europe. This is a world threatening to come apart in the "flying skirmish" of dialectical forces.

The bullfight is really an image of the same skirmish, as if the chief bull were a figure for what Girard calls the "monstrous double" of the sacrificial crisis, the *unheimlich* monster that really lurks within.[5] The bull charges the stranger, Almanzor, who spears him once, sidesteps, and then decapitates him in one swordstroke. This is an image for Almanzor's conflict with himself, with his unruly passion. But it is also an image for Almanzor's contest with Boabdelin, for Christianity's contest with the Moors, and finally for the entire culture's struggle with a displaced version of its worst enemy—deadly rivalry brought about by the breaking of words, the perjury that eventually destroys Granada from within.

Almanzor is a great warrior summoned to help the Moors raise the Christian siege of Granada. His immediate past is extremely significant, but Boabdelin fails to read its lesson aright. Almanzor had been summoned to a similar scene of rivalry in Fez, where the Xeriff brothers feuded for the throne of Morocco. At first Almanzor fought for the Elder, the "juster cause," but when he waxed ungrateful, Almanzor changed sides and placed the Younger on the throne (1.I.i.248-52). There are two lessons here: a people without a clear principle of succession, as Islamic peoples were popularly portrayed, is always in danger of civil war; a leader who is ungrateful for services rendered is liable to reap unhappy consequences.

The lesson of the consequences of ingratitude is clear.[6] Nevertheless, Boabdelin fails to read the lesson and thus is doomed to have history repeat itself. In Almanzor's first battle for the Granadans, he wins a victory and captures the mighty duke of Arcos, but then he heroically pledges to set him free to fight again. Boabdelin refuses to honor Almanzor's "promise" and absolves him from his "word" (1.III.i.5-6). Almanzor's response not only insists upon his right to his word but characterizes the king as a troth-breaker whose faction-ridden state is the result of his inconstancy:

> He break my promise and absolve my vow!
> 'Tis more than *Mahomet* himself can do.
> The word which I have giv'n shall stand like Fate;
> Not like the King's that weathercock of State.
> He stands so high, with so unfix't a mind,
> Two Factions turn him with each blast of wind. [7-12]

Predictably, Almanzor, who, as Dryden insists in the prefatory essay, "Of Heroique Playes," "is not born their Subject whom he serves" (*Works* 11:16) and therefore owes them no allegiance, deserts Boabdelin and joins the rebellion of his rival brother, Abdalla.

Abdalla himself, however, though witness to Almanzor's Moroccan history, learns its lesson no better than Boabdelin. Nor does he profit from his brother's mistake, but breaks his own word to Almanzor, reneging on his agreement to let him set another captive free—this time, the beauteous Almahide, with whom Almanzor has fallen instantly in love. Abdalla yields to Zulema's threat to withdraw the support of the Zegrys, and Almanzor accuses him of rationalizing his "ingratitude" with empty "words" (1.III.i.502-4). Thus, Almanzor returns to Boabdelin, not to vindicate the

Gramley Library
Salem Academy and College
Winston-Salem, N.C. 27108

latter's claim to the throne but simply to rescue Almahide and set her free. But after Almanzor keeps his "Promise" to Boabdelin (1.V.i.185) and again turns the tide, Boabdelin makes the mistake of swearing by "*Alha*" to grant him any desire (225). When Almanzor then asks for Almahide, Boabdelin naturally refuses to surrender his betrothed. Furious, Almanzor responds, "I'll call thee thankless, King; and perjur'd both: / Thou swor'st by *Alha;* and hast broke thy oath" (268-69). Almanzor deserts both brothers and departs for Africa. Even if there be an inadequate political system for succession and legitimation, pledged words ought to bind. Almanzor rejects a world where they do not.

With the loss of the heroic defender and with Abdalla's escape to join the Christians, Boabdelin's fortunes precipitately decline, and his people begin to rebel. In other words, his troth-breaking has produced anarchy. The "many-headed Beast" (2.I.ii.29), the mob, rebels in "The name of Common-wealth," where "the People their own Tyrants are" (47-48). Boabdelin argues that "Kings who rule with limited Command / Have Players Scepters put into their Hand" (49-50), and Abenamar describes the results of the destabilizing dialectic that occurs when kings must contend for power, a dialectic that divides within and leads to conquest from without. Then, the mob will "want that pow'r of Kings they durst not trust" (58). Thus Dryden rouses memories in his audience of his own country's civil war—as well as fears lest it return, with its ultimate tyranny, as a result of factionalism—and of quarrels over principles of succession.

Boabdelin has been incapable of commanding the trust of his people from the beginning. He has always been a troth-breaker. As he often does, Dryden provides some original sin of distrust that lies like a curse over the land. Ferdinand's claim to Granada is twofold. The Spaniards have a prior "just, and rightful claim" to Spain because they were there before the Moors, who simply took it by conquest and therefore rule merely by "force," de facto and not de jure (1.I.i.295, 303). Moreover, Arcos had once captured Boabdelin and his father and released them upon their "Contract" to resign the crown of Granada and rule as Ferdinand's vassals until the death of the father, when Boabdelin would "lay aside all marks of Royalty" (317-22). When that time came, however, Boabdelin refused to yield the throne, and Arcos accuses him, "[L]ike a perjur'd Prince, you broke your oath" (316). Such a king, according to the pattern of feudal literature, of which this baroque drama is a late example, will inevitably suffer a poetical justice that is a sign of a divine justice that avenges forswearing. Boabdelin is "slain by a *Zegry*'s hand" (2.V.iii.171)—killed not by a Spaniard but by one of his own rebellious, troth-breaking Granadans.

Boabdelin might as well have been killed by his own brother, but Dryden has another fate in store for Abdalla, whose political rivalry with his brother, though it is based in part upon Zulema's Hobbist perversion of words, of such concepts as "Vertue" (1.II.i.208-13), "Justice" (226-27), and primogeniture (247-51), is complicated by a sexual rivalry with Abdelmelech over that central chivalric figure, the inconstant woman. Abdalla rebels because only with a crown can he obtain Lyndaraxa, who is preengaged, she maintains, to Abdelmelech.

Lyndaraxa's manipulation of her lovers at times borders on the comic. But she epitomizes the very grave threat of uncontrolled desire that seduces men away from the code of loyalty to participate in a rebellion against the very order of patriarchy. Jealous of Almahide, she wishes to be a queen—not simply a royal consort. No, she would "be that one, to live without controul" (1.II.i.148). Figuratively, she is the Dread Maternal Anarch, who threatens all the bonds of patriarchal society. She provokes Abdalla to Oedipal rebellion: "For such another pleasure, did he live, / I could my Father of a Crown deprive" (172-73). Abdelmelech laments, "With what indifference all her Vows she breaks!" (1.III.i.150), as she mockingly taunts him with libertine doctrine, "'Twas during pleasure, 'tis revok'd this hour. / Now call me false, and rail on Woman-kind" (141-42). She is also capable of manipulating by perverting the code of the word and accusing her two puppets of being the ones who are "faithless" and "false" (1.IV.ii.63, 75). When Abdelmelech tries to leave her because of her "falshood" (59), she hypocritically accuses him, "[Y]our breach of Faith is plain" (77). When Abdalla demands constancy from her, she explains that frailty's name is woman: "Poor womens thoughts are all *Extempore*" (180). He complains, "Is this the faith you promis'd me to keep?" (1.V.i.38), then calls her a "faithless and ingrateful maid!" (67). Old Selin properly brands her "faithless as the wind" (2.II.i.110).

Lyndaraxa is a symbol of the faithlessness always threatening feudal aristocracy. Mythologically, she is associated with Circe (1.III.i.93-96), that seducer of heroes who distracts them from the paths of true glory and turns them into beasts. More prominently, Lyndaraxa associates herself with the goddess Fortune, who, as she believes, governs events (265-69). And yet, as the Middle Ages and the Renaissance portrayed her, Fortune is ultimately a whore. Abenamar proclaims, "I have too long th' effects of Fortune known, / Either to trust her smiles, or fear her frown" (1.IV.i.7-8). Lyndaraxa proves incapable of being Fortune, of controlling events, and thus she turns eventually to Almanzor, who himself claims to Boabdelin, "I am your fortune; but am swift like her, / And turn my hairy front if you defer" (30-31). Lyndaraxa plans to assault him with her wiles, because "In gaining him, I gain that Fortune too / Which he has Wedded, and which I but Wooe" (2.III.iii.61-62).

To win Almanzor, Lyndaraxa must destroy "his vow'd Constancy" to Almahide (2.III.iii.65), and her ultimate weapon is to declare her nominalism and proclaim:

> There's no such thing as Constancy you call:
> Faith ties not Hearts; 'tis Inclination all.
> Some Wit deform'd or Beauty much decay'd,
> First, constancy in Love, a Vertue made. [162-65]

When he resists her, she spitefully taunts, "The Fate of Constancy your Love pursue! / Still to be faithful to what's false to you" (181-82). Thus according to her—and to the secular, self-interested philosophy for which she stands—the faithful are the fools. And yet, despite all her wiles, despite perjury against Almahide and dirty tricks against Almanzor and Ozmyn, Lyndaraxa does not triumph. Abdelmelech kills Abdalla and then resists and rejects Lyndaraxa, throwing her philosophy back in her teeth and berating her for her inconstancy, which has been justly rewarded (2.IV.ii. 130-33). Not finished yet, she finally joins the Christians in the last assault and is rewarded with the crown of Granada. She exults, "I knew this Empyre to my fate was ow'd: / Heav'n held it back as long as 'ere it cou'd" (2.V.iii.238-39). But she taunts Abdelmelech once too often, and he stabs her. Lyndaraxa, Queen of Rebellion itself, ironically charges her "fate" with "Rebellion" (262), but Abenamar passes the final judgment on her and her quest to master Fortune: "Such fortune still, such black designs attends" (267). In other words, however capricious be Fortune in her own person—and therefore a fitting figure for Lyndaraxa the Inconstant—Fortune is finally only an instrument of Nemesis. No "Blind Queen of Chance" rules this world (2.III.ii.17) but a Providence that underwrites the code of constancy.

Contrasted with the faithless Lyndaraxa, as Penelope with Circe, is the faithful Almahide, model of chivalric female behavior. When Almanzor falls in love with her, she protests she is "promis'd to Boabdelin" (1.III.i.376). He would disregard such bonds as mere "Ceremony" (388), but she tries to explain to this "noble Savage" (1.I.i.209), "Our Souls are ty'd by holy Vows above. . . . I gave my faith to him, he his to me" (1.III.i.392, 396). Later, when Almanzor again presses his suit, she protests, "My Fathers choice I never will dispute" (1.IV.ii.428), though this time she allows Almanzor to try to change that father's mind and retrieve her hand from Boabdelin. When Boabdelin breaks his oath to Alha to grant Almanzor any wish, denies him Almahide, condemns him to death, and then proceeds to demand that Almahide keep her promise to marry him, Almahide exclaims, "How dare you claim my faith, and break your own?" (1.V.i.347-48). How can there be troth among troth-breakers? Nevertheless, when her father insists, "No second vows can with your first dispence" (350), and when he guarantees that Almanzor shall only be exiled, Almahide capitulates—"honor ties me" (356)—and she gives her "oath" to be Boabdelin's wife (404).

Married to Boabdelin in the second part of the play, Almahide remains constant despite Boabdelin's jealousy, insisting, "That hour when I my Faith to you did plight, / I banish'd him [Almanzor] for ever from my sight" (2.I.ii.158-59). Forced to recall Almanzor to save her husband's throne, she fully intends to "square" her love by virtue (219). Unfortunately, she miscalculates Boabdelin's response to her yielding to Almanzor's request and giving him her scarf "for my Husbands sake" (2.II.iii.111)—that is, as a sign that he is their Champion. Of course, the scarf has the same significance as Desdemona's handkerchief: it is the very badge of marital chastity, a "publick" sign of a "private" "Gift," an "Embleme" of "Love" (2.III.i.55-56). Consequently, at its sight in Almanzor's possession, Boabdelin breaks into a jealous rage and concludes Almahide "False" (54). Insisting on her "Loyalty" (127), she demands the scarf back and returns it to her husband. And she even makes the sullen Almanzor fight to save him.

Almahide's most crucial trial comes when Almanzor sneaks into her palace chambers and demands a tangible reward for his services. Unable to deter him by any of her arguments and unable to deny her own desire for him for a moment longer, she resorts to the ultimate remedy of the chaste matron, at least from the time of Lucrece—suicide: "You've mov'd my heart, so much, I can deny / No more; but know, *Almanzor,* I can dye" (2.IV.iii.265-66). Immediately Almanzor aborts both her and his attempts, and her chastity is preserved alive. Ironically, however, this temptation of Almahide takes place in the context of her imminent rape by Zulema and Hamet—as if to underscore the nature of Almanzor's assault as a form of rape. After Almanzor leaves, the second rape is begun, and Almahide, who calls on "heav'n" for help (293), seems to be saved only by the providential appearance of Abdelmelech: "I thank thee, heav'n; some succour does appear" (296). But hers appears to be a hasty interpretation, for Lyndaraxa and her brothers perjure themselves and accuse Almahide and Abdelmelech of adultery. Despite all the signs of fidelity his wife has given, Boabdelin immediately concludes her—and all women—false: "O proud, ingrateful, faithless womankind!" (362). He condemns her to summary execution without trial. But what is much more surprising is that Almanzor, who has just had such indelible proof of her chastity, likewise misogynistically concludes her—and all women—"false" (369): "She was as faithless as her Sex could be: . . . She's faln! and now where shall we vertue find? / She was the last that stood of Woman-kind" (2.V.i.3-6).

Thus, Hobbist philosophy seems momentarily to have triumphed: the faithful appear to be the fools, their code inefficacious, with no supernatural validation. It is as if the old gods have been overthrown, as Abdelmelech complains (2.V.i.15-18). Without such validation, to be virtuous is a joke on oneself, as Almahide complains nominalistically:

> Let never woman trust in Innocence;
> Or think her Chastity its own defence;
> Mine has betray'd me to this publick shame:
> And vertue, which I serv'd, is but a name. [2.V.ii.5-8]

In other words, the play has brought us to the point of asking crucial questions about the chivalric code: What protection is there against perjury and hypocrisy? Why be virtuous if the innocent suffer? Are oaths and vows mere breaths of air? Either the rebels are right or some sign of divine protection must appear. That is why Dryden has Ozmyn demand a Trial by Combat, a *jugement de Dieu* as the French call it. Boabdelin begins by proclaiming, "And may just Heav'n assist the juster side" (2.V.ii.24). All the combatants swear the justice of their cause and kiss the Koran. The implication of the contest is clear: even if Almanzor is fighting only for reputation's sake, the audience knows Almahide is chaste and expects that Heaven will indeed assist the juster side. Almahide's Christian lady-in-waiting, Esperanza, urges her to "Trust" in a higher power than mere stoic virtue, "the Christians Deity" (2.V.ii.9-14), and Almahide asks that god for a sign of his "succour" (18).

Despite Lyndaraxa's dirty tricks, Almanzor and Ozmyn win. The truth emerges as Zulema confesses his party's treachery and perjury. Appropriately, Abdelmelech, who before had doubted the gods, concludes, "Heav'n thou art just" (2.V.ii.88), and Almahide thanks her new god, upbraids her husband for his distrust, and plans never to see him or Almanzor again, but to sublate her love upward "to Heav'n," to a new "plighted Lord" (2.V.iii.63-64). At the end of the play, Almahide's constancy is not just vindicated but rewarded. By Boabdelin's death she is free from her former vow, and her new "Parent," her godmother Queen Isabella, dispenses with her constancy to his ghost and gives her hand to Almanzor, whom she will marry after her "year of Widow hood expires" (331-37). Then she—and not her antithesis, Lyndaraxa—will receive a "Coronet of *Spain*" from Almanzor's family and will reign as princess (307), but one properly subordinated to her new husband, her new king, and her new god.[7]

Meanwhile, the young and heroic Almanzor is only potentially a culture hero. He is one of those diamonds in the rough who must be polished; he is a great source of martial and sexual energy that must either be socialized or remain anarchic and destructive. He must learn to control the raging bull of his own passion and to respect the code of the word, the bonds of society—ethical, political, metaphysical. Though he takes the side of the oppressed Abencerrages when he first arrives, he owes allegiance not only to no king but to the wrong god and to virtually no code of ethics. When Abdalla seeks his help rebelling against Boabdelin, Almanzor eschews talk of what's "right" or of the bonds of nature and society Abdalla is violating and bases his response on his "friendship" with Abdalla and on his desire for revenge against Boabdelin (1.III.i.22): "True, I would wish my friend the juster side: / But in th' unjust my kindness more is try'd" (27-28). In an important sense, within a culture with no clear principle of legitimation and where brother often fights with brother, there is no "juster" side; there is always the threat of Girardian anarchy. When Almanzor helps Boabdelin regain the throne, again he does so out of revenge against Abdalla for breaking his word—and also to have his will in setting Almahide free. What in this world exists to control his Will to Power?

But it is Almahide who tames him, and she does so especially by teaching him the value of constancy. She refuses to yield herself as a spoil of the war not only because brute force is wrong but also because she has plighted troth to Boabdelin. Thus she ennobles the savage. At one point Almanzor exclaims: "There's something noble, lab'ring in my brest: / This raging fire which through the Mass does move, / Shall purge my dross, and shall refine my Love" (1.III.i.422-24). Nevertheless, considering Almahide his "Right" by war (1.IV.ii.423), he still has no respect for the king's right to her (442) and little more for her father, who has given her to Boabdelin. He is justified in being angry with Boabdelin for breaking his word to grant his request, but he is not justified in *demanding* Almahide with no respect for her vows, and she upbraids him for it. Only her honoring her word saves him from death, as he is sent into exile. Upon his departure, she tries to teach him to have faith that "Heav'n will reward your worth some better way" than by having her (1.V.i.422). Finally, he stubbornly decides to live and "not be out-done in Constancy" (482), but his understanding of the term includes more obduracy than fidelity.

When Almahide calls him back from exile, she demands an even higher form of service: "Unbrib'd, preserve a Mistress and a King," and he pledges, "I'le stop at nothing that appears so brave" (2.II.iii.100-101). She has apparently raised his love from the self-interest of a Lyndaraxa to the selflessness and even self-sacrifice of herself and the other models of such a love, such a constancy, Ozmyn and Benzayda. But he backslides, stubbornly contending with Boabdelin over the scarf, stubbornly refusing to fight after Almahide makes him give it back. Then when Boabdelin is captured, Almahide berates Almanzor for breaking his word (2.III.i.174-80). Stung by her rebuke, he honors his promise and fights again.

Against Lyndaraxa's temptation to inconstancy, Almanzor maintains his own constancy to his pledge, despite the lack of reward, though he still is too sullen:

> Though *Almahide,* with scorn rewards my care;
> Yet; than to change, 'tis nobler to despair.
> My Love's my Soul; and that from Fate is free:
> 'Tis that unchang'd; and deathless part of me. [2.III.iii.177-80]

But from this joyless resolution Almanzor proceeds once more after victory to press his suit to Almahide. In the name of the needs of "flesh and blood" (2.IV.iii.264), he demands payment for his services. As the ghost of his mother warns him, he pursues "lawless Love"—adultery, that is, the adulteration of aristocratic patrilinearity (132). Almanzor rejects the ghost's warning, however, and takes refuge in his theory of predestination. Though she has just informed him he is a Christian, he has not learned to trust in their god.

Almanzor now resembles his libertine counterpart in Restoration comedy. He excuses himself from his "bond" with the specious argument that it was compelled by "force" (2.IV.iii.164). He rejects as idealistic nonsense the notion that "purest love can live without reward" (166). When Almahide appeals to "honour" as "the Conscience of an Act well done," "[t]he strong, and secret curb of headlong Will; / The self reward of good; and shame of ill" (190-95), he nominalistically responds that honor is "but a Love well hid" (191) and that her words are but "the Maximes of the day" (196) to be discarded at night, the time for "warm desire" (201). "Enrag'd" with such desire, he paints a vivid, lurid picture of the sexual "Extasie" they will have if she but yield (210-34). In vain are her appeals to his previous "Myracle of Vertue" (258) in serving her "unbrib'd," her attack on his request as "mercenary" (244-46). Only her attempted suicide enables him to defeat that raging bull of his "desire" (274).

Having overcome his passion thus, Almanzor appears to have earned what his mother's ghost has promised: the secret of his birth. In the ensuing battle, as the duke of Arcos relates, "Heav'n (it must be Heav'n)" intervenes and reveals to him his son through unmistakable signs (2.V.iii.187), and Almanzor's mother, expressly sent from Heaven (2.IV.iii.106), restrains him by crying twice, "Strike not thy father"

(2.V.iii.196). Himself a child of passion, born in exile, raised in captivity, Almanzor is an embodiment of his father, who rebelliously married the king's sister without permission. Therefore, he is a perfect double of the monstrous bull, an energy that must be contained and socialized or it will wreak havoc. And the restraining order is the patriarchal monarchial code: he is brought to know and kneel at the feet of his father (205), to acknowledge and pay allegiance to his kinsman as king—his cousin Ferdinand (278-85)—and to respect the laws of sexual constancy, which protect the patrilineal genealogy, and legitimate succession. Finally, he is brought to serve the ultimate validating ideological patriarch, the Christian god, to spread his "Conqu'ring Crosses" to the rest of Spain (346). It is that god who has ratified the code of the word by his repeated providential interposition.

Hence, rivalry and revenge have finally been conquered in this Christian conquest of Granada, and they have been overcome by a countervailing set of values, best epitomized in the Ozmyn and Benzayda subplot. In the face of their fathers' inveterate hatred, they refuse to accept the code of revenge. Despite her father's commands, Benzayda refuses to kill Ozmyn as payment for her brother Tarifa's death. Out of her "pity" grows love between them (1.IV.ii.240). They are rescued by his father, Abenamar, only to have to flee his hatred, as Ozmyn refuses to renege his "vows and faith" to Benzayda (1.V.i.141). Succored by the Christians, who respect such noble pity and love, they yet refuse to turn against their own country. Then, Ozmyn rescues Selin from his own father, being careful to preserve both elders. Selin is vanquished by his generosity and embraces both youngsters, surrendering his revenge. When Selin is later captured by Abenamar, Ozmyn and Benzayda go separately to offer themselves as sacrifices in his stead: as Selin says of his daughter, she "comes to suffer for anothers fau't" (2.IV.i.49). Finally, this spirit of sacrifice, of selfless love, vanquishes even Abenamar.

Self-sacrifice rescues civilization from endless rivalry. Ozmyn and Benzayda do not actually die. But their actions recall the significance of the Cross in which sign the Christians conquer. It is as if their faith—as well as that of Almahide—is sublated upwards, converted into *the* Faith. What Abdalla has said to Lyndaraxa in scorn is, of course, true in the world of the play: "There is more faith in Christian Dogs, than thee" (1.V.i.71). The Zegrys scorn the Abencerrages for possessing not only some Christian blood but even the Christian value of charity to prisoners. The real conquest of Granada is the triumph of Christian values. As Isabella expresses it, Granada is finally "At once to freedom and true faith restor'd: / Its old Religion, and its antient Lord" (2.I.i.26-27). That "Lord" is at once its rightful king and its god, a god that the Spaniards—and all peoples,

Dryden seems to imply by those "Conqu'ring Crosses" that spread out over not only Spain but the New World—should serve by keeping faith: to lovers, fathers, kings, and the Christian father-king-god.[8]

Richard Braverman has provocatively argued that this play does not follow the typical pattern of the aristocratic family romance—and a pattern with particular appeal during the Restoration—where the *perdu,* the lost son, is restored in the end to his legitimate throne (*Plots and Counterplots* 118-25). Indeed, like Corneille's Cid, Almanzor will earn Almahide by his service to a legitimate monarch, and he will be rewarded by sharing the throne of Granada—but not that of Spain itself. Thus the aristocratic ethic of trust is underwritten, but perhaps a subtle message is sent not only to potential rebels in England but even presciently to the king's illegitimate son, the duke of Monmouth: that the throne of the realm is not open to him, despite his heroic energy.

Oedipal rebellion lurks at the heart of feudal patrilineal monarchy.[9] As the emperor in Dryden's *Aureng-Zebe* (1675) puts it, "What love soever by an Heir is shown, / He waits but time to step into the Throne" (II.i.426-27). Other heroic romances have tended to displace rebellion onto others, particularly Machiavels, and from the beginning in Orrery's *Generall* they have developed a figure for loyalty—he who does not himself merit the throne but who, sometimes late, like Almanzor, comes to support it. But in his last rhymed heroic romance Dryden confronts the problem head on. Morat, the emperor's youngest son, is an Oedipal rebel whose "Will" to "Pow'r" (IV.i.322, 376) drives him to fully supplant the father who invited him to the throne by laying claim to his father's intended paramour, the beautiful queen of Kashimir, Indamora: "I've now resolv'd to fill your useless place; / I'll take that Post to cover your disgrace, / And love her, for the honour of my Race" (350-52). Girard's reinterpretation of the Oedipus complex in *Violence and the Sacred* enables us to interpret the son's desire as not for his mother as object libido but for the sign of his father's power, potency. Morat is the Oedipal "Monster" his father fears (354). He defies Father as Superego:

> Could you shed venom from your reverend shade,
> Like Trees, beneath whose arms 'tis death to sleep;
> Did rouling Thunder your fenc'd Fortress keep,
> Thence would I snatch my *Semele,* like *Jove,*
> And midst the dreadful Rack enjoy my Love. [360-64]

A new Jove defies the thunder of the old, even as he assumes Jove's divine potency. Morat will "secure the Throne" by "Paricide" (IV.ii.170).[10]

The Oedipal triangle is tripled in the play. Aureng-Zebe too desires Indamora, who has been granted to him by his father—a grant on which the emperor would now renege because his own desire for her has been aroused. And his right to her is the one right that Aureng-Zebe refuses to relinquish to his father. Meanwhile, the emperor's current queen, Nourmahal, like Phaedra, falls in love with her stepson but, unlike Phaedra, nominalistically defies traditional morality:[11]

> I stand with guilt confounded, lost with shame,
> And yet made wretched onely by a name.
> If names have such command on humane Life,
> Love sure's a name that's more Divine than Wife.
> That Sovereign power all guilt from action takes,
> At least the stains are beautiful it makes. . . .
> Custom our Native Royalty does awe;
> Promiscuous Love is Nature's general Law.
> [III.i.364-69; IV.i.131-32]

She herself leads a rebellion that ironically costs her own son, Morat, his life, and she dies in classical fashion, poisoned with her own monstrosity. Morat, too, receives a condign punishment, dying at the hands of other rebels against his father's throne.

Juxtaposed to these figures of inconstancy, disloyalty, radical rebellion are Morat's wife, Melesinda, Indamora, and Aureng-Zebe. Despite Morat's unfaithfulness to her, Melesinda remains absolutely faithful to him—to the point of committing suttee. Dryden's editors fall over backwards trying to make sense of this Hindu action by a Moslem. Dryden seeks not cultural geographical but ideological consistency, however. Melesinda is a Penelope figure of absolute constancy. The "better Nuptials" she goes to knit anticipate those of Dryden's Cleopatra (V.i.620). As opposed to those dominated by "Int'rest," her "love was such, it needed no return" (628). The piety of her constancy is contrasted with the impiety, the impiousness, the impudence of Nourmahal's promiscuity. She figures forth the pure, unadulterated vessel of patrilineal seed absolutely necessary to (the ideology of) late feudal aristocracy.[12]

Aureng-Zebe is a figure of filial piety. Dryden attempts to negotiate the Oedipal crisis by having Aureng-Zebe *not* rebel against his father. He fights *for* his father throughout and actually at the end *restores* the emperor to the throne Morat has briefly usurped: "[A]ll the rightful Monarch own" (V.i.504). In direct contrast to the emperor's statement that every heir waits impatiently for the death of his father, Aureng-Zebe proclaims, "Long may you live! while you the Sceptre sway / I shall be still most happy to obey" (I.i.320-21). Critics who find Aureng-Zebe unbelievable do not understand the genre; they are like his follower, Dianet:

> The points of Honour Poets may produce;
> Trappings of life, for Ornament, not Use:
> Honour, which onely does the name advance,
> Is the meer raving madness of Romance. [II.i.532-35]

Aureng-Zebe is indeed a figure out of romance whose piety is not supposed to be psychologically but ideologically believable.

Not that he is perfect. Like pious Aeneas, he has an Achilles heel: "by no strong passion sway'd / Except his Love" (I.i.102-3). That passion causes him momentarily to draw his sword against his father, a "Crime" his "Virtue . . . Exerts it self" to rectify immediately, thanks to Indamora (462-64). And that passion causes him to distrust her through jealousy twice, almost at the price of losing her. But Aureng-Zebe's distrust is not just some domestic concern. It is related to the mega-theme of trust in the play. All trusts are interrelated, the domestic and the political, for the world of aristocratic ideology is built on trust.

Indamora, like a Spenserian heroine, teaches Aureng-Zebe and even Morat the value of aristocratic virtue. When Aureng-Zebe draws his sword against his father to assert his right to her, she speaks in the imperative:

> Lose not the Honour you have early wonn;
> But stand the blameless pattern of a Son.
> My love your claim inviolate secures:
> 'Tis writ in Fate, I can be onely yours.
> My suff'rings for you make your heart my due:
> Be worthy me, as I am worthy you. [I.i.455-60]

This is Cornelian *worth*, related to the *gloire* that Indamora's superannuated admirer seeks in his self-sacrifice to save Aureng-Zebe, to the *gloire* that Melesinda seeks as "a glorious Bride" in self-immolation (V.i.635). It is the *gloire* to which Indamora summons Morat, experienced "when to wild Will you Laws prescribe" (V.i.108). Morat becomes her "Convert" (511), and finally turns to his wife to ask her forgiveness before he dies.

As emperor at the end of the play, Aureng-Zebe would seem to have merited succession to the throne by worth instead of birth, for he is not the eldest of the four sons of the emperor. Is Dryden suggesting a counterplot to the normal aristocratic plot, as Braverman would have it (125-34)? I think not. First, the play is not proposing a bourgeois theory of political succession. Despite the fact that early in the play we are apprised that

Aureng-Zebe's "elder Brothers, though o'rcome [by war], have right" (II.i.466), Dryden submerges them (and history: see *Works* 12:385-86) into forgetfulness and makes the conflict between Aureng-Zebe as elder and Morat as younger brother. Aureng-Zebe insists on no "right" to the throne (476). When his father willfully misunderstands his claim to "the birth-right of my mind" (that is, his self-possession) as a claim to succession (III.i.208), Aureng-Zebe insists again, "I, from my years, no merit plead" (217). Yet later the emperor will berate himself for ignoring both "Right" and "Nature" in his surrendering Aureng-Zebe's succession to his younger brother (IV.i.366). Moreover, Morat sees the contest in classical primogenitive terms:

> Birthright's a vulgar road to Kingly sway;
> 'Tis ev'ry dull-got Elder Brother's way.
> Dropt from above, he lights into a Throne;
> Grows of a piece with that he sits upon,
> Heav'ns choice, a low, inglorious, rightful Drone.
> But who by force a Scepter does obtain,
> Shows he can govern that which he could gain.
> Right comes of course, what e'r he was before;
> Murder and Usurpation are no more. [V.i.66-74]

The play certainly does not support this de facto position. Implicitly, "Heav'ns choice" appears no "inglorious rightful Drone" but the glorious, rightful, active Aureng-Zebe. There also seems to be an implicit form of criticism of the Muslim model, where the father's choice may be arbitrary and where his son's path to the throne is a different form of parricide (literally, killing one's relatives): fratricide. Victor in his father's name, Aureng-Zebe extends his virtue of piety by decree: "Our impious use no longer shall obtain; / Brothers no more, by Brothers, shall be slain" (V.i.412-13). Finally, Aureng-Zebe finesses the Oedipal crisis by restoring his father to the throne—only to have the latter abdicate in his favor. So he accedes to the throne with no parricidal blood on his hands, not even over the emperor's dead body. And the emperor also withdraws from sexual rivalry with his son(s), regranting to Aureng-Zebe his beloved, constant Indamora:

> The just rewards of Love and Honour wear.
> Receive the Mistris you so long have serv'd;
> Receive the Crown your Loialty preserv'd.
> Take you the Reins, while I from cares remove,
> And sleep within the Chariot which I drove. [671-75]

No supplanting Jove, Aureng-Zebe passively succeeds, married to his non-passive, instructive royal consort, whose wit and wisdom may suggest a figure of Sophia.

Implicit in the endings of Dryden's two great exotic heroic romances, *The Conquest of Granada* and *Aureng-Zebe,* is that a country without a clear mechanism for succession, one preferably sanctified with religious rhetoric, is in danger of the endless reciprocal violence of feuding brothers, clans, factions. England could take comfort in having such a mechanism. But as all Englishmen knew, it was a mechanism damaged by regicide and only tenuously restored. The message of the plays would seem to be that patrilineal, primogenitive succession must be rigorously adhered to lest another civil war erupt.

As James Thompson has suggested, throughout *The Conquest of Granada* runs a subtext of imperialism, what Laura Brown has called "the romance of empire."[13] King Ferdinand's "Conqu'ring Crosses" represent not only *La Reconquista* of Spain from the Moors but also the conquest of the New World. They represent the rationale for the conquest and colonization of the entire world by Western Europe because its god is the One True God. The dramatic prologue to Dryden and Robert Howard's *Indian Queen* features an Indian boy and girl waking from an idyllic sleep at the invasion of the New World by the Old. They are mindful of prophecies that foretold this event, but the sight of the conquerors puts them at ease, for "Their Looks are such, that Mercy flows from thence. . . . By their protection let us beg to live; / They came not here to Conquer, but Forgive." Forgive for what? Obviously, for being pagans.

Thus, even as Restoration heroic romance represents a late feudal swan song for aristocratic ideology, in its ubiquitous exotic settings it reveals a subtext of Western Europe's struggle for cultural and economic hegemony—over the Mediterranean Sea, the Atlantic, the Pacific, the Indian oceans. In a couple of remarkable operatic tableaux, Sir William Davenant, manager of one of the two legitimate theaters in London after the Restoration, portrayed incipient English hegemony in particular: *The History of Sir Francis Drake* and *The Cruelty of the Spaniards in Peru,* both written and performed during the Interregnum but resurrected and cobbled together as part of a drollery to pass the summer doldrums in 1663, *The Play-house to Be Let*. Drake's English sailors sing,

> Then Cry One and all!
> Amain, for *Whitehall!*

The *Diegos* we'll board to rummidge their Hold;
And drawing our Steel, they must draw out their Gold. [*Works* 90]

A chorus sings of granting "clemency" to those Indians who submit to England, who shall then "seem as free as those whom they shall serve" (93). Thus England portrays itself as Liberator. And her destiny reaches beyond America. A maroon takes Drake to a famous tree in Panama whence he can see the two Atlantics, north and south. Drake cannot wait first to see, then to sail, the south Atlantic, which yet no English ship has sailed. The maroon, a former Spanish slave now liberated by Drake, prophesies that Drake will appropriate that ocean for his isle as well. The chorus sings

This Prophesie will rise
To higher Enterprise.
The *English* Lion's walk shall reach as far
As prosp'rous valour dares adventure War.
As Winds can drive, or Waves can bear
Those Ships which boldest Pilots stear. [96]

Of course, the lament of the Peruvians anent their colonization by the Spanish subverts for the wise the jingoism of the English liberators, who will treat their West Indian *servants,* whom they benignly *forgive* and *protect,* no differently:

Whilst yet our world was new,
When not discover'd by the old;
E're begger'd slaves we grew,
For having silver Hills, and strands of Gold.
Chorus. We danc'd and we sung
And lookt ever young,
And from restraints were free,
As waves and winds at sea. [105]

Dryden and his colleagues can appropriate and romanticize American and Asian Indians, but it is an act of cultural imperialism that is part and parcel of incipient British imperialism.[14]

2
Villains & States
Romantic Tragedy

Romantic tragedies tend to be quite black and white, pitting good against evil, as in romance, with gray characters in the middle, more sinned against than sinning. Such tragedies most often conclude in stages littered with the bodies of the suffering innocent as well as the sinners and the villains. That is, romantic tragedies do not conclude in the distributive justice of romance, where not only are villains defeated but heroes are ultimately rewarded after trial. Romantic tragedies do, nevertheless, conclude in retributive justice against their dark villains and usually with some kind of promise of reward in the afterlife for the suffering innocents. In the Restoration, conflict in romantic tragedies pits Hobbist-Machiavels, with their nominalism and at least crypto-atheism, against virtuous aristocrats, struggling to remain constant to others, to themselves, to their values of honor and trust. If the virtuous die, their values do not. The ruling class demonstrates its worth, its right to rule, precisely because its values are transcendent.

As the alternate endings of Howard's *Vestal Virgin* (1665) indicate, the rhymed heroic play could accommodate tragedy, concluding one night with distributive justice, the next with none, no restoration of the innocent. The most notorious of these rhymed romantic tragedies is Elkanah Settle's *Empress of Morocco* (1673), which features not one but two Machiavels, one the evil statesman Crimalhaz and the other the fiendish empress herself. Machiavels are often explicit blasphemers, and these two defy the gods outrageously. Although the Machiavels are responsible for the death of the old and the young emperors and are on the brink of triumph, their inconstancy to each other (no honor among thieves) causes the mad suicide of the empress. Interestingly, the statesman is foiled by one of his factors, Hametalhaz, who is converted to aristocratic generosity, a conversion he attributes to the power of Platonic love and "Heav'n" (V, 69). The loyal general, a prince of the royal blood, succeeds to the throne, and the scene draws to reveal the statesman impaled on hooks, while a spokesman reads the moral: "See the reward of Treason" (70).

The audience is assured that the murdered emperors have found new crowns in heaven.

More interesting than Settle's outrageous villains—and he created several more in romantic tragedies throughout the period[1]—are the more subtle villains in Thomas Porter's *Villain* (1662) or Jaspar in Henry Neville Payne's *Fatal Jealousy* (1672), both (mostly) unrhymed romantic tragedies. The title character of the former, out of the sheer malignance his proper name implies (Malignii), manipulates essentially virtuous characters into destroying themselves. He himself is tortured to death at the end, and the spokesman cautions us not to despair at the apparent triumph of evil, for "Vertue" really triumphs, if only in an afterlife, and "We must submit to him that makes all even, / And never Spurn against the will of Heaven" (V, concluding lines [faulty pagination]). Playing Iago to Antonio's Othello, Jaspar in Payne's tragedy goads Antonio to avenge his wife's misperceived inconstancy, killing first her soiled sister, Eugenia, by mistake, then the heavenly Caelia. The men kill each other; both women seek entrance into heaven. Jaspar concludes, "'Tis done, I am catch'd at last in my / Own Trap. Oh, I deserve my Death for want / Of fore-sight" (V, 71). Such sentiments are typical: evil defeats itself because it is not providential; only Heaven is. And the witches associated with Jaspar's evil are juxtaposed especially to the constant Caelia, with the Magdalenic Eugenia in between along a value spectrum designed to inculcate chastity in the vessels of patrilinearity.

Agents of the supernatural abound in these romantic tragedies, most dabbling in black magic (witches, ghosts, friars, priests).[2] Some become explicitly religious martyr plays, from Dryden's *Tyrannick Love* (1669) to Banks's *Vertue Betray'd* (1682) and *The Island Queens* (unacted because banned). Here the suffering innocents at last manifest contempt for the world and seek the reward for their virtue in a Christian afterlife, despite the blasphemous defiance of Maximins and Machiavels. Here the Manichaean nature of romantic tragedy most manifests. Virtuous apparent naifs are constantly being told they don't know the power of the dark side, the power of Power. Yet their mettle, tested in the fires of trial, vindicates their values after all as not naive but transcendent over suffering and death. Therefore, the nobility, portrayed as the class most naturally bred to such values, must deserve their rank. And, therefore, the villains from that same class who oppose those values warrant to be cloaked, like Wolsey, as the fallen Lucifer, the ultimate class traitor.

Such a traitor is John Wilson's fine creation, Andronicus Comnenius, in his play of that name (unacted but publ. 1664). Mamalus, former secretary of state of the Eastern Roman Empire, warns those who would recall the exiled Andronicus to stabilize the state,

> He is a Prince of the most daring soul,
> E're dropt from Heaven; industrious, vigilant,
> Kind, affable, magnificent:—
> Yet all this good, Nay, all his lusts and passions
> Are slaves to his Ambition: Take him there,
> Nothing can hold him; Lawes, Religion, All
> Sacred or civil. [I.i.148-54]

The lords hope to tie him by oaths, but Mamalus reports that his reason for exile was that he "Swore, and forswore again" till the old emperor had to banish him despite his talents (161). Returned, Andronicus plots against the young emperor with Machiavellian bravado:

> There's but a step
> 'Twixt me, and the imperial Crown:—Nor shou'd
> That coward wear't, that dares not venture for't:
> Was this the reason, my blind Mistris [Fortune], that
> You strook at me? . . . if she
> Will not assist, the world shall know I can
> Do it without her help; . . .
> Who is past hope, he should be past dispair:
> I'll run the hazard then, and if I fall,
> What in me lies, I'll pluck all after me. [I.v.7-22]

Once Andronicus has dispatched his cousin, like Richard III, he courts his widow.

Choosing the people as his power base instead of the peers of the realm, Andronicus manipulates his way to nearly all his goals, while his factor Philo admires: "Excellent fox" (III.ii.79). Pretending to refuse the crown, he mocks the supposed vox populi he has maneuvered to offer it (116). When his son Manuel, himself redeemed from cynicism, opposes law to Andronicus's designs, the latter expostulates in exasperation,

> By law! you blockhead; Doth not Justice sit
> At *Jupiters* elbow? What cannot power do,
> And justifi't when don? He that can nothing
> But what is lawful, raigns by curtesie:
> Besides, what use of Laws? Good Kings may live
> Without 'um, bad ones will not much regard 'um; . . .
> Weigh Crowns by th'ballance and you'll make fine work:
> Preach laws to sword-men! [IV.i.128-41]

To Manuel's "vertue" (118), then, Andronicus opposes Machiavelli's antinomian *virtù*.

Nevertheless, Andronicus becomes more and more like Macbeth, not knowing "whom to trust" (V.ii.2), relying on another, lesser Machiavel. Finally his fate is condign:

> The people
> Having by this time utterly defac'd
> Whatever bore his name, or memory;
> Fell foul of him—Or rather He, of them;
> Had you but seen the hubbub!—One twicks his beard;
> Another, beats out an Eie; A third, a Tooth;
> A forth cuts off a Hand; —No cruelty
> He e'r commanded, but was there agen
> Epitomis'd on himself. [V.viii.80-88]

The lesser Machiavel, likewise defeated, proclaims, "Heav'n is just" (47). The loyal lord whose name is telling—Constantinus—engineers the restoration of the rightful heir. And the play concludes with a double warning, one addressed to such class traitors, the other to the threat of the fickle rabble:

> May the same Fate ever attend Rebellion,
> And usurpation;—And let the world,
> Hence lea[rn], on what a ticklish point they stand,
> Whose unjust actions; and borrow'd greatness,
> (How speciously soever colour'd o're)
> Have no foundation, but what's built upon
> The peoples favour;—The uncertain people,
> Constant to nothing, but in constancie. [95-102]

When Manuel says, "Honour without vertue, / Is what the people pleases, not our own" (III.iv.115-16), the possessive refers to his aristocratic class. The "vertuous man" he delineates to the mocking Philo (121) is a portrait designed to return virtue to *virtù* as the play inculcates a restored aristocratic ideology.

In Orrery's *Tragedy of Mustapha, the Son of Solyman the Magnificent* (1665), the Machiavel is a vizier, the unscrupulous statesman Rustan, who as a nominalist considers friendship "a mere Name 'twixt those who covet Power" (II.116) and who gives explicitly Machiavellian advice to Solyman: "[W]isest Monarchs by Success have prov'd, / That it is safer to be fear'd, than lov'd" (IV.322-23). But his villainy merely abets the ambition of the deceitful Roxolana, second wife to Solyman, who exacerbates his jealousy against Mustapha, his elder son by a former wife, in order to secure the succession to her son, Zanger. Rustan's attitude toward friendship is contradicted by the mutual vows between these brothers, despite the fact that they become rivals in love. Their vows are exchanged in the face of the Islamic practice of succession through fratricide that we saw in *Conquest of Granada* and *Aureng-Zebe*. As in the latter play, no one finally succeeds through either parricide or fratricide. But fratricide is avoided only because Zanger commits suicide over the corpse of his brother. Rustan is executed for his villainy, and the empress Roxolana is forgiven but banished. The Christian queen of Hungary, who has thrown herself and her infant son on the generosity of Roxolana, is allowed to return to Buda with her son, who becomes king. So far a typical romantic tragedy: suffering innocents whose values transcend not only those of the villains but the world; villains punished by a just "Heav'n" (V.245).

What is interesting about this play, however, is the way in which Solyman's guilt gets displaced at the end onto the villains, for he is guilty of rash retaliation against putative Oedipal rebellion. His insecurity leads him to precipitate distrust of Mustapha, as the family secret of patriarchal monarchy peeps out of the closet: the son can succeed only over the dead body of the father. Rustan poisons Solyman with a report that the army greatly affects Mustapha. Solyman jumps to conclusions: "He robs my heart of all the Calms of Rest: / Il'l [*sic*] tear the dire Usurper from my Breast" (II.185-86). The antecedent of "He" is both Rustan and Mustapha himself. Mustapha's very existence troubles an aging patriarch. Solyman protests he himself resides still in the heyday of heroic glory—"They [the soldiers] steal my Laurels to adorn my Son; / Who can but dream of Fields that I have won" (II.237-38)—even as he reveals doubts:

> They, by the many Battles I have won,
> Think all the stock of my Success is gone:
> Though fortune often grac'd me in the field,
> And many favours hung upon my shield;
> Yet now cold looks men to my winter bring,
> Whilst they rejoyce at my Successour's spring:
> Fortune they think is to his youth in debt;
> And what she pays to him they hope to get. [III.255-62]

His "winter" is his discontent, his son's "spring." He accuses his son of the nominalism with which Rustan and Roxolana have infected him:

> Since on Ambition's wings he means to rise,
> He will both hate and slight all Nature's Ties.

> A Fathers Name cannot his Nature fright
> From Glory when it does his youth invite.
> Th' inchanting sound of Pow'r so Charms his Ear,
> That he will now no other Musick hear. [IV.338-43]

Tragically, it is Solyman who in the fantasy of a diseased mind forgets the name of *son*. His feverish imagination interprets his dilemma as Oedipal fate: "My Son's ordain'd to what he should not do / And I to bear what I should punish too" (IV.382-83).

Unwilling "to live under a Fathers Hate" (V.168), the pious Mustapha would go quietly but, like Aureng-Zebe, asserts his right of self-defense when his executioners deny him the opportunity to clear himself with Solyman. The latter is outraged at his effrontery, and Mustapha acquiesces: "I am too guilty since you think me so" (V.227). After Mustapha's execution, his brother insists to their father, "By all the duty to a Father due, / And to our Prophet, *Mustapha* was true" (V.360-61). Solyman momentarily acknowledges his "guilt" (364), but immediately imputes his "Fate" to "destinie" (375). After Zanger's suicide, Solyman blames "Friendship and Cruelty" (395) for robbing him of both sons. Curious it is to displace his own double guilt onto Zanger and Mustapha's exemplary friendship. And if the "Cruelty" he refers to is his own, he quickly displaces it through his "Revenge" onto the villains (413). He maintains that this revenge keeps him from the Roman stoic suicide of Zanger. And perhaps Orrery feels constrained by decorum from portraying a monarch with too much guilt, too much pathos even. But the horror of his crime leers from behind the arras. A messenger narrates Solyman's successful quelling of the army faction risen in rebellion over Mustapha's arrest. He describes the lament of the victorious over the slain in this intestine warfare: "Some, who had kill'd their Sons, more tears did shed / For their own guilt, than that their Sons were dead; / Guilt wrought by Fate" (561-63).

The "Fate" is endemic to the system of succession. It may get consigned to the corner of the action, as in a Brueghel painting. But it contaminates the ideology of monarchy portrayed in the play. Opening with dissenting councils on both Turkish and Christian sides, the play moves toward the following declamation in the middle. Solyman narrates how he raised his son to the heroic ethos of the romance of chivalry:

> I taught him . . .
> That only valour is true faith, and those
> Do most trust Heav'n, who alwaies life expose;
> I taught him Vertue, and to love her so
> As tame Philosophers durst never do;

Enduring for her sake the pangs of power,
And all the toyls that make a Conquerour:
For none but Chiefs who firmly these endure,
Can reach such pow'r as may the good secure:
I taught him such a greatness as might be
From all the yokes of Subjects counsel free:
None but our Prophet Empire understood,
Which, when 'tis bounded, ceases to be good; . . .
He [Mustapha] blest Heav'ns King, who Monarchy first made.
[III.181-99]

The play seems to insist that Love qualifies this ethic: the love that the Hungarian queen inspires in the two brothers; even the love between Solyman and Roxolana that finally moves him to merely banish and not kill her; the "love" Solyman insists to his Machiavel should motivate the prince (IV.ii.321). Mustapha even asserts that "[a] Cottage-Lover may deserve a Throne" (III.i.142). But the play's hostility to anyone beneath the highest order who dares to have an opinion militates against any democratic sentiments. Solyman denigrates his parliament:

Divans, like Commonwealths, regard not fame;
Disdaining honour they can feel no shame:
Each does, for what they publick safety call,
Venture his Vertue in behalf of all,
Doing by pow'r what Nature does forbid,
Each hoping, amongst all, that he is hid,
Hidden because they on each other wink,
When they dare act what Monarchs scorn to think. [I.i.65-72]

There is, of course, a grave irony in Solyman's accusing anyone else of "Doing by pow'r what Nature does forbid." Nevertheless, his critique is echoed later in the play by Roxolana:

By counsel Men perswade, or else direct;
Direction like Appointment we suspect:
And even perswasion does the Throne invade;
For Slaves may govern whom they can perswade. [IV.i.187-90]

Monarchs cannot allow anyone to *tell* them what to do; such directions are suspicious because they may be motivated by self-interest. And any theory of government based on persuasion would ultimately destroy royal prerogative and the very class system itself. We might dismiss these sentiments as associated with demonstrably imperfect rulers. But they are echoed by the Hungarian queen:

> Our greatest Counc'lours think we are unjust,
> When our least Thoughts are hidden from their trust;
> And till (by knowing th' utmost that we know)
> Those restless Counc'lours may our Rulers grow,
> They do not love us, and they sullen seem;
> But after, care not, though we love not them. [IV.i.285-90]

Even the greatest of counselors, then, will not be satisfied until they know so much of monarchs' thoughts that they virtually become the rulers of rulers. After they have gained so much power, they could not care less whether the monarchs love them. And it is, after all, the virtuous Mustapha who at the end of Solyman's recitation of his heroic ethic "blest Heav'ns King, who Monarchy first made, / And prais'd him, cause he no companion had" (III.ii.199-200). Is this ideology qualified by Mustapha's deity being Allah and not the Christian Trinity? Not when juxtaposed to the queen's sentiments. Orrery's monarchism would seem to be as absolute as Charles II or even Louis XIV could want.[3] And it is a monarchism that eclipses Solyman's parricide as the curtain falls.

The title character of Aphra Behn's *Abdelazer; or, The Moor's Revenge* (1676) is perhaps the most interesting of all Restoration Machiavels, for he is a Moor, a racialized other, an *unheimlich* monster onto whom is displaced the evil that threatens the aristocratic code of loyalty and generosity. Abdelazer seeks the revenge of the subtitle because his father, the king of Fez, was conquered by King Philip of Spain. The young Abdelazer became Philip's slave but also a favorite, whom he raised to honors. The mature Abdelazer, insisting throughout on his own royal blood, seeks a kingdom for a kingdom, and he employs the arts of seduction and dissimulation—and villainous murder—to gain his ends.

Abetted by the queen of Spain, whom he enslaves through lust, Abdelazer poisons her husband, sets up the new king and his own wife to be caught in compromising circumstances and murdered, manipulates the queen to disgrace herself and declare her second son and heir to the throne a bastard, uses the queen to manipulate the prince cardinal into betraying the rightful prince, has the queen herself murdered, and finally courts the princess as his bride and future queen.

Despite Abdelazer's repeated claim to his right to the throne,[4] it is not he but Prince Philip, the second son, who is restored at the end.

Abdelazer's royal nature makes him, too, a class traitor. He is an unscrupulous Machiavel, a dark trickster, who is thoroughly demonized throughout. Other characters repeatedly refer to his black skin as the sign of his devilishness. Prince Philip refers to him as his mother's "Sooty Leacher" (I.ii.91). Such references might be viewed as mere cultural prejudice, a prejudice the play belies (as perhaps in *Othello*). But Abdelazer himself luxuriates in his blackness as the cloak for his villainy:

> So I thank thee Nature, that in making me
> Thou didst design me Villain!
> Fitting each faculty for Active mischief:—
> Thou skillful Artist, thank thee for my face,
> It will discover nought that's hid within.—
> Thus arm'd for ills,
> Darkness! and Horrour! I invoke your aid;
> And thou, dread Night! shade all your busie Stars
> In blackest Clouds,
> And let my Daggers brightness only serve
> To guide me to the mark,—and guide it so,
> It may undoe a Kingdom at one blow. [II.i.292-303]

As he tempts the Princess Leonora, who is precontracted to another, Abdelazer hypocritically pretends to blame her resistance on his blackness and to curse "Nature, that has dy'd my skin / With this ungrateful colour" (V.510-11). Yet he proceeds once again to luxuriate:

> —Yet as I am, I've been in vain Ador'd,
> And Beauties great as thine have languish'd for me.
> The Lights put out! thou in my naked arms
> Wilt find me soft and smooth as polisht Ebony. [513-16]

The use of the simile of "polisht Ebony" allows him to occlude his color and celebrate it at the same time.

Ironically, Abdelazer, the royal slave who would be master, is defeated by one of his own slaves, by the blackamoor Osmin, who saves Leonora from rape, preserves Prince Philip, and later rescues him from prison and despair. His blackness cloaks virtue, symbolic whiteness: "Thou art some Angel sure, in that dark Cloud" (V.692). But Osmin is the exception. Philip refers to the "Sooty hand" of the Moor, Zarrack, come to execute him (675). And when Abdelazer complains that he has been betrayed by his own slaves, Philip retorts, "Now thou damn'd Villain! true born Son of Hell! / Not one of thy In[f]ernal Kin shall save thee" (720-21). On the blasphemously defiant, heroic devil of a villain, who rehearses his crimes in Philip's teeth, Philip levels the epithet "Poor angry Slave" (785). His execution is communal: Philip *"Runs on him, all the rest do the like in the same minute: Abdelazer aims at the Prince, and kills Osmin: and falls dead himself"* (798 s.d.).[5] Thus Philip is restored through the agency, yet once more, of his black angel, who takes the thrust intended for him. Radical otherness, in one sense, destroys itself. In another sense, it is expunged by the community in a collective purgation of the *unheimlich* monster. The purgation allows the community the fiction that it is no longer contaminated. But the nature of the *unheimlich* is that it is no stranger. Abdelazer represents the radical threats built into the system that must perpetually be kept at bay. His "witchcraft" (I.i.98) is not some exotic voodoo but homegrown "Magick of Dissimulation" (IV.253).

The queen is another such representation, a gendered other that threatens patriarchal control: "Assist me all that's ill in Woman-kind" (III.ii.39). What is more, she is Mother as other. Her very lust for a Moor is ipso facto a sign, within white male European symbolism, of her radical perversity. Philip plays the role of plain dealer:

> My Father whilst he liv'd, tir'd his strong Arm
> With numerous Battels 'gainst the enemy,
> Wasting his brains in Warlike stratagems,
> To bring confusion on the faithless Moors,
> Whilst you, lull'd in soft peace at home,—betray'd
> His name to everlasting Infamy;
> Suffer'd his Bed to be defil'd with Lust,
> Gave up your self, your honour, and your vows,
> To wanton in yon Sooty Leacher's arms. [I.ii.83-91]

The monstrous other is at home in bed with the queen, that symbol of patriarchal cultural stability. She traffics with radical evil.

The radicalness of her evil is manifested in her hatred of her own son—"that Boy I hate" (II.i.214)—whom she has determined to kill. She sounds like Lady Macbeth:

> Nature be gone, I chase thee from my soul,
> Who Love's Almighty Empire does controul;
> And she that will to thy dull Laws submit,
> In spight of thee, betrays the Hypocrite.
> No rigid Virtue shall my soul possess,
> Let Gown-men preach against the wickedness;
> Pleasures were made by Gods! and meant for us,
> And not t'enjoy 'em, were ridiculous. [230-37]

Women who obey men's laws are hypocrites, for at bottom they are all desire: patriarchal man's greatest fear, greatest monster. Ironically, Abdelazer's birthing imagery—"My wrongs and I will be retir'd to Night, / And bring forth Vengeance, with the Mornings light" (245-46)—signals his appropriation of the agency she claims.

The queen is so unnatural as to declare Prince Philip a bastard and to urge her older son, the new King Ferdinand, to rape her rival, Abdelazer's wife:

> Assist me all that's ill in Woman-kind,
> And furnish me with sighs, and feigned tears,
> That may express a grief, for this discovery [the bastardy].—
> My Son [Ferdinand], be like thy Mother, hot and bold;
> And like the Noble Ravisher of *Rome,*
> Court her with Daggers, when thy Tongue grows faint,
> Till thou hast made a Conquest o're her Virtue. [III.ii.39-45]

As the virtuous wife poises a dagger to kill herself if Ferdinand should persist in his rape, the queen enters, pretends she threatens the king, and kills her. Ferdinand curses her "Devils" hand (III.iii.135) and contemplates condign punishment:

> —What dost thou merit for this Treachery?
> Thou vilest of thy Sex—
> But thou'rt a thing I have miscall'd a Mother,
> And therefore will not touch thee,—live to suffer
> By a more shamefull way. [136-40]

Behn's finest dramaturgy exhibits itself in the queen's manipulation of the prince cardinal—first into deserting Prince Philip not just through the ruse of bastardy but through the use of the cardinal's lust for her and his ambition for the throne; last into losing the object of his passions through her betrayal of him. The dramatic moment has come for the queen to name the father of her bastard. She is forced to articulate her shame. She names—the cardinal himself! And she turns her shame into merely that of Malory's duchess of Cornwall: the cardinal slipped into her husband's place while he was away at war. The cardinal exclaims to the cosmos: "Gods! is there any Hell but Womans falshood!" (V.107). Yet he sees "The Powers above are just" (148) in their punishment of his passions.

Nevertheless, the cardinal's question still rings at the end of the play. Abdelazer represents an *unheimlich* monster, but the queen a *heimlich*. "Womans falshood" is the greatest of all hells in patriarchal literature, for her adultery constitutes adulteration of patrilinearity. On the fragility of her symbolic hymen depends succession of power and property, from Guinevere to Gertrude to Almahide (see *Word as Bond*). Thus, lest the play lend itself to cultural despair, Behn creates two constant women in antithesis to the queen: Abdelazer's wife, Florella, and Princess Leonora, both of whom remain true to their betrotheds and resist seduction and rape. King Ferdinand's uncontrollable love for Florella stems from the fact, familiar in Behn's plays, that they loved each other before her father, in deference to old King Philip, gave her to Abdelazer. Though he insists Abdelazer's possessing her was "a Sacrilegious theft" (III.iii.70), she insists à la Almahide that she is now bound to Abdelazer by "Sacred vow" (68), and like Almahide she threatens to kill herself to preserve her chastity. Killed instead by the queen, according to Ferdinand "her sacred soul is fled / To that Divinity, of which it is a part" (113-14), and killed himself by Abdelazer, the dying Ferdinand envisions Florella waiting for him beyond the pale, where, the implication is, they will be united at last: "I hear thee cry, my Love!—I come—I come, fair Soul!" (188). Princess Leonora's faith to her vows to Alonzo, despite his lower birth, causes her to resist the temptation of union with Abdelazer's power in co-regency—and then to resist his rape. Calling on "ye Powers that favour Innocence," she attributes the black angel Osmin's salvific advent to "the Gods" (V.567, 579). Her faith is finally rewarded by Alonzo's being raised to sufficient rank for them to marry—duke of Salamanca. She concludes the play acting like an honorable princess, as opposed to the dishonorable queen, her mother: she says to the restored King Philip, "Come, my dear Brother, to that glorious business / Our Birth and Fortunes call us" (818-19).

The passivity of Florella and Leonora, relative to the queen, constitutes the typical patriarchal dichotomy between assertive and recessive women, the former being improperly uppity, centrifugal, the latter properly meek, centripetal. Leonora is somewhat atypical in her royal assertiveness at the end, but after all, she will not be queen. Assertiveness matching that of the queen and Abdelazer is reserved for Prince Philip. If Ferdinand is too weak a king to oppose them, languishing in his "Lethargy of Love" (II.ii.137), Philip is a Drydenesque fiery martial hero, who refuses to control his tongue in disapprobation of his mother and the "Slave" Abdelazer, as he repeatedly calls him. Philip resembles Hamlet cum Laertes: he returns to his father's funeral clothed in martial victory and properly pious. Yet he cannot restrain his vitriol against his mother and her paramour. He cannot let his mother leave without proclaiming her "sin and shame" (I.ii.81). And he proclaims Abdelazer "Villain, . . . Hell-begotten Fiend" (93) and would answer him sword for sword immediately. When Abdelazer asks,

"How got you, Sir, this daring?" (105), Philip boldly asserts its origin and the origin of Abdelazer's power:

> From injur'd *Philips* death,
> Who, whilst he liv'd, unjustly cherist thee,
> And set thee up beyond the reach of Fate;
> Blind with thy brutal valour, deaf with thy flatteries,
> Discover'd not the Treasons thou didst act,
> Nor none durst let him know 'em:—but did he live,
> I wou'd aloud proclaim them in his ears. [106-12]

Similar to a Jacobean malcontent, Philip is the only one in the play to remain in Abdelazer's face. He even criticizes his brother's adulterous lust to his face and draws against Abdelazer in the royal presence. Ferdinand finally reduces the rash young Philip to obedience to his new king, but his hatred of the Moor breaks out again, and he drinks to his "Confusion" in his presence (II.ii.66). When his brother asks him why he must display his resentment "in publick," Philip responds, "Because he gives me cause, and that in publick. / And Sir, I was not born to bear with Insolence" (121-23)—adding to his friends that Ferdinand "will sleep away his anger, / And tamely see us murder'd by this Moor" (131-32). Warned by the black angel, Philip escapes Abdelazer's plot against him and, after Ferdinand's and Florella's deaths, takes up arms against him and the queen. Fearlessly Philip meets Abdelazer in the field and against all odds defeats him. But the queen has seduced the cardinal into betraying Philip, and the prince is led defiantly to prison: "Villains, you cannot be my Jaylors; there's no Prison, / No Dungeon deep enough; no Gate so strong, / To keep a man confin'd—so mad with wrong" (IV.438-40). In prison he defiantly complains against the "cruel Powers" for abandoning him (V.645). Yet implicitly it is the Powers that have sent the black Osmin, whom Philip himself names "Angel" (692). Finally matching word for word, sword for sword, Philip presides over the communal purgation of the blasphemous villain. The cardinal announces the restoration to Spain of "the greatest Treasure / That ever happy Monarchy possess'd" (811-12).

The necessity for this confrontation between the potent Philip and the potent Abdelazer is cultural. There must be a white boy who can jump. For the conflict symbolized by black versus white, European versus African, Christian versus Muslim, is a cultural clash, represented through ideological portrayals that mask its economic nature. The thousand years' war between West and East (and South) was a battle for the Mediterranean, for the control of trade, of wealth. Abdelazer represents, then, not only the *unheimlich* that European ideology displaces onto a racialized other but a formidable rival for economic supremacy, portrayed as "faithless Moors" (I.ii.86), as Infidels, as Devils in a Manichaean dichotomy performing cultural work. The restored King Philip concludes the play in an apparently conventional epic simile:

> So after Storms, the joyful Mariner
> Beholds the distant wish'd-for shore afar,
> And longs to bring the rich-fraight Vessel in,
> Fearing to trust the faithless Seas again. [V.821-24]

Yet the simile has hidden riches itself: So the Spanish have only a little further until *La Reconquista* be complete, the "faithless" Moors defeated, and the Mediterranean Sea safe for monopoly European trade.

Dryden's *Indian Emperour; or, The Conquest of Mexico by the Spaniards* (1665) explicitly foregrounds the romance of empire. It is a romantic tragedy, featuring Machiavellian villains Almeria and Odmar (joined temporarily by Alibech). These are Indians of high noble blood, and in a sense we witness a typical aristocratic family romance. Alibech, daughter of the usurper Zempoalla from *The Indian Queen,* argues that betraying the emperor, Montezuma, and letting in the enemy is an evil necessary to the safety of these doomed Indian nobles and therefore, "That ill is pardon'd which does good procure" (IV.ii.72). Moreover, she argues that subjects have the right to rise "for publick good" against stubborn monarchs (75). Guyomar, loyal son to Montezuma, warns,

> Take heed, Fair Maid, how Monarchs you accuse:
> Such reasons none but impious Rebels use:
> Those who to Empire by dark paths aspire,
> Still plead a call to what they most desire;
> But Kings by free consent their Kingdoms take,
> Strict as those Sacred Ties which Nuptials make;
> And what e're faults in Princes time reveal,
> None can be Judge where can be no Appeal. [76-83]

As John Loftis has pointed out,[6] this is European monarchism. The analogy between political and sexual constancy is appropriate to patrilineal monarchy. And the rebellion of Montezuma's older son, Odmar, is, like Morat's, Oedipal, for he would mount the throne by "Parricide" (V.i.11). Almeria is the reincarnation of her unscrupulous mother, who preaches that "Courage makes ill actions good" (III.i.103) and who fatally enthralls the emperor. In the end, Guyomar and his chastened bride, Alibech, live, although they seek refuge to the barren north, which the Conquistadores could not possibly covet. The villains on both sides, including the wickedly greedy Pizarro, are dead. And the virtuous Cortez succeeds to empire, married to the royal princess, Cydaria. Virtue triumphs after great loss.

The Spanish conquer, however, not because of greater virtue. They would seem to conquer because their god is the True God. The Aztec earthly spirits prophesy, "A God more strong, who all the gods commands, / Drives us to exile from our Native Lands" (II.i.25-26). But Montezuma wins the theological debate with the Spanish priest: his deistic religion is shown to be superior to a parochial religion operating by force and threat and torture. The Christians' pretense to superior religion is belied by their—and its—inherent sadism. Honoring international aristocracy, Dryden's rather subversive point is that Europe triumphs simply because of the manifest destiny of history.[7] Montezuma and his empire's "fall" is their "doom" (I.ii.340). He prays that if it be so, "Grant only he who has such Honour shown, / When I am dust, may fill my empty Throne" (341-42). In the immediate future, that person is the noble, honorable Cortez. But he himself recognizes that Spain (and the pope and the Jesuits) have all lost their moral authority through their greed and sadism. Indian gold "into *Spain* wilt fatally be brought, / Since with the price of Blood thou here art bought" (V.ii.136-37). The clear implication is that the honorable (Protestant) English will inherit the Indies by moral default.

3
Fathers & Sons
Political Tragedy

All these state-sponsored romances and tragedies are political in the broad sense that they generally produce hegemonic ideology. But some Restoration tragedies are political in a narrower sense: this sense may include topical reference, but I am using the term here to imply a larger pattern of figuration intended to reaffirm hegemonic ideology by defending its regnant political theory. The majority of Restoration political tragedies polemically defend Stuart monarchial theory of hereditary succession, especially at the time of the most severe political crisis of the era, 1678-88, from the Popish Plot through the Exclusion Crisis to the Glorious Revolution. A handful of plays offer a counterideology—or at least expose the fatal Oedipal crisis lurking at the heart of monarchial ideology.

Most of these plays are especially concerned with loyalty in the face of rebellion. No matter how weak the king, no matter what crimes he himself may have committed, loyal subjects must leave vengeance to the Lord. Perhaps the most important group of these political tragedies comprises the Shakespearean adaptations of Nahum Tate and John Crowne. Tate's adaptation of Shakespeare's *Richard II* as *The History of King Richard the Second,* acted as *The Sicilian Usurper* (1680), makes significant changes, not one of which, as he says in the dedication, "but what breaths Loyalty," especially in touching up the character of the king (sig. A2v). For example, Richard is not named as a murderer of Gloucester, he takes the Lancastrian revenues merely as a loan, and he develops a very saintly contempt for the world. Other changes stress loyalty. Instead of switching sides, York remains loyal until the end, accusing Bullingbrook of trying "[t]o Compass right with wrong" (II.iii, 20). Tate adds a scene (II.iv) in which the rabble purport to be establishing a commonwealth, when each contradictorily claims the right to be a noble and even a king. They encounter Bullingbrook, who claims to be defending their "Liberty and Rights" (II.iv, 22)—resembling not a little the contemporary duke of Monmouth in his progress through England. The rhetoric of the scene is clearly Royalist: these are not republicans but self-interested rebels. Tate adds another scene later between Richard and his constant queen before his resignation, where his friends counsel him for safety's sake to accept the will of the "usurping House" (IV, 39), a phrase calculated to raise contemporary hackles. And the queen impatiently complains, "Has Loyalty so quite renounc't the World, / That none will yet strike for an injur'd King?" At the end the queen retires to a land free from "Heaven's ripe Vengeance" (V, 54), which already begins to manifest itself immediately after Richard's murder and continues, as an English audience would know, down to the reign of Henry VI, whose story was simultaneously portrayed on the Restoration stage in Crowne's adaptations of Shakespeare's trilogy.

In these adaptations (*Henry the Sixth; The First Part, with the Murder of Humphrey, Duke of Glocester* in 1680 and *The Misery of Civil-War* in 1681), Crowne, in a response to the Popish Plot typical of both Royalist and opposition playwrights, adds a heavy dose of antipapism (a de rigueur rhetoric, no matter what one's politics), but he also portrays the rebellious rabble as leveling butchers. He emphasizes Shakespeare's point that King Henry is weak precisely because his title to the crown is weak, and he portrays Edward of York, who emerges at the end as Edward IV, as flawed but legitimate. In Crowne's version of *2 Henry VI,* Henry is a weak king. But his weakness, Crowne emphasizes, stems from his own saintly *contemptus mundi,* on the one hand, and, as we learn in Crowne's adaptation of *3 Henry VI, The Misery of Civil-War,* from Henry's weak title to the throne, on the other. He finally abdicates this title, since it is "founded on Rebellion, / The murder of a King and usurpation" (II, 26). Moreover, in Shakespeare's *2 Henry VI,* despite that weakness and despite the machinations of those surrounding the king, Humphrey, duke of Glocester and Protector of the Realm, remains fiercely loyal to Henry. Yet even Glocester's own wife, in Crowne's version, scoffs at his squeamishness at the word "Disloyalty" (*Henry the Sixth* I, 5). And the Machiavel in the play, Cardinal Beaufort, in Crowne's version perverts his office and the Sacred Word by casuistically justifying the murder of Glocester. But in a scene added by Crowne, the cardinal's conscience drives him mad, and in another added scene, Henry's queen, whose adultery with the duke of Suffolk is a sexual analogue to the political inconstancy, laments the beheading of her lover and repents. Thus Crowne has emphasized the poetic justice attending those who violate the word. And whatever Glocester's private fortune, we are to see the ending as a Providential validation of the code he serves.

In *The Misery of Civil-War,* such Providential justice accompanies Henry's own death, for Crowne adds to Shakespeare two ghosts to justify it, first the ghost of Richard II, who says his usurpation must be expiated, and then a Spirit, who says chasteningly that the crown is the gift of

Heaven, secured by law (obviously, that of succession), and yet who comforts Henry with promise of spiritual reward for his saintliness. Meanwhile, in another added speech, Henry justifies Edward's claim to the throne against Warwick's arguments that Edward's virtue does not merit it:

> If Kings may lose their Rights for want of Virtue,
> And Subjects are the Judges of that Virtue;
> Then Kings are Subjects, and all Subjects Kings:
> And by that Law that Subjects may destroy
> Their Kings for want of Virtue, other Subjects
> May think those Subjects Rogues, and cut their throats.
> Thus *Babel* might be builded, but no Kingdom. [V, 58]

To follow such a political theory is to destroy the words that bind society and to create a chaos where all classes are leveled and all have right to all. Crowne reinforces this lesson by expanding the depiction of Cade's rebellion (actually from *2 Henry VI,* IV), fleshing out a dialogue between Cade, a butcher, a tailor, and a cobbler, who vow to kill all who can speak Latin and French, all lords and gentlemen, and to become lords and gentlemen "our selves" (I, 3). And since "all the Law of *England* is but mouth," they will mouth the law themselves, taking over Westminster and St. Paul's and burning all the "Mouldy Records of what our Grandsiers did" (I, 7). Thus levelers are portrayed as extending nominalism to the point of erasure of all words. In a similar vein, Crowne adds a scene in which pillaging soldiers break their word with some countrymen by ravishing their daughters and sending the men off to be hanged, which action they justify by accusing the men of breaking their "Allegiance" to the king: "Yet break your Oaths to him? and do you expect, / We shou'd keep Verbal promises with you?" (III, 36).

Crowne also emphasizes his theme by mirroring the political in the sexual. Edward of York, who upon the death of his father has the rightful claim to the throne (and who later becomes Edward IV), is depicted by Crowne as courting Lady Elianor Butler. Later on the battlefield, she comes to accuse him of inconstancy, and he apparently risks victory for a night of dalliance. At this juncture Warwick and Richard (eventually Richard III) criticize Edward, who seems to have lost his kingdom "in a kiss" (III, 37). But it happens that Edward was only pretending to be irresponsible to test them, and he turns upon his critics, chastising them for calling the kettle black. The point is that all Edward's (or Charles's) faults do not vitiate his right to the throne.

At the same time, Edward (as well as Charles?) *is* criticized. He keeps his word with Henry not to seek the throne during Henry's lifetime, and it is clearly Henry (or rather, his queen) who is wrong to "break" his "Oath" not to proceed against Edward (IV, 42). Yet Edward breaks his own oath to Lady Elianor and marries Lady Grey—and all this at the very time Warwick seeks a bride for him in France. Consequently, Edward suffers: not only does Warwick turn against him but Crowne adds a couple of scenes in which Lady Elianor comes to accuse Edward of perjury. Sounding like Etherege's Dorimant, he responds, "I thought you wou'd have given me a clear draught / Of Love without the dreggs of Oaths and Vows" (II, 21); "I believ'd those Oaths / A form of speaking, which did please you best" (IV, 55). Toward the end of the play, Lady Elianor disguises herself as a soldier and provokes Edward into killing her. She dies beseeching Heaven's forgiveness for his broken vows, and he finally realizes the gravity of what he has done, admits his sins, and vows to amend his profligate ways. The fact that the audience knows he does not amend his life but later will take Jane Shore as his mistress does not vitiate the lesson of the interpolated subplot.

That lesson serves to underscore the main political lesson of the play: there is no honor among troth-breakers, and broken words simply beget more broken words; therefore, friends and lovers must remain constant and subjects loyal no matter what. In lines added by Crowne, Henry attacks rebellion and civil war:

> Oh you, who when you suffer by your Kings,
> Think to mend all by War, and by Rebellion!
> See here, your sad mistakes! how dreadfully
> You scourge your selves! learn here the greatest Tyrant
> Is to be chose before the least Rebellion. [IV, 44]

At the same time, again in lines added by Crowne, Edward (whom Crowne keeps innocent of the murder of Henry and his son) reaffirms the Royalist principle of succession. He concludes of Henry's fate,

> His, and the Kingdom's dreadful Ruines prove,
> A Monarch's Right is an unshaken Rock,
> No storms of War nor time can wear away,
> And Wracks those Pirates that come there for prey. [V, 71][1]

In perhaps the best of these loyalist plays between the crisis and the Revolution, Nathaniel Lee and John Dryden's *Duke of Guise* (1682), the party of Guise perverts the language of the aristocratic code to justify rebellion. In Hobbist fashion, they argue that those who have power *are* the government: they have the real power; therefore, the king is the real rebel and thus has "betray'd his Trust" by resisting their will to exclude his brother from the throne. They withdraw their allegiance and pledge their oath to Guise, their Moses, their Messiah (and obviously Monmouth), who is himself a nominalist, agreeing to be whatever they "call" him (I.i.69, 79) and justifying an act of treason by "good intentions" (110). Moreover, the oaths of troth-breakers are worth nothing, for like the curate of St. Eustace, they all "swallow Oaths as easie as Snap-dragon, / Mock-Fire that never burns" (142-43). The implication of such imagery is, of course, that none of them really believes in heaven or hell or any metaphysical sanction for the violation of oaths. The perversion of the code reveals in full its inherent blasphemy in the subplot, where the Shaftesburian Malicorn consorts with devils,[2] one of whom advises that Guise not be frightened with fables of hell: "[B]id him not stand on Altar Vows, / But then strike deepest, when he lowest bows" (I.ii.23-24). Another devil, Melanax, reveals how devils, posing as Puritan Saints, pervert the Logos to foment sedition:

> We mix unknown with the hot thoughtless Crowd,
> And quoting Scriptures, which too well we know,
> With impious Glosses ban the holy Text,
> And make it speak Rebellion, Schism and Murder,
> So turn the Arms of Heaven against it self. [IV.ii.13-17]

And later he justifies the deposing of a prince by the majority with this ingenious perversion of language: "When the most are of one side, as that's our case, we are always in the right; for they that are in power, will ever be the Judges: So that if we say White is Black, poor White must lose the Cause, and put on Mourning, for White is but a single Syllable, and we are a whole Sentence" (IV.iv.39-43).

On the other hand, there are those who speak the truth. The loyal Bussy calls a spade a spade, branding the "City Bands" "well season'd Traitors," "proof against an Oath" (I.i.113-16). The indulgent Henry III himself calls Paris "Ungrateful, perjur'd and Disloyal Town" (IV.i.92). And especially Guise's beloved Marmoutiere remains loyal to the king, despite her love for Guise and the king's ill-timed addresses to her. Though she rejects the king's love, she says even if he were dethroned she would—and all her sex should—abandon everything and "follow you like Pilgrims through the World" (III.i.270). And she tries desperately to recall Guise from his rebellious course, at the last concluding him incorrigibly "faithless" (IV.iii.122) and abandoning him to his fate. When the three Estates finally break their oath to the king and vote to exclude his brother, the faithful Grillon raises the crucial question: "[I]f they Vote that they have not broken their Oaths, who is to be Judge?" Alphonso Corso answers, "There's One above" (V.i.52-53), that is, a god who validates the entire code. So this god does by proxy at last. The king, who until now has been patient and merciful, asserts himself and defends his own cause, arguing with the rebels that the relationship between king and subject is one of "mutual" "Tyes" as well as "Benefits" (V.i.183-84). To their appeal to religious sanction for their deeds, he replies emphatically,

> If Kings may be excluded, or depos'd,
> When e're you cry Religion to the Crowd,
> That Doctrine makes Rebellion Orthodox,
> And Subjects must be Traytors to be sav'd. [V.i.213-16]

The king finally, reluctantly concurs in the death of Guise and the other leaders, concluding with a warning against those who thus tempt "the Vengeance of indulgent Kings" (V.vi.29). The "One above" has vindicated the divine right of succession through its agent, the king. And the play has an obvious message for Dryden and Lee's contemporaries, whose tampering with the right of succession Dryden in the dedication and in *The Vindication of the Duke of Guise* (1683) everywhere labels treason. In the *Vindication,* Dryden says explicitly that the lesson of the play is "to reduce men to Loyalty, by shewing the pernicious consequences of Rebellion, and Popular Insurrections" (*Works* 14:320). The loyalists, of course, have nature, law, and religion on their side. Or such is their rhetoric.

The rhetoric of loyalty persists in most political tragedies up through the time of the Glorious Revolution. Sometime during the 1680s, John Banks composed another martyr play, *The Innocent Usurper; or, The Death of the Lady Jane Gray* (not acted; publ. 1694), though this time the play is decidedly political. Lady Jane and her husband, Gilford, must learn to scorn the world and expect immortality, and they suffer a "Noble Martyrdom" to their "vow'd Faith," Protestantism (V, 56, 60). However, theoretical political issues in this play are central. The earl of Northumberland masterminds Lady Jane's succession to the throne of England upon Edward VI's death. His principles are Hobbist; he believes in de facto power, and his assault on the aristocratic code is portrayed in blasphemous terms:

> Help now you Powers! whether from Heaven or Hell;
> Descend, ascend, bring but a Crown, I care not; . . .
> I'de wrest the War out of the Gyants hand,
> And undertake a second fight with Heaven. [I, 6-7]

Moreover, the main issue in the play again is the right of succession. However attractive a character she may be, from the beginning Lady Jane knows that she and Gilford are usurpers and therefore culpable: "This is Damnation; we too surely know, / A Sin will Edge the Flaming Sword of Justice" (II, 16). Once she has accepted the crown (which she does only to save from suicide Northumberland and Gilford, who have already cast the die), she has a dream wherein crowns fall from heaven and angels proclaim, "When Virtue Slave to tempting Glory lies, / 'Tis just it fall Ambition's Sacrifice" (III, 26). When she is deposed, she and Gilford both rejoice in the easing of their consciences and thank "Heaven" for answering their prayers (IV, 31). At her trial Lady Jane disclaims the title "Virtuous" and calls herself "Delinquent" (IV, 39). Thus, the play may be stridently anti-Catholic (witness the duchess of Suffolk's ravings), and it may laud Lady Jane's refusal to be an apostate to her Protestant faith, but it clearly condemns Northumberland's principles and Lady Jane's usurpation.

In early 1688, a performance of Crowne's *Darius, King of Persia* was graced by the presence of James II. No wonder, for the play seems addressed directly to both his friends and his enemies. Crowne portrays a king deserted by his own people and betrayed by his generals, who propose to establish a republic, though they really only want power for themselves. For them, "Religious awe of Kingly Majesty" is just an opiate of the people (II, 19). Darius vows to "defend all Kings"—that is, the feudal aristocratic order itself—by his exemplary vengeance on the rebels (II, 27). He disdains foreign support (a hint of Louis XIV?), yet when he is seized, he cries out,

> Oh! rise in my Revenge and Aid, all Kings!
> This is your common Cause, I am a King.
> Rise all Mankind, for all Humanity
> Is by these Villains scorn'd, disgrac'd, and curst,
> By what they do to me their most kind Friend.
> Nay, rise all Gods! your Power suffers in me
> Your Minister, and a deputed God! [IV, 50]

In prison Darius nearly despairs over the "stupifying Patience o'the Gods," who "seem only infinite, / In suffering ill" (V, 63). Yet as the rebels kill him, he prophesies, "All Kings and Gods / Will be the Ministers of my Revenge" (65). In contrast, the rebels declare nominalistically that there is no such thing as treason but ill "success" makes it so: "They alwaies have the Cause, who have the day" (66). Nevertheless, the loyal Artabasus has counseled Darius to have contempt for the fickle world and to trust that "There is a Heaven, or there are no Gods," who would never allow such crimes to go unpunished (IV, 48). Indeed, even as the noble Alexander, another king, conquers, the rebels are defeated by the loyalists, and the dying Darius demands of Alexander, in the spirit of transnational aristocracy, "for the common Cause of all Crown'd Heads, / I challenge the Revenge due to my Blood" (V, 67). He dies and all nature mourns, but the rebels are wracked before the ghost of Darius, a happy vision, Artabasus says, of "Vertue triumphing over Villany" (V, 69). The ideological message of the play is summed up clearly by Darius, as he earlier confronts the rebels: "[D]o your Duty, Sirs, and I'le do mine. / Leave the dispose of Crowns to Kings and Gods" (III, 35).

Thomas Southerne's *Spartan Dame* was apparently written around the time of the revolution, although it was not produced until some thirty years later (1719). It is perhaps the most stridently Royalist of all these loyalist political tragedies. In the uncut fifth edition (1721), Southerne restored enough lines to hang twenty Jacobites (the restored lines are marked by quotation marks in the left margin). The play features the usurpation of a throne by a daughter and a son-in-law! The play is filled with Royalist defenses of the right of succession, almost all with reference to divine sanction. For example, the Spartan dame of the title, Celona, appeals to the reverence due to the names "'King'" and "'Father'" (I.i.79-81) and upbraids her husband Cleombrotus's claims to a hereditary "Right" to the throne (87) if the people are pleased to depose her father, Leonidas:

> "Your Right, my Lord,
> "Is nothing, the King living, tho' depos'd,
> "Unless you stand upon the People's Voice,
> "Preferring their Election to a long
> "Hereditary Line of *Spartan* Kings,
> "Deriv'd from the rich Blood of *Hercules.* [I.i.102-7]

She warns Cleombrotus about basing a throne upon the vox populi:

> "When once the People get the jadish Trick
> "Of throwing off their Kings, no Ruler's safe. . . .
> "O! think what 'tis to be the Peoples Slave,
> "To owe your Pow'r to their Inconstancy:
> "For shou'd the good Gods leave their heavenly Thrones,
> "To rule below, they could not please us long:
> "The sawcy Censurers of Soveraign Sway
> "Wou'd tax their Government; Divinity
> "It self were not secure, without a Guard
> "Of Bolts, and Flames, to awe rebellious Man. [125-52]

Finally, Celona deserts her usurping husband to seek out even just "'one Man . . . who has preserv'd / His Loyalty'" and to defend her "'Father's Cause'" (II.i.395-98).

Meanwhile, sexual inconstancy again mirrors political: Cleombrotus is unfaithful not only to his king but to his wife. He lusts after her married sister and justifies the incestuous adultery in nominalistic terms: "Brother, and Sister, are but Terms of Art, / Occasionally fashion'd to the Ends / Of Government" (II.i.503-5). The pervert Cleombrotus (William) manages to have his way through a bed-trick. As in the romantic tragedies, the violated woman, Thelamia, calls upon the gods to avenge her, and once again the crucial question is whether the ethical and political code of the feudal aristocracy is supported by gods who care. The usurpers, of course, think not. Cleombrotus's assault upon all the bonds of society takes its final step into open blasphemy, when he violates the Temple of Neptune "in bold Defiance of the Guardian God" (V.i.12), vowing to rape yet another daughter of Leonidas. But he is finally killed, Leonidas is restored, and Celona praises the "just Gods" (154; cf. Leonidas V.64), who have vindicated monarchy and the right of succession. The sense of the ending is Jacobite wish fulfillment, clothed in all the religious rhetoric of royalism.

The last and best of these loyalist political tragedies is Dryden's *Don Sebastian, King of Portugal,* a cut version of which was produced in 1689 and an uncut version published in 1690. The play's topical political relevance is obvious in the uncut version.[3] But more interesting is the play's ideology. Here again the world of the play is one of broken words. The emperor of Morocco, Muley-Moluch, is at first sympathetic with the captured Don Sebastian's undisguisable "Majesty" in the face of death (I.i.343) and also with his subjects' "untainted Faith"—subjects who, as Sebastian says, refused to forsake him at his "greatest need; / Nor for base lucre sold their Loyalty" (397-98). Consequently, the emperor spares both Sebastian and his subjects from death and promises Sebastian quick release from captivity. But the emperor is already a compromised figure, for he has gained his throne by "force" and secured it by murder (453). And now his passion for the beautiful Almeyda tarnishes his late generosity. At first he is willing to risk his "Royalty" (II.i.46) and his "People's love" (34) to marry an enemy; then, discovering that she and Sebastian have married, he breaks his "promise" to Sebastian (III.i.100) and threatens to execute him in order to divorce them permanently. Thus he also plans, as Almeyda says, "to break what Heav'n has joyn'd" (206). He is still barred by the Koran from marrying a Christian; nevertheless, he would pervert the Sacred Word by claiming, "I am Law" (84), and exacting from the mufti sanction for rape.

This breaking of bonds is mirrored in the political anarchy of the rabble scenes and the sexual anarchy of the comic subplot. The renegade Dorax characterizes the rabble as "Lords of Anarchy" (I.i.146), and however attractive their leader, Mustafa, as a dramatic character, we must not be blind to the mob's nominalism and fickleness.[4] The day is saved not by them but especially by Dorax, who dismisses them as rebels:

> Away ye skum,
> That still rise upmost when the Nation boyls:
> Ye mungrill work of Heaven, with humane shapes,
> Not to be damn'd, or sav'd, but breath, and perish,
> That have but just enough of sence, to know
> The masters voice, when rated, to depart. [IV.iii.353-58]

"The voice of the Mobile" is *not* "the voice of Heaven" as the mufti hypocritically asserts (IV.ii.219-20). At best, the mob is an instrument. It has no real allegiance to anyone, not even the gods.

Corresponding to this political anarchy is the sexual anarchy of the subplot. At first Antonio, one of those oversexed soldiers familiar from Restoration comedy, intends adultery with the mufti's wife and later fornication with his daughter. All along this libertine behavior is rationalized in a parody of religious language that mirrors the corruption of religion by the mufti in the main plot. "Conscience" seems dead (III.ii.193-200), and the only use of an oath seems to be either to preserve one's neck or to obtain the sexual prize. The mufti's wife, Johayma, is inconstant not only to her husband but to all her lovers, whom she discards and dispatches. Antonio's "Christian intention" with regard to the mufti's daughter, Morayma, is merely "to revenge my self upon thy Father" (289-90). In short, the subplot portrays the same things as the main: perversion of words, breaking of bonds, rebellion against corrupt authority. Appropriately, most of its action takes place in chaotic darkness.

The worst perverter of words and bonds is the Machiavellian statesman Benducar, who, desirous of the crown and Almeyda, plans a revolt against the emperor, confident of success because he is so trusted: "[T]rust has given me means / Once to be false for all" (I.i.32-33). He rationalizes his murder of the emperor in Hobbist terms: "I can sin but once to seize the Throne. / All after Acts are sanctify'd by pow'r" (IV.i.187-88). But he mistakenly tries to enlist the aid of the brave Dorax, who indignantly responds,

> He trusts us both; mark that, shall we betray him?
> A Master who reposes Life and Empire

> On our fidelity: I grant he is a Tyrant, . . .
> [Yet] wou'd his Creature, nay his Friend betray him?
> Why then no Bond is left on human kind:
> Distrusts, debates, immortal strifes ensue;
> Children may murder Parents, Wives their Husbands;
> All must be Rapine, Wars, and Desolation,
> When trust and gratitude no longer bind. [II.i.288-311]

Dorax perfectly articulates the rhetoric of the aristocratic code: the threat of the loss of all such order if the feudal political order is violated even to overthrow tyrants. Such kings must be left to Heaven, and accordingly, in the face of the emperor's threat to her and to Sebastian, both of whom are sovereigns, Almeyda challenges the gods:

> But is there Heav'n? for I begin to doubt;
> The Skyes are hush'd; no grumbling Thunders roul.
> Now take your swing, ye impious; Sin unpunish'd;
> Eternal providence seems overwatch'd,
> And with a slumb'ring Nod assents to Murther. . . .
> O Pow'rs, if Kings be your peculiar care,
> Why plays this Wretch with your Prerogative?
> Now flash him dead, now crumble him to ashes;
> Or henceforth live confin'd in your own Palace:
> And look not idely out upon a World
> That is no longer yours. [III.i.294-319]

Almeyda's imagination transmogrifies the caring god of both Christianity and Islam to Epicurean gods who retire from human affairs to play palace shuffleboard. "Eternal providence seems overwatch'd" is a delicious Drydenesque oxymoron.

Yet ultimately the gods do care. At the crucial moment their instrument, Benducar, beheads the emperor, who, we must remember, is not a rightful ruler and who is caught improvidently unarmed and bent on his lust. Moreover, evil providentially overreaches itself, for Benducar's and the mufti's poisons cancel each other out, as "Heaven pleases" they should (IV.iii.330), so that Dorax lives to save the day for Sebastian and Almeyda. Dorax attributes his plan to prompting by either his or Sebastian's "Angel" (V.i.36), and Almeyda praises Dorax and "those blest holy Fires, our Guardian Angells" (IV.iii.360). The Catholic Dryden lurks behind the arras.

Nonetheless, Dorax himself must be taught the secret "Moral" of this play that Dryden claims lies *"couch'd under every one of the principal Parts and Characters, which a judicious Critick will observe, though I point not to it in this*

Preface" (*Works* 15:71). It is, in effect, the moral of all these loyalist plays: not only faith in Providence but especially loyalty to one's legitimate sovereign, no matter what. Dryden teaches this moral particularly through the career of Dorax. The one boon he had requested for all his service to Sebastian as his loyal general, Alonzo, was the hand of Violante, with whom he had, unbeknown to Sebastian, exchanged "vows" (IV.iii.473). But Sebastian had already promised Violante to his favorite, Enriquez. As a result of Sebastian's denial, Alonzo had become insolent, struck Enriquez, whom he considered an effeminate parasite, and thus violated the presence of "awfull Majesty" (486). The angry Sebastian had spurned Alonzo from that presence, and Alonzo repudiated his king, his name, and even his Christian faith, for he is a "Renegade" (dramatis personae), which means literally a denier, an apostate. Thus Dryden underscores the radical nature of Dorax's rebellion: he is no Almanzor, who owes no allegiance; he commits a literal act of defiance, of *défiance,* hurling down a metaphorical gauntlet and *disaffiancing* himself from his sovereign. Thus he rebels against the entire feudal code of faith—ethical, political, and metaphysical. Moreover, as Bruce King has ably shown, Dryden portrays Dorax in language and imagery that allude to Milton's Satan.[5] Alonzo's rebellion is not only against "Annointed power" (505) but against the Power that anoints.

Now Dorax faces Sebastian, whom he has rescued only to challenge to a duel, which he claims is promised him by Sebastian's "Oath" to reward him: "Fight or be Perjur'd," he demands (545-47). All these references to conflicting oaths, vows, and promises and to "the Sacred Character of King" (520) indicate what is at stake: this is a deadly rivalry that threatens the very fabric of established order. And Dryden brilliantly resolves the conflict. Sebastian paints a tableau of Enriquez, despite his effeminate nature, bravely dying in the act of shielding his king—the ultimate exemplum of loyalty, portrayed in the ratifying Christian colors of self-sacrifice: "And on his naked side receiv'd my wound" (574). By such a dazzling rebuke Dorax is stunned into self-awareness: "my Soul's a Regicide" (611). Like Milton's Adam, he sees clearly the similarity between himself and Satan. But like Adam and unlike Satan, Dorax can repent: he throws "this Rebell, this proud Renegade" at his master's feet, and in the archetypal gesture of forgiveness, Sebastian raises him from the dust (634-36). The order is saved; the bond of the word, girded here by references to the Word, is reestablished; broken vows are mended, even those between Dorax and Violante, for she never yielded to Enriquez but kept her pledge to her lover. Thus has "Heaven blest" Dorax, reconciling him at once to the three aristocratic orders: "To Heaven, and to my King, and to my Love!" (646-49).

And so the play should have ended happily, like a heroic or tragicomic romance. But it does not, for Sebastian and Almeyda have unwittingly committed incest, however cryptically they were warned. Are we to infer the dissolution of aristocratic ideals?[6] I think not. The explicit lesson is that the innocent suffer for the sins of the fathers. Implicit is the suggestion that behind all the violations of bonds in the world of the play lies an original violation: Sebastian's father, himself "newly marry'd" (V.271), committed adultery with the exiled queen of Morocco; Almeyda is their daughter. The deeper lesson seems to be that this original violation is itself a sign of *the* Original Sin, which Milton calls one of "foul distrust" between man and God.[7] Therefore, as Dryden must have felt poignantly in 1689, history is not always just. The world as the Christians portray it is radically fallen and relentlessly mutable. Innocence is often unrewarded, and the rightful sovereign does not always reign. Art may portray the truth of philosophy and religion, as theorists from Aristotle to Sidney and the advocates of poetical justice desired.[8] But it may also portray the truth of history, sometimes a pattern of injustice that humans cannot blame on God but must blame on themselves, their parents, the Fall—according to the Story that still informs late feudal Europe's ideological history.

Nevertheless, Sebastian and Almeyda resist the greatest sin against trust, a sin Dryden himself must have had a hard time resisting after the flight of James II, "despair" (V.i.460). Acting the part of Spenser's Despayre by seeming to argue for suicide, Dorax once again really plays the role of a guardian "Angell" (532) and saves Sebastian from "Damnation" (520). Together Sebastian and Almeyda reject the "impious" desire to "break through Laws Divine, and Humane" (635, 629), as "Heav'n" inspires them with the solution of dying to each other and living "alone to Heav'n" (545). In the spirit of *contemptus mundi,* they renounce the world and depart severally for religious retreats. And they leave the world in order, the code of trust intact, with the kingdom renewed in a now legitimate and compassionate king, with Dorax and his faithful lover reunited, and with even the libertine Antonio's promiscuous sexual appetite socialized into the bonds, the "vows" (702) of marriage. We the audience know at the end that Sebastian's brother, the cardinal, and the emperor's brother, Muley-Zeydan, himself once a usurper in intent, will not be the great sovereigns Sebastian and Almeyda would have been. But we also are manipulated to believe that however inscrutable the ways of Providence, it has nonetheless been portrayed as defeating the nominalists, Hobbists, and atheists and as reaffirming the code of feudal aristocratic order—a vision of justice that may or may not be realized in history but certainly will be realized in the eschaton. At least, to adapt a line from Hemingway, isn't it pretty for aristocrats and their poets to think so?

During the Exclusion Crisis, the trope of the loyal general, present in Restoration tragedy from Orrery's *Generall* (acted Dublin 1662, London 1664), offers a displaced version of the Oedipal crisis that lurks at the heart of feudal patrilineal monarchy. The loyal general suffers torture, death, dismemberment rather than rebel against the Father-King. He becomes a mute sacrifice, a martyr.[9] As the Oedipal paradigm approaches the surface, it suffers obfuscating distortion: often the general is older than the king, a father figure himself. Or, as in *The Ambitious Statesman,* the Oedipal paradigm is doubled and displaced, so the title character rebels against his king, while his son, the loyal general, is dishonored by his prince, the dauphin, with whom he is locked in mimetic desire for his wife, who loves the general. The general disobeys his father and refuses to join the rebellion, while the dauphin, out of jealous rage, dupes the statesman into torturing and murdering his own son. Thus castrating paternal tyranny and supplanting filial ingratitude, the stuff of the paradigm, vector across a quadrangle of desire. The ambitious statesman is finally sent to execution, but it is the agonizing death of the innocent general that the audience witnesses as the sacrifice to the system.

The world of some of these political tragedies fosters rebellion precisely because no clear legitimacy obtains. In John Bancroft's *Tragedy of Sertorius* (1679), Sertorius rebels against the tyrant Sulla but is himself overthrown by rebels. In Crowne's *Henry the Sixth,* Glocester remains staunchly loyal to a pious but illegitimate king yet will not participate in Oedipal rebellion and dies for it. In Tate's adaptation of Shakespeare's *Coriolanus,* which he called *The Ingratitude of a Common-Wealth* (1681), the very title is a giveaway: no respect for greatness or authority is possible in such a state. Yet the loyal general must die.

In these *loyal general* plays of the crisis, however, Oedipal rebellion is displaced onto figures who are not the sons of kings and who are sometimes even old enough to be the king's father. This latter figure points to the dilemma of monarchial order: kings themselves were once sons who have supplanted fathers. Successfully negotiated earlier in the Restoration in a play like *Aureng-Zebe,* the Oedipal crisis seems forced to the surface full-blown at the moment of the Restoration's greatest crisis of succession. The repressed returns to the spotlight, and some plays directly enact open Oedipal rebellion—one of them entitled *Oedipus.* Thomas Otway's eponymous protagonist in *Don Carlos, Prince of Spain* (1676) was precontracted to his father's queen, and he is torn between filial submission and self-assertion. The queen deters him from joining rebels in Spain, but it is too late: the king intercepts dispatches and catches his son and his wife in an embrace. The son tries to kneel but rises in defense of the queen and in defiance of the king and draws his sword in his father's presence, albeit against an evil counselor. He surrenders his phallic sword, only to catch the swooning queen in his arms once more, as the king impotently rages. The king's fear of castration causes him to have both son and wife killed, but they die together in one last embrace that drives the king madly to try to mount the sky to separate them.[10]

Lee's *Mithridates, King of Pontus* (1678) bifurcates the Oedipal son into the disloyal Pharnaces, who leads a rebellion against his father, King Mithridates, and the loyal Ziphares, who resists rebellion against Mithridates despite incredible provocations. The father appropriates both sons' women, and when Pharnaces encourages his soldiers to kill children in their mothers' wombs, we infer the internecine self-destruction inherent in patriarchal dynastic struggle: Pharnaces, Oedipal rebel against his father, would precastrate future rebellious sons. Ziphares mistakenly kills his beloved, constant Semandra, then kills himself, and Mithridates dies from a wound inflicted by Pharnaces, who is ordered thrown from the battlements. Mithridates's final speech extols the lesson of *sic transit gloria mundi,* but this act of erasure cannot obliterate Pharnaces's parting taunt:

> Yet, when my Ghost is from this body dash'd,
> If such a Goblin as a Ghost there be,
> I'll rise, and wing the mid-way Air to wait thee;
> Hurl'd shalt thou be, as Saturn was by Jove,
> And flag beneath me, while I reign above. [V.ii.384-88][11]

Dryden and Lee turned *Oedipus* (1678) into a play as much about rebellion as about the consequences of parricide and incest. Creon is a Machiavel who would usurp the throne, with the fickle mob's assistance, from the "lawful" king "[b]y publick voice elected" (I.i.324, 283). The rebels violate their oaths of allegiance: "[I]t's a hard World Neighbours, if a mans Oath must be his master" (285-86). Ironically, of course, Oedipus is more than an elected monarch. He is the son of the former king. But he has come to the throne through unwitting parricide, and he possesses the queen, the sign of the king's power and potency. Moreover, though innocent of conscious incest, Oedipus and Jocasta are not just the victims of fate. Dryden and Lee add significant changes to the traditional story. Laius had been warned by the oracle, yet he chose to have children regardless. So the sins of the father are (again) visited upon the children. Jocasta herself defies the oracle and tries to cover up the dawning truth. As their incest breaks into full consciousness, they nevertheless embrace.[12] Only Laius's ghost can reassert patriarchal taboo. Like Medea, Jocasta murders her children, and she and Oedipus both commit suicide. This purgation causes Haemon to read the political lesson of the play: "How sacred ought / Kings lives be held, when but the death of one / Demands an Empire's blood for Expiation?" (V.i.409-11).[13] Yet Dryden and Lee have perhaps unwittingly implied that the very system of patrilineal monarchy, consciously or unconsciously, invites Oedipal rebellion.

Even when the Oedipal is ostensibly displaced by rebellion against a queen, as in Banks's *Unhappy Favourite; or, The Earl of Essex* (1681), the repressed returns. Employing his wonted metier of English history play, Banks pits the loyal general Essex's fiery temperament against Queen Elizabeth's conflicted passion. Faced with not only ingratitude for his services but even suspicion of sedition, Essex comes to justify himself to the queen but loses his temper and too boldly asserts himself in the court presence. The queen, torn between private love for him and the public necessity of asserting her authority, slaps him, pushing him into open rebellion. To the condemned but penitent Essex the queen, praying that the gods judge her conflicted passions equitably, gives a ring as pledge for redemption upon demand. The *"Machiavile"* countess of Nottingham (V, 64) intercepts the ring when Essex tries to redeem it, however, and Essex is executed as a traitor.

This rebel, like the typical loyal general, reportedly (though from an unreliable source) dies a "Martyr," forgiving his queen (V, 7[7]). But we have just heard the tortured Essex complain bitterly against the gods. Moreover, the queen's earlier diatribe against the loss of order in the modern world hangs still over the ending of the play:

> There's Order in all States but Man below,
> And all things else do to Superiors bow; . . .
> But Man the veryer Monster, Worships still
> No God but Lust, no Monarch but his Will. [I, 13]

The more active of such wills have been those of the queen's evil counselors; nevertheless, the essentially loyal but willful Essex's rebellion, even though against the Virgin Queen, is cryptically Oedipal after all. He describes his situation in mythological terms:

> Yesterday's Sun saw his great Rival thus,
> The spiteful Planet saw me thus ador'd,
> And as some tall-built Pyramid, whose Height
> And golden Top confronts him in his sky,
> He tumbles down with lightning in his rage;
> So on a sudden has he snatcht my Garlands,
> And with a Cloud impal'd my gawdy Head,
> Struck me with Thunder, dasht me from the Heav'ns,

> And oh! 'tis Dooms-day now, and darkness all with me.
> Here I'll lie down—Earth will receive her Son. [II, 24][14]

Stressing its implications, Banks sustains the metaphor of the sun throughout the play. Nottingham remarks of Essex's passion: "His Soul with sullen Beames shines in it self, / More Jealous of Mens Eyes, than is the Sun / That will not suffer to be look'd into" (IV, 42-43). Essex's last words image him absorbed by the patriarchal sun at the moment of his dissolution into nothingness: "Why do I stand thus shivering on the Shore! / 'Tis but a Breath, and I no more shall think, / Mix with the Sun, or into Attomes shrink" (V, 74).

Two Restoration tragedies enact successful rebellion against a tyrant: John Wilmot, the earl of Rochester's play *Valentinian* (1684) and Lee's *Lucius Junius Brutus, Father of His Country* (1680). In the former, Rochester employs the loyal/disloyal "son" dichotomy (metaphorically speaking, for each is older than the father/emperor). Aecius, the loyal general of Valentinian, constantly preaches Royalist rhetoric against rebellion; no matter what the emperor has done, he must be left to the gods, for "Faith to Princes broke, is Sacriledge" (V, 58). At the end, after Valentinian has committed Tarquinian rape on Lucina, wife of the other loyal general, Maximus, Aecius confronts Valentinian, kills his eunuch lover, but runs on Valentinian's sword, praying for him as he dies. Praying himself for the gods to kill Valentinian midst his debauches, Maximus leads a rebellion. Asked why he would rebel with such an example of loyalty as the dead Aecius at his feet, Maximus bitterly replies that he lacks Aecius's honesty and virtue. While he himself does not strike the killing blow, Maximus becomes the new emperor over Valentinian's dead body. He warns the dying Valentinian to "think there may be Gods" (V, 80). If there are, they have sanctioned rebellion, for the play ends with a tyrant deposed and a rape upon the body politic revenged. Yet Maximus represents not a founder of a new order but the last Roman emperor before the Vandals sack Rome: in a sense, then, he represents the decline and fall of the Roman Empire (cf. Braverman, *Plots and Counterplots* 158-60). Moreover, Oedipal guilt, though displaced, rears its head, as Valentinian laments:

> I grieve for *Aecius!* Yes, I mourn him, Gods,
> As if I had met my Father in the dark,
> And striving for the Way had murder'd him. [80]

In the fully oppositional ideology of his play, Lee's Lucius Junius Brutus does found a new state based on law and trade. He represents the emergent bourgeois trope of the One Just Man, the stoic father not of his family but of the country. As such, because they have rebelled against him in favor of the ancien régime of the rapist tyrant, Tarquin, he sacrifices his sons for the good of the state. The evil son, Tiberius, curses him as a "Thiestes" who devours his own children (V.i.118) and goes to his death in satanic defiance. The good son, Titus, seduced into the rebellion by fears for his beloved, nevertheless accepts his sacrifice as necessary to the state and exchanges blessings with his father before he dies. Titus's Christ-like patience serves to negotiate the Oedipal crisis of patriarchal monarchy. Brutus's harshness imitates divine justice, and the "Sacrifycing" of his "Bowels" (V.ii.38) redeems the state from its Oedipal blood (he exhorts Titus to "heal her wounded Freedom with thy blood" [IV.524]), just as Christ's sacrifice redeemed the world from a debt it could not pay. Moreover, Titus's death is actually the result not of the castrating execution through beheading ordered by the paternal Brutus but of the dignity-saving stabbing administered by the fraternal Valerius—as if to say, republican fraternal order has replaced patriarchalism.

Brutus's solution is not democratic—good as the people are at heart, they need to be led—but republican, a system still in need of strong leaders, men who can overcome their feminine softness. A sensitive audience might feel, however, that the new order has not really escaped patriarchalism. Just as the ancien régime used to say, to represent the continuity of succession, "The king is dead, long live the king," so might the new regimen say, "The father (of our country) is dead, long live the father." Lee seems to me not really to have negotiated the Oedipal crisis: it is still a world *between men*, where the son will still have to supplant the father and where women will be silenced.[15]

An interesting subtext of *The Unhappy Favourite* is Essex's failure to subdue the rebels in the Tyrone rebellion. His precipitate return to England to defend his actions in Ireland challenges Queen Elizabeth's power to control not only him but her Protestant imperial power in England's overseas colony closest to home. Especially threatening is not only Essex's slow progress against the rebels but his daring meeting with their leader, Hugh O'Neill. We never learn in the play the gist of the meeting, and historically Elizabeth berated Essex for its secrecy.[16] But the threat obviously is to a system that thrives on mastery of the other. When the leader of the other is accorded status as an equal,[17] then control and exploitation are threatened—in this instance the deployment of religion as an excuse to seize land and to appropriate it through plantation, as the English had been doing since the Anglo-Norman period and as they had done with a vengeance during the Commonwealth. If O'Neill is equal to Essex, the logic of the play implies, then Essex is equal to the queen. Indeed, her boxing his ears is itself an intimate act, and her authority is constantly undercut by the fact that she loves him. Girard has shown throughout his work that difference is essential to hierarchy. Postcolonial theorists have shown that it is, of course, essential to colonization. Banks's queen *cannot* marry Essex, *cannot* raise him to her bed and thus to equality. Instead, he must die, a martyr to the system of difference that enables Elizabeth to be the queen and England to continue to conquer and dispossess the Irish, to ship thousands off to the West Indies as indentured—slaves. Elizabeth Regina must step over Essex's corpse to become Britannia. It is interesting that the last rhymed heroic play in English is Irish Robert Ashton's *Battle of Aughrim* (apparently not acted), marking the final defeat of Irish rebels at the very end of the Restoration period, 1690. Their demise is coeval with that of the Stuarts—and feudal aristocracy in England.

4
States of Mind
Personal Tragedy

There is a tradition of personal tragedy in Western culture since Aristotle that focuses on essentially great protagonists who through some fatal mistake or crime suffer catastrophe. Abetted by neoclassical theorizing about tragedy and by the magnificent neoclassical tragedies of Jean Racine in France, in the 1670s some of the best playwrights of the Restoration tried their hand at this bow of Ulysses. Aristocratic tragedy is based on the premise that the nobility have great souls capable of great passion. The hands of the best stringers of the bow—Lee and Dryden—mold heroes whose conflicting passions destroy them and ruin their states.[1] These tragedies focus on the problem of sexual constancy—because, as the conduit for the succession of power and property and the state itself, woman is the aristocratic sign of societal stability. Yet Lee and Dryden at their best portray the constant women as unobtainable—with the consequence that the greatness of their protagonists is not perpetuated through legitimate genealogy.

From early in his career, Lee was interested in the figure of heroes in decline, Hannibal in *Sophinisba; or, Hannibal's Overthrow* (1675) and Augustus Caesar in *Gloriana; or, The Court of Augustus Caesar* (1676). Augustus condemns the lascivious excesses of his notorious daughter, Julia, but is incapable of controlling his own adulterous passion for Gloriana, daughter of the first triumvir, Pompey. Moreover, Augustus is threatened by the knowledge that Caesario, son of Caesar and Cleopatra, lives and lurks in the wings to topple him. Caesario has his own flaws, however. His delusions of divinity Lee portrays in language that ironically alludes to a competing divinity newly born: Caesario refers to his own "Swadling-bands," and he is called "King of Kings" (II.i.18, 61). This is a tragedy of distrust. Julia's husband, Marcellus, distrusts her, believes her infamous, only to be reconciled with her when she convinces him otherwise. Caesario saves Gloriana from Augustus, and they fall in love, but Augustus takes them together, and only Gloriana's surrender to him saves Caesario. Gloriana plans to kill the tyrant in his bed, but Caesario shows up instead, raging against her inconstancy. To prove her fidelity, Gloriana stabs herself. When

Augustus enters, Caesario begs a death and dies in Gloriana's arms, proclaiming her love worth all the world. Marcellus and Julia die from grief at the scene. Augustus, conscience-stricken by the havoc he has wrought—he had recognized the greatness in Caesario but could not overcome his jealousy—vows to die like Hercules, that is, poisoned by the shirt of his own runaway passion. When Agrippa counsels patience, Augustus rejects it. Such passion threatens aristocratic heroism from within, by an excess of the very energy that supposedly distinguishes the noble from the common—an excess that disrupts continuity.

Sophonisba is a better play. Like Marc Antony, Hannibal mourns his passion for Rosalinda, since it caused him to dally when he could have taken Rome. Scipio chastises Massinissa, the Numidian king, for a similar passion (for Sophonisba) that has unmanned him. The conflict seems familiar: Roman values of glory, virtue, honor, fame versus oriental values of effeminate passion. Yet the stoic Scipio himself is attracted to Rosalinda, now his captive. And his harsh treatment of Sophonisba causes her and Massinissa to commit suicide.

Rosalinda is sent back to Hannibal's camp accompanied by Massinissa's nephew, Massina, as a pledge that Sophonisba will be exchanged. Despite her protests that she has remained constant to him, Hannibal's uncontrolled jealous rage at the handsome young escort causes Massina to kill himself. Henceforth, Hannibal's career plummets. He loses the battle at Zama, and though he vows to reinvigorate himself and conquer all, we know by the prophecy that opens the fourth act that he will die poisoned (again, that Senecan symbol for one too passionate).

Indeed, the play is rather Senecan, reinforcing lessons of *sic transit gloria mundi* and *contemptus mundi.* In Act I, Massinissa responds to Massina's question, "What is ambition, Sir?"

> The lust of Power,
> Like glory Boy, it licenses to kill,
> A strong temptation, to do bravely ill;
> A bait to draw the bold, and backward in,
> The dear bought recompence of highest sin:
> For when to death we make the conquer'd yield,
> What are we, but the Murd'rers of the Field? [I.i.131-37]

But this is more than *sic transit.* It is an exposé of the hollowness of aristocratic heroism, its flip side of violence in service of "Power."

After Massina's death and Rosalinda's chastisement of his jealous rage, Hannibal utters similar sentiments, which, as the editors note, seem based on *King Lear:*

> The bus'ness of our life's a senseless thing;
> Why burns th'Ambitious Man to be a King?
> Or to what purpose does the Warriour call
> For Arms? Or Gown-men bustle in the Hall?
> Sport for the Gods, they whirl us here and there,
> As Boyes blow watry bubles in the Air. [III.ii.146-51]

So much for the Sydneyan concept of aristocratic service, whether knight of the sword or knight of the robe!

Deploying the familiar allusion to the story of Phaeton, but appropriating Banks's Oedipal trope for succession not of patrilineal monarchs but of superheroes on the stage of history, Hannibal plans to teach Scipio the dangers of ambition:

> But like Sol's off-spring swell'd with dangerous fires,
> He to the management of all aspires.
> Alone the scepter of the world would sway,
> Alone would rule the heaven and drive the day.
> Like that indulgent God I'le first advise,
> Show him the tracks through which ambition flies.
> If deaf to all let him ascend the Throne,
> Snatching at glories which must weigh him down,
> Like Jove we'le toss him from his glistering Chair:
> Sindging ye Clouds hissing through liquid Air,
> And darting headlong like a falling Star. [IV.i.160-70]

But when they finally meet, the old general sounds war- and world-weary, as if he has taken his own lesson to heart:

> Thy boyling Courage does to war incline,
> And glory more then profit you design;
> Such fortune once did on our Genius shine.
> But long experience and the chance of War,
> Makes me at present certain peace prefer.
> Grasp not at Scepters which may turn to rods,
> To Day is yours, to morrow is the Gods. [V.i.23-29]

The warning is no longer of the wrath but of the wisdom of the Father, who has learned not to trust the harlot "fortune." Heroes who court her can only be disappointed.

Running counter to this last trope of mutability is the constancy of a love that transcends Fortune's world. Rosalinda loves Hannibal so much that she dons armor and dies fighting in his cause. But it is Massinissa who articulates love's transcendence. Killing one of Scipio's generals who have come for Sophonisba, in metaphors anticipatory of Dryden's Antony, Massinissa realizes the die is cast:

> I'm in, and now no hope of safety's nigh,
> Yet still a King we will attended dye.
> Like a brave Merchant:
> Who when his long toss'd loaded Vessel hits
> Against some Rock, and with loud horrour splits;
> First grasps one Casket which does all contain,
> Then fearless, shoots himself into the Main.
> So I with thee, my only wealth, my all,
> Amidst the numerous slaine at last must fall. [IV.i.249-57]

When Scipio refuses to let them marry, Massinissa determines that they will die together transcendently:

> Scorn'd be your glory more, and Roman pride,
> While I in winding-sheets embrace my Bride.
> For 'tis decreed that we must never part,
> Wee'l be one spirit as wee're now one heart.
> Traverse the glittering Chambers of the Sky,
> Born on a Cloud in view of fate I'le lie:
> And press her soul while Gods stand wishing by. [V.i.292-98]

Although, in his despair of earthly success, Massinissa blames love as much as ambition, nevertheless he dies in Sophonisba's arms while assuring her, "Thy love is Empire and eternal bliss" (418). The play concludes with Scipio sadly learning these neoclassical lessons of the transience of glory and the value of love. He determines to make peace, not war, and retires to "study not to live, but how to die" (434)—a retirement that reminds the audience that only the aristocracy has the leisure to retire and contemplate the transcendence of its values. But worse: the play concludes with no continuity of greatness, no succession in legitimate political power, no transmission from father to son. *Sic transit,* unfortunately, does not build lasting states.

Lee brings the figure of the declining hero to perfection in *The Rival Queens; or, The Death of Alexander the Great* (1677). Dryden followed suit in *All for Love; or, The World Well Lost* (1677). These two plays, arguably the best neoclassical tragedies on the English stage outside of Shakespeare and Jonson (and two of the Restoration's best blank-verse tragedies), focus on another major paradigm in patriarchal aristocracy, the figure of the adulterous father. Like the adultery that begins and ends the Arthurian story, the adulterous behavior of Alexander and Antony costs them the world and leaves it seeking a worthy leader.

Lee and Dryden cast the injured wife quite differently. The great tragic actress Rebecca Marshal played Alexander's first wife, Roxana, as Medea. The great comic actress Katherine Corey played Antony's current wife, Octavia, as a matron. The former would respect her rival queen, Statira, but cannot because of her raging jealousy. The latter has no more respect for Cleopatra than a Roman matron would for an exotic mistress who had distracted her great husband from the business of the world through her erotic "black endearments" (III.442).[2] But the implication of both plays is the same: How can the state retain legitimacy when sexual inconstancy invites discontinuity? Dryden's Octavia brings Antony's children onstage to reclaim him as father—of the family and of the state (at least the Eastern Empire). Lee's Roxana utters an extraordinary curse. She is carrying Alexander's child, begotten when he returned to her from his bigamously wed Statira. Because Alexander claims to be descended from Jupiter, the child is his semidivine successor. But Roxana prays that the bastard of another of Alexander's mistresses will destroy the legitimate child and rule in his stead:

> May the Illustrious bloud that fills my womb,
> And ripens to be perfect Godhead born,
> Come forth a Fury, may Barsina's Bastard
> Tread it to Hell, and rule as Soveraign Lord,
> When I permit Statira to enjoy
> Roxana's right, and strive not to destroy. [III.129-34]

In addition, she curses Statira with lack of "fruition" (IV.107).

In the end, Alexander dies as a result of his impetuosity, both as ruler and as lover. His beloved old warrior Clytus has berated him from the beginning for his effeminate slackness, articulating stoic versus exotic values:

> O that a Face should thus bewitch a Soul,
> And ruine all that's right and reasonable.
> Talk be my bane, yet the Old Man must talk,
> Not so he lov'd when he at Issus fought;
> And join'd in mighty Duel great Darius,
> Whom from his Chariot flaming all with Gems

He hurl'd to Earth and crush'd th'imperial Crown,
Nor cou'd the Gods defend their Images
Which with the gawdy Coach lay overturn'd:
'Twas not the shaft of Love that did the feat,
Cupid had nothing there to do, but now
Two Wives he takes, two Rival Queens disturb
The Court; and while each hand do's beauty hold,
Where is there room for glory? [I.56-69]

Alexander between his rival queens images his radical ambivalence, torn between not only two women but also love and "glory." Again, Lee introduces the theme of stoic retirement, but this time his hero is being petulant; moreover, his retirement would endanger the state. His favorite tries to console the torn Alexander:

Hephestion. Look up, my Lord, and bend not thus your Head,
As you wou'd leave the Empire of the World
Which you with toil have won.
Alexander. Wou'd I had not,
There's no true joy in such unwieldy Fortune.
Eternal gazers lasting troubles make,
All find my spots, but few my brightness take.
Stand off, and give me air,—
Why was I born a Prince, proclaim'd a God?
Yet have no liberty to look abroad?
Thus Palaces in prospect barr the Eye,
Which pleas'd, and free, wou'd o're the Cottage fly;
O're flow'ry Lands to the gay distant Skie.
Farewel then Empire, and the Racks of Love;
By all the Gods, I will to wilds remove,
Stretch'd like a Sylvan God on Grass lye down,
And quite forget that e're I wore a Crown. [II.413-28]

This is aristocratic self-indulgence, a pastoral posturing that is disingenuous.

Alexander's ambivalence is mirrored in the state. His lack of attention to affairs of the state, indeed his inattention to those he has inadvertently injured, breed conspirators against him. And tragically, it is not the conspirators who feel his wrath but his loyal general, whom he kills for criticizing his slackness to his face. Alexander's guilt is Oedipal:

—here I will lye *[falls.]*
Close to his bleeding side, thus kissing him,

These pale dead lips that have so oft advis'd me,
Thus bathing o're his Reverend face in tears,
Thus clasping his cold body in my arms,
Till death, like him, has made me stiff and horrid. [IV.548-53]

The very aristocratic magnanimity that gives birth to the great passions of ambition and love also potentially breeds its self-destruction, the ideology reflexively warns. In a fit emblem, Alexander dies burning from poison administered by injured rebels but traditionally the sign of uncontrolled passion. And Statira dies as a result of breaking a vow never to see the inconstant Alexander again, their rapprochement goading the enraged Roxana to stab her to death. Alexander's and Statira's broken vows are emblems for the breakdown of the allegiance that is supposed to solidify the state,[3] and Roxana turns out to be the "Fury" that represents retribution. Like Medea, although she does not kill her child, she flees with it in utero, leaving Alexander without an heir. When asked who should succeed him, Alexander offers his empire "To him that is most worthy" (V.371). The worthy Lysimachus seems ready to rise to the occasion, but Lee's audience knew that Alexander's empire was fragmented for lack of such a successor. Alexander's adultery is a trope for the inherent fragility of genealogy as a system for transmission of power, subject as it is to the centrifugal forces of desire and liable to result in aristocracy's failure to perpetuate itself, of heroes to perpetuate states.

Dryden's version of the story of Antony and Cleopatra begins with Antony in "black despair" after the battle of Actium (I.i.61). To no one in particular he rails at unnamed forces that "rais'd" him like a "Meteor" only to "cast" him "downward / To be trod out by *Caesar*" (206-9). He later complains to Ventidius that he himself caused these forces, which he now names, to desert him:

I was so great, so happy, so belov'd,
Fate could not ruine me; till I took pains
And work'd against my Fortune, chid her from me,
And turn'd her loose; yet still she came again.
My careless dayes, and my luxurious nights,
At length have weary'd her, and now she's gone,
Gone, gone, divorc'd for ever. [303-9]

Like that of most characters in English drama, Antony's metaphysics is not very sophisticated, and his use of the term "Fate" here, because it is illogical, can perhaps best be interpreted as mere hyperbole. But his use of the term "Fortune" makes more sense, for the Roman goddess Fortuna is consistently portrayed throughout the play as a personification of capricious chance. Of course, she retains her traditional, patriarchally imposed character of inconstant woman.

The Roman point of view, best represented by Ventidius and Octavia, associates Cleopatra with this female figure of inconstant Fortune. To them, she is the force that has *ruined* him, a word they use throughout the play to describe his plight. To her face, Octavia maintains that Cleopatra cannot really love Antony, for "you have been his ruine" (III.i.451; see also 437). With the force of Roman law behind her, Octavia can claim that Cleopatra has seduced Antony into violating his marriage vows to her and thus destroying his fortunes. When Cleopatra insists that Antony "grew weary of that Houshold-Clog," a wife, and chose her "easier bonds" (424-25), Octavia triumphantly exclaims,

> I wonder not
> Your bonds are easie; you have long been practis'd
> In that lascivious art: he's not the first
> For whom you spread your snares: let *Caesar* witness. [425-28]

Octavia passes the Roman judgment that Cleopatra is nothing but an inconstant "Strumpet," a "faithless Prostitute" (IV.250, 389).

When Ventidius witnesses Cleopatra's feigned reception of Dolabella's courtship, it simply confirms his estimation of her character. He calls her "Every Man's *Cleopatra*," who is now merely providing "against a time of change" by taking a new lover (IV.298-301), and he commands Alexas to verify her infidelity because "You are of *Cleopatra*'s private Counsel, / Of her Bed-Counsel, her lascivious hours; / Are conscious of each nightly change she makes" (321-23). In a cosmic hypothesis Ventidius asserts, "If Heav'n be true, she's false" (315). And in a misogynistic generalization he exclaims, "Woman! Woman! / Dear damn'd, inconstant Sex!" (126-27). Describing the Egyptian fleet's desertion to Octavius's navy, the high priest Serapion identifies the fleet's behavior with the "fawning Strumpet," Fortune (V.85). Again, the Romans substitute Cleopatra for Fortune and interpret the desertion as Cleopatra's final betrayal of Antony. Ventidius excoriates her once more: "The Nation is / One Universal Traitor; and their Queen / The very Spirit and Extract of 'em all" (156-58). To the Romans, Cleopatra is the very sign of inconstancy. She is another Eve, another Criseyde—a metonymy for faithlessness—and thus for political instability.

In what the Romans would call Antony's soberer moods, he agrees with their appraisal of Cleopatra. He berates her for her inconstancy to him when she became Julius Caesar's mistress and for her inconstancy to Rome when she failed to provide support for Antony's campaign in Cilicia (II.i.262-73), and he blames her, in effect, for his fatal "unkindness" to Fulvia, his infidelity to Octavia, and his "shame" at Actium (292-312). Now he accuses her of wanting, by retaining him, to "multiply more ruins on me" (316). When he believes Cleopatra and Dolabella have dallied together, the enraged Antony banishes them, for they have attacked the ethical system of constancy at its very heart:

> I can forgive
> A Foe; but not a Mistress, and a Friend;
> Treason is there in its most horrid shape,
> Where trust is greatest: and the Soul resign'd
> Is stabb'd by its own Guards. [IV.543-47]

Finally believing she betrayed the fleet to curry favor with Octavius, Antony rails against her as a fair-fortune lover (V.208-13).

In other words, throughout the play the Roman point of view embodies traditional Western patriarchal morality placed in service of late feudal, aristocratic ideology. Ventidius, Dolabella, Octavia, and Antony and Octavia's children win him back to that morality with successive titles that represent Antony's public duty, his social bonds: "Emperor!" "Friend!" "Husband!" "Father!" (III.i.361-62). Dolabella defends his own attraction to Cleopatra by contrasting it with Antony's: "But yet the loss was private that I made; / 'Twas but my self I lost: I lost no Legions; / I had no world to lose, no peoples love" (199-201). Antony is bound by his word, both explicit and implicit, to his wife and family, his friends and his "loyal" legions (I.i.349), his country and its people. And Cleopatra, like all those other dark women and foul temptresses of feudal literature, appears to have seduced him away from his manly, patriarchal tasks and, arch-Inconstant herself, to have made him a troth-breaker—thus to have destroyed him as one of the remaining dual pillars of the world.

Dryden's Cleopatra is *not* "Every Man's *Cleopatra,*" however, nor is she every other poet's Cleopatra, certainly not Shakespeare's (with whom Dryden invites comparison on the title page of his play, where he announces that it is "Written in Imitation of *Shakespeare's* Stile"). Dryden has removed all the ambiguity in Shakespeare's Cleopatra that keeps us wondering whether she be courting favor with Octavius, whether she be not feathering her nest for the next in her covey of Great Men upon whose backs she has risen to the pinnacle of ambition (not to say pleasure). Dryden's Cleopatra defends herself against the charge of promiscuity.

Dryden is indebted to the historian Appian of Alexandria, as he suggests in his preface (*Works* 13:10), at least for one important particular. Appian is the only ancient historian to suggest, and Dryden the only Renaissance playwright (that is, from 1542 to 1677) to maintain, that Antony and Cleopatra met and fell in love in 55 B.C. when Antony, serving under Gabinius, returned Cleopatra's father to his throne in Alexandria (II.i.262-65).[4] Antony complains that, while he left Cleopatra to "ripen," Caesar stepped in and "Pluck'd" her first, though he himself deserved her (266-71). Dryden's obvious reason for the innovation is, despite appearances, to make Cleopatra constant to Antony from the beginning.[5] When given the chance to retort to Antony's attack on her, she responds,

> You seem griev'd,
> (And therein you are kind) that *Caesar* first
> Enjoy'd my love, though you deserv'd it better:
> I grieve for that, my Lord, much more than you;
> For, had I first been yours, it would have sav'd
> My second choice: I never had been his,
> And ne'r had been but yours. But *Caesar* first,
> You say, possess'd my love. Not so, my Lord:
> He first possess'd my Person; you my Love:
> *Caesar* lov'd me; but I lov'd *Antony.*
> If I endur'd him after, 'twas because
> I judg'd it due to the first name of Men;
> And, half constrain'd, I gave, as to a Tyrant,
> What he would take by force. [II.i.346-59]

Like the modern figure of the Whore with the Golden Heart, Cleopatra's soul and love have remained inviolate. She claims she cleared herself of Antony's charges in Cilicia (274). She denies she "betray'd" him at Actium, insists she fled out of "fear," and implies that, if it were a betrayal, she would have fled not to Egypt but "to th' Enemy" (375-76). She admits that, because she loved him, she welcomed him to her arms in his flight from his wives, but she denies that she thereby "design'd" his "ruin" (361-72).

Throughout the play, Cleopatra repeatedly demonstrates that she is a "*Mistress true*" (prologue 18), from her refusal of Caesar's offers to her suicide. Alexas comments concerning those refusals:

> O, she dotes,
> She dotes, *Serapion,* on this vanquish'd Man,
> And winds her self about his mighty ruins,
> Whom would she yet forsake, yet yield him up,

> This hunted prey, to his pursuers hands,
> She might preserve us all. [I.i.76-81]

As Aubrey Williams has argued in "The Decking of Ruins," the image of Cleopatra's winding about Antony suggests the traditional image of the vine winding around the elm tree, an emblem for marriage. Moreover, the word "ruins" is important here because it picks up the Roman estimate of what constitutes ruin—loss of honor, fame, and fortune—and prepares us for the contrast with Cleopatra's estimate, for whom the loss of Antony is ruin. Showing Antony a letter from Octavius offering terms if she "forsake" his "fortunes," Cleopatra protests:

> You leave me, *Antony;* and, yet I love you.
> Indeed I do: I have refus'd a Kingdom,
> That's a Trifle:
> For I could part with life; with any thing,
> But onely you. O let me dye but with you!
> Is that a hard request? [II.i.399-406]

When Alexas, interpreting Antony's rapprochement with Octavia, exclaims to Cleopatra, "You are no more a Queen; / *AEgypt* is lost," she responds, "What tell'st thou me of *AEgypt*! / My Life, my Soul is lost! *Octavia* has him!" (III.i.395-97).

When Alexas then advises her to attempt to retrieve Antony from Octavia by making him jealous, she resists, affirming that her love is "so true" that she "can neither hide it where it is, / Nor show it where it is not" (IV.89-91). Even though she tries to flirt with Dolabella, she faints when he paints Antony as coldly inconstant to her and wakes lamenting her return to "Th'abode of Falshood, violated Vows, / And injur'd Love" (174-75). Yet her "one minutes feigning" she fears has ruined her "whole life's truth" (521-22), for Antony banishes her. Still, at this crux she rises above the possessiveness of her love, saying, "I love you more, ev'n now you are unkind, / Than when you lov'd me most" (582-83). As the wounded Antony implores Cleopatra to promise him she was not false, she responds, "'Tis now too late / To say I'm true: I'll prove it, and die with you" (V.374-75). Unlike Shakespeare's, Dryden's audience knows that Cleopatra has indeed been true, and there is no hesitation here before she kills herself, protesting that she goes to "knit" her and Antony's "Spousals with a tie too strong / For *Roman* Laws to break" (417-18).

Thus, however antithetical to conventional morality, Cleopatra's love for Antony is absolutely constant. Dryden dissociates her from Fortune, who has denied Cleopatra the title of "Wife" and "made a Mistress" of her, whereas she was meant by "Nature" to be a "wife, a silly harmless houshold Dove" (IV.91-94). Though earlier she appears to contemn the word "Wife" as describing "That dull insipid lump, without desires, / And without pow'r to give 'em" (II.i.82-84), at the end of the play Cleopatra appropriates the title of "Wife" after all (V.413-14). And Dryden sets up the play to suggest that Cleopatra deserves that title more than Octavia not only because of the superiority of her love but precisely because that superiority manifests itself in absolute constancy of soul. When Cleopatra responds to Octavia's charges that she has ruined Antony, she asserts,

> Yet she who loves him best is *Cleopatra.*
> If you have suffer'd, I have suffer'd more.
> You bear the specious Title of a Wife,
> To guild your Cause, and draw the pitying World
> To favour it: the World contemns poor me;
> For I have lost my Honour, lost my Fame,
> And stain'd the glory of my Royal House,
> And all to bear the branded Name of Mistress.
> There wants but life, and that too I would lose
> For him I love. [III.i.457-66]

The fact that she honors her boast argues its sincerity and the legitimacy of Cleopatra's claim. Moreover, Dryden contrasts Octavia's behavior with Cleopatra's. However much Octavia claims to love Antony (III.i.329-30), it is she, not Cleopatra, who is finally faithless to him, for in her Cornelian pride and jealousy she deserts Antony, saying petulantly, "My Lord, my Lord, love will not always last" (IV.416). Maybe her love will not endure, but Cleopatra's will. Thus, in the value system of the play, Cleopatra does "deserve" Antony "more" (III.i.450). Dryden has granted her claim priority on both chronological and value scales. Hence (contradicting himself by reverting to the traditional account of Antony and Cleopatra's first meeting at Tarsus on the Cydnos River in Cilicia), Dryden has Cleopatra describe her final wedding to Antony as if it were a renewal of previous marriage vows. She decks herself out in the same trappings she wore when she impersonated Aphrodite on the barge (V.458-62).[6]

Cleopatra's constancy stands out in contrast to the inconstancy not only of Octavia but of others. Her own Egyptians remain faithful to Antony only to save their country but eventually do betray his fleet. Alexas, not Cleopatra, is "the very Spirit and Extract of 'em all," who has no loyalty and would "betray" Antony if he could thus save his own neck (V.110). His lies, not Cleopatra's, provoke Antony's suicide. But other

Romans are guilty of inconstancy, too, the very charge they lay on Cleopatra and the Egyptians. The very contest between Antony and Octavius was rooted in the aftermath of Roman parricide. Antony's dear friend Dolabella proves "[u]nfaithful" and betrays Antony's trust by courting Cleopatra (IV.57). And Octavius is portrayed as a pragmatic opportunist, the "Minion of blind Chance" (II.i.110) and thus the one to be associated with Fortune.

But, of course, Antony himself is the most inconstant character in the play. Ironically, he says if Cleopatra "took another Love" he would be heartbroken (IV.38-39)—even while he is deserting her again, as he has done all his life. Dryden's Antony has spent his life leaving Cleopatra for one wife or another, thus relegating her to the perpetual status of mistress, the exotic other that threatens Western order. After falling in love with her and awakening her love for him at a time when Dryden suggests they were both free to marry, he left her to "ripen," as he says (II.i.266), and she subtly upbraids him for it: "For, had I first been yours, it would have sav'd / My second choice" (350-51). It would have saved Antony's second choice, too, for during Caesar's affair with Cleopatra, Antony married Fulvia. After Philippi, Antony left Fulvia for Cleopatra, only to desert her again and, Fulvia being dead, to marry Octavia, only to desert her and return to Cleopatra, whom twice within Dryden's play he is prepared to desert again.

Antony's tragedy, then, is, like Alexander's, his vacillation, the very human inability of this aristocratic hero, this putative demigod, to make a choice once and for all, a choice based upon proper evaluation (cf. Vance). Dryden emphasizes the importance of values and of proper evaluation by all the language of commerce in the play. The motif crystallizes into one set of opposing images, toys versus jewels. Ventidius describes Antony as "[u]nbent, unsinew'd, made a Woman's Toy" (I.i.177), and later he uses the word to describe Cleopatra, as he desperately and disdainfully demands of Antony, "And what's this Toy / In ballance with your fortune, Honor, Fame?" (II.i.428-29). Antony responds that "it out-weighs 'em all" (430), and he exclaims,

> Give, you Gods,
> Give to your Boy, your *Caesar*,
> This Rattle of a Globe to play withal,
> This Gu-gau World, and put him cheaply off:
> I'll not be pleas'd with less than *Cleopatra*. [443-47]

Despite this boast, despite his earlier statement that Cleopatra "deserves / More World's than I can Lose" (I.i.368-69), and despite his later ironic protestation, "When I forsake her, / Leave me, my better Stars; for she has truth / Beyond her Beauty" (III.i.232-34), Antony still vacillates and only comes to realize the full value of Cleopatra when it is too late.[7] Cleopatra's value is underscored by imagery of jewels and precious treasure. Jewels are associated with her from the beginning, first negatively when Ventidius says she "new-names her Jewels" taxes and provinces (I.i.363-65). Then, Alexas brings jewels to Antony's commanders, and it is a "Ruby bracelet, set with bleeding hearts" which symbolically "bind[s]" Antony to Cleopatra as he is about to leave (II.i.199-200). Dolabella is the first to realize Cleopatra's full value, which, echoing Othello, he describes in terms of precious stones:

> I find your breast fenc'd round from humane reach,
> Transparent as a Rock of solid Crystal;
> Seen through, but never pierc'd. My Friend, my Friend!
> What endless treasure hast thou thrown away,
> And scatter'd, like an Infant, in the Ocean,
> Vain sums of Wealth which none can gather thence. [IV.201-6]

Like Desdemona, Cleopatra is a jewel worth more than all her tribe.

Having banished his mistress and his friend, Antony picks up the imagery and shows that he has a proper sense of values at heart, though he has not really followed it and is therefore responsible for his own loss: "I'm like a Merchant, rows'd / From soft repose, to see his Vessel sinking, / And all his Wealth cast o'er" (V.206-8). When he thinks Cleopatra has killed herself to prove her constancy, however, he seems finally to mean his declaration of contempt for all the things of the world—with one exception: "Let *Caesar* take the World,— / An Empty Circle, since the Jewel's gone / Which made it worth my strife" (273-75). He repeats the image to Cleopatra as he is dying:

> *Cleopatra.* How is it with you?
> *Antony.* 'Tis as with a man
> Removing in a hurry; all pack'd up,
> But one dear Jewel that his haste forgot;
> And he, for that, returns upon the spur:
> So I come back, for thee. [365-69]

Dryden beautifully completes the image pattern by having Cleopatra don her "Crown" and richest "Jewels" before she dies (437), and as the curtain closes upon her and Antony sitting in state, we are left with an emblem of the value for which the world is well lost, a jewel of great price, to purchase which one should go and sell all that he has. Had Antony done so at the beginning, he might have had Cleopatra and the world, too, at least for a while longer. If not, he at least would have had a jewel worth all the world. His final evaluation is conclusive: his parting kiss is "more worth / Than all I leave to *Caesar*" (401-2).

Dryden's final dissociation of Cleopatra from Fortune is the implication that the love of Antony and Cleopatra is "Immortal" (467) and thus transcends the mutable world governed by Fortune. Though the Egyptians and the Romans both desire Antony to seize "Fortune" again (I.i.48, 333), in his heart Antony knows "Fortune is *Caesar*'s now" (III.i.149). From the opening imagery of extreme flux and the ghost's cry, "*AEgypt* is no more" (I.i.28),[8] we are reminded that we are in Fortune's world and that it is her nature to be inconstant. Thus the pervasive imagery of ebb and flow, storms and shipwrecks and sinking, ripeness and rottenness, loss and ruin, "Time and Death" (I.i.450).[9] Fortune, not Cleopatra, is the real "fawning Strumpet" of the play. Therefore, one must find something of permanent value that transcends her, and the jewel imagery suggests that the constant Cleopatra contains such value and that Antony has finally grasped it for eternity. In his dying breath Antony exults,

> What Ages have we liv'd!
> And now to die each others; and, so dying,
> While hand in hand we walk in Groves below,
> Whole Troops of Lovers Ghosts shall flock about us,
> And all the Train be ours. [V.393-97]

Cleopatra believes in the same afterlife, for she prepares to convey her "Soul" to Antony and to "knit" their "Spousals with a tie too strong" for not only "*Roman* Laws" but for Fortune's power "to break" (488, 417-18). After momentary bewilderment as she is dying, Cleopatra confidently utters these final lines: "*Caesar*, thy worst; / Now part us, if thou canst" (500-501).

Unlike Shakespeare, Dryden does not undercut Antony and Cleopatra's assertion of transcendence as mere rhetoric.[10] Instead, Dryden allows Serapion, the admirable and honorable high priest, who has acted as a choric character throughout, the analogue to Shakespeare's (and Plutarch's) soothsayer, to pass the final judgment of the play:

> See, see how the Lovers sit in State together,
> As they were giving Laws to half Mankind.
> Th'impression of a smile left in her face,
> Shows she dy'd pleas'd with him for whom she liv'd
> And went to charm him in another World. [V.508-12]

Serapion means literally that Antony and Cleopatra appear still to be ruling the Eastern Empire, but there is nothing conditional in his statement that they have gone to "another World." The metaphoric implication, then, is that they still rule from beyond the grave the half of mankind who are true and constant lovers. And they are free at last from the forces about which Antony first complained:

> Sleep, blest Pair,
> Secure from humane chance, long Ages out,
> While all the Storms of Fate fly o'er your Tomb;
> And Fame, to late Posterity, shall tell,
> No Lovers liv'd so great, or dy'd so well. [515-19]

Dryden's celebration of adulterous love is quite extraordinary. He later maintained that this was the one play he "writ for . . . myself" (*Essays* 2:207). Yet while the theme of the play is constancy, while Dryden uses Appian of Alexandria for the story that Antony met Cleopatra and fell in love with her before Caesar did, the fact (in the fiction) is that he abandoned her again and again: an emblem, as with Alexander, of his inconstancy—and consequent incompetence—as a ruler. He has destroyed himself and left his state to the self-interested Octavius. It is as if the last of the aristocratic heroes, revealed for all his literal magnanimity to be no moral superior, yields on the stage of history to the new man of dispassionate bourgeois efficiency.

What is more remarkable is that Lee and Dryden in these plays make the mistress more attractive than the wife, reflecting again at the moment of England's dynastic crisis one of the aristocracy's central myths of endemic instability because it ultimately cannot control the genealogy upon which it depends for continuity. Instead, it must desperately posit, even at the moment of its greatest awareness of its limitations, the socially irresponsible fantasy of transcendence of a world too tough to govern. In exalting a private, adulterous relationship as transcendent, even as he himself had indulged in an adulterous affair with the actress Anne Reeves (see Winn s.v.), Dryden has transformed a feudal transgression into the bourgeois fantasy of the private. Antony's successor is Archduke Rudolph.

Though not intended for the stage, John Milton's *Samson Agonistes* (publ. 1671) demands attention here as a classical Hebraic tragedy (anticipating Racine's later plays), which embodies an oppositional ideology—and as simply the greatest poetic tragedy of the age. *Samson* is very much a

Restoration tragedy, for the figure of Samson, like the figures of Alexander and Antony and, indeed, of Milton himself, is that of champion apparently defeated by history—implicitly the cause of the Puritan Saints overturned by the restoration of Charles II, or worse, lost by the Saints themselves through slackness:

> But what more oft in Nations grown corrupt,
> And by thir vices brought to servitude,
> Than to love Bondage more than Liberty,
> Bondage with ease than strenuous liberty;
> And to despise, or envy, or suspect
> Whom God hath of his special favor rais'd
> As their Deliverer. [268-74]

God had provided Cromwell as Deliverer. The rest is history, a history of renewed enslavement because of failure to cement the Revolution.

Appropriating the figure of the hero and the theme of trust to his own purposes, Milton portrays Samson as no hero by birth but by grace, chosen by God to deliver the Israelites from the Philistines. Now, like Lee's and Dryden's heroes, past his prime, he has fallen from his greatness because he has allowed himself to be enslaved by his passions, to betray the secret of his God-given strength to a woman. This passion is an emblem of the moral slackness Milton attacks as precipitating bondage even in the midst of liberty:

> I yielded, and unlock'd her all my heart,
> Who with a grain of manhood well resolv'd
> Might easily have shook off all her snares:
> But foul effeminacy held me yok't
> Her Bondslave. [407-11]

But after he has successfully resisted the wiles of Dalila, who would further enervate him and alienate him from his calling, Samson responds to the braggart Philistine champion, Harapha, "My trust is in the living God" (1140), thus reestablishing his bond with God and opening himself for the grace once again to be His champion. Samson's toppling of the temple of Dagon on the heads of the decadent Philistine aristocracy represents Puritan wish fulfillment. But it also images Milton's apocalyptic vision of history and his paradoxical bourgeois vision of leadership by a new aristocracy of the "best," the "ablest," the men of "merit" and "true virtue."[11] The Chorus articulates the bourgeois, undemocratic appropriation of the trope of the chosen people:

Nor do I name of men the common rout,
That wand'ring loose about
Grow up and perish, as the summer fly,
Heads without name no more remember'd
But such as thou hast solemnly elected. [674-78]

Samson Agonistes has colonial implications as well,[12] for it justifies the destruction of pagan cultures ("inhuman foes" [109], whose "foreskins" [144] are a synecdoche for their radical otherness/inferiority) by the agents of the One True God acting on behalf of His Chosen People. It justifies intermarriage for the purposes of infiltration: "I thought it [marriage to Dalila] lawful from my former act [marriage to the Timnan], / And the same end; still watching to oppress / *Israel's* oppressors" (231-33). One thinks of Cortez's marriage not to Dryden's fictive Cydaria but to history's legendary La Malinche, the Aztec who betrayed her people to the white invaders, a betrayal that earned her the title La Chingada. In other words, it justifies "Conqu'ring Crosses" for the purposes of subjugation and conversion. What is worse, it justifies systematic genocide against "Infidels" (221). Just as Dryden's Indians hope their conquerors will forgive them, so Samson forgives Dalila—at a distance—before he destroys her and the Philistines. (My generation has seared into its memory the image of Heddy Lamar as the forgiven Delilah amidst the pillars behind Victor Mature/Samson as he pushes the columns apart in Cecil B. De Mille's *Samson and Delilah*.) Samson may have vacillated, may have shamefully babbled the secrets of Jehovah, but like Cromwell he has been the instrument of sacred history. Milton may have believed that his fellow Saints failed to seize the day, that now the world shall run "[t]o good malignant, to bad men benign" (*Paradise Lost* XII.538). But his fellow Puritans in New England, having seized the land from heathens, thought their City on the Hill was doing just fine.

5
Apocalypse Now
Tragical Satire

The ending of tragical satire is foreboding, featuring either draconian, apocalyptic justice or no justice at all. The sense of the ending is that evil perseveres, threats to the hegemonic class persist unchecked, unaneled. At its best, Restoration tragical satire splits the seams of the aristocratic ideological cloak and allows us to see its inherent contradictions. In his early play *The Vestal Virgin* (1664), Sir Robert Howard (like John Fowles in *The French Lieutenant's Woman*) writes alternative endings, one tragic with no metaphysical consolation (hence a romantic tragedy), the other comic with a distributive poetical justice attributing the dynamic of the dénouement to divine justice (hence a heroic romance). Such an alternative suggests, as in Fowles, that the "happy" ending is the product of wish fulfillment, that poetical justice as the rhetoric of order is merely the rhetoric of desire.

In the later, much better *Duke of Lerma; or, The Great Favourite* (1668), we are in the world of villains and states. Howard gives his audience the illusion of attending a typical romantic tragedy, with its expectation of at least retributive poetic justice. The duke is a Renaissance Overreacher, a Grand Machiavel characterized by enormous ambition, unscrupulousness, and magniloquence. As he proceeds in his quest for unlimited power to exalt his base followers, persecute the loyal nobility, prostitute his own daughter, Maria, in order to control the young King Philip, and murder the Queen Mother, he is portrayed as blasphemously irreverent, defiant, and positively satanic: he would supplant God himself. When the old king, who has thwarted Lerma's ambition and ordered him banished, finally dies, Lerma mocks traditional descriptions of such events as having cosmic, cataclysmic consequences:

> I heard methoughts a Groan as Horrible
> As if great Nature's Frame had crackt in two,
> And yet that blow kill'd not a Fly, *Caldroon* [his own Mosca];
> Something is gone old Folks will talk on. [I.i, 212]

When a courtier announces the king is dead, Lerma responds aside, "Thanks be to Heaven." Appropriating the language of the code of word-as-bond, Lerma demands loyalty, faith, and trust from his equally vicious followers and accuses his truly loyal brother, the duke of Medina, who is attempting to defend the young king from Lerma's schemes, of violating the bonds of "Nature" and abandoning brother, "Friends and Alliance" out of a specious "Pious Love to Honour" (V.i, 247). Medina sees him as "a subtle Sophister," and in soliloquy Lerma articulates his antitrust ethic:

> He's gone; he durst not stay to hear me;
> He did begin to melt: good-natur'd Gentleman.
> I love to try Mens tempers to laugh at 'em;
> For I shou'd hardly trust a promis'd kindness.
> I will not beg, that can command my Peace;
> He that secures himself well in the end,
> Must destroy Foes, and never trust a Friend. [V.i, 248]

Delivering Maria to King Philip supposedly out of "Loyalty" (II.ii, 221), Lerma in ironically religious language justifies his and her confessor's virtual pimping:

> you may tell her
> The Mistress of a King, is half a Saint,
> For she'll be worshipt. . . .
> You have a fine, large Text, to preach upon:
> And I will second you, and add new motives,
> Hugging her Sin, and bless her for offending. [I.iii, 214]

Falling down before his daughter and worshiping her as a "Divinity" who can save him from banishment by seducing the young king, Lerma blasphemously declares, "I ask no other help but thine, / To make *Spain* know I am their Deity" (II.i, 218). When Maria mysteriously disappears and Lerma's designs begin to fail, he defiantly indicts Heaven:

> Where is its Mercy then? for it ne'er had
> Another way to Bless, but by *Maria*.
> Could my prophane and passionate Revenge
> Reach but the Hearts and Lips of the Religious;
> No Incense evermore shou'd upward fly,
> Of Prayer or Praise; I'd stop all Piety
> Till they restor'd *Maria* to me. [V.i, 246]

From the beginning Lerma claims to control events, as he says to the confessor, "If we but prosper now; not we on Fate / But she on us, shall for direction wait" (I.iii, 215). Even as things begin to fall apart, Lerma proclaims, "Fortune and I did long ago agree, / I to make work for her, and she for me" (IV.ii, 243). Seemingly more resigned to failure, he appropriates traditional stoic discourse: "Vertue can singly stand on its own trust. . . . He only is above Envy and Fate, / Whose Mind in sinking Fortunes keeps its height" (III.iii, 235; IV.ii, 245).

Lerma's creature, Caldroon, however, employs a typical image for impending doom: "The Storm has overtook our greatest speed. / Nor can the Duke himself find out a shelter" (III.iii, 233). Indeed, it would appear that Howard has set Lerma up for the traditional poetical/providential justice. While Lerma defiantly mocks romantic "Love" and naive "Confidence," the virtuous characters pledge their "Loyalties" to young King Philip and advise him to garner "the Peoples Oaths," as Medina exults, "It is the Boast of *Spain,* and our best Glories, / That we have ever truly serv'd our Kings" (I.i-ii, 213-14). As Lerma gains power, the virtuous appeal to Heaven. Horrified at the pimping confessor, Maria cries, "Is this Divinity? Defend me, Heaven!" (II.i, 215). In contrast to Lerma's perverted stoicism, Maria practices proper Christian stoicism: "Vertue, thou shalt protect me before heaven, / Though not from this bad World" (II.i, 219). Yet she responds to Lerma's blasphemy with both filial and religious piety: "Heaven defend my Father" (II.i, 216). And she resists the attempt to prostitute her, converts King Philip to ideal love, and proves her constancy and fidelity to the skeptical patriarchal judge, Medina.

Meanwhile, the loyal duke of Alva praises Medina's attempts to thwart Lerma and prays, "Heaven prosper and direct you" (II.ii, 224). Finally the loyalists begin to purge the court of Lerma's favorites. In a spectacle designed to move Lerma to repent his atrocities, Caldroon is led to execution by friars carrying a crucifix and tapers. The confessor poisons himself. And Medina draws his sword of "Justice" (V.i, 246), obviates Maria's plea for mercy, and confidently believes the approaching Lerma, despite his laughing defiance, "a tir'd o'er-hunted Deer" who "Treads fatal Paths offer'd by chance, / And not design'd by him" (V.ii, 250). The oxymoron, "fatal Paths" of "chance," epitomizes all the contradictory references to Fate and Fortune throughout the play and reveals them to be sloppy metaphysics, for the force that governs events is finally portrayed neither as pure accident nor as pure necessity but as the "design" of a providential justice that employs Medina as its instrument. Or so it would seem.

The great shock at the end of the play is the complete frustration of expectation. Lerma enters in a *"Cardinal's Habit"* (V.ii, 250 s.d.), purchased from the pope in Rome in the nick of time. As early as the end of the third act he has predicted, "[I]n despight of my curst Enemies, / I'll find a Conquest in a safe retreat, / And though they rise, I'll sink to be as great" (III.iii, 235). As his followers earlier hide his treasure remaining from his secret papal purchase, he triumphs blasphemously, perverting the religious language that is supposed to underwrite feudal society:

> Here, set that Treasure in, for they are Reliques,
> And will preserve their faithful Worshipper;
> Why, here are Mysteries Canonical,
> That must not be search'd into by disputes;
> 'Twas a good purchase too—considering
> The deep necessity; or if compar'd
> To the vast sums I gave my Instruments
> To turn them Fiends, and make my self a Devil,
> For I am Sainted at a cheaper Rate,
> Thanks to his Holiness, my pack of Councellors,
> I have out gone you all. [V.i, 245]

Indeed, one of the apparently triumphant counselors concludes, "He has o'er-reach'd us all" (V.ii, 250).

Thus this Renaissance Overreacher does not end, as usual, by defeating himself, by going one step too far, by improvidently playing into the hands of Providence. And he taunts his would-be justicers by pretending to have received from the conferral on him of his cardinal's "Office" a gift of tongues, a call to preaching, as he upbraids them for being so "uncharitable" as to abominate his escape from their justice and as he counsels them to have "Patience" (V.ii, 250). Even though King Philip and Maria will apparently finally be married as her religious vows yield to public (genealogical) necessity, and even though the play thus has something of the conventional resolution, the audience cannot shake the effects of Lerma's last great cynical attack, worth quoting in its entirety:

> I will not longer trouble you, my Lords,
> But leave you now to prey upon your selves.
> He that devours the rest, in time may be
> A Monster, more o'ergrown than e'er I was.
> When you are low and poor, you are all Friends,
> And in one fair pretence together join,
> While every one conceals his own design.
> It is your Countrys cause, until full grown
> In long sought power. then it proves your own.
> When you seem good, your Crimes are not the less,
> Men have all new Creations by Success.

Ambition, like a wanton Womans hast,
Invites new Slaves, grown weary of the last.
Mankind each others stories do repeat,
And Man to Man is a succeeding cheat.
So to this fate I leave you, and shall joy,
To see those Crimes you blame, your selves destroy.
May you all sink in fates for me you meant,
And be too dull, your ruines to prevent;
That when you're lost in this ambitious toil,
I in my safe retreat may sit and smile. [V.ii, 251]

Not only does Lerma frustrate expectations of justice, he indicts the virtuous as hypocrites. Like Hobbes (anticipating Nietzsche), Lerma interprets the language of virtue, the rhetoric of ethical order, as a mask for desire, for the inevitable Will to Power that animates men. Medina is so captivated by Lerma's "greatness" of "Spirit" in this speech that he "cou'd almost forgive him" (V.ii, 251). Howard leaves us with a Nietzschean rather than Aristotelian magnanimity, a frightening great-spiritedness that threatens to translate virtue back into its root sense of manly power. Lerma's final mockery is directed as much at us as at his antagonists: "This holy Robe tells me, it is my duty, / And I forgive: but sure I may laugh at you" (250). An audience that expects poetical as a sign of providential justice, the rhetoric of metaphysical order, has been forced to take a nasty look into the nominalist abyss. And yet, to paraphrase Maynard Mack on the ending of *King Lear,* the play is designed for the audience to cling to the assurance that it is better to be Maria than Lerma. However much at some level that audience acknowledges the (patriarchal) truth that Renaissance nation-states are whores taking successive, supplanting dynastic lovers, ambitious villains who become heroes if successful, it is supposed to take consolation in Howard's condemnation of hypocrisy.

Lee's Duke Nemours from *The Princess of Cleve* (1682?) is another type of overreacher; he is an extreme example of the Restoration Rake, the libertine Don Juan whose unlimited pursuit of sexual variety threatens to destabilize patriarchal society by attacking the grid upon which its power is based, genealogy. The typical rake of Restoration social comedy (Etherege's Dorimant, Behn's Willmore) has his promiscuous sex urge socialized into marriage. The rake of subversive comedy (Wycherley's Horner, Otway's Truman) remains a rover at large, but the plays end in celebration and marriage (Harcourt and Alithea, Valentine and Camilla). Perhaps following Thomas Shadwell's lead in *The Libertine* (1675), Lee portrays a rake so extreme in his defiance of conventional morality and its validating metaphysics as to be utterly shocking. Shadwell's Don John is ultimately punished for his outrageous defiance—that is, his *défiance* in its root sense, his radical breaking faith with the feudal patriarchal system and its underwriting Logos.[1] But Lee's Nemours escapes punishment altogether even as he mocks the fifth-act conversion of the libertine.[2]

The play is structured like a split-plot tragicomedy, but Lee took the unusual measure of refusing to designate its genre,[3] perhaps because he sensed its radical difference from other plays. At the risk of seeming facetious, I might term it a *comitragical satire.* Like Sir Robert Howard, Lee frustrates generic expectations. As in a Dryden tragicomedy especially, the comic plot mirrors the concerns of the heroic or high plot. St. Andre and Poltrot are buffoons, libertine wanna-bes who mimic the lascivious behavior of their betters. St. Andre appears to be a parvenu lord and Poltrot his boorish cousin from England. They search for sexual game, pretending to lie with duchesses and other women of quality, much to the consternation—and sexual frustration—of their wives, Elianor and Celia. And Poltrot yearns to cuckold his friend. That is, he would play Nemours, but ironically he ends up a comic version of the prince of Cleve, except that, unfortunately, he has actually experienced his bed rocked, his wife mounted, and himself apparently shot in the groin by one of the wits. Thus Poltrot receives a typical folk poetical justice.

Lee's apparent tragicomedy moves away from the typical Drydenian split-plot, however, toward Shadwell's subversive comedy, *Epsom Wells* (1672), or toward one of his or Durfey's outright comical satires (see *Tricksters and Estates,* intro. and chap. 11). The wives of these comic butts also ape the vices of their betters, and in the high plot the Lady Tournon outrageously justifies being a bawd for Nemours and the other wits by appropriating the conventional language of morality ("Honesty" means "Pimping," for example, at I.i.45-46; "True" means virile at II.ii.153), portraying all grave and apparently moral women as "Devils in a corner" who employ proper language with seductive double entendre (III.i.18), and praising clever women who succeed in the patriarchal system not by the high road of chastity but by the low road of "Discretion" (IV.ii.7). Tournon calls attention to her having appropriated the main tool of male oppression—language—by joking, "[C]ertainly I shou'd have made a rare Speaker in a Parliament of Women, or a notable Head to a Female Jury, when his Lordship gravely puts the question, whither it be Satis or Non Satis or Nunquam Satis, and we bring it in Ignoramus" (IV.ii.15-18). The fools' wives similarly employ language to free themselves from their husbands' tyranny, first in overt dialogue, then in masquerade by engaging in a witty repartee that they clearly win, as they waltz off with the wits. When the butts adopt Jonsonian disguises, humors, and cant to get even with their wives by abusing them misogynistically, the women turn the tables and defeat them verbally once more. Finally, they cuckold them with two of the wits, and even though discovered, they maneuver their husbands into reconciliation.

Although the couples conclude the play swearing henceforth to be true to one another, Lee suggests through style alone that the women have learned too much. When Celia sues to Poltrot to be forgiven, in a parody of the princess suing to the prince of Cleve, she breaks into heroic couplets and Settlean quatrains. When that posturing fails, she resorts to prose and hilarious physical threats: "I'll have your Throat cut. . . . He that miss'd your Guts in the dark, shall take better aim at your Gullet by day-light" (V.i.73-77). It might be argued that the men have received no more than what they deserve and that the women want nothing more than constancy and regular sexual service. But the fact that Poltrot complains throughout the play of Celia's romps with Lord Harebrain earlier in their relationship implies that she, like her male libertine counterpart, will never be satisfied and that the comic conclusion of apparent return to constancy is merely, satirically, cynically cosmetic.

Celia has another counterpart in the high plot—Marguerite. She begins the play as a Mrs. Loveit, railing violently at the perjured, inconstant Nemours. Like Loveit, she vows revenge, but that revenge takes the shape of a bed-trick, with Marguerite courting Nemours in a masquerade, punctuating their dialogue with asides condemning him for his devilish falsehood. She plans not to redeem him for herself, however, but simply to rekindle his desire for her, "enjoy him / With the last Pang of a revengeful Pleasure," exact from him vilification of herself and promises of constancy, then reveal herself and "leave him to the Horror of his Soul" (III.i.96-107). Like Celia, then, she would inflict on her unfaithful a poetical justice, one that here takes on religious overtones. Yet like Celia in another way, after she has worked her scam and, after exciting—and mocking—repeated vows of constancy from Nemours, unmasked in triumphant scorn, she proclaims that she will beat Nemours at his own game of promiscuity:

> Yes, I will try the Joys of Life like you,
> But not with Men of Quality, you Devils of Honour;
> No, I will satisfie
> My Pride, Disdain, Rage and Revenge more safely,
> By all the Powers of Heav'n and Earth I will;
> I'll change my loving lying Tinsel Lord,
> For an obedient wholsome drudging Fool. [IV.i.193-99]

Sounding like the voluble gadabout in Rochester's "Letter from Artemisa to Chloe," Marguerite announces a program of freeing herself from male oppression by choosing a fool for a husband, whom she can dominate in order to purchase her own sexual freedom.

Women who commit adultery and get away with it are relatively rare in Restoration drama, especially if they remain witty and desirable like Otway's Mrs. Goodvile, Behn's Lady Fancy, and Southerne's Sir Anthony Love—or like Marguerite and Celia in this play. But Marguerite's triumph and program are short-lived, for at the end of the play she is resubordinated to patriarchy as Nemours claims her for his wife. Then perhaps the princess of Cleve represents real freedom and independence from men, the kind of (silently) triumphant feminist heroine like the one Nancy Miller finds in Madame de La Fayette's original ("Emphasis Added" 43). At a crucial moment in the play, the princess learns that her husband, the prince, is to be accompanied by Nemours on an important mission. Actually, the prince is just testing her to discover the identity of the lover she has already confessed. As she speaks, she fatefully discloses her concern for the threat Nemours represents to her, to them, and to society. She pleads, "Perhaps 'tis not too late yet to supplant him" (III.ii.21). She means *replace* Nemours in the entourage, but she calls attention to his role as supplanter, as what Jacques Derrida calls the "dangerous supplement" (*Of Grammatology,* pt. 2, chap. 2), that constant threat to the perfection or completion of any human institution, from marriage to language itself. Nemours has already supplanted Cleve in her heart, but the princess makes a heroic resistance, confesses to her husband her attraction, and remains constant to him. Nevertheless, the dangerous supplement continues to work. The prince grows jealous; trust yields to distrust and finally to deadly rivalry between these best friends, Nemours and Cleve; the prince receives at least a psychic wound if not an actual physical one, fades swiftly, and eventually dies. As he is languishing, he sees the princess and Nemours together, concludes the affair has been consummated, and comes to exhort his wife to repentance before he dies. She maintains her innocence, and he declares their final reconciliation, but he refuses ever to see her again, and we must interpret why. He says, "I do believe thee; / Thou hast such Power, such Charms in those dear Lips, / As might perswade me that I am not dying" (IV.iii.149-51). Yet of course he knows he's dying, so he is referring to the power of language to make faith, trust, permanence, Presence seem possible despite the reality of the supplement. He says he believes, yet "Were I to live I shou'd not see thee more" (157), because to see her again would admit the possibility of further supplementation, further supplanting.

Even the princess's heroic effort to overcome supplanting fails. After Cleve's death, when there is no legal reason why she and Nemours cannot fulfill their love in marriage, that is, why his final supplanting of Cleve should not take place, the princess refuses because she has learned the danger of the supplement, how satiety leads ineluctably to the need for variety, a truth that seems the wisdom of both high and low plots. Nemours's rhetoric of constancy, of his word as bond, she sees as "the Blandishments of Perjur'd Love" (V.iii.201), and she poignantly asks, "What Power on Earth can give / Security that Bond shall prove Eternal?" (164-65). Thus she triumphantly declares, "I will, I must, I shall, nay, now I can, / Defie to Death the lovely Traytor Man" (202-3). She appears to have transcended earth with its patriarchal dominance and dangerous supplement and turned toward Heaven with its permanence and Presence, as she calls on Heaven throughout the scene for its forgiveness and support. She herself longs to die, for she has developed nothing but contempt for the false world.

And yet, in an extraordinary departure from the line of her reasoning, she admits to Nemours,

> 'Tis true, my Lord, I offer much to duty,
> Which but subsists in thought, therefore have patience,
> Expect what time, with such a love as mine,
> May work in your behalf. [230-33]

In a weak moment she acknowledges that the language of transcendence is but abstraction, that time and supplementation are the underlying realities. She leaves imploring Nemours, "Believe that you shall never see me more" (247), but he recognizes that this is not really a declaration. Upon his knowledge of "the Souls of / Women," he self-assuredly and cynically proclaims to the vidam, "Believe that you shall never see me more—she Lyes, I'll Wager my State, I Bed her eighteen months three weeks hence, at half an hour past two in the Morning" (254-59).

Such unmitigated cocksureness is the trademark of this extreme libertine. From the beginning he has defied time and death, morality and the gods themselves. Like the duke of Lerma, he mocks man's moralizing memento mori over the death of the ultimate libertine, Count Rosidore (read Lord Rochester), whom he eulogizes as "the Spirit of Wit" who personified and exulted in the dangerous supplement itself: "He never spoke a Witty thing twice, tho to different Persons; his Imperfections were catching, and his Genius was so Luxuriant, that he was forc'd to tame it with a Hesitation in his Speech to keep it in view" (I.ii.101-6). Nemours appreciatively paraphrases Rosidore's poetry celebrating carpe diem in defiance of death (III.i.125-33).

In typical libertine fashion, Nemours is a thoroughgoing nominalist. Sounding like Lerma, he chides Tournon for appealing to "Conscience" and continues: "Vertue! An ill-bred crosness in the will; / Honour a

Notion, Piety a Cheat, / Prove but successful Bawds and you are great" (I.ii.58-69). To his boy Bellamore he makes a mockery of the important aristocratic virtue of obligation, for he had once saved the life of the prince he is about to cuckold: "I sav'd his Life, Sweet-heart, when he was assaulted by a mistake in the dark, and shall he grudge me a little Fooling with his Wife, for so serious an Obligation?" (II.iii.7-9). To the vidam he declares he would leap his mistress "in thy Face" (26). And like Lerma, he chides all others as hypocrites:

> Why 'tis the way of ye all, only you sneak with it under your Cloaks like Taylors and Barbers; and I, as a Gentleman shou'd do, walk with it in my hand. . . . Now do I know the Precise will call me damn'd Rogue for wronging my Friend, especially such a soft sweet natur'd Friend as this gentle Prince—Verily I say they lye in their Throats, were the gravest of 'em in my condition, and thought it shou'd never be known, they wou'd rouze up the Spirit, cast the dapper Cloak, leave off their humming and haing, and fall too like a Man of Honour. [II.iii.34-36; IV.iii.14-19]

But here, in Nemours's echoing of biblical phrasing and his perversion of the concluding phrase, we see that, like Count Rosidore, Nemours's most potent weapon is his tongue, as he appropriates the language of trust, friendship, and constancy merely to obtain the objects of his desire. He *trusts* his Ganymede, Bellamore, with the secret of his adulterous desire for the princess of Cleve (I.i.20-35). How can there be trust, the play asks its audience, in such a decadent world of lubricious sexual thieves and perverts—and class traitors? He calls "glorious" his supplanting the prince in the princess's heart (II.iii.218). And he perverts religious language throughout, as in the hilarious exchange in Calvinistic cant between Nemours and Tournon, who is disguised as a Huguenot (IV.i.35-49), or in this outrageous exchange between the disguised Nemours and Marguerite as they accomplish their tryst during the masquerade:

> *Nemours.* For the forward brisk she that promis'd me the Ball Assignation, that said, there was nothing like slipping out of the crowd into a corner, breathing short an Ejaculation, and returning as if we came from Church— . . .
>
> *Marguerite.* [Clapping him on the shoulder.] I love a man that keeps the Commandment of his word.
>
> *Nemours.* And I a Woman that breaks hers with her Husband, yet loves her Neighbour as her self. [IV.i.30-55]

Nemours's most frightening appropriation of language occurs when he postures as friend and lover. As the jealous Cleve approaches to demand satisfaction from him, Nemours prays, "Hypocrisie and Softness, with all the Arts of Woman, / Tip my Tongue" (IV.i.272-73), and he pours forth all the blank verse rhetoric of friendship and trust. Begging "by the name of Friend" that Cleve desist, he draws his sword as reluctantly "[a]s if I were to fight against my Father" (354-55). This last statement is extremely significant, for indeed Nemours, as dangerous sexual supplement, is rebelling against the patriarchal superego. Such rebellion is different from yet related to the rebellion of the sons of Mithridates and Lucius Junius Brutus. An assault upon the patriarchal superego is tantamount to assault upon the king and the god at the apex of the hierarchical, monarchial pyramid.

Finally, Nemours deploys all the pseudo-religious rhetoric of Platonic, transcendent love to attempt to win the princess. Lee emphasizes the purely rhetorical nature of Nemours's discourse by having him slip into heroic couplets (see Richard Brown 398-99). When the princess appeals to Heaven to help her resist him, Nemours appropriates the religious rhetoric:

> The Heavenly Powers
> Accept the poorest Sacrifice we bring,
> A Slave to them's as welcome as a King.
> Behold a Slave that Glories in your Chains,
> Ah! with some shew of Mercy view my Pains;
> Your piercing Eyes have made their splendid way,
> Where Lightning cou'd not pass—
> Even through my Soul their pointed Lustre goes,
> And Sacred Smart upon my Spirit throws;
> Yet I your Wounds with as much Zeal desire,
> As Sinners that wou'd pass to Bliss through Fire.
> Yes, Madam, I must love you to my Death,
> I'll sigh your name with my last gasp of Breath. [IV.iii.93-105]

The princess's response represents an astonishing reversal. Apparently convinced by his rhetoric, she offers him a kind of hope as she exhorts him to abide by the code he articulates: "Fix to your word, and let us trust our Fates" (108).

But, of course, Nemours no more means these words than those to Cleve. Like the husband of the famous widow of Ephesus, he sardonically goes to seduce the princess on the very "Tomb" of her husband, dressed in the full panoply of not Platonic but libertine rhetoric: "I mean a Visit by the way of Consolation, not but I knew it the only opportunity to catch a Woman in the undress of her Soul; nay, I wou'd choose such a time for my life, and 'tis like the rest of those starts, and one of the Secrets of their

Nature—Why they melt, nay, in Plagues, Fire, Famine, War, or any great Calamity—Mark it—Let a man stand but right before 'em, and like hunted Hares they run into his lap" (V.ii.16-22). Knowing he has Marguerite in reserve, he is undaunted, and Tournon gives him his just character: "Go thy ways Petronius, nay, if he were dying too, with his Veins cut, he wou'd call for Wine, Fiddles and Whores, and laugh himself into the other World" (31-33).

From the beginning Nemours has blasphemously defied that other world and its putative gods. When Tournon playfully taxes him with damning both his own soul and those of his victims, he pledges to her a fidelity not of the soul but of the body and its sexual performance: "[B]y Heaven I'm thine, with all the heat and vigorous Inspiration of an unflesh'd Lover—and so will be while young Limbs and Lechery hold together, and that's a Bond methinks shou'd last till Doomsday" (I.ii.47-50). So much for word-as-bond!

When the disguised Marguerite, protesting aside that Nemours is a "Fiend, and no Man," pretends she might indeed be a devil herself, a succubus, Nemours insouciantly and defiantly proclaims, "But be a Devil and thou wilt, if we must be Damn'd together, who can help it" (III.i.52-63). In Tirso's, Molière's, and Shadwell's plays, such defiant rhetoric constantly reminds the audience of the sure divine vengeance that awaits Don Juan, who commits rampant rape, murder, and incest. And in Lee's play, the audience's expectations of a similar divine justice are aroused when Marguerite announces she plans a revenge that will conclude with Nemours's contemplating "the Horror of his Soul" (III.i.107), or when the mortally wounded Cleve warns his wife, "There is a Power that can and will revenge" (IV.iii.130).

The problem with the ending, however (see Weber, *Rake-Hero* 76-78), is that Nemours is brought to no such contemplation nor is he punished by some Power that protects the conventional morality. Instead, he enacts his last posture, that of the reformed rake, a posture so successful that even Lee's modern editors believe it (*Works* 2:150). Exhorting the couples of the low plot to "Swear a whole Life's Constancy," he proclaims, "For my part, the Death of the Prince of Cleve, upon second thoughts, has so truly wrought a change in me, as nothing else but a Miracle cou'd—For first I see, and loath my Debaucheries—Next, while I am in Health, I am resolv'd to give satisfaction to all I have wrong'd; and first to this Lady [Marguerite], whom I will make my Wife before all this Company e'er we part" (V.iii.289-99). With an obvious reference to the recent death of Rochester, Lee's audience is ostensibly supposed to believe in the "Ingenuity" (ingenuousness) of Nemours's "Repentance" because, unlike Rochester, Nemours "had the power to go on," that is to continue in iniquity: "He well Repents that will not Sin, yet can, / But Death-bed Sorrow rarely shews the Man" (300-303).

Yet how can the audience believe the conversion of this extreme libertine, when moments before he has predicted he will bed the princess, naming the very minute? How can they believe him when he has parodied the very notion of "Conversion" by telling Tournon to use it to win back Marguerite from the dauphin, threatening that the prince's death has caused him to repent and resolve "to leave off Whoreing and marry"—not Marguerite but the princess (V.ii.8-11)? How can they believe him when he has repeatedly stated that Marguerite is merely his "reserve" to fall back on if the princess refuses him? Unlike Dorimant, Nemours has not been led to the gradual awakening of something dormant in his soul, a different kind of passion from what he has experienced before. True, he rediscovers Marguerite's wit, but he also loves and pledges to serve always that of Tournon, and he still intends to seduce the princess.

Thus, it would seem, the ending of the play defies three possible conventional endings: a poetical justice that takes the Don Juan off to hell, as in Tirso's, Molière's, and Shadwell's plays; a poetical justice that leaves him contemplating "the Horror of his Soul"; or a socialization that causes him truly to repent his sexual excesses and marry. Instead, Lee's audience is left with the dangerous supplement still on the loose, the champion of the antimorality of the unpunished libertine wits both male (Bellamore, the vidam) and female (Tournon, Celia). Nemours masquerades behind the rhetoric of reformation, but he lurks there to ultimately supplant the prince, his father, and all the males so ill protected by the patriarchal code of words. He is pure Will to Sexual Power and cannot be socialized. The message to Lee's audience is to beware the *unheimlich* libertine monster lurking within the aristocracy itself.[4]

One remembers Shakespeare's *Life of Timon of Athens,* if at all, as marked by passages of bitter yet grandiloquent diatribe against human greed, hypocrisy, and ingratitude. The exchanges between Timon and Apemantus remind one of those between Lear and Gloucester on the strand—especially in the austere, nihilistic vision of Peter Brook. Shakespeare's Timon raises the figure of malcontent, popular on the Jacobean stage, to the heroic proportions of misanthrope.

The late John Wallace has argued that the play satirizes the failure of the aristocratic ethos of Senecan stoic morality, particularly concerning benefits and gratitude ("*Timon of Athens* and the Three Graces"). I might add that, given its constant references to broken oaths, vows, and promises, Shakespeare's play satirizes a world where a gentleman's word is no longer his bond. But in contrast with Wallace, I see *Timon* concluding with a healing closure in the redemptive generosity of Alcibiades, a generosity that extends that of the faithful servants to the regeneration of an aristocratic ethos Alcibiades shares not with those who ungratefully deserted Timon and banished him but those who negotiate his reentry into the city, its government, and its life. Shakespeare's ending marks the play a satirical tragedy and not a tragical satire—that is, not that kind of play that features serious loss of life, with strident attacks on society, but that ends either without resolving closure or with draconian or apocalyptic justice.

Because of its draconian revolutionary ending, however, wherein the government of Athens is radically altered, I would classify as tragical satire Thomas Shadwell's adaptation of Shakespeare's *Timon* as *The History of Timon of Athens, Man-Hater.*5 Performed in January 1678 at the Duke's Theater, Shadwell's play preserves, as his subtitle indicates, Shakespeare's portrait of a misanthrope, though some of his diatribes are cut and his language is somewhat sanitized, as was typical of Restoration adaptations.[6] But more important than such cuts and stylistic alterations, Shadwell drastically alters Shakespeare by additions that make the play a thoroughly *Restoration* tragical satire—and a radical one at that.

As I have attempted to demonstrate in *Tricksters and Estates* (chap. 11), Shadwell's subsequent *Woman-Captain* (acted 1679) is a comical satire on libertine extravagance that leads to the squandering of estates. Shadwell had already written an antilibertine tragical satire, *The Libertine* (acted 1675), a shrill, excessive treatment of Don Juan and his draconian demise. Shadwell makes his Timon a libertine, too. Not just his prodigality but his hedonism drains his estate: "[W]e should seize / On pleasure wheresoever we can find it, / Lest at another time we miss it there" (II, 216). Like Don Juan with his cast mistresses, Timon coolly dismisses his discarded Evandra with libertine doctrine:

> Why are not our desires within our power?
> Or why should we be punisht for obeying them?
> But we cannot create our own affections;
> They're mov'd by some invisible active Pow'r,
> And we are only passive, and whatsoever
> Of imperfection follows from th'obedience
> To our desires, we suffer, not commit;
> And 'tis a cruel and a hard decree,
> That we must suffer first, and then be punish't for't. [I, 212]

Evandra, also sounding like Mrs. Loveit, protests their mutually exchanged vows and deems him a "perjur'd man" (I, 211).

Like Etherege's Dorimant, however, Timon's affections have moved to another object, the rich Melissa. She enters the stage coquettish, fretting over the appearance of her new dress and, like Etherege's Harriet, bantering with her maid about a curl. If the audience did not see the parody of Restoration comedy in Timon's scene with Evandra, it cannot escape it now. Unlike Etherege's headstrong but virtuous Harriet, Shadwell's Melissa is satirized as a fickle gold digger, who has transferred her affections from Alcibiades to Timon because the former has lost his "Estate . . . And I hate a poor Fellow, from my heart, I swear" (II, 215). Her chastity is not virtue but "interest" (214)—that is, marketable reputation—and her coquetry is mere vanity: "I vow methinks I look so pretty to day, I could / Kiss my self" (215).

Of course, despite her vows and protestations, reattracted to Alcibiades on his prospect of regaining his estate, Melissa deserts Timon the moment he loses his. When he upbraids her with infidelity, ironically she echoes his own libertine philosophy: "We can't command our wills; / Our fate must be obey'd" (III, 241). In another volta-face, announcing she is "always true / To interest and my self" (IV, 259), Melissa turns back to Timon when Alcibiades is banished again and the rusticated Timon is rumored to have discovered gold.

This uppity woman gets her comeuppance when she is dismissed by both lovers. Excusing her former behavior toward him as but a "tryal" of his love (IV, 259), Melissa now accuses Timon, victim of monumental ingratitude, of ingratitude toward her. The atmosphere is that of Milton's *Samson Agonistes.* Timon is being tempted again by his weakness. As Samson abruptly dismisses Dalila, Timon calls a spade a spade:

> False! proud! affected! vain fantastick thing;
> Be gone, I would not see thee unless I were
> A Basilisk: . . .
> Be gone, or thou'lt provoke me to do a thing unmanly,
> And beat thee hence. [260]

Appropriating Alcibiades's rhetoric against the city of Athens, Melissa throws herself in his path as he reenters triumphant. He, too, calls a spade a spade: "What gay, vain, prating thing is this?" (V, 270). He, too, is proof against her wiles and brushes her aside by offering her to his corporal.

In the figure of Melissa, Shadwell satirizes not just another example of inconstant, fair-weather allegiance but another example of mercenariness, to which theme I shall return in a moment. But first, in another variation on his borrowed theme from Restoration comedy, Shadwell harmonizes other echoes from Restoration tragedy. Just one month earlier debuted *All for Love* by Shadwell's nemesis, John Dryden. In Shadwell's *Timon,* Evandra, like Cleopatra, has never had her relationship with Timon solemnized by marital ritual:

> 'Tis true, my Lord, I was not
> First lifted o're the Threshold, and then
> Led by my Parents to *Minerva*'s Temple:
> No young unyok'd Heifers blood was offer'd
> To *Diana;* no invocation to *Juno,* or the *Parcae:*
> No Coachman drove me with a lighted torch;
> Nor was your house adorn'd with Garlands then;
> Nor had I Figs thrown on my head, or lighted
> By my dear Mothers torches to your bed:
> Are these slight things, the bonds of truth and constancy?
> I came all Love into your arms, unmixt
> With other aims. [I, 212]

Such rituals have indeed traditionally signified "the bonds of truth and constancy": they are their public manifestation, designed precisely to avoid the problems of private vows, which traditionally had been acknowledged to constitute marriage. Though the Council of Trent had forbidden such marriages, literary artists still employed them to emphasize the supremacy of constancy as a cultural virtue. Shakespeare's use of the bed-trick to enforce such constancy is one famous (perhaps now infamous) instance of such poetic license.

The bed-trick leads to public acknowledgment, however. Like Dryden, like Aphra Behn in her Rover comedies, Shadwell is bolder, attacking the mercenary motives of marriage itself, that system for the trafficking in women in order to build estates. Evandra attacks Melissa's motives:

> But her Love is mercenary,
> Most mercenary, base, 'tis Marriage-Love:
> She gives her person, but in vile exchange
> She does demand your liberty: But I
> Could generously give without mean bargaining:
> I trusted to your honour, and lost mine,
> Lost all my Friends and Kindred. [210-11]

Like Dryden's Cleopatra, Evandra has not the specious title of a wife to gild her reputation. And yet:

> Ah *Timon,* I have lov'd you so, that had
> My eyes offended you, I with these fingers
> Had pluckt 'em by the roots, and cast them from me:
> Or had my heart contain'd one thought that was
> Not yours, I with this hand would rip it open:
> Shew me a Wife in *Athens* can say this;
> And yet I am not one, but you are now to marry. [210]

In other words, while Evandra thinks marriage as a system is mercenary and while she disdains the title of a wife thus obtained, she nevertheless considers herself a wife. She attacks "that base *Cecropian* [Athenian] Law" that "Made Love a merchandize, to traffick hearts / For Marriage, and for Dowry" (211). Yet she wonders without it "who's secure?" (211). That is, what woman, relying on vows of constancy alone, can compete with a system based on greed? Moreover, while she "Could generously give without mean bargaining," what protection does she have against inconstancy? Unlike Timon's, her position is not libertine. She still desires to possess. In the face of Melissa's last threat she asserts her claim to Timon: "Why shou'd you strive to invade anothers right? / He's mine, for ever mine" (IV, 259).

Shadwell proposes not promiscuity, then, but an extramarital fidelity: "No, *Timon,* I will have you whole, or nothing" (II, 227). Like Dryden's Antony, Timon gradually comes to appreciate her value: "For the Empire of the Earth I wou'd not lose her; / There is not one of all her Sex exceeds her / In Love, or Beauty" (228). At this point he still intends to marry Melissa. But when she rejects him as impecunious, Timon laments his ingratitude to Evandra, is astonished at her "most amazing generosity" when she relieves him (III, 242). Just as, in contrast to Octavia, who deserts Antony insisting love will not always last, Dryden's Cleopatra remains faithful to him despite his fate, so also does Evandra in contrast to Melissa: "Let false *Melissa* basely fly from thee, . . . I am no base Athenian Parasite, / To fly from thy Calamities" (241-42). In Shadwell it is not Shakespeare's steward but Evandra who is faithful to the rusticated, misanthropic Timon, and he finally pronounces "to all the world, there is / One woman honest" (IV, 253). When Melissa calls her "dishonest" because unmarried, Timon protests, "There is much more honesty / In this one woman than in all thy Sex / Blended together; our hearts are one" (260). Like Antony again, Timon dies proclaiming Evandra the "only! dearest! kind! constant thing on Earth" (V, 269). And like Dryden's Cleopatra, Evandra keeps her "word" and kills herself rather than outlive her lover. Alcibiades eulogizes Evandra at the end as "That Miracle of Constancy in Love" (V, 273). Moreover, in Evandra Shadwell expands Shakespeare's figure of the faithful servant (compare Kent) by giving Timon a kind of Cordelia, who would redeem nature from the curse Timon subjects her to: "Repose your self, my dearest love, thus—your head / Upon my lap, and when thou hast refresht / Thy self, I'll gather Fruits and Berries for thee" (IV, 254).

Yet given the extramarital nature of that love, its threat to traditional society, as Shadwell portrays it, is perhaps implied in Alcibiades's earlier retort to the inconstant, gold-digging Melissa: "[T]ell me, is not one / Kind, faithful, loving Whore, better than / A thousand base, ill-natur'd honest Women?" (V, 270). Shadwell retains Timon's sarcastic attack on Alcibiades's whores, whose promiscuity threatens continuous patrilineal descent. If marriage as a system, with what Etherege's Harriet would call *church security,* is discarded, who will protect women from inconstancy, who will protect the rights of heirs?

As in Western patriarchal literature in general, Shadwell's figure of the constant woman remains a figure for continuity through genealogy. And she is not just some abstract symbol, for patriarchal society transmits its power and property through the bodies of women, who must therefore be the pure vessels of such transmission. So Shadwell is not merely spicing up Shakespeare in order to exploit the presence of actresses in the repertory companies.

Furthermore, in aristocratic literature the constant woman is a figure for social continuity as well, for political succession is also patrilineal. Not only the theme of ingratitude links the two plots of Shadwell's adaptation. The desertion of Timon is compounded by inconstancy. Evandra's faith is juxtaposed to Melissa's but also to his country's infidelity, an infidelity not just to Timon but to Alcibiades. The play ends not with Timon and Evandra's mutual death and a subsequent restoration of the old order. It ends with a radical revolution of that order, a draconian poetical justice on the inconstancy of Athens.

Like Shakespeare, Shadwell links that inconstancy to ingratitude. But he links it also to mercenariness.[7] The other side of the libertinism that Shadwell satirizes is the fiscal. He opens the play with a steward, a role expanded from Shakespeare but similar to the one employed in *The Woman-Captain,* in order to emphasize the cultural loss in the squandering of estates. For if "to nauseous Flatterers, / To Pimps, and Women, what estates he gives" (I.i, 199), as an aristocratic lord he wastes the very basis of his status—land and its revenue that were increasingly slipping into the hands of unscrupulous Restoration cits: lawyers, merchants, and bankers of the city of London.

In other words, to the Plutarchan and Senecan moralizing of Shakespeare's play, epitomized in Timon's and Apemantus's diatribes against greed, hypocrisy, and ingratitude, Shadwell adds the Restoration twist of concern with the shift from a land-based to a trade-based economy and concomitant ruling oligarchy. And this supposedly proto-Whig Shadwell emphasizes his attack on mercenariness by subtly transforming the senators of Athens into cits and thereby transforming his play into a satire on the emergent bourgeoisie.

First, Evandra refers to "th'extorting Senators" (III, 242), a key characterization Alcibiades repeats: "Banish me! Banish your doatage! Your extortion!" (IV, 250). Just a few years before Shakespeare's *Coriolanus* will be adapted as *The Ingratitude of a Common-Wealth* (1681), Alcibiades insinuates the same innuendo: "Banish your foul corruptions and self ends! / O the base Spirit of a Common-wealth!" If the audience were not heretofore hearing *Parliament* for *Senate,* they are now perforce. And Shadwell has made an ad populum appeal to residual memories of the Civil War and abhorrence of The Good Old Cause.

Shadwell's rendering of Timon's offering to Alcibiades his newfound gold to finance Alcibiades's apocalyptic scourge of Athens borrows the word "Usurer" (V, 265) from the original, but he emphasizes the word and its pejorative connotations by having Alcibiades conclude the exchange with this exhortation to his army: "Now march, sound Trumpets and beat Drums, / And let the terrour of the noise invade / The ungrateful, Cowardly, usurious Senate" (266). Indeed, Shadwell transforms the Athenian senators upon the walls of the besieged Athens from nameless senators to the specific senators who profited from his largesse then deserted him: Nicias (Melissa's father), Aelius, Phaeax, Cleon, Isander, Isidore, and Thrasillus. Instead of the dignified, reasonable argument from Shakespeare's senators that all within have not injured Alcibiades, that he might decimate the population but not destroy the city of his birth, Shadwell has these ungrateful cowards grovel and demean themselves, offering their necks to be trod upon. Shadwell emphasizes their niggardliness by having Alcibiades call them a "Den of Thieves" (267) and by extending the Shakespearean characterization of them as "Pursy" to an image of them as bourgeois pigs who, while soldiers suffer incredible hardships, "snort / In peace at home, and wallow in their bags" (268).

Finally, Shadwell takes one last, remarkable step in transforming these aristocrats into bourgeois. Significantly shrinking their number down from seven, he has Alcibiades demand, "You six of the foremost here must . . . on your Knees present your selves / With Halters 'bout your necks!" (V, 268). He has metamorphosed them into the Six Burghers of Calais, whose deaths were the price to save the population of the city as Edward III occupied it in the Hundred Years' War. One thinks of Rodin's monumental sculpture and the halters round the necks.

Yet Shadwell's satire on mercenary cits is unlike typical Restoration reveling in Cavalier superiority. The upper class's ethos of birth-as-worth is roundly satirized, as is the concept of honors won through service. Apemantus levels aristocratic lords mercilessly:

> Show me a mighty Lordling, who's puft up,
> And swells with the opinion of his greatness;
> He's an Ass. For why does he respect himself so,
> But to make others do it? wretched Ass!
> By the same means he seeks respect, he loses it.
> Mean thing! does he not play the fool, and eat,
> And drink, and void his excrements and stink,
> Like other men, and die and rot so too?
> What then shou'd it be proud of? 'Tis a Lord;
> And that's a word some other men cannot
> Prefix before their names: what then? a word
> That it was born to, and then it could not help it.
> Or if made a Lord, perhaps it was
> By blindness or partiality i'th' Government.
> If for desert, he loses it in Pride;
> Who ever's proud of his good deeds, performs
> Them for himself; himself shou'd then reward 'em.
> Oh but perhaps he's rich, 'Tis a million to one
> There was villany in the getting of that dirt,
> And he has the Nobility to have knaves for his Ancestors. [III, 231]

Apemantus pulls the rug out from under any admiration we might have for Alcibiades by reminding us of his riotous lifestyle and especially his pride in his conquests, about which he boasts throughout the play and which were in reality won by his soldiers, themselves "a poor rabble / Of Idle Rogues who else had been in Jails" (V, 271). The bourgeois ethos of meritocracy Apemantus further explodes:

> The Government's to blame in suffering the things I rail at.
> In suffering Judges without Beards, or Law, Secretaries that can't write;
> Generals that durst not fight, Ambassadors that can't speak sence;
> Block-heads to be great Ministers, and Lord it over witty men;
> Suffering great men to sell their Country for filthy bribes,
> Old limping Senators to sell their Souls
> For vile extortion: Matrons to turn incontinent;
> And Magistrates to pimp for their own Daughters. [III, 231]

Gulliver had many ancestors.

Given the failure of both residual aristocratic and emergent bourgeois ethoi, Alcibiades makes the radical gesture of turning over the government to the people:

> Thus when a few shall Lord it o're the rest,
> They govern for themselves and not the People.
> They rob and pill from them, from thence t'increase
> Their private stores; but when the Government
> Is in the Body of the People, they
> Will do themselves no harm; therefore henceforth
> I do pronounce the Government shall devolve upon the
> People, and may Heav'n prosper 'em. . . .
> Now all repair to their respective homes,
> Their several Trades, their business and diversions;
> And whilst I guard you from your active Foes,
> And fight your Battels, be you secure at home.
> *May* Athens *flourish with a lasting Peace;*
> *And may its wealth and power ever increase.* [V, 272-73]

Is this a default political theory? Ruling classes have failed, so let's turn the government over to the people in general, whom he previously contemned, and who have been portrayed throughout as a riotous, fickle rabble. Will this motley crew "do themselves no harm"? In other words, Shadwell backs into this theory. He does not carefully develop it throughout the play. One might see the leveling impulses of Apemantus's attacks on aristocracy and meritocracy as leading toward democracy, the democracy, after all, of Athens—until one remembers that Timon insists the only common denominator leveling reduces us to is "base and shameful Villany" (IV, 251).

Wallace says of the ending of Shakespeare's *Timon,* "Shakespeare had no conception of a contractual political society because nobody conceived one until much later, so Timon is a martyr to profoundly held beliefs which Shakespeare knew were inadequate but was powerless to change and could only challenge with a vision that shirked nothing" (363). I am wary of assuming what Shakespeare "knew," and I see more reaffirmation of aristocratic values through Alcibiades's generosity than does Wallace. It is Shadwell's ending that strikes me as hollow. For Shadwell had such a contractual theory available to him, not the absolutist contractual theory of Hobbes but the republican contractual theory of Milton if not yet of Locke. Instead, he leaves us with a trapdoor solution, a radical gesture toward a democracy with no credibility, with a corrupt general—a Buckingham (see Sorelius), a proto-Marlborough—serving as Protector to a people he disdains. The wish fulfillment exhortation to let trade thrive during peace is unexceptionable as a slogan, but it is not a real program.[8] Shadwell has satirically turned the Restoration world upside down and left us momentarily pleased at the revolution, at the rallying cry of "*Liberty, Liberty*" (V, 273), but nevertheless blinking in anticipation of the ensuing anarchy. Despite the signal fidelity of Evandra, she and Timon figure forth a forlorn single couple of the Just in an apocalyptic ending. Shadwell's *Man-Hater* cannot escape its misanthropy, its radical hatred of man and his systems.

Thomas Otway is the master of Restoration absurdist tragical satire.[9] His early tragedies end on absurdist notes.[10] His last two, best tragedies reveal the absurdity inherent in aristocratic patriarchalism itself. For the raising of men to be heroes to rule and protect states demands the expunging of the female within them and makes them fundamental misogynists. Moreover, in these plays there is no escaping the Oedipal rebellion that lurks in the tapestry of patriarchy. In *The Orphan* (1680), Castalio transgresses his father's injunction not to marry (therefore, not to enjoy the privileges of the patriarch—see Tumir). Here, son contends not with father over the woman but with a twin brother. As René Girard has shown, twins are extremely dangerous, threatening genealogy and even identity.[11] In a symbolic sense, the bride, Monimia, whom both brothers love, represents their patrimony, and since they are twins, with no clear indication of primogenitive precedence, they in effect destroy each other over her. Castalio keeps his marriage a secret, and his twin, Polydore, simply acting as a Don Juan, supplants him in his bridal bed. Once the incest is discovered, Monimia's pollution must be purged by the *pharmakon* that is both her poison and society's remedy. And Polydore must remove the confusion of identical twins, sacrificing himself for the survival of the other, who ostensibly would carry on patrilinearity.

Castalio himself dies a victim to patriarchy's imploding myths. He keeps his marriage secret, on one level, because for him to marry an orphan without his father's approval, since she is not an appropriate exchange item for building an estate, is likely to result in his disinheritance, as is hinted twice in the play and as Otway portrays elsewhere in his canon. On another level, he does not want to hurt his brother with news of his victory in their rivalry. But on a deeper level, his own father's attitude toward marriage—"Let Marriage be the last mad thing ye doe" (III.88)—may threaten Castalio with the castration his name implies (see Morrow). In the libertine, homosocial world, marriage is a sin. It cheats man of his "Freedom," as Castalio himself protests to Polydore (I.162), insisting he would never marry till he be old—too old to sow wild oats is the implication.

Yet on a deeper level, Castalio cannot admit he is married because that would mark him as effeminate. All the sexual discourse in the play demonstrates that, in order to control property through genealogy, patriarchal society must inculcate from a very early age distrust of the opposite sex. Thus Monimia and Serina, the twins' sister, who is falling in love with Chamont, constantly betray a learned misandry, reinforced by Chamont, who warns Monimia to beware men, for they are all false. On the other side—and far more serious for the outcome of the play—is the inculcation into young men of a fundamental misogyny. That which has wounded worst the patriarch, Acasto, is his whorish Fortune.

Throughout the discourse of Acasto's household, this supposed paradise free from the corruption of the court, woman is a metonymy for deceit, betrayal, frailty. We are not surprised at Polydore's repeated misogyny, for libertinism turns women into sex objects, instruments of male pleasure. But Castalio himself is thoroughly indoctrinated by the discourse. His insouciant pose with Polydore may be hypocritical, but as soon as he gets the first harsh look from Monimia, who is understandably upset that he loosed his brother on her, he concludes, "I am a Fool, and she has found my Weakness; . . . I am a doating honest Slave, design'd / For Bondage, Marriage bonds . . . Betray'd to Love and all its little follies" (II.307-19). When he cannot gain admission to her chamber on their wedding night, he sits down outside and rails at "th'inconstant Sex" (III.558). He considers being chained, like Hercules, to a distaff. And he buys into the cultural stereotype of the relation between the sexes as a battle for dominance. When he finally learns the truth, he curses not his deceiving his brother but his engaging in heterosexual love: "My Fatal Love, alas! has ruin'd thee," he says to Polydore (V.443).

What is worse, Monimia herself buys into the patriarchal stereotype: when the page reports to her Castalio's affected libertine insouciance, she determines to "[b]e a true Woman, rail, protest my wrongs, / Resolve to hate him, and yet love him still" (I.278-79). At the end, the dying Monimia asks Castalio, "Wilt thou receive pollution to thy Bosom, / And close the eyes of one that has betray'd thee?" (V.456-57). Built into patriarchal discourse is not merely a rhetoric of sexual virtue that protects genealogy but a misogyny that reflects deep male fears that women might perform the ultimate castration of taking back the control of genealogy themselves.

Castalio dies cursing the world and its system of "trust" (V.503), and Chamont reads a moral that does the opposite of the last lines of a typical Stuart tragedy: "'Tis thus that Heaven its Empire does maintain, / It may Afflict, but man must not Complain" (529-30). Otway gives us no comforting rhetoric of providential justice or transcendence for the just. If there be a god, he is sheer Power. The world of *The Orphan* has collapsed because the discourse designed to enforce patriarchal control has done its job all too well. The men fundamentally distrust all women, and the women themselves accept the rhetoric of purity and pollution. Castalio, Monimia, Polydore, Acasto—all their personal tragedies constitute an absurdist satire on their patriarchal culture. Otway's universe is as absurd as Oedipus's: fate makes no sense.[12]

The satire of Otway's *Venice Preserv'd; or, A Plot Discover'd* (1682) is darker yet, its absurdity a vision not of the illusory power of language but of its total breakdown. By the end of the play, the code of the word as bond of loyalty, trust, fidelity, constancy—indeed, late feudal aristocratic *official discourse* itself—has been destroyed, replaced by meaningless gestures, mad ravings, and nonsense.[13]

The conflict in the play is triple sided, and Jaffeir is caught in the middle of the triangle. He has three contending loyalties: to his friend and fellow conspirators and their code of liberty and justice; to his country, its leaders, and its code of honor and humanity; and to his supposedly transcendent jewel, his wife, Belvidera. Ironically, he who articulates to the Venetian Senate the aristocratic standard of constancy in the face of adversity—"a Steady mind / Acts of it self, ne'r asks the body Counsell" (IV.153-54)—manifests a most unsteady mind.

The play opens similarly to *Othello.* Jaffeir has betrayed his host and foster father Priuli's trust and stolen away his daughter "like a Theif" (I.49). Deprived of control over his progeny, Priuli curses Jaffeir and Belvidera with "[a] steril Fortune, and a barren Bed" (53). Although, as Jaffeir reminds him, they have escaped the latter part of the curse already, for Belvidera is pregnant, Priuli endeavors his utmost to implement the first part of the curse, prompting Jaffeir's creditors to foreclose and evict his own daughter. Nevertheless, convinced that by saving Belvidera's life, as he once did, he has purchased the right to the "nobler gratitude" of her love (46), Jaffeir defies Priuli's curses and Fortune's changes, adopts a *contemptus mundi,* and sounding like Dryden's Antony, will "trust" his "Fate no more" but concludes the "world" and its "Busy Rebellion" well lost in favor of his "choicest Treasure," Belvidera (382-95).

Jaffeir's *contemptus mundi* is short-lived, however. Already he has solemnly sworn to his friend Pierre, "By Sea and Air! by Earth, by Heaven and Hell, / I will revenge my *Belvidera*'s Tears!" (297-98). The same night when he boasts his defiance of the world he keeps his appointment on the Rialto with Pierre to learn more of the conspiracy against the state. Within minutes he pledges his word to rejoin the active political world and participate in "Busy Rebellion." He plights a new troth to Pierre and the conspirators:

> [B]y all those glittering Stars,
> And yond great Ruling Planet of the Night!
> By all good Pow'rs above, and ill below!
> By Love and Friendship, dearer than my Life!
> No Pow'r or Death shall make me false to thee. [II.177-81]

Jaffeir confirms his oath by entrusting them with "[a] Pledge, worth more than all the World can pay for" (II.346). He surrenders to them his jewel, Belvidera, to be killed if he prove false. Thus, he subordinates his love to this greater purpose, the cause of liberty from oppression, as especially Pierre describes it: "A Battle for the Freedom of the World" (282).

Throughout the play, this rough, once loyal general, heroic Pierre, has the best lines as he articulates a revolutionary's definition of villainy, of heroes and states:

> To see the suffring's of my fellow Creatures,
> And own my self a Man: To see our Senators
> Cheat the deluded people with a shew
> Of Liberty, which yet they ne'r must taste of. . . .
> All that bear this are Villains; and I one,
> Not to rouse up at the great Call of Nature,
> And check the Growth of these Domestick spoilers,
> That make us slaves and tell us 'tis our Charter. [I.152-64]

He exhorts the hesitant Jaffeir to curse his own "and the worse Fate of *Venice,* / Where Brothers, Friends, and Fathers, all are false; / Where there's no trust, no truth" (252-54). If trust itself has fled, then do not brave men have an obligation to restore it?

Yet immediately after Pierre has concluded the first of these ringing speeches, Jaffeir comments, "Oh *Aquilina!* Friend, to lose such Beauty, / The Dearest Purchase of thy noble Labors; / She was thy Right by Conquest, as by Love" (165-67). In other words, Jaffeir has already interpreted Pierre's real motivation to be not the altruistic saving of a people but the more selfish sense of injured merit on the part of a general whose loyal service to the state should have earned him unchallenged possession of his mistress, who has been appropriated by the senator Antonio. And without hesitation Pierre acknowledges the justness of Jaffeir's suspicion, lamenting Aquilina's inconstancy and deeply resenting the new object of her attentions if not affections. He then rationalizes his rebellion on the grounds that the Senate's chastising him for beating Aquilina's dotard, Antonio, constitutes breaking the "Tyes" of loyalty forever (194-204). From this point on, "revenge" becomes the key word in Pierre and Jaffeir's discourse, contaminating the idealism of their cause, as they ban "all tender humane Follies" from their breasts and talk increasingly of ruin rather than reformation (II.182-95).

Similarly, the rhetoric of the other conspirators is contaminated. First, Renault in soliloquy reveals his real motivation to be "ambition" (II.196). Then, several of the conspirators quarrel, and their leader, Bedamore the Ambassador, upbraids them (222-28): If such men feel justified in overthrowing a corrupt regime that has, as Renault says echoing Pierre earlier, destroyed trust (265-66), must they not indeed evince implicit trust with one another? Must they not be above the rest of corrupt mankind, the elect of Providence, transcendent as a jewel and therefore possessing the right "To restore Justice and dethrown Oppression," as Jaffeir expresses it (322)? Their very quarreling denies them such special status; it is a sign (in aristocratic ideology) of the anarchy that ensues when men assume the right of revolution. Moreover, Renault's attempt to rape Belvidera, especially as punctuated by the incredulous Pierre's exclamation, "He durst not wrong his Trust!" (III.ii.240), demonstrates that there can be no trust among those who, in effect, murder trust through their disloyalty and rebellion.

Furthermore, the rhetoric of revolution masks the iron law of oligarchy: Renault reveals that the bonds of trust of the new order will simply be the bondage imposed on slaves by a new set of masters. He says of trustless Venice,

> [L]et's destroy it;
> Let's fill their Magazines with Arms to awe them,
> Man out their Fleet, and make their Trade maintain it;
> Let loose the murmuring Army on their Masters,
> To pay themselves with plunder; Lop their Nobles
> To the base Roots, whence most of 'em first sprung;
> Enslave the Rowt, whom smarting will make humble;
> Turn out their droning Senate, and possess
> That Seat of Empire which our Souls were framed for. [II.271-79]

The last lines clarify Renault's later injunction:

> [S]pare neither Sex nor Age,
> Name nor Condition; if there live a Senator
> After tomorrow, tho the dullest Rogue
> That er'e said nothing, we have lost our ends;
> If possible, lets kill the very Name
> Of Senator, and bury it in blood. [III.ii.333-38]

This is class warfare of a kind, and the intent is to annihilate one oppressive ruling class only to replace it with another, while effectively exposing that the very idea of nobility is absurd: at its base are the "base Roots, whence most of 'em first sprung." Yet "the Rowt" must remain "enslaved."

Perhaps the worst aspect of the conspirators' motivation is their apparent sadistic lust for blood. As Renault's rhetoric reveals most clearly, their rebellion is an intended rape:

> Then sheath your swords in every breast you meet. . . .
> Shed blood enough, spare neither sex nor age. . . .
> Without the least remorse then let's resolve
> With Fire and Sword t'exterminate these Tyrants,
> And when we shall behold those cursed Tribunals,
> Stain'd by the Tears and sufferings of the Innocent,
> Burning with the flames rather from Heav'n than ours,
> The raging furious and unpitying Souldier
> Pulling his reeking Dagger from the bosoms
> Of gasping Wretches; Death in every Quarter,
> With all that sad disorder can produce
> To make a Spectacle of horror: Then,
> Then let's call to mind, my dearest Friends,
> That there's nothing pure upon the Earth,
> That the most valu'd things have most allays,
> And that in change of all these vile Enormities,
> Under whose weight this wretched Country labours,
> The Means are only in our hands to Crown them. [III.ii.321-88]

The logic of this last passage is twisted and perverse. Since nothing on earth is pure and since the most precious things are the most alloyed, the contamination of our idealism by the blood of the innocent is a necessary evil that actually sanctifies (crowns?) the enterprise. So kill them all and enjoy it. Hence, words can be used to justify the worst atrocities, and such a "Trust," such a rapist brotherhood, is, as Belvidera says, "hellish" indeed (III.ii.107).

Even Jaffeir adopts the rhetoric of erotic slaughter (followed by erotic reward):

> Nay, the Throats of the whole Senate
> Shall bleed, my *Belvidera*. He amongst us
> That spares his Father, Brother, or his Friend,
> Is damn'd. How rich and beauteous will the face
> Of Ruin look, when these wide streets run blood;
> I and the glorious Partners of my Fortune

Shouting, and striding o're the prostrate Dead,
Still to new waste; whilst thou, far off in safety
Smiling, shalt see the wonders of our daring;
And when night comes, with Praise and Love receive me.
[III.ii.140-49]

Amid the erotic slaughter is, of course, the parricide (and fratricide) so assiduously avoided in *Aureng-Zebe,* in *Mustapha,* so threatening in *Don Carlos, Mithridates,* so devastating in *Oedipus*—so endemic to monarchy. If Dryden and especially Lee reveal a glimpse of destructive desire in Jocasta's lingering, now semiconscious eroticism as the truth dawns in *Oedipus,* Otway lays it bare here. Swords and daggers are to be sheathed in the metaphoric vaginas (Latin for *sheath*) of the breasts and bosoms of "gasping Wretches," while the phallic daggers of the victors are sheathed in the literal vaginas of their worshiping female co-conspirators, whose adulation attests to these heroes' dominance. Otway portrays not just Oedipal murder but Oedipal rape. Belvidera, the treasure seized from his pseudo father, is his pseudo Jocasta, over whose prostrate body the victorious Jaffeir will stride.

Horrified at parricide, Belvidera attempts to "free" Jaffeir "from the Bondage of these [enslaving] Slaves" (III.ii.110) by countering their rhetoric with that of the traditional code of implicit and explicit bonding words:

Murder my father! Tho his Cruel Nature
Has persecuted me to my undoing,
Driven me to basest wants; Can I behold him
With smiles of Vengeance, butchered in his Age?
The sacred Fountain of my life destroy'd?
And canst thou shed the blood that gave me being?
Nay, be a Traitor too, and sell thy Country? [154-60]

She attempts to recall him "To eternal honour" by saving "Virgins . . . From horrid violation" (IV.4-10). Her rhetoric is equally graphic, intended to arouse not sadistic lust but loyalty and compassion by exposing their rebellion as being in effect infanticide and mother rape (46-57).

At this point, Jaffeir—and the spectator—appear to have a clear standard by which to get their bearings. In retrospect we remember that Jaffeir's first oath of revenge was "by Heaven and Hell" (I.297); that Pierre appeared to Jaffeir on the Rialto just when he was expecting to be tempted by the "Devil" (II.100); that Jaffeir has paradoxically—and blasphemously—called upon "Kind Heav'n" for curses "To kill with" (II.109, 123); that he has, as he says, taken "a Damning Oath / For shedding native blood!" (III.ii.270-71). As the conspirators plot their carnage, Jaffeir appropriately asks, "Heav'n! where am I? beset with cursed Fiends, / That wait to Damn me: What a Devil's man, / When he forgets his nature" (302-4). And he poignantly complains, "[C]an there be a sin / In merciful repentance?" (271-72).

But actually, Belvidera can only motivate Jaffeir to act according to this altruistic code by constant appeal to the self-interested code of revenge. Time and again she must appeal to the threatened ravaging by Renault: "Then where will be revenge, / The dear revenge that's due to such a wrong?" (IV.67-68). Something very wrenching occurs when she employs such an oxymoron as "dear revenge"—there's that destructive eroticism again—and when he responds by praising Belvidera for "Prophetick truth" in her every word (69-71). The phrase clings to her last prediction, which appears to be the only "truth" that motivates him to defend the old order. And what happens to our estimate of Belvidera when she resorts to such maneuvering? Is she too not contaminated?

What also works to undermine Belvidera's argument is the utter bankruptcy of the order she defends. Not only is Priuli contemptible in his inhuman wrath, but he and all the senators and the doge himself violate the most sacred oath—"By all the hopes / Ye have of Peace and Happiness hereafter" (IV.169-70)—to preserve the lives of the conspirators whom Jaffeir incriminates. Moreover, how can Belvidera apply the term "Reverend bloud" to "all" the "Nobles," including Antonio (IV.46-47)? If the rebels are characterized by sadism, Antonio's perverse masochism becomes symbolic of the senators' total decadence.

Meanwhile, Jaffeir, that "inconstant man," as Belvidera calls him (IV.19), has been unable to steady his mind, to stick to any moral bearings. Instead, he resolves his conflict into a sexist dichotomy. He moans to Belvidera,

> Rather, Remember him, who after all
> The sacred Bonds of Oaths and holyer Friendship,
> In fond compassion to a Womans tears
> Forgot his Manhood, Vertue, truth, and Honour,
> To sacrifice the Bosom that reliev'd him.
> Why wilt thou damn me? [14-19]

According to the code of honor of the rebels, Jaffeir's listening to Belvidera's pleas is unmanly, effeminate. The rebels' attitude toward the feminine really is that of a rapist, founded upon a fundamental misogyny, as is evident in Pierre's berating Jaffeir for conversing with Belvidera after he has surrendered her:

[W]ilt thou never,
Never be wean'd from Caudles and Confections?
What feminine Tale hast thou been listening to,
Of unayr'd shirts; catharrs and Tooth Ach got
By thin-sol'd shoos? Damnation! that a Fellow
Chosen to be a Sharer in the Destruction
Of a whole People, should sneak thus in Corners
To ease his fulsom Lusts, and Fool his mind. [III.ii.221-28]

Pierre's "feminine" is the mother in whose breasts the conspirators would sheath their swords. For him, as is obvious in his comments to Aquilina, women belong at home, preferably in a supine position: "How! a Woman ask Questions out of Bed?" (II.54).

Jaffeir is vulnerable to this rhetoric because he shares its fundamental assumption. He exclaims of his dear jewel, "Can there in Woman be such glorious Faith?" (I.335). Behind such a question lurks an essential doubt. And Jaffeir never overcomes this radical ambivalence. Even as he acts to preserve Venice, he ambiguously brands himself a "Villain" (IV.134). Immediately after he yields to the feminine, as he views it, he accuses himself of "wickedness" and "falsehood" (210-15). And he treats Pierre like a betrayed Jesus, himself a Judas. Here, not only Jaffeir but language itself begins to lose its bearings.

The problem is that Jaffeir cannot have it both ways. Pierre cannot be both Jesus and the Devil. So to avoid his ambivalence, Jaffeir reveres his hellish oath, his code of brotherhood with avengers, above his jewel and nearly sacrifices her for his "broken vows," contending that "Heaven must have Justice" (IV.501). By this time such rhetoric can only be seen as delusive. Unable to kill her, unable to implement his apocalyptic rhetoric calling down the "destruction" of "all the world" (V.219-27), but cursing his own blessing on his marriage day as "a rash oath" (265), he parts from Belvidera forever, absurdly enjoining her to raise their son "in vertue and the paths of Honour" (337). By now, what does honor mean?

Jaffeir goes to honor his "oath" (V.342). But Otway undercuts this male brotherhood one more time. Absurdly, Pierre maintains to the priest on the scaffold,

I tell thee Heaven and I are friends,
I ne'r broke Peace with't yet, by cruel murthers,
Rapine, or perjury, or vile deceiving,
But liv'd in moral Justice towards all men. [V.375-78]

At best he is an equivocator, for he certainly intended murders and rapine; he was willing to put an entire nation to the sword out of revenge. Even more absurdly, Pierre maintains that the other conspirators "all dy'd like men . . . Worthy their Character" (422-23). Worthy *what* character? That of Renault? Equally absurdly, Jaffeir vows to sacrifice all of Venice to Pierre's *manes*—that glorious destruction of a whole people again, and again for no redemptive sacrifice but for revenge—and once more he vacillates and vows his wife and child shall bleed. Finally, rather than live to face the empty posturing of their heroic rhetoric, Pierre and Jaffeir desperately seek to write their last act tragic. Jaffeir consummates their relationship with dagger strokes to each breast so that the presiding officer can say, "Heav'n grant I dye so well" (480) and the world can interpret their deaths as heroic. Behind all this posturing lurks the suggestion that Renault is right when he says, "Man, / Irregular Man's ne're constant, never certain" (II.206-7). How can he be certain when, again as Renault says, "[T]here's nothing pure upon the Earth" (III.ii.384).

What about Belvidera and the code she articulates? Whether anyone else lives up to them, are not she and her ideals (if not her vengeful desires) pure? If so, the play provides no consolation, no divine confirmation, no validating poetical justice. When Jaffeir leaves her the last time, Belvidera resorts to apocalyptic rhetoric, sounding more like him and the conspirators than any angel, more like Job's wife than Job, as she curses all creation. And Belvidera sees no recompensing afterlife but seeks only the peace of sure obliteration. At the end, raving in mad delusion, she digs at the earth to join Jaffeir's ghost. No flights of angels sing her to her rest. Instead, she feels as if Jaffeir and Pierre "drag" her "to the bottom" (V.508). Left alone as her spokesman is no Horatio but Priuli, whose repentance and forgiveness have come too late, whose attempt to save Pierre proves a futile gesture, and who closes the play with no salvific rhetoric, no glimpse of hope, but only a desperate, self-loathing death wish:

> Lead me into some place that's fit for mourning,
> Where the free Air, Light, and the chearful Sun
> May never enter: Hang it round with Black;
> Set up one taper that may last a day,
> As long as I've to live: And there all leave me.
> *Sparing no Tears when you this Tale relate,*
> *But bid all Cruel Fathers dread my Fate.* [511-17]

What is worse is that someone else survives the debacle and symbolizes the utter loss of Logos: Antonio. He is not at all harmless, as he might first appear. He symbolizes emptying words of their power to bind. He is noted for his parliamentary speeches, and as the conspirators die ignominiously, as Pierre and Jaffeir wrap themselves in meaningless heroics, and as

Belvidera maniacally digs herself into her grave with her father not far behind, Antonio survives and practices a speech composed of nonsense for the preserved Senate. This is Tony Leigh, the great comic actor, inhabiting another of his Restoration W. C. Fields roles (see *Tricksters and Estates*):

> Most Reverend Senatours,
>
> That there is a Plot, surely by this time, no man that hath eyes or understanding in his head will presume to doubt, 'tis as plain as the light in the Cowcumber—no—hold there—Cowcumber does not come in yet—'tis as plain as the light in the Sun, or as the man in the Moon, even at noon day. It is indeed a Pumpkin-Plot, which, just as it was mellow, we have gathered, and now we have gathered it, prepar'd and dress'd it, shall we throw it like a pickled Cowcumber out at the window? no. that it is not onely a bloudy, horrid, execrable, damnable, and audacious Plot, but it is, as I may so say, a sawcy Plot; and we all know, most Reverend Fathers, that what is sawce for a Goose is sawce for a Gander: Therefore, I say, as those bloudthirsty Ganders of the conspiracy would have destroyed us Geese of the Senate, let us make haste to destroy them; so I humbly move for hanging. [V.131-47]

Antonio breaks off as Aquilina enters to terrorize if not kill him for voting to put Pierre to death. She explodes into heroic diction, invoking the standard of faith: "Thou hast help'd to spoil my peace, and I'll have vengeance / On thy cursed life, for all the bloody Senate, / The perjur'd faithless Senate" (184-86).

But Antonio converts her ravings into sexual provocations, employing throughout the scene the moribund expletive "faith." As her fury peaks, so does his sexual excitation. Dropping down at her feet, he explains his behavior in terms that deflate her rhetoric and drain the last drop of meaning from the code of the word: "Nothing but untie thy shoe-string a little, faith and troth" (210-11). His sexual death right on the stage as she leaves enervates both codes of faith and revenge and marks the death of a culture: "Adieu. Why what a bloody-minded, inveterate, termagant Strumpet have I been plagu'd with! Oh h h, yet more! nay then I die, I die—I am dead already. [*Stretches himself out.*]" (216-18).

His prone figure remains on the stage during Jaffeir and Belvidera's parting scene. How does one play the part? Looking up and taking more perverse pleasure in their suffering? Reminding us with a leer of the inefficacy of all their rhetoric? Would a good director not bring Antonio on stage during the final scaffold scene to enjoy it? Would he not be the last to leave, an emblem of the collapse of a culture whose code, without divine underwriting, has been reduced to *words, words, words*? Or to put it another way, this feminized, female-dominated masochist is a sign of the loss of the masculine, patriarchal, heroic—and yes, essentially sadistic and misogynistic—Logos. *O tempora! O mores! Ubi sunt?* Where have all the *real* men gone? *Et Verbum caro factum est.* The Word has been made flesh with a vengeance in the fat, lubricious body of the leering Leigh. And the seams of aristocratic ideology have been rent asunder.[14]

Dryden's *Amboyna* (1672?), subtitled on its first page *The Cruelties of the Dutch to the English Merchants,* is a piece of propaganda designed to elicit support for the Crown in the Third Dutch War. But as James Thompson has recently shown, it is also a rallying cry for the expanding English empire. Thompson astutely argues that, though rivals, the Dutch and the English pursued an imperialism based on systematic exploitation through colonization rather than conquest, through mercantilism rather than militarism. Thus Dryden, defender of late feudal, Stuart ideology, even as he defends monarchy in this play, also heralds forth a new, emerging ruling class, its ethos, its economics of world trade, and its natural right to world hegemony.

In the prologue Dryden asserts, *"Well Monarchys may own Religions name, / States are Atheists in their very frame"* (21-22). By "States" Dryden means the Dutch republican state, the name for the legislature in each of the provinces of Holland, which themselves were represented in a national States-General. Monarchies are religious because kings and peoples are bound together by sacred oaths. Republics are atheistical because they are not bound together by trust—they cannot be, for there can be no honor among troth-breakers, and, as the heroic Beaumont argues in the play, the English should never have trusted as partners a people "who had cast off the Yoke of their lawful Soveraign" (V.167-68). The heroic Towerson deplores the Dutch tortures of his men, saying the Spanish general d'Alva was less cruel against Dutch rebels, even though they were guilty of "original Villany"—like that of Satan, presumably—and were "damn'd" for it (311-12).

Just as in a few Restoration comedies—for example, Behn's *False Count* and Ravenscroft's *London Cuckolds*—members of the *haute bourgeoisie,* that is, the upper or merchant middle class, become absorbed into the Town wits, the representatives of the naturally superior class who deserve to rule (see *Tricksters and Estates,* sub verba), so Dryden in this play portrays his merchant factors as heroes, their merchant bosses as "Noblemen" (II.392). At best Dutch "Gentlemen," if there are any such, mocks Beaumont, "live like Bores" (392-93). As opposed to the petty bourgeois Dutch governor of Amboyna, who was once a "Cooper" (I.147), Towerson, an agent of the English East India Company, is exalted with the titles of "Captain" (passim) and even "General" (I.109; V.50-51), though he was at best a ship's purser (*Works* 12:282), and is cloaked in the rhetoric of the English gentleman/hero: Beaumont describes his friend,

> Were I to chuse of all mankind, a Man, on whom I would relie for Faith and Counsel, or more, whose personal aid I wou'd invite, in any worthy cause to second me, it shou'd be only *Gabriel Towerson;* daring he is, and thereto fortunate: yet soft and apt to pitty the distress'd; and liberal to relieve 'em: I have seen him not alone to pardon Foes, but by his bounty win 'em to his love: if he has any fault, 'tis only that, to which great minds can only subject be, he thinks all honest, 'cause himself is so, and therefore none suspects. [I.125-34]

Beaumont's description is validated when Towerson's disgruntled lieutenant, Perez, suborned into assassinating him, discovers Towerson's generosity toward him, howbeit belated. Even the Dutch describe Towerson as "brave" and a man of "honor and great wealth" (107-14). And indeed he is treated as an aristocrat not only by the English and the Dutch but by the natives, who allow him to marry the aristocratic, very wealthy Ysabinda. When Towerson rejoices to Ysabinda, "I have gain'd your Kindred" (II.41), we seem to be in a Restoration comedy, where gentry couples are brought together to improve estates. Once again, transnational aristocracy, fluid enough to absorb rising merchants, situates itself vis-à-vis the unworthy, whether "Indian" natives or European riffraff.

The fiction of Dryden's propaganda is that England discovered Amboyna first and agreed to share it with the Dutch, who then savagely turned on them in an act of signal ingratitude, for the Protestant English had helped the Protestant Dutch gain their freedom from oppressive Catholic Spain. Of course, the Dutch seized the island from the first "discoverers," the Portuguese, who had built a fort there as part of their militant form of imperialism. In a show of British superiority, Towerson articulates a humane, enlightened philosophy of world trade: "This Ile yields Spice enough for both [England and Holland]; and *Europe,* Ports, and Chapmen, where to vend them. . . . [W]hat mean these endless jars of Trading Nations? 'tis true, the World was never large enough for Avarice or Ambition; but those who can be pleas'd with moderate gain, may have the ends of Nature, not to want: nay, even its Luxuries may be supply'd from her o'erflowing bounties in these parts: from whence she yearly sends Spices, and Gums, the Food of Heaven in Sacrifice: And besides these, her Gems of richest value, for Ornament, more then necessity" (I.215-27). So this systematic imperialism is fostered not by "Avarice or Ambition" but by the desire to share the superfluities of nature, as if the Third World sent them to the First in the form of a "Sacrifice"—as if, the text implies, to their superiors, their gods.

When Perez's wife, Julia, who in reality was a native slave woman (*Works* 12:282), but whom Dryden seems to portray as more European, paints a verbal tableau of her relationship with all the men in her life, she wittily transforms herself into a symbol for the island of Amboyna, itself a synecdoche for all such possessions: "If my *English* Lover *Beaumont,* my *Dutch* Love the *Fiscall,* and my *Spanish* Husband, were Painted in a piece with me amongst 'em, they wou'd make a Pretty Emblem of the two Nations, that Cuckold his Catholick Majesty in his *Indies*" (II.226-30). Like the Restoration stage rake, because of his superior parts, the Englishman will win the sexual competition eventually. The willing colonies, like Ysabinda, will be as attracted to the English as is the wife who willingly suffers martyrdom along with Towerson and his men at the hands of the Dutch. She defies the Dutch governor: "[T]here is no Sex in Souls; wou'd you have *English* Wives shew less of Bravery then their Children do? to lie by an *English* Man's side, is enough to give a Woman Resolution" (V.210-13).

But Ysabinda is the central symbol in the play. She is married to Towerson as her colony is to the heart of noble England. Then before her bridal night with her husband she is raped by the son of the Dutch governor, whose rationale for her capitulation sounds eerily like Towerson's rationale for shared trade: "You are a Woman; have enough of Love for him and me; I know the plenteous Harvest all is his: he has so much of joy, that he must labor under it. In charity you may allow some gleanings to a Friend" (IV.iii.30-33). In revenge Towerson kills the rapist, and the Dutch use his action as the excuse for the massacre they have long aimed at. Many English, including Towerson, are tortured and killed. The play ends without justice but with apocalyptic prediction—an obvious appeal to the English of Dryden's time to take delayed vengeance. But the symbolic message of the play is even stronger. The governor says in response to his son's death, "My sorrow cannot be so soon digested for losing of a Son I lov'd so well, but I consider, great advantages must with some loss be bought: as this rich Trade which I this day have purchas'd with his death" (V.1-4). When the spectator juxtaposes this statement with his son's and with Towerson's on trade, he or she realizes that monopoly and monogamy are related in the play. The Dutch killed the English to gain a monopoly. Towerson should have had a monopoly in his wife. The Dutch are untrustworthy trade rapists and have lost their moral right to share. By extension, the English should share with no one but seize the day, seize world trade. The last line of the epilogue jingoistically proclaims, "*Let* Caesar [Charles II] *Live, and* Carthage [Holland] *be subdu'd.*"

As proof of moral superiority, with its attendant right to dominate, Towerson goes to his death as a gentleman should, with Christian stoicism and a blessing—a prayer remarkable for its bourgeois ethos: "[T]ell my friends I dy'd so as became a Christian and a Man; give to my brave Employers of the *East India* Company, the last remembrance of my faithful service; tell 'em I Seal that Service with my Blood; and dying, wish to all their Factories, and all the famous Merchants of our Isle, that Wealth their gen'rous Industry deserves" (V.398-403). While the play is an obvious satire on the Dutch, then, it is a paean to Britannia. Yet sticking out like a sore thumb is Ysabinda's plea with Towerson after her rape: "[F]or my sake, fly this detested Isle, where horrid Ills so black and fatal dwell, as *Indians* cou'd not guess, till *Europe* taught" (IV.v.15-17). "*Europe*" includes not only the cruel Spanish and Dutch but the English as well. A minor note, surely not intended by Dryden to undercut his paean. Yet it as surely sounds, however diminished, in the ear of the attentive spectator.[15]

6

States and Estates

Tragicomic Romance

Like tragicomedy in general, original Restoration tragicomedy has no precise generic limits. Playwrights used the term to refer to plays that range in form from some of the rhymed heroic plays (Sir William Killigrew's *Ormasdes* and John Weston's *Amazon Queen*) all the way down the mimetic scale from court to domestic settings to such an obvious low comedy as Thomas Porter's *Witty Combat.*[1] Title-page labels do not help. Restoration tragicomedy is part of the larger genre of romance. Tragicomic romance is a more domestic form of romance than heroic, featuring less *intérêt d'état* and including comic, even farcical scenes. As Mikhail Bakhtin has best shown, this kind of romance is traditionally dominated by variations on the theme of fidelity amidst the fires of trial (*Dialogic Imagination* 105-9). It usually features constant lovers tempted to infidelity or lost children or beleaguered wives or sometimes rightful princes exiled or cast adrift because of some original act of infidelity. The threats are usually not displaced outward onto monsters or invading armies. Instead, they reside in one's spouse, one's brother, one's supposedly loyal general, one's best friend, a nearly irresistible paramour. Not that political considerations are excluded. The political and the sexual continue to mirror each other, the state in the estate.

Whatever the precise limits, tragicomedy was a popular and thriving genre during the Restoration. European tragicomedy historically had been mostly an aristocratic mode, rescuing sequestered children who ultimately prove to be of noble birth, or affirming the legitimacy of royal succession, or preserving the constancy of some besieged wife, or uniting witty but equally generous or noble couples. So it should come as no surprise that the heyday of Restoration tragicomedy should be the first years of renewed Stuart hegemony. Far from being meaningless or existing purely for aesthetic satisfaction, as Eugene Waith has argued anent Beaumont and Fletcher and Laura Brown has argued anent our period ("Divided Plot"), tragicomic form in the Restoration, as Northrop Frye says of romance in general, gets absorbed "into the ideology of [its] ascendant class" (*Secular Scripture* 57).

Restoration tragicomedy is generally a reaffirmation of feudal aristocratic values, portrayed as under stress by challenges from bourgeois parvenus, libertine lovers, and ambitious statesmen; from ethical nominalists, political pragmatists, and metaphysical atheists. Against such challenges almost all these plays affirm a hierarchical social order, bonded together by the virtues of loyalty, constancy, fidelity, trust, and ultimately validated by a divine providence. Man's word as the fundamental bond of society is portrayed as underwritten by the Divine Word. As such these plays are very similar to the Restoration heroic romances. The main difference is that Restoration tragicomedies do not generally feature culture heroes in epic situations. As opposed to those heroic romances, these tragicomic romances, with some exceptions, focus more upon ethical, particularly sexual relations and the problem of constancy. The sociopolitical function of such a theme is obvious: the entire superstructure of feudal aristocracy is built upon the grid of a patrilinear genealogy passed on through the estate. Birth determines entrance into the power elite (theoretically, at least), and therefore sexual promiscuity must be restrained. Thus along with chastity belts was invented a literature of sexual fidelity, an ethical analogue to political loyalty which likewise has its metaphysical sanction, as the religious rhetoric and the deus ex machina endings insist.

For purposes of study, let us divide Restoration tragicomedy into unified- and split-plot. Let us call unified-plot those tragicomedies that either have only one plot or have two or more romance plots with only incidental comic business and thus with a unified effect. These can be further divided heuristically into the following groups. The first group I would designate as domestic plays, that is, plays where the emphasis is more on building estates than affairs of state. The best known are Sir Samuel Tuke's *Adventures of Five Hours* (1663) and Dryden's *Rival Ladies* (1664). Both are about freedom from enforced marriages, and they feature defiant women who dare to rebel against their male guardians, stereotypical Spanish brothers. But such rebellion against patriarchal tyranny is curtailed. Neither playwright advocates absolute sexual freedom for these women. Instead, the plays affirm the doctrine of constancy. In fact, in each play the reason for resisting enforced marriage is a prior commitment to a lover, inconstancy to which, as Dryden's Julia says, "is such a Guilt, as makes / That very Love suspected which it brings" (V.iii.73-74). But the doctrine is affirmed not only against male tyranny but also against sexual promiscuity. Each play features one constant male lover and his rakish or at least inconstant counterpart or double. These doubles are false to previous lovers, however brief their encounter, and must be reclaimed. And in both plays the sexual dynamics lead to deadly rivalry almost resulting in bloodshed and the squandering of the energies of all these young people. In the dénouements, the phallic swords are diverted to their proper sheaths, the blocked constant couples are united, the errant inconstants are recalled, the hostile brothers are socialized, and all this by means of a metaphysical dynamic, the "Providence" (Tuke 47), which serves as a sanction to the social code and which unites couples with the right stuff for the continuing of the estates of the ruling class.

Aphra Behn wrote two such domestic tragicomedies, *The Dutch Lover* (1673) and *The Town-Fopp; or, Sir Timothy Tawdrey* (1676). The first is a play of hidden identities that threatens murder and incest but is resolved when (aristocratic) identities are made manifest, vows are honored, libertines converted, lovers united, and estates and class secured. *The Town-Fopp,* with its title parvenu attempting to marry up in order to have money for his kept mistress, Betty Flauntit, is even closer to the world of Restoration comedy. But its mood is dark and its dangers are life-threatening, as young Bellmour is forced by his uncle, Lord Plotwell, to marry the Lady Diana instead of his beloved, betrothed Celinda, who herself appears destined for Sir Timothy Tawdrey. Threatened with loss of his estate and with a fine in addition, Bellmour is tempted to Oedipal rebellion against his surrogate father's control of access to women—and estates. Bellmour nearly becomes the beast into which he threatens to degenerate, and his wife out of revenge nearly has him murdered, but he is saved through the trickery of lover, friend, and siblings. Faced with the consequences of his tyranny, Lord Plotwell agrees to an annulment; Diana is united to a better lover, Bellmour's friend; Sir Timothy is pawned off onto a tricky sister; and Bellmour is finally united with both betrothed and estate. Bellmour attributes the dénouement to "the Powr's above" (V.472), which, of course, underwrite aristocracy.

Several other tragicomedies end after multiple mistakes and intrigues in similar multiple aristocratic marriages.[2] Two seem worth noting. John Leanerd's *Country Innocence; or, The Chamber-Maid Turn'd Quaker* (1677) features the conversion of a country squire from his droit-du-seigneur lust for a tenant's daughter, whom he threatens with her father's loss of his copyhold. Her resistance upholds class difference even as it subtly undercuts it through her moral superiority: she says the very thing he thinks makes him irresistible is that which causes the most resistance, his "Noble Breeding" (II, 15). Interestingly, his wife foils his assaults by decking out this family of tenants in her finery—as if to say, they do not need his largesse—and at the end the daughter is married up to a captain and the entire family is raised a notch in social status. Leanerd's play has a proto-bourgeois quality to it even as aristocrats (Sir Robert's wealthy widowed sister and a neighboring squire) consolidate estates through marriage at the end.

Durfey's *Banditti; or, A Ladies Distress* (1686) insists on class difference much more strictly. Don Diego, heir apparent to the wealthy Don Ariell, is really the son of banditti, and his boorishness implies he cannot escape his heritage. Don Fernand, soldier of fortune without apparent origins, has such aristocratic sentiments and mien that his captain, Don Garcia, opines, "By all the Glories of the Arms he speaks of, I rather think him Son of some great Prince, then of *Plebean* Generation" (I, 4). He turns out to be really the son of an aristocrat, Don Ariell's brother, and heir to the estate. Thus as late as after the death of Charles II, tragicomic romance retells the aristocratic family myth of the perdu restored. As attractive as the banditti are in their folk humor and class existentialism (see Durfey's wonderful song [III.i, 24-25]), their leader, Leon, Don Fernand's foster father, accedes to traditional morality and confesses the truth of Fernand's birth in hopes of making some amends for his past life. The banditti, Diego among them, are reprieved but flogged, and all but Leon are banished, while the aristocratic couples are finally united.

Related to these domestic tragicomedies is another small subgroup of unified plays, pastoral tragicomedies. The number of these in the Restoration is surprisingly low considering the Renaissance tradition and the number of Restoration translations and adaptations of plays by Tasso, Guarini, Shakespeare, and Fletcher. Among unified tragicomedies, there are only a few I would classify as pastoral.[3] Interestingly, they span the Restoration period. Thomas Forde's *Love's Labyrinth; or, the Royal Shepherdess* (not acted; publ. 1660) and the anonymous *The Constant Nymph; or, The Rambling Shepherd* (1677) both feature the requisite swains and nymphs complaining of inconstancy and unrequited love. Both feature constant shepherdesses courted by inconstant shepherds. But more interestingly, both feature constant women who are courted by their supposedly dead lovers disguised. In Forde's more intriguing play, neither spouse recognizes the other, and as they fall in love with what appear doubles of one another, each hopes the deceased lover will not upbraid his or her inconstancy. At the same time, Forde's heroine is courted by her own son and her father, each of whom is lured to her pastoral retreat by rumors of her beauty. Thus Forde stretches to breaking the bonds containing sexual appetite. His world is on the brink of anarchy. But as disguises fall, the heroines of both plays can have their husbands and their lovers in one, a discovery that preserves the bonds of marital constancy, as it were, even beyond the grave (something Hamlet would have appreciated). And in the anonymous play, where the inconstant shepherd seems utterly incorrigible and unsocializable, miraculously he undergoes a religious conversion and plights his troth to God. Wives and daughters thus are "heaven-protected" (Forde 72).

Sir William Davenant's adaptation of Shakespeare and Fletcher's *Two Noble Kinsmen* as *The Rivals* (1664) is moved from Thebes to Arcadia. It opens as a restoration play, celebrating the Providential victory of the Arcadians over the tyrant Harpacus, especially through the heroic efforts of the provost, who maintains he merely did his duty to his country and the "Sacred Person" of his prince (I, 3). Theocles and Philander are prisoners of war and become the rivals or the title over the prince's daughter, Heraclia. As in the story from Boccaccio and Chaucer to Fletcher, Theocles is freed but finds a way to stay; Philander escapes; they meet and fight in the woods. Davenant's wrinkles are that Celania, daughter to the provost, has fallen in love with Philander, follows him into the forest, and becomes lost and distracted (shades of Imogen cum Ophelia). The prince's way to resolve the dispute is to force Heraclia to choose between the rivals. When Heraclia cannot choose and when Celania reveals the madness of her passion for Philander, the prince solomonically decides that Theocles will get Heraclia and Philander Celania. Philander's capitulation would strike a modern audience as insincere, but it has significance within the ethos of the aristocratic family romance: "[S]ince that Love does want / Growth in *Heraclia*'s bosom I'le transplant / It into [Celania's]" (V, 56). Love's "Growth" in Heraclia's bosom has been of signal importance since the beginning, for the prince is without a male heir. However pastoralized, the aristocratic economy demands that she be cultivated, so that her father's royal line will not lie fallow. The *transplantation* of Philander's love to Celania means that she, too, will be cultivated. Thus the ending ensures that rivals to the state will be socialized not only to defuse their deadly rivalry both to each other and to Arcadia but to turn their swords into metaphoric plowshares for the cultivation of estates.

Durfey's *A Common-Wealth of Women* (1685) plays off contemporary politics. Du Piere is a Cavalier gallant who has wounded someone in a duel for insulting his admiral: he describes the offender as "a damn'd huffing fellow yonder, a Rebel, Whiggy Buffle head" (I, 4). In the year of Charles II's death and the accession of his brother, James, duke of York and lord high admiral, then, Durfey writes of rebellion and commonwealths. Within the commonwealth of women, former wives and daughters of Portuguese plantation owners exiled on an island by French pirates, there is, despite the "Protectress" Roselia's insistence that women are as capable as men of ruling, a lack of order because the women are willful, democratic.

Throughout the play the aristocratic men are shown to be superior to parvenus and cits (who at one point outrageously contemplate cannibalism), and the women are shown to need intercourse with men, in both senses. In another sense, this play too is a restoration play: after years of exile, the rightful governor of the Happy Isles, Don Sebastian, is restored to both position and wife, Roselia. The women abandon their Amazonian rebellion, men are restored to their proper dominance, and a commonwealth is superseded by the politically superior patriarchy (by implication, monarchy)—and all by the agency of "Heaven" (V, 53).

By far, the largest group of unified tragicomedies is that of the plays situated at court. Some of these affirm explicit aristocratic political ideology, allegiance to one's lord and his rightful heirs. In Sir Robert Stapylton's *Step-Mother* (1663), Edward Howard's *Change of Crownes* (1667), and John Crowne's *Juliana; or, The Princess of Poland* (1671), ambitious statesmen or wicked stepmothers—or both—attempt to usurp thrones from legitimate successors. They justify their actions with nominalist and Hobbist arguments: Stapylton's Queen Pontia, who wants the crown for her son instead of the crown prince, says scornfully,

> [H]e that puts himself into a fright
> With empty sounds, meer Terms of Wrong and Right,
> Is fitter (when his Conscience checks at them)
> To wear a Mitre than a Diadem. [I, 14]

Crowne's Machiavellian cardinal thinks the virtuous are mere fools, and he openly defies the "providence" that is supposed to support legitimacy (II, 14). Yet in each play the usurpers are foiled and the beleaguered faithful are redeemed as "Providence" is explicitly praised (Stapylton V, [9]2, Howard V.iv, 89; cf. the "Miracle" in Crowne V, 59). And even Stapylton's Queen Pontia, an example of that dark woman of romance who represents the matriarchal threat to patriarchy, is resocialized and subdued by the male code of the word.

A few of these political court tragicomedies seem pure romances. The plots of Sir William Killigrew's *Selindra* (1662) and *The Seege of Urbin* (1664-65) are filled with such dizzying events and reversals of fortune as to seem to exist simply for the sake of the aesthetic effect. Nevertheless, even these formal features have ideological significance: Killigrew's world is one of mutability where Fortune seems to reign, and her inconstancy is mirrored in the action of characters who mistrust each other, betray their king's trust, or distrust the gods. But in the end, "those powers, which protect Princes in all just causes" (*Seege* I.ii, 9) do just that. Loyal subjects and constant lovers are rewarded, betrayers are defeated, and the virtuous—and noble—characters conclude that "the Gods smile upon us now" (*Selindra* V, 54).

One plot of Aphra Behn's *Young King; or, The Mistake* (1679) is similarly exotic, with one pair of lovers who distrust each other and another pair, the obvious model of aristocratic behavior, who trust each other absolutely. But the play's political plot is more interesting. As in the interpolated subplot of Dryden's adaptation of Shakespeare's *Tempest,* the play's young king is raised as a noble savage in the state of nature; that is, in complete isolation from women and courts. When finally exposed to the first, he manifests unrestrained promiscuous desire and when exposed to the second, unrestrained tyrannical urges. But in typical aristocratic fashion, love and beauty tame him, and he learns the social need for sexual constancy and the political need for mutual trust between king and people.

Most unified court tragicomedy is less political.[4] Typically, the conflict centers on a constant wife or betrothed who, in her husband's or lover's absence, is besieged by tempters, including the ruler. Often the absent lover distrusts and tests her, but in the end she proves true. This female figure is a descendant of Penelope; the male figure, of Odysseus. The stakes are still the same. Her infidelity would destroy the patriarchal control of generation; it would fatally crack the sacred vessel of genealogy. Shadwell's play varies the theme, making the faithful wife of the prince appear to be baseborn and thus an unworthy vessel to carry his child. In the end, of course, she proves to be of royal birth and thus a worthy vessel after all. The male lover in these plays is sometimes himself "the Emblem of Inconstancy" (Harris II, 26) and must be recalled to his "Vows" (Winchilsea V, 327). But the more threatening male figure is the libertine, the Don Juan, who would violate another man's vessel. This nominalist calls "Vice, Vertue," "Hell, Heaven," "Lust, Love," and "Dishonor, Honor" (Flecknoe, *Erminia* III, 47). And his inevitable fate is to be either neutralized or converted to the code of the word. Meanwhile, the Odyssean husband is convinced of his wife's fidelity, and her constancy is finally rewarded by reunion or reinstatement. Again, these dénouements are usually attributed to underwriting divine intervention, to "miracles" (Flecknoe V, 94; Shadwell V, 1:169) performed by the "Powers" of Providence, of "Heaven" (Durfey V.iii, 52; Harris V, 70; Winchilsea V, 330).

Let us call divided or split-plot those tragicomedies with both romance and comic plots that appear to work against each other to achieve what Laura Brown calls a disjunctive effect ("Divided Plot"). A few divided tragicomedies are indeed disjunctive. These include Sir Robert Howard's *Blind Lady* (not acted; publ. 1660), his brother James Howard's *All Mis-*

taken; or, The Mad Couple (1665), and George Villiers, the duke of Buckingham's adaptation of Fletcher's *Chances* (1667). In each, the heroic plot achieves typical romantic closure: constancy is rewarded, inconstancy is punished and socialized, and the heavens are praised. Yet the comic plots do not come to the usual closure: the libertines are not socialized. In James Howard's and Buckingham's delightful and interesting plays, the carefree gay couples eschew marriage and celebrate sexual promiscuity. These disjunctive endings are indeed subversive of official discourse, for they frustrate the socializing of sexual energy for the perpetuation of aristocratic estates.[5]

But these early Restoration tragicomedies are the exception and not the rule. However apparently disjunctive, most divided tragicomedies have an ideological coherence: the ideals of romance are juxtaposed to the pragmatics of comedy, but both support class-based institutionalized constancy. In one group the plots seem disjunctive because either one or the other miscarries and fails to come to closure. For example, William Chamberlayne's *Wits Led by the Nose; or, A Poet's Revenge* (1677) features a romance plot coupled with a farcical comic plot. What could be more disjunctive? In the heroic plot, a loyal general who puts down a rebellion becomes the sexual rival of his king, who forces him to fight and even wound his sovereign. But in the end this "Act so wicked" (IV, 41) is forgiven, the rivalry dispersed, and the king *"Crown'd at once with Loyalty and Love"* (V, 56), an ending attributed to a "Miracle" (55). The comic plot is punitive, where the action serves to discipline and punish parvenus. Two clever servants ridicule and thoroughly dupe a couple of cowardly nouveaux knights aspiring to aristocratic tastes—and brides—simply because they have money.[6] Yet the ideological function of both plots grants them coherence. The reclaiming of the Oedipal rebel functions to preserve monarchy even as the punishing of parvenus functions to preserve the class superiority on which monarchy is based.

In the comic plots of Richard Flecknoe's *Love's Kingdom* (1664; a rehash of his earlier *Love's Dominion,* publ. 1654) and Dryden's *Spanish Fryar; or, The Double Discovery* (1680), the figure of the rake fails to be socialized. But neither is he successful in his erotic quest. In Flecknoe's play he is mocked and exiled; in Dryden's he discovers his lover to be his sister and is thus restrained by society's ultimate taboo, though he remains a rebel at heart. Meanwhile, the heroic plots of both plays affirm constancy—sexual in Flecknoe's play, where separated lovers are finally reunited, and political in Dryden's, where the rightful king is restored, usurpers are chastised, and lovers are also united. Dryden's play, as one would expect, is complicated, however. The current queen is the daughter of a usurper, who in the course of the play orders the imprisoned king murdered. As a result of this fundamental violation of allegiance, the country is in political and social turmoil—a typical consequence in Dryden (and others) of an original sin of breach of trust. The friar of the title is the play's ultimate symbol for the absence of trust at the core of society: a lubricious, hypocritical manipulator of the word. "A Vow is a very solemn thing" (II.iv.95), he says even as he abets the rake Lorenzo's adultery. In a parody of the heroic plot, Lorenzo comes to present his "grievances" to his "Sovereign," the married Elvira (III.i.18-19). For her the bond of the word has become "Bondage" (65), and she seeks deliverance. For him, "'[T]is Interest governs all the World" (27). When the hero, Torrismond, overcomes his horror at the queen's regicide and marries her secretly, it would seem that interest has indeed triumphed in both plots. The evil counselor, Bertram, justifies the regicide in Hobbist terms as "self-defense" (IV.ii.69). Might (and desire) appear to make right. Only when his foster father reveals to Torrismond his identity as the prince and recalls him to his duty to overcome his passion and chastise the queen does the truth emerge that the old king is still alive. Thus the play can end happily with the lovers united after all, for "Heaven makes Princes its peculiar care" (V.ii.432).

Does the failure of libertines in the comic plots of Dryden's and Flecknoe's plays undercut the reaffirmation of the code in the heroic? Exile and taboo seem very strong social prophylactics to guarantee that subversion of that code remains *interruptus* indefinitely. In the case of *The Spanish Fryar,* the incest taboo that aborts Lorenzo's designs on his sister seems related obliquely to the Oedipal taboo, nearly breached by both Torrismond and Lorenzo, who both rebel against their fathers not only in spite of the legitimate authority of the state but in favor of their own self-interested desires. The resurrection of the king reestablishes the power of the Oedipal taboo even as Torrismond takes his place peacefully and Colonel Lorenzo's sword, already in the service of Torrismond as rebel, becomes legitimized and sheathed at once.

A more interesting example of this kind of play (and therefore one deserving more extended treatment) is Dryden's *Secret Love; or, The Maiden Queen* (1667), where the comic plot achieves closure but the heroic plot apparently fails. Moreover, the realism of the comic plot pulls hard against the romance of the heroic. The secret love of the maiden queen for the noble but not royal Philocles is ultimately not rewarded in the typical concluding marriage of tragicomedy. Nor, unlike other monarchs in these plays whose passions are temporarily misplaced, does she at the end return her affection to a previous lover. Nevertheless, the heroic plot affirms aristocratic values, for the queen finally retains her royal dignity and stature, masters her passions, and allows Philocles to marry his beloved Candiope.

Philocles himself overcomes the temptations of ambition and inconstancy and honors his former vows.

Meanwhile, the comic plot features one of the most famous of Restoration couples, the rakish Celadon and the waggish Florimel. Concerning constancy, Celadon insists, "Constant to one! I have been a Courtier, a Souldier, and a Traveller, to good purpose, if I must be constant to one; give me some Twenty, some Forty, some a Hundred Mistresses, I have more love than any one woman can turn to" (I.ii.7-10). Yet he falls so much in love with Florimel as to begin to contemplate marriage. And she, however she affects wild behavior, sure-handedly guides him toward that corral. She gives him a year in which to grow "reserv'd, discreet, sober, and faithful," and if he prove "unfaithful," she will extend the trial period (II.i.93-102). When caught courting others, he excuses himself (and all men): "Well, we must all sin, and we must all repent, and there's an end on't" (III.i.415-16), while Florimel chides, "See what constant metal you men are made of!" (426). Yet she loves him in spite of his "infidelities" (V.i.5). His spirit shows his value, and so he must be socialized, as he finally is when Florimel, disguised as a spark, invades his stable of mares. He promises to be "desperately constant" (140), and they contract in the famous proviso scene.

Is this plot disjunctive with the heroic? It seems to me not to contradict but to complement aristocratic ideals with pragmatic considerations, even that one might fall out of love. In the light of this possibility, Celadon and Florimel still base their relationship upon a promise—to confess such a falling off if it should occur—a promise that does not deny the need for the plighting of troth. And such a consideration does not undermine ideal love but reveals it to be the rhetoric of desire for transcendence in a mutable world. The dialectic of both plots pits the centripetal force of the code of the word against the centrifugal forces of selfish passion. The queen may lose, but Candiope, Florimel, and aristocratic society win. For the code of the word is not articulated in a vacuum but in conflict: subjects may rebel; monarchs may surrender to their flaws; love may become adulterated. But the protagonists in aristocratic drama, at least, must act *as if* constancy were possible.[7] The supposed naturalness of aristocratic ideology may be unmasked, de-essentialized, existentialized. But the mask is nevertheless raised at the end to be held before the face.

In the other divided tragicomedies, both plots achieve closure. The comic appears to strain against the heroic in disjunctive tension, but in reality it merely complements the heroic. In the comic plot of William Clark's *Marciano; or, The Discovery* (1662), two Cavaliers fool both city and country dolts and win two well-guarded aristocratic ladies. This obvious celebration of aristocratic triumph, in the heroic plot, coincides with the restoration of a "lawfull Prince" (I, 4), who is addressed with a recitation of the code surely intended for Charles II, but at the same time intended to be paradigmatic of the aristocratic ideological superego, the eye at the top of the hierarchical pyramid:

> Great Prince, whose daring eye strikes traytors dumb,
> Revives all loyal souls: disperses all
> Rebellions foggy mists: You have this day
> Conferr'd such honour on your highness servant,
> As were I a base Infidel, yow'd perswade
> My heart to faith. [V, 70]

Thomas Thompson's *English Rogue* (privately acted?) concerns a conversion from infidelity to faith. The infidel is not the typical libertine rake but the uppity noblewoman, Ermenia, who contemns her betrothed but estateless "decayed Gentleman," Eusames. She announces to his friend, Florentio, *"First let him change his coat of poverty, / To wealth and honour: and then think of me"* (I.ii, 4). Florentio reminds her in a whisper, *"Maids contracted are as good as wives!"* (5). Having heard the story of his parents' prodigality, which cost him his estate, Ermenia begins to feel shame, and her cousins congratulate her for escaping from the "second hell" of "breach of contracts" (V.ii, 52). They are convinced that her love—and fortune—will raise Eusames up from his current state, and she marries him in the end. Meanwhile, two delightful Cavalier tricksters, Plot-thrift and Cozen, con the city usurer, Avaritius, out of his daughters, Ermenia's cousins, and their portions. Though they are rakes, their energy is gradually socialized by the women's "handsome" faces and "good fortunes," which work inevitably to "tye [them] close to their tails in tyme" (III.ii, 29)—the comic necessity that perpetuates aristocratic estates. The hymeneal embrace at the end includes the couples from both plots.[8]

Edward Howard's *Womens Conquest* (1670) focuses on the question of sexual constancy by examining two societies with opposing extreme positions: in the comic plot the Scythians are virtually polygamists in that they may divorce their wives at whim; in the heroic plot the Amazons are virtually polyandrists for the opposite reason. In both heroic and comic plots, the play moves toward recognition of the societal *need* for constancy. In the one, "heroick constancy" (V.i, 76) finally saves a royal marriage, and even the Amazons convert to the patriarchal aristocratic model of "Mutual Loves" (I.i, 13) where nevertheless men have "sole supremacy" (V.i, 85). Meanwhile, in the comic plot, a summarily divorced common woman complains against a country "Where sacred Tyes, and chastest Love / Is no security" (I.i, 4). But gradually even the Scythian common men become glad of the bonds of matrimony, if only to ensure a steady supply of sexual gratification. The plots are not then disjunctive but reciprocal, reinforcing the same lesson—one on idealistic grounds, the other on pragmatic. In both there is the need for "sacred Tyes," that is, for bonds that have the force of religious sanction.

A group of divided plays daringly split the plot three ways: they contain farcical plots as well as the typical heroic and gay-couple plots. In the heroic plot, beleaguered constancy is finally rewarded; in the gay-couple plot, the inconstant rake is finally converted to marriage; and in the farcical plot, some pretending fool or some nouveau knight raised by Cromwell is bubbled. The most famous example is Sir George Etherege's *Comical Revenge; or, Love in a Tub* (1664).[9] The constancy that is rewarded in the heroic plot, however, is atypical. The Royalist Colonel Bruce, upon his release from Commonwealth imprisonment, comes to claim the hand of Graciana, ostensibly promised by her and her father, Lord Bevill. But she has fallen in love with the Cavalier, Beaufort, and while she praises Bruce for his "Loyalty," she reveals a conflicting promise from her father, a "sacred Vow" never to force her marital choice (II.ii.69, 95-96). When her brother, Lovis, asks Bruce point-blank whether Graciana ever plighted troth to him, Bruce is forced to admit that she merely promised to try to decrease her antipathy toward him. But his passion overcomes his reason, and he duels with Beaufort, falling on his sword when he loses. Graciana's younger sister, Aurelia, has loved Bruce all along, stifling her passion for her sister's sake, but now she confesses to the apparently dying Bruce, who lives after all and rewards Aurelia's constancy: "*Aurelia,* here, accept that life from me, / Which Heaven so kindly has preserv'd for thee" (V.v.11-12). Lord Bevill sees their union as "Heavens decree" (18) and adds his blessing. Beaufort and Graciana are united as well.

Meanwhile, in the farce plot Sir Nicholas Cully, Commonwealth parvenu, is gulled repeatedly by Royalist factors Wheadle and Palmer and finally by Sir Frederick Frollick, who pawns him off on his cast mistress, Lucy.[10] And the Cavalier Sir Frederick himself, the libertine energy figure of the play, is socialized into marriage with the Widow Rich, attributing the dénouement to "Chance" (V.v.58). In a provocative analysis of the play, Richard Braverman grants precedence to Sir Frederick's dynamic of *chance* over that of the *heaven* of the heroic plot (*Plots and Counterplots* 64-82). He sees Sir Frederick's prudence and pragmatism as revealing the reality of the Restoration settlement, as opposed to the outmoded idealistic rhetoric in which it was cloaked. But if one views the play as the wish fulfillment of class triumph, then both rhetorics can be seen as supporting the same end. Moreover, if Colonel Bruce is the Scot Braverman takes him for, then the allegorical implications of the ending might be read as the hegemony not of "new cavalier" over "old" (Braverman, passim) but of native English (Anglican) over Scottish (Presbyterian). Finally, Braverman's reading of the epilogue's witty appeal for applause as the Widow Rich's really having placed her estate in trust to the people of England—and thus constituting "a politically subversive gesture, suggesting England will be governed only upon condition of her own will" (82)—is ingenious but unconvincing (epilogues rarely if ever alter the action of a play). Like other rich widows in Restoration comedy, Lady Rich has *manned her land* (see *Tricksters and Estates,* chap. 2), Sir Frederick has gained an estate, and the play, set in the Commonwealth period, looks forward to the restoration of the state to aristocratic, patriarchal control.

The best of these triple-plot plays—and one of the masterpieces of Restoration tragicomedy—is Sir Charles Sedley's *Mulberry Garden* (1668), literally a Restoration play set during the Commonwealth period. The punitive plot focuses on Sir Samuel Forecast. He and his brother, Sir John Everyoung, are like Terence's famous brothers: the one from town, the other from the country; the one liberal, insouciant, indulgent, and the other parsimonious, prudent, strict—and in this play, the one Royalist and the other Roundhead. Their names betray them. Sir John has the eternal, natural attraction of the Cavalier.[11] Sir Samuel, who would affect the providential Puritan, is neither so prudent nor so virtuous as he protests. He courts the Widow Brightstone, pays lip service to her fidelity to her deceased husband (a friend of his), yet greedily wants her for himself. He offers to bribe a judge for her—in short, he is willing, as he says, "to trample on those unprofitable and foolish principles the honourable Beggars of former times Govern'd their lives by" (II.iv.77-79). At one point, despite his own supposed principles, he disguises himself as a fantastic courtier, and his brother has him properly cudgeled and exposed to teach him a lesson.

In the heroic plot, Eugenio and Philander have left their lovers, Althea and Diana, to fight in Honor's cause as Royalists. Political and sexual loyalty remain linked throughout, clothed in the usual metaphysical rhetoric. When Eugenio discovers that Althea has become engaged to someone else, he complains against her and against Heaven. Philander remonstrates in words that employ several concepts of the aristocratic code:

> Despair's the portion of the damn'd below,
> And in a generous mind shou'd never grow;
> Trust to *Althea*'s virtue, trust her love,
> And you will safe in either of 'um prove. . . .

> The smiles of Fortune you so false have found,
> Methinks, you shou'd not mind her when she frown'd:
> How wou'd *Althea*'s Vertues grieve to find
> Themselves suspected in *Eugenio*'s mind!
> Like Princes murder'd on the Royal Throne,
> Where 'till that minute they had brightest shone. [III.i.19-22, 44-50]

The concluding simile is a baroque yoking of the ethical and political dimensions of aristocratic ideology.

Eugenio commends Althea to the gods and returns to his higher task of fighting for his king, but later, disguised as a soldier of the Commonwealth, he comes to try Althea's sexual constancy under the guise of questioning her political loyalty, and she reproaches him with distrust. Meanwhile, Diana disguises herself as a boy and travels to Philander's hideout in order to test his love for her, complaining that he left her at the altar for fame. But he protests that he had preengaged his faith to both his king and his friend Eugenio. Reconciled, they renew their vows of mutual fidelity. At the end, Charles II is restored to the throne and the Royalists are rewarded with both honor and love. Althea embraces Eugenio, rejoicing, "Such truth in love and loyalty y'ave shown, / What less for both cou'd by just Heaven be done?" (V.v.59-60).

The comic plot features several complications involving two young rakes, Henry Modish and Ned Estridge; a third madcap youth, Jack Wildish, who has no truck with ideal love; and two women, the romantic Victoria and the witty Olivia, who delightfully mocks romantic rhetoric. She and Wildish become the gay couple. Despite himself he falls in love with her and awkwardly protests fidelity; she likes him better the way he was—voluble and witty. When he appears so later, she says with relief, "[E]ver since I saw you last, I have been in most terrible apprehension of a whining Copy of Verses" (III.ii.48-50). Nevertheless, his fit appears permanent, and they finally have their witty engagement scene. They depart seeking a preacher, and she warns him of his punishment when his love falls off.

So this rake, too, is converted, his sexual energy contained. Meanwhile, in the end, instead of either converting to constancy or exulting in promiscuity, the other libertines are duped. Already exposed by Wildish as vain boasters, they plan revenge by frustrating his plot to marry his cousin, the Widow Brightstone, to Sir Samuel. They will get her and her fortune themselves and split the profit. Estridge marries her and comes to triumph, but the Widow turns out to be not Wildish's rich cousin but her maid. Thus the real libertines in the play, those incapable of love and constancy, are thoroughly satirized. In contrast are not only the converted Wildish but another young inconstant, Horatio, who has broken his vows to Victoria in pursuit of Althea. Although her father, Sir Samuel, prefers Horatio, Althea contemns him as "faithless" (II.ii.102). The essential nobility of Horatio's character shines when he defends his rival for Althea, Eugenio, from arresting soldiers. Though promised Althea by her father, Horatio releases her and renews his faith to Victoria: "*Victoria*'s wrongs did my success oppose, / And my lost passion its own penance grows" (V.v.79-80).

The concluding union of brothers (Sir John rescues Sir Samuel from the Tower even as General Monck approaches) and of their daughters with the desirable young men, especially Sir Samuel's city daughters with the Royalists, represents the wish fulfillment of the rhetoric of restoration, which is as tenuous as loyalty itself. Olivia's witty threat to cuckold Wildish if he prove inconstant reminds the audience, as the shouts proclaiming Monck ring down the curtain, that an oath of loyalty today is a word that may be broken tomorrow. Again, the mask of ideology is held at some distance and allows us to see the smiling face of the actor. But as audience we are complicit in the necessary fiction of constancy—necessary for the construction of both states and estates.

The last set of divided tragicomedies takes the classic form of heroic plot linked to gay-couple plot, both concluding successfully. Here at last is the jewel of the genre, Dryden's *Marriage A-la-Mode* (1671).[12] The heroic plot begins in civil war. Approximately twenty years before the action of the play, Theagenes, king of Syracuse, had set out to quell "a Rebellion in the heart of *Sicily*" (I.i.258), was victorious, but received a mortal wound and died leaving his queen and infant son to the care of his loyal general, Polydamas. But rebellion was not really quelled, for "false *Polydamas* betray'd his trust" (269) and usurped the throne. Ironically, however, at this moment of apparent success, Polydamas's world refused to coalesce into harmony. Not only the queen and the prince but Polydamas's own pregnant wife fled into oblivion with the loyal vicegerent, Eubulus. Polydamas is left heirless, and the noble Amalthea interprets his plight as a providential retribution: "[S]ee how heav'n can punish wicked men / In granting their desires" (276-77). Moreover, Polydamas is shadowed by Amalthea's brother, Argaleon, son of one of the rebels who helped him to the throne. "Standing in the dark to him," Argaleon studies Polydamas and plays upon his desires, "which he so times and sooths, that, in effect, he reigns" (223-25). And he clearly hopes to succeed Polydamas, further displacing the throne from the lost royal family. Thus when Polydamas comes to Sicily "in hope to find an Heir" (245), Argaleon tries to cast doubt upon the signs of his lost child. And when Leonidas and Palmyra are found, Argaleon swears Palmyra is the perdita, "By all my hopes" (388). His only hope now is to become royal consort of the princess and eventually reign not merely in effect but in deed.

In other words, once Polydamas has broken the bonds of loyalty and legitimate succession, both principles remain destabilized. Even when he thinks he has found a son and heir, he cannot control Leonidas's will, and this time he himself infers providential retribution: "But you are just, you Gods; O you are just, / In punishing the crimes of my rebellion / With a rebellious Son!" (II.i.316-18). Rebellion begets rebellion, disloyalty disloyalty, and the original act of usurpation comes perilously close to being repeated. Once Argaleon realizes Leonidas is the young Theagenes and thus the legitimate king, he counsels Polydamas, "Command his execution instantly; / Give him not leisure to discover it; / He may corrupt the Soldiers" (V.i.416-18). As the concepts of loyalty and legitimacy become perverted, so does language: Leonidas's declaration of his legitimacy will "corrupt the Soldiers"—from what? loyalty to a usurper? Both Argaleon and Polydamas go so far as to call Leonidas, their sovereign, a "Traitour" (419, 423).

Besides this threat to the word as the pledge of allegiance, the heroic plot features a threat to the word as pledge of betrothal. Polydamas has promised to wed his lost heir, according to its sex, to either Argaleon or Amalthea. When he believes Leonidas to be his son, he insists that his "vow" to Amalthea be honored, even though Amalthea generously releases Leonidas from it when she observes Leonidas's disinclination (II.i.337 ff). For Leonidas has already plighted his troth to Palmyra, and not all Polydamas's threats can shake his constancy:

> *Palmyra.* Speak quickly; what have you resolv'd to do?
> *Leonidas.* To keep my faith inviolate to you. . . .
> Think not that time or fate shall e'r divide
> Those hearts, which Love and mutual Vows have ty'd.
> [II.i.458-59, 490-91]

Polydamas's attitude toward the supposedly low-class Palmyra is typically aristocratic—at best she can be "Fit onely for a Prince his vacant Hours" (III.i.295)—and he condemns her to drift at sea with only three days' provision.

At this point, three themes emerge from the conflict. The first is apparent egalitarianism in the face of the condemnation of Palmyra. Leonidas argues that love "knows no difference in degrees" (III.i.280). Earlier, Hermogenes asserts a natural nobility greater than that found in courts (I.i.352-54). Connected is the theme of the noble savage. At the beginning, Leonidas seems to have a native greatness, as he contrasts the glory of the court with the glory of nature (I.i.396-400). When he apparently is revealed to be not the prince but a peasant, he exclaims, "Though meanly born, I have a Kingly Soul yet" (IV.i.22), arrogantly comparing himself to the self-sufficient "Godhead" (III.i.471). Like Almanzor, he alone is king of himself, and he feels kingly motions in his mind. Nevertheless, Dryden has raised these themes only to dissipate them in the revelation that both Palmyra and Leonidas are noble, the latter indeed a king. Their real nobility shines through their circumstances. Thus, as in much romance, the apparent threat to the purity of aristocratic genealogy proves to be specious, and Dryden's apparent egalitarianism constitutes merely a theatrical gesture.[13]

The third theme that emerges from the lovers' conflict in the heroic plot is more substantial—Leonidas's distrust of Palmyra and of the code of word-as-bond itself. He begins to fear that Palmyra "Is grown asham'd of a mean ill-plac'd love" (IV.i.13). He complains to her, "But you, I fear, are chang'd" (IV.ii.22). In a scene reminiscent of that between Almanzor and Almahide, Leonidas demands to know whether he must hope or despair, and Palmyra justly rebukes him: "After so many proofs, how can you call / My love in doubt?" (IV.iv.37-38). But she refuses to give herself to Leonidas without her father's permission. Rather, she can vow only "ne'r to wed another man" (69): "I'll keep my promise, though I lose my life" (71). Nevertheless, Leonidas demands the body's reward, and he has no respect for her appeal to her relationship with her father: "Duty's a Name; and Love's a Real thing" (46). Here, his faith in the efficacy of the code is yielding to nominalism: "Duty" is a mere word, whereas "Love" corresponds to real passion.

This incipient nominalism is leading Leonidas to disregard the bonds of society and to become a rebel himself (and an Oedipal rebel at that). Earlier he appeals to the "Gods" to protect his "piety" and to "Keep me from saying that which misbecomes a son" (III.i.314-15). Yet in a moment he draws his sword against his supposed father, and Palmyra is hard-pressed to recall him from the ethic of the usurper, the use of "lawless force" (339). In the later scene, Leonidas no longer rebels against a father or even a king but the usurper of his own throne. Yet Palmyra still calls his method "ruinous" (IV.iv.89), for he would seize both "Love and Crown, by force" (57). Palmyra is prepared, "if you force employ," to "divorce" him forever (78-79). She is pleading that there must be a better way than another civil war. Her recalcitrance causes him to delay long enough to be captured by Polydamas and condemned to death. Palmyra appears to be a dreamy-eyed idealist who should have listened to Leonidas's practical wisdom. As he is led off, Argaleon appears to have triumphed over not only Leonidas but the code of the word itself, for he mockingly perverts one of its key concepts, telling Palmyra, "You must be constant" (V.i.377). Constant to what? To her principles despite adversity? To him? Such goading is mere nasty gloating.

The comic plot offers its own challenge to the traditional code of the word in two of its major manifestations, the bonds of marriage and friendship. Antithetical mirror images of Leonidas and Palmyra (who have just concluded a scene of renewed betrothal), Rhodophil and Doralice pretend "true love" in public (III.i.2). Doralice claims to be "every day worse and worse in love" (21-22). Nevertheless, she opens the play with a song that reveals the opposite movement:

> *Why should a foolish Marriage Vow*
> *Which long ago was made,*
> *Oblige us to each other now*
> *When Passion is decay'd?*
> *We lov'd, and we lov'd, as long as we cou'd,*
> *Till our love was lov'd out in us both:*
> *But our Marriage is dead, when the Pleasure is fled:*
> *'Twas Pleasure first made it an Oath.* [I.i.3-10]

The last line especially attacks the idealization of the code in that the word is portrayed as merely the mask of desire. The comic plot thus opposes a libertine to the chivalric ethic. To the libertine, marriage is not a manifestation of Natural Law, for humans are not naturally monogamous. According to this view, the bonds of matrimony really cannot hold, especially against the power of desire for variety and novelty.

Rhodophil suffers the same desire. He complains to his friend Palamede that he has violated his libertine "Vows and Resolutions" and committed the utmost sin, marriage (I.i.126). Later he says aside, "There's something of antipathy in the word Marriage to the nature of love" (IV.i.169-70). All he now knows of Doralice's "perfections" that enticed him "is only by memory" (I.i.144-45). He has loved her "a whole half year, double the natural term of any Mistress," but they have finally "arriv'd at that point, that there was nothing left in us to make us new to one another" (147-48, 151-52). Palamede counsels an endless series of mistresses as the only remedy: "as fast as one fails, you must supply it with another" (161). Rodophil's later response to this ethic is very instructive: "This were a blessed Doctrine, indeed, if our Wives would hear it; but, they're their own enemies: if they would suffer us but now and then to make excursions, the benefit of our variety would be theirs; instead of one continu'd, lazy, tyr'd love, they would, in their turns, have twenty vigorous, fresh, and active loves" (II.i.108-13). Thus, while he too seeks variety, his ethic is not so completely libertine as that expressed in Doralice's song. For there she would not *"bar"* her husband's similar satisfaction of his desire for variety (I.i.16). But Rhodophil's ethic is based upon a double standard. His wife would benefit only vicariously from his promiscuity. And he outrageously upbraids her: "Why there's the devil on't! if thou coudst make my enjoying thee but a little less easie, or a little more unlawful, thou shouldst see, what a Termagant Lover I would prove. I have taken such pains to enjoy thee, *Doralice,* that I have fanci'd thee all the fine women in the Town, to help me out. But now there's none left for me to think on, my imagination is quite jaded. Thou art a Wife, and thou wilt be a Wife, and I can make thee another no longer" (III.i.77-84). In his imagination he has already availed himself of Palamede's remedy, and he is about to graduate from imagination to reality, as he courts Melantha to be his mistress.

For both Doralice and Rhodophil, then, the bonds have become the "Banes of Matrimony" (III.i.63), with the connotation of *ruin* replacing that of *proclamation.* This is marriage à la mode. Each cruelly wishes for the other's death, if only to pursue sexual variety, and Rhodophil accurately characterizes their relationship: "Prethee, *Doralice,* why do we quarrel thus a-days? ha? this is but a kind of Heathenish life, and does not answer the ends of marriage" (III.i.66-68). For him, the "ends of marriage" are no more than sexual gratification, and chivalric idealism has been converted to libertine realism.

The bond of friendship is also fractured in the comic plot. Rhodophil and Palamede are supposedly best of friends. But the tenuousness of that relationship is underlined when Palamede confides to Rhodophil *"sub sigillo"* (II.i.122)—that is, he swears "under the seal" of their friendship—that the lady he points to is his mistress. Ironically, of course, the lady is Doralice, and Rhodophil exclaims aside, "By all that's vertuous, my Wife!" (II.i.124). Believing Palamede "abuses" him to his face (II.i.127), Rhodophil waxes wroth, and a crisis is avoided only because Palamede senses his error and wittily escapes. But ironically he identifies Rhodophil's own mistress as his fiancée—and then realizes he himself will be cuckolded by the friend he sets out to cuckold, a shame he must endure; otherwise, he must either be disinherited or (his unspoken reservation) confront Rhodophil and force the issue to a crisis.

Dryden makes explicit the violated standard. At their assignation in the grotto, Palamede pretends to have "one scruple of conscience," and Doralice impishly asks, "I hope you are afraid of betraying your friend?" Palamede's answer perverts the very concept: "Of betraying my friend! I am more afraid of being betray'd by you to my friend" (III.ii.42-47). Obviously, the only sin in his libertine world is getting caught. The trust between friends becomes exchanged for a "trust" between illicit lovers not to tell (49). When Rhodophil and Melantha arrive for their own tryst, confrontation between the friends seems inevitable, and Palamede struggles frenetically to avoid it—to the point of willingly sending his friend away with his fiancée and further perverting the language of the code: "Well, dear friend, to let you see I scorn to be jealous, and that I dare trust my Mistris [Melantha] with you, take her back . . . : there's an effect of pure friendship for you now" (100-106). Finally, crisis is again narrowly averted by deft verbal manipulation. Still, as Palamede in soliloquy foresees the progress of this "odd kind of game" (140), he fears not betrayal of friendship but that "both our women will certainly betray their party" (144-45)—not by violating moral standards nor even by kissing and telling but by enjoying both lovers, which is the very thing he and Rhodophil intend to do. The concept of betrayal has become warped indeed.

Dryden's device of disguising the two women as boys allows the public enacting of what is usually hidden. Rhodophil unwittingly delivers his wife to his friend (IV.i), and later the two court one another's betrothed before his "face" (IV.iii.90-91, 102-4) in a hilarious scene of carnival freedom, where the sexual rivalry has free play in masquerade. Crisis threatens when the women rivals move from verbal to physical attack, but again their business is interrupted, this time by the king's business. The actual moment of crisis finally arrives when Rhodophil catches Palamede dead to rights kissing Doralice's hand. Each friend accuses the other of seducing his betrothed, and finally each draws his sword. The kind of deadly rivalry that the aristocratic codes of friendship and chastity were designed to prevent has exploded in all its violence.

Thus, both plots strain the bond of the word to the breaking point. The heroic plot is on the verge of regicide; the comic, adultery and homicide. And in both, as we have seen, not only are the bonds corrupted but so, too, are the key words that name the bonds and their violations: "Traitour," "constant," "betrayal," and "trust." Such words are all in danger of becoming what Doralice calls Palamede's amorous cant: "words of course" (I.i.51).

This motif of the perversion of words is extended in the comic plot to include the religious language that traditionally invests the ethical and political codes with metaphysical significance and sanction. For the libertine Palamede, as for Rhodophil, marriage is a sin "past redemption" (I.i.73). A "vertuous Woman" is "damnable" (67). Rhodophil explains the phenomenon of his marrying: "Yes, faith, the Devil has had power over me" (125-26), but, following Palamede's "blessed Doctrine" (II.i.108), he has already begun the remedy of getting a mistress: "[F]aith, considering the damn'd disadvantages of a marry'd man, I have provided well enough, for a poor humble sinner" (I.i.165-67). Meanwhile, Doralice makes an assignation by resolving to "pray" for Palamede at her private "devotions" (II.i.240-43), assuring him thus of privacy and opportunity, to which he wittily and bawdily responds in soliloquy, "Well, I will not be so prophane a wretch as to interrupt her devotions; but to make 'em more effectual, I'll down upon my knees, and endeavor to joyn my own with 'em" (246-48). When they keep their tryst, they work a series of puns off such religious language (III.ii), and later Palamede has three delightful displays: When Rhodophil wishes him good hunting with his mistress, Palamede responds, "He has wish'd me good fortune with his Wife: there's no sin in this then, there's fair leave given. Well, I must go visit the sick; I cannot resist the temptations of my charity" (IV.i.179-81). When the four of them are interrupted by the king's business, he complains, "Yes, yes, I will go; but the devil take me if ever I was less in humour. . . . Truth is, I had a little transitory crime to have committed first; and I am the worst man in the world at repenting, till a sin be thoroughly done" (IV.iii.166-71). Finally, when Doralice accosts him at the end with the immanence of his marriage, Palamede protests, "I have abundance of grace in me, that I find: But if you have any spark of true friendship in you, retire a little with me to the next room that has a couch or bed in't, and bestow your charity upon a poor dying man" (V.i.207-11).

Especially witty in this dialogue, as in much Restoration comedy, are the religious expletives, whose moribund status indicates the emptiness of such language and the apparent death of the old standard. Yet these seemingly dead metaphors are paradoxically quick with ironic significance. Some of the best examples of this technique occur when Palamede nervously answers Rhodophil's demand to know who calls him at the grotto assignation, "Faith I can't imagine," and Doralice's impudent response to being caught, "O, Gentleman [Rhodophil], have I caught you i'faith?" (III.ii.98, 113-14). To swear by faith in such situations implies that the violators of marital faith no longer need fear the metaphysic that was once portrayed as punishing them.

The play's central symbol of this decadence of language is Melantha. As one fanatically thirsting for a language that is in vogue, she purchases new French words from her maid, Philotis, every day and discards yesterday's, making Philotis "heir to all my cast words, as thou art to my old Wardrobe" (II.i.15-16), as if words were transient garb no sooner put on than put off, no longer à la mode. She cares not about the meanings of words: she replaces "Intrigue" with "Amour," thus whitewashing the affair (II.i.14-15); when Philotis tries to define a few new entries, Melantha exclaims, "Truce with your interpretation" (III.i.212). Desiring to be absolutely *au courant,* she lays claim to the very invention of the words she hears, only to have them stolen out of her mouth by Palamede before she can employ them for their only value, their daily currency at court, which will, she hopes, buy attention. But her incessant palaver produces nothing but cacophony. Palamede describes her affected verbal manner: "to be very aiery, with abundance of noise, and no sense" (V.i.178-79). The text continues here, "Fa, la, la, la, &c." Even more than the nonsense syllables, the "&c." is Melantha's mark. One of her favorite phrases is "and all that." She is a figure for Derrida's "dangerous supplement" (*Of Grammatology*, pt. 2, chap. 2), that necessity for language to endlessly supplement itself in a series of metonymns that constantly supplant their predecessors, destroying the possibility of a logocentric language that can ever adequately name the *Ding an sich*.

The problem with such endless supplementarity in the play is that it does not confine itself to Melantha but becomes symbolic of the action of both plots. In the comic plot, Doralice considers a husband per se "the creature of the world the most out of fashion" (V.i.238), and Rhodophil complains of being "out of fashion" as a constant husband (I.i.150). His and Palamede's remedy—and Doralice's—is an infinite series of lovers, that is, infinite supplementarity, as one lover supplants the other in a perpetual masquerade of shifting identities, of constant displacements because the absolute Presence of love, the Logos of its language, will not abide. In the heroic plot, just as Melantha herself invades the "Presence" of the court (III.i.110), so also does supplementarity in the deferral of the *presence* of a king who represents a divine presence, a Logos, and in the threat of a series of usurping supplanters, from Polydamas to Argaleon and beyond.[14] Not by accident are the legitimate kings, both father and son, named Theagenes, or "divine descendant," the patronymic name itself pretending a different order of succession than supplementarity through metonymy, an order of repetition without difference that preserves the Logos. But Theagenes *père* is dead and Theagenes *fils* is displaced and in danger of perpetual deferral.

Moreover, the slippage of language that Melantha represents, as we have seen, permeates the comic plot and subtly invades the heroic, moving even Leonidas toward nominalism. More insidious is the invasion of echoes from the comic plot—echoes of a dying language—into his relationship with Palmyra. Melantha punctuates her monologues with the meaningless ejaculation, "Let me die," a phrase paraphrased often by Leonidas and Palmyra as they pledge constancy till death—and a phrase actually echoed by Leonidas verbatim as he rails at Palmyra's exile, "But let me die before I see this done" (III.i.316). How compromised is such a line in the middle of the play? How compromised is all their language of constancy and honor? What do we make of their presence at the same masquerade that the four lovers attend? Of their making an assignation? During the masquerade, Leonidas and Palmyra's planning a tryst is immediately followed by a bawdy song about premature ejaculation. Thereupon, like any other rake, Argaleon supplants Leonidas with Palmyra and betrays the two of them. When Doralice pledges "to him that has the fairest Lady of *Sicily* in Masquerade to night" (IV.iii.114-15), whom are we supposed to take as the referent? Even the virtuous Amalthea seems tainted, for it is she who bids Doralice learn the opening song celebrating inconstancy. The worlds are all tending to collapse together, destroying fixed hierarchy and fixed differentiation and creating the kind of crisis René Girard analyzes in *Violence and the Sacred.* The entire world of the play appears to be one marked by absence: of god, of order, of love, of meaning to all the words that bind society together. The dangerous supplement seems to have triumphed; it seems to have disseminated all the orders of discourse in a kind of coitus interruptus mirrored by all the interrupted assignations. As Melantha says at the end, "[O]ur damn'd Language expresses nothing" (V.i.495). She means explicitly English as opposed to French, but in the light of the play's pervasive perversion of words, the statement carries dire universal significance.

Nevertheless, the play seems to close in a way that wills-to-mean (Derrida's *vouloir-dire*) and to reaffirm the traditional aristocratic code of the word. The rightful king is, after all, restored to the throne. The usurper is replaced by one who really precedes him, by one who represents the Father-King-Logos. Leonidas's original right—as well as his name—is restored to him as Theagenes. Hence Divine Presence is restored to the court, a restoration symbolized in the explicit attribution of the dynamic of the dénouement to Providence: Leonidas credits "the Gods" and Palmyra exclaims, "Now all my prayers are heard" (V.i.454, 489). The chain of political supplements is therefore broken. The son's bearing the name of the father he replaces implies the displacement of the sequence of metonym by the sameness of metaphor: *le roi est mort, vive le roi.* The Oedipal crisis is avoided because the son is the father.

Other knots are untied in the dénouement of the heroic plot. The usurper becomes repentant and resumes his proper role in society, his proper name, as "Father" to both Palmyra and, by extension, Leonidas (475). The recalcitrant supplanter, Argaleon, is rebuked and sequestered. And even Amalthea, supposedly tragically excluded from the happy ending because of her frustrated love for Leonidas,[15] goes off to become a Vestal Virgin and pray for Leonidas. Perhaps her completely selfless act of saving Leonidas can be interpreted, like the selfless love between Ozmyn and Benzayda in Dryden's *Conquest of Granada,* as a suggestion of that sacrificial act Girard discusses which redeems society from impending disaster, or better, as a reminder to a Christian audience of the efficacy of the central event in their mythology. At any rate, though frustrated, her love is being sublated upwards to a relationship with the gods, trust in whose Presence, however they may appear absent or *absconditi,* has been reaffirmed.

This reestablished order permeates the dénouement of even the comic plot. The relation between the plots is reversed and the heroic invades the comic when Amalthea races in to plead for the couples' rightful king, appealing to their "loyalty" (V.i.438). Their instantaneous response demonstrates their heretofore obscured place in the hierarchy, and Palamede, of all people, reaffirms the political code: "[N]o Subject e'r can meet / A nobler fate, than at his Sovereign's feet" (451-52). To this "Loyalty and Valour" (458) Leonidas also attributes the dynamic of the dénouement, thus linking the political code with the metaphysical, its sanction: "Next to the Gods, brave friends, be yours the honour" (454).

Moreover, the lovers resolve their sexual conflict. For pragmatic rather than idealistic reasons, they repudiate the libertine code. First, Doralice and Palamede reach an agreement not to sleep together. He is to be married on the morrow, and she contemns an affair with a married man, not because of the invasion of another's "propriety," her reservation at the beginning (I.i.76), but because a married man is not a vigorous lover. According to her, everything about him is married, "and if we could look within his Breeches, we should find him marri'd there too" (V.i.242-43). Her most poignant pragmatic reason is actually the fear of the desire for supplements, the fear of the absence of Presence in love: "[W]e might upon trial have lik'd each other less, as many a man and woman, that have lov'd as desperately as we, and yet when they came to possession, have sigh'd, and cri'd to themselves, Is this all?" (252-55). She indulges in a kind of Keatsian fantasy of Presence: "The onely way to keep us new to one another, is never to enjoy, as they keep grapes by hanging 'em upon a line; they must touch nothing if you would preserve 'em fresh" (271-73). Palamede recognizes the flaw in her fantasy: "But then they wither, and grow dry in the very keeping" (274). And he still believes in the doctrine of supplements. Thus, he suggests the one possibility that the aristocratic code allows: sequential rather than simultaneous supplementation. They pledge to keep fit and marry each other if their spouses die.

This contract anticipates another that brings the comic plot to resolution. Preparatory to it, a different dynamic has been at work. First, the rivals discover they love (desire) their betrotheds more than they thought. Rhodophil is revealed to be incompatible with Melantha, whereas Palamede waxes quite compatible as he fences with her *en français* and *à la mode.* To his surprise he finds, "I begin to like her" (V.i.190). And Doralice cleverly interrupts Palamede and Rhodophil's duel by asking the crucial question, "[A]re not you two a couple of mad fighting fools, to cut one another's throats for nothing? . . . You can neither of you be jealous of what you love not" (314-15, 318-19). Rhodophil concludes, "Faith I am jealous, and that makes me partly suspect that I love you better then I thought" (320-21). Second, the rivals reason according to what Girard calls "mimetic desire,"[16] that each's betrothed must be valuable since the rival desires her.

The next crucial consideration for the rivals is the patriarchal aristocratic concern with the woman's, the vessel's purity. And here, though arrived at for pragmatic reasons, the code of trust is reestablished. When Rhodophil says he is ready to reconcile with Doralice if he can be sure she is chaste, that is, faithful to him, she answers wittily, "If you are wise, believe me for your own sake: Love and Religion have but one thing to trust to; that's a good sound faith" (V.i.336-37). Doralice links trust in love to that in religion, and the effect is more than an analogy. The language of the comic plot now reapproaches that of the heroic. The ethical code of trust is reaffirmed and reconnected with the metaphysical. And when both rivals move to witness each woman's chastity, their testimony is dependent upon faith in a word that carries divine sanction; at the same time, they restore the bonds of friendship:

> *Palamede.* *Rhodophil,* you know me too well, to imagine I speak for fear; and therefore in consideration of our past friendship, I will tell you, and bind it by all things holy, that *Doralice* is innocent.
> *Rhodophil.* Friend, I will believe you, and vow the same for your *Melantha.* [346-50]

Note Rhodophil's use of the auxiliary "will": this, too, is will-to-meaning.

The last crucial consideration, as Rhodophil says, is how the rivals can keep their wives faithful. To put it another way, how to avoid such sexual rivalry in the future? One solution—the libertine answer—is the radical suggestion of a "blessed community" (V.i.351), a sexual commune. But Dryden apparently knew the psychological hazards of such a solution, for Palamede and Rhodophil immediately demonstrate fear of a different and equally deadly rivalry over sexual performance. The apparent random equity of the women drawing lots for their night's partner would degenerate, as Palamede says in a typical male fantasy born of insecurity, into each desiring "the longest cut" (358).

For these realistic, pragmatic considerations the two men enter into "a firm League, not to invade each others propriety" (V.i.359-60). They have rediscovered patrilineal patriarchy's need for binding words—based ultimately on faith—to bar deadly sexual rivalry, for proprietary sexual laws and contracts, a need that continues even when feudalism yields to the bourgeois code (see Tanner, *Adultery in the Novel*). But Doralice's witty promise of sexual retribution as a sanction implies the perpetual threat of sexual anarchy, thereby underscoring both the tenuousness and the exigency of such covenants.

There is a similar tenuousness in the resolution of the heroic plot. The legitimate king and the principle of orderly succession are restored. But Argaleon is not killed, just sequestered, and his dark shadow remains as the reminder of the threat of future usurpers. And Amalthea's sublation is still a sign of the sublimation of unfulfilled desire, a desire which will always threaten monogamy even within the privileged confines of the court. At the same time, both plots do achieve a comic closure that reinforces the code of the word. Language has not proved to be meaningless in either plot but rather to constitute the very bonds of society through will-to-meaning.[17]

Curiously, Dryden, who picks his names very carefully for their etymological significance (for example, *Polydamas* means "conqueror of many," *Argaleon* means "troublesome"), names his dead king and the rightful heir *Theagenes,* a name which means not just "divine descendent" but "descendent of a goddess." There seems the suggestion that patriarchal states and estates can endure only through the respect for the power of female sexuality figured forth in Dorigen's delicate but unmistakably sensuous attractiveness. The mysterious power of women is strangely figured forth in Dryden's absent goddess who appears to be the progenitress of Dryden's kings. This goddess seems to provide a glimpse of a benevolent and tolerant originating power that man can never really control. She has inhabited feudal aristocratic literature at least since the Lady of the Lake. Patriarchal ideology thus occasionally acknowledges in a supplicating manner the real reproductive power of women it attempts to control.

In sum, Restoration tragicomic romance performs its cultural work by reaffirming the official discourse of constancy—but sometimes in a manner that allows us a glimpse behind the mask of heroic ideals to reveal their necessity. This necessity is itself a supplementary ideology justifying aristocratic power relations, particularly patriarchy.

Dryden (in collaboration with Davenant) had already adapted Shakespeare's *Tempest* (1667) in a manner which extended the theme of political rivalry to a sexual rivalry that threatens to undo Prospero's grand scheme of reconciliation and restoration. By doubling Miranda with a sister,

Dorinda, and Ferdinand with the aptly named Hippolito—rightful prince of Mantua, raised as an *enfant sauvage*—Dryden creates a cross-rivalry that leads to a sacrificial crisis apparently concluding in the death of one prince and the condemnation of the other. Hippolito is a natural libertine who demands sexual access to all women, who accepts no restraints upon his desire, and who sees even his foster father, Prospero, as a sexual rival. When friendship fails as a restraint, a jealous Ferdinand threatens force. Unlike Rhodophil and Palamede, Ferdinand and Hippolito actually duel, and Ferdinand runs the sexual overreacher through. Even the sisters fall out in rivalry and in recrimination over the death of Hippolito. But Hippolito is saved by the application of "Weapon-Salve" applied to "the Sword which pierc'd him" (V.ii.78-79)—a magical folk-fairy remedy that has obvious symbolic significance, turning the implement of violence into a medicinal magic wand. As in *Marriage A-la-Mode,* the resolution of this plot occurs through a pragmatic rediscovery of the need for constancy and monogamy: the human passions of possession and jealousy demand sexual restraint, covered over with the thin candy shell of the ideology of true love (that protects patriarchy). The two royal couples, Ferdinand and Miranda and Hippolito and Dorito, will return to Europe to inherit their real estates.

Dryden complicates this rather typical tragicomic romance, however, by compounding Shakespeare's comic as well as his heroic plot. Caliban has a twin sister of his mother's name, Sycorax. Colonial interpretations of Shakespeare's *Tempest* have become commonplace. Dryden retains Ariel as indentured servant (like the criminals and the Irish who were transported to the British West Indies). And he retains Caliban as indigenous inhabitant, from whom Prospero learns everything he can about the island, then enslaves, with the rationale that Caliban is an irredeemable, ineducable savage who even tries to rape his colonial master's daughter. And as in Shakespeare, Caliban has no more sense than to follow seamen whose very class makes them incapable of ruling. At the end a chastened Caliban slinks off to remain Prospero's slave—and to justify the white man's taking him up as his burden.

Dryden's creation of Sycorax allows him to reinforce his theme of the societal necessity for sexual restraint through constancy and monogamy. Sycorax's sexual appetite is voracious, and there is much comic business in the farcical action of her pursuing an embrace from Trincalo, flirting with Stephano, and apparently even having an incestuous roll in the grass offstage with her twin brother. Like her mother, she is a witch; as such she represents the return of the repressed matriarch, and her outrageous actions justify and rationalize patriarchal control over female sexual desire, over those enslaving feminine wiles Prospero warns Hippolito about.

But Sycorax has "Blobber-lips" (III.iii.12). Her mother is from Africa. Like her brother she is "freckl'd" (I.ii.205, as in Shakespeare). She is, then, a composite of Irish, African, and, being a Bermudan, Indian colonized peoples. Ugly by refined European standards, she has the typical hyper sex drive, as the California editors point out, portrayed in "women of dark-skinned races" (*Works* 10:335). Thus she is the exotic other, representing European male wish fulfillment: unlimited sex with native women in the colonies. Even more, she represents the islands themselves, the land to be claimed, plowed, cultivated by a superior race. In order to assert his dominion, Trincalo will "lay claim to this Island by Alliance" (II.iii.222), by marrying Sycorax, gelding Caliban (!), and engendering mulatto colonists. His actions are a parody of the heroic resolution: "The *Trincalos,* like other wise men, have anciently us'd to marry for Estate more than for beauty" (III.iii.7-9). The estate he lays claim to—and lays a crop by—is the brave New World itself. But, of course, when *Trincalo* appears bound home for the metropolis, that's no place for his pregnant native, so he refuses her passage and tells her, being part fish, to swim for Europe. He leaves the homely plowed field behind to bear fruit for its masters. Sycorax is left at the primitive altar: no marriage, no equality between the conquerors and the indigenous.

Aphra Behn's tragicomedy, *The Widdow Ranter; or, The History of Bacon in Virginia* (1689), is literally both a tragedy and a comedy. It is Bacon's tragedy. Apparently a "Noble Gentleman" (I.i.102), like Towerson, Bacon is described as "a Man indeed above the Common Rank, by Nature Generous; Brave, Resolv'd, and Daring" (113-14): "that great Soul'd Man, no private Body e're contain'd a Nobler" (V.313); "great Souls are born in common men, sometimes as well as Princes" (I.i.120-21). In other words, as in feudal tragedy in general, the great-souled are capable of great action and great passion. Bacon has great ambition, "who," as his fellow Cavalier Friendly says, "studying the Lives of the Romans and great men, that have raised themselves to the most Elevated fortunes, fancies it easy for Ambitious men, to aim at any Pitch of Glory, I've heard him often say, Why cannot I Conquer the Universe as well as *Alexander*? or like another *Romulus* form a new Rome, and make my self Ador'd?" (114-19). His problem is that he has no warrant for his ambitious action, no commission for his acts of warlike heroism.

Having taken up arms against marauding Indians to save both his own plantation and the colony of Virginia itself, he is a victim of the envy and ingratitude of lesser men, who foist him on the technicality of law. Behn's ignominious parvenu councilors sound like stereotypical Puritans from anti-Commonwealth satire: "[T]ho' he fought like *Alexander,* and preserv'd the whole world from perdition, yet if he did it against Law, 'tis Lawful to hang him; why what Brother, is i[t] fit that every impudent fellow that pretends to a little Honour, Loyalty & Courage, should serve his King and Country against the Law? no, no, Brother, these things are not to be suffer'd in a Civill Government by Law Establish'd" (I.ii.108-13). Yet when he dies at the end, Bacon counsels his fellow Cavaliers thus: "[N]ever let Ambition—Love—or Interest make you forget as I have done—your Duty—and Allegiance" (V.307-8). Like Essex, he is guilty of ambitious boldness; like Antony, he is guilty of adulterous love. And who can tell where the one leaves off and the other begins. Friendly again: "This Thirst of Glory cherisht by Sullen Melancholly, I believe was the first Motive that made him in Love with the young *Indian*-Queen, fancying no *Hero* ought to be without his Princess. And this was the reason why he so earnestly prest for a Commission, to be made General against the *Indians*" (I.i.122-26). But the queen is married to his protégé, the young Indian king. The rivalry between their cultures becomes collapsed into their deadly rivalry over her, and Bacon kills the king. Ironically, he kills her, too, she disguised in battle as a brave. He then kills himself, for he has lost that which was alone worth fighting for. Bacon echoes Antony: "Why prithee let him [the deputy governor] make the World his Prize, I have no business with the Trifle now; it now contains nothing that's worth my care, since my fair Queen—is Dead" (V.227-29).[18]

The question that lurks unanswered is what Bacon means by "Interest." Perhaps he means just his ambition and his love. But perhaps he refers to his other reason for fighting the Indians. When the king accuses the Europeans of "Abusing all our Charitable Hospitality" by usurping their "Right" to the land and enslaving them (II.i.13-14), Bacon justifies not his forebears but himself: "I will not justify the Ingratitude of my forefathers, but finding here my Inheritance, I am resolv'd still to maintain it so, And by my sword which first cut out my Portion, Defend each inch of Land with my last drop of Bloud" (15-18). The audience is immediately distracted from the full implications of this speech by the Indian queen's aside that she dotes on his every word. But the queen is a trope not only for Bacon's ambivalence but for the Indians' secret desire to be conquered by a superior race. The argument is, moreover, all too familiar: I'm not the one who oppressed you so I owe you no recompense; the land is now mine, and I proceed by right of defense of property and self-defense.

Bacon's death, then, results from his personal tragedy, his overreaching. But his appeal to his fellow Cavaliers to make peace with the colonial government ushers in a comic ending with imperialist implications. The (mostly class) differences between the colonists are swept aside in the general amnesty and the hymeneal close of marriages at the end. The deputy governor addresses mainly the Cavaliers, but his embrace includes the inept parvenus as well:

> Come my brave Youths let all our Forces meet,
> To make this Country Happy, Rich, and great;
> Let scanted *Europe* see that we enjoy
> Safer Repose, and larger Worlds than they. [V.398-401]

Friendly has said at the opening, "This Country wants nothing but to be People'd with a well-born Race to make it one of the best Collonies in the World, but for want of a Governour we are Ruled by a Councill, some of which have been perhaps transported Criminals, who having Acquired great Estates are now become your Honour, and Right Worshipfull, and Possess all Places of Authority; there are amongst 'em some honest Gentlemen who now begin to take upon 'em, and Manage Affairs as they ought to be" (I.i.105-11). Bacon himself was one of these last, who indeed tried to fill the power vacuum left by the absent governor. But the deputy governor is the one who speaks for this well-born class at the end: his name is Wellman. He allies himself with the brave Cavalier youths. Order and hierarchy have been restored. And now a pacified, unified colonial class can set about to turn the colony into the "Happy, Rich, and great" country it can be, indeed, the envy of the "scanted" Old World in its plenty and "Repose."

The marriages are fraught with meaning. Dareing, Bacon's obvious great-souled symbolic heir, marries the rich Widdow Ranter of the title, a character designed to make the frontier woman comically acceptable. She was originally transported herself or sold into white slavery, but her master married her. So the union between her and her Cavalier represents creole respectability. The marriage between the down-and-out younger brother, Hazard (whose name indicates how he lost his annuity), and a wealthy widow (whose husband's last-minute death frees them from the adultery toward which their love has been heading) infuses his energy into the creole mix. Moreover, he gets into a fight the moment he arrives because some of the parvenus, sons of petty bourgeois or indentured servants themselves, suggest he will have to work for a living, either as a merchant or a laborer. With Cavalier class-righteousness, he announces, "I was not bred to Merchandizing Sir, nor do intend to follow the Drudgery of Trading. . . . I was not born to work Sir" (I.i.225-30). Thus Hazard represents a creole plantation class, ready to succeed to the dead husbands of the two remarried widows.

If Bacon did not live to conquer worlds, like Alexander, or at least the "*America*" Dareing says he could have, he has left descendants who will.

There will be no marriage between British gentleman and Indian queen, symbolic of a harmonious coexistence between peoples.[19] The Europeans will kill the Indian kings. And they will be justified. As indicated in the stage directions at the opening of act four, Behn presents us with an Indian ceremony in which *"Priest[s] and Priestesses Dance about the Idol, with ridiculous Postures and crying"* words that even Derek Hughes calls "gibberish" (*English Drama* 372). Obviously such ridiculous, childish people are no match for manly Europeans, whose women can even, like the Widdow Ranter, take the field in battle (as opposed to the Indian queen, who lacks *"Amazonian"* strength [V.192]). So they deserve to be swept off the stage of history, as they are swept off this stage, making no appearance at the end.

Also making no appearance are the "Negro's" (II.ii.1 s.d., 34 s.d.) who are part of Ranter's house entourage. When shortly thereafter one of the foolish councilors, Dullman, calls anyone who says he heard anything of his origins from Dullman himself "a kid-Naper" (II.ii.109), the audience gets the fleetest reminder that fills out the picture of the labor that supports this colonial paradise: indentured servants in the tobacco fields, who were quickly replaced with African slaves (the easier to differentiate racially; also, they weren't so uppity as whites); African slaves and kidnapped Indians as domestic servants in the plantation mansions. Just as the narrator of Behn's *Oroonoko* absents herself from the crucial scenes of torture and dismemberment (lest she be accused of even tacit complicity), so Behn's *Widdow Ranter* is also tacit at the end about the price paid in human oppression in order that Hazard and his class will not have to work and in order that metropolitans can have cheap New World commodities. Both Behn's tragedy and her comedy obscure the reality behind the romance of empire.

7
Dramatic Shifts
Shifting Tropes of Ideology in Revolutionary Tragedy

After the Revolution of 1688, shifting tropes of ideology in the various subgenres of tragedy help to constitute the transformation from an aristocratic, late feudal to a newly dominant bourgeois ideology.[1] By bourgeois I mean those meanings and values associated loosely with the ascension into the old ruling aristocracy of a rising middle class that gained increasing wealth from the end of the Middle Ages into the Modern period and demanded its share of power.

As I see it, the change in ideology, unlike the change in social history, is rather a sudden transformation—what Thomas Kuhn calls a paradigm or Michel Foucault an epistemic shift. It is as if, right up to the Glorious Revolution, an aristocratic force field holds the elements of official discourse together in the drama; afterwards, we can detect a new bourgeois configuration of ideology. New space suddenly seems to open up (some of it literally at Thomas Betterton's breakaway company's digs in Lincoln's Inn Fields in 1695)[2] for ideological production that is not so much reflective of but enabling of political and social change. While histories of literary form have proven particularly fruitful in the analysis of the emerging bourgeois form par excellence, the novel, they have not proven fruitful for the drama, probably because dramatic genres were so well established. Instead, we might fare better by analyzing these ideological configurations in terms of what Fredric Jameson calls ideologemes but which I prefer to call by the more common, more euphonious name of tropes.

Employing useful concepts from Raymond Williams, we can follow tropes that shift from emergent status in the aristocratic era to dominant status in the bourgeois era. While dramatic *genres* remain quite consistent, the tropes within them shift rapidly over the fulcrum of the Glorious Revolution. By representative sampling in the six main genres of English tragedy I have deployed in this book—heroic romance, romantic tragedy, political tragedy, personal tragedy, tragical satire, and tragicomic romance—I should like to trace some key tropes, especially of class and gender, from their emergent status in Restoration drama (1660-88) to their dominant status in Revolutionary (1689-1714) and early Georgian drama. Previous formalistic, teleological analysis, by focusing on wholes more than parts, has obscured what a tropic analysis can reveal. It becomes obvious that, despite their democratic, meritocratic political rhetoric, the plays are exclusionary: they portray the consolidation of power in the hands of a new (male) elite—a power based ostensibly on law but really on the sword and the gun. And their neostoic exemplary morality masks oligarchic male dominance over gender, class, and even race. Developing social contract theory, which underlay the bourgeois revolution in England and later in America, actually meant in practice, as these plays despite their inculcation of the new ideology unwittingly reveal, that only a few (good) men are created equal.

Heroic Romance

If the heroic play par excellence of the Restoration, Dryden's *Conquest of Granada* (1670-71), essentially reaffirms Royalist ideology, most intriguing is how Dryden invests so much of the play's energy into two anarchic characters, Almanzor, the "noble Savage" (1.I.i.209), who owes allegiance to no power, and Lyndaraxa, the seductive ambitious woman, who would be queen no matter who wears the crown. Michael McKeon's analysis of Leonidas in Dryden's *Marriage A-la-Mode* (155) also applies to Almanzor. Following the typical romance plot, Almanzor discovers his royal lineage and kneels to his cousin-sovereign. Nonetheless, he also articulates a radical individualism ("I alone am King of me" [1.I.i.206]) that claims for the savage a new kind of nobility based on merit. Moreover, Almanzor's discovery of his lineage is complicated by his origins as a love child. The king's sister secretly married beneath her status. She and her husband, the duke of Arcos, were forced into exile, and she died in childbirth. They were thus rebels against the strict control of the patrilineal system, especially in the royal family. The princess's death can be read as a condign retribution for such a crime against status. And Almanzor's relegation to the role of a subject can also be seen as a consequence of that crime. Furthermore, as the most attractive and most powerful agent in the play, for the ideological intentionality of the play to work he must be won from fluctuating allegiances and socialized into the service of legitimate power, lending his powerful phallic sword to the growing imperialism of Spain's "Conqu'ring Crosses" (2.V.iii.346). By the end, then, the dominant class ideology subsumes the emergent trope of the bourgeois self-made man. But can we forget it?[3]

Something similar occurs with Lyndaraxa. Characterized as enormously seductive and ambitious, she transcends the normal stereotype in these plays through her brilliant and attractive wit. Observe the way she verbally toys with her suitors, Abdelmelech and Abdalla. At the end she suffers her own condign punishment: killed at the moment of her apparent triumph by a cast suitor who knows her evil wiles, she is finally troped into the figure of the uppity woman put in her place by the phallic sword of gender dominance. Yet does she not also represent an emergent figure that will not go away forever?[4]

In other words, we might see *The Conquest of Granada* as a play that allows the genie of emergent bourgeois ideology, particularly concerning the class status of men and the gender status of women, to strut and fret on the stage until charmed back into the lamp. Is there any significance to the contrast between Almanzor's being socialized and Lyndaraxa's being so harshly punished? Perhaps one could speculate that English society was more prepared to embrace the bourgeois trope of the self-made man than it was that of the self-made woman. Meanwhile, the romance form attempts to contain emergent male individualism by enlisting it in the service of imperialism just as Dryden's *Annus Mirabilis* attempted to co-opt rebellious London into a joint venture for a world emporium.[5]

In the 1690s the best of the heroic romances, William Congreve's *Mourning Bride* (LIF 1697), focused its energy on negotiating the lingering problem of Oedipal rebellion inherent in patriarchy and in the Revolution itself. The tyrant of Granada, King Manuel, is accidentally killed by his loyal general, who is also the ambitious statesman Gonsalez. The Oedipal significance is manifested by the subsequent beheading of the corpse—an image sure to recall Charles I—and by Gonsalez's begging his son, Garcia,

> On me, on me, turn your avenging Sword.
> I who have spilt my Royal Master's Blood,
> Should make atonement by a Death as horrid;
> And fall beneath the Hand of my own Son. [V.ii.69-72]

The succession of the prince of Valencia, who became king upon his father's death and married Manuel's daughter, leaves Granada free from Oedipal taint. The ratification of his choice by a people who have rebelled to claim their "Liberty / And Native Rights" (III.i.71-72) marks a legitimacy that is no longer strictly hereditary but elective, constitutional, bourgeois.

By the time of Rowe's *Tamerlane* (LIF 1701), the most popular heroic romance of the eighteenth century, at least Almanzor's male genie was out of the bottle for good. Previous critics have read the play as a political allegory, attempting to identify characters as prominent persons, from Tamerlane as William III and Bajazet as Louis XIV on down.[6] John Loftis goes further, reading the play as "war-inspired Francophobia" at the beginning of the War of the Spanish Succession and Whig propaganda for Lockeian constitutional theory (*Politics* 32-34). Susan Staves (107-9) reads *Tamerlane* as "democratic romance" but focuses on the single trope of reduced authority for sovereigns. Laura Brown (151) reads it as "the direct embodiment of the bourgeois ideals of the Glorious Revolution" but limits her treatment to the contrast between "Herculean" and "exemplary" hero. The figure of Tamerlane is important but not so much in isolation as in his connection to a network of ideological tropes.

Tamerlane indeed portrays the ideal bourgeois leader, the constitutional monarch, *primus inter pares,* contrasted with his class antithesis, the absolutist monarch Bajazet, whom the new ideology portrays as a runaway autocrat bound by no laws, human or divine. The emergent bourgeois political model is fraternal rather than paternal. Bajazet mocks Tamerlane's dependence upon the advice and consent of "debating Senates," with whom he shares "a precarious Scepter" (II.ii, 24).[7] In the prologue Rowe underlines this bourgeois appropriation of the Roman model of government. When Tamerlane is roused to war against the tyrant, Rowe anachronistically narrates,

> *The peaceful Fathers, who in Senates meet,*
> *Approve an Enterprize so Just, so Great;*
> *While with their Prince's Arms, their Voice thus join'd,*
> *Gains half the Praise of having sav'd Mankind.*

In other words, like the new bourgeois political theorists, Rowe makes Parliament a supposedly equal partner with the king, though the latter's "Scepter" now depends upon the former's will.

Loftis plus Staves plus Brown will take the interpretation this far. But the figure of Tamerlane is part of a larger pattern. Rowe suggests that meritocracy has supplanted aristocracy. Tamerlane's followers insist that "had not Nature made him Great by Birth, / Yet all the Brave had sought him for their Friend" (I.i, 2). When accused by Bajazet of "vile Obscurity," Axalla, who has come to court Bajazet's daughter as well as peace, scorns to "borrow Merit from the Dead" by citing his Roman lineage but asserts instead "that inborn Merit, / That Worth" of his own "Virtue" which distinguishes him. Besides, the most salient feature of those "Heroes, and God-like Patriots" among his ancestors is that they "Scorn'd to be Kings" (III.i, 40).

Of course, Tamerlane and Axalla may indulge themselves in this republican rhetoric, for they both indeed were born great. Moreover, meritocracy remains a system essentially *between men* (to borrow a key concept from Eve Sedgwick). What further complicates the democracy of this romance is the gender politics of its subplot, the tragic story of Moneses and Arpasia, Greek lovers whose solemn betrothal has been ruptured by Bajazet, who has forced Arpasia into marriage with him. When Moneses appeals to Tamerlane, in effect, to annul the forced marriage and reinstate the prior vows, Tamerlane is as absolute as a legislature or tribunal of men refusing to allow an abortion after rape: "[W]ould'st thou have my partial Friendship break / That holy Knot, which ty'd once, all Mankind / Agree to hold Sacred, and Undissolvable?" "All Mankind" has established a system of genealogical control in which woman is nothing more than an incubator, and bourgeois ideology upholds this patriarchal sentiment. Tamerlane enjoins Moneses to "cure this amorous Sickness of thy Soul" and engage with him in the "manly" art of conquering war: "Nor will I lose thee poorly for a Woman" (III.ii, 50-51). Meanwhile, Arpasia is allowed divorce only in her sleep with its song-induced dream. As with Lyndaraxa, women are not allowed full participation in the new order. They are confined to chambers while the men engage in a displaced version of Britain's new imperialism under King Billy and his wars. The providential rhetoric of the play insists that bourgeois right now makes might. Bajazet's own daughter may rebel against her father's tyranny and aid the juster side, but the real agency of power remains the phallic sword installing and expanding oligarchic male dominance.

A new ethic shrouds the naked point of this political sword, neostoicism. Rowe focuses on the master trope of the bourgeois era, self-reliance. Tamerlane stands fixed on his own firm center (the figures of Marlborough, Nelson, and Wellington are merely his avatars). Rowe complicates the focus with the heartrending emotions of the subplot, but finally, when Arpasia is forced to watch Moneses's strangulation, she too becomes a figure for self-reliance as Rowe appropriates the aristocratic trope of constancy and changes its emphasis from constancy or fidelity to a person to constancy of mind. Yet like the martial arts, this, too, is manly activity: Arpasia must overcome the "Woman" in her "Soul" (IV.i, 63) and endure this "Tryal" of her resolve (V.i, 73). She does, then dies from the strain, confident that she and Moneses will be united in an afterlife. At the end of the play, Bajazet, confined to his cage as an exemplum, has been defeated by those who stand fixed on the firm center of self-control as opposed to those who yield to lawless passion, now a trope for the decadent aristocracy. But the new ethic remains patriarchal, between men, and is enforced by a still quite patriarchal god.

From Delariviere Manley, author not only of notorious attacks on prominent (male) Whigs that incurred the wrath of the government (and

Alexander Pope) but also of several numbers of the *Examiner* that earned her temporary coeditorship with Jonathan Swift, one might have expected a more enlightened treatment of gender in her late heroic play, *Lucius, the First Christian King of Britain* (1717). Indeed, Jack Armistead and Debbie Davis, editors of a recent facsimile edition, maintain that the heroine, Rosalinda, erstwhile queen of Aquitaine and future queen of Britain and Albany (here, Scotland), is a "crucial feminine agent" (iii). They mean that, as the object of what René Girard would call mimetic desire among warring rivals, as the cause of Lucius's killing the usurper of his own throne, and as the converter of Lucius to Christianity, she is responsible for the transmission of Christian authority in England from pope to monarch—a version of history that helps constitute and reinforce early eighteenth-century Tory ideology (vi-vii).

I shall return to this putative Tory ideology in a moment. Let me first examine Rosalinda's putative agency. As the *object* of mimetic desire, she can hardly be said to be an *agent.* Only as the passive object of Lucius's desire, about to be raped by the executioner (really the usurper Vortimer in disguise), does she *cause* Vortimer's death. She does convert Lucius to Christianity, but that action occurs before the play and results in their death sentence by the pagan Gauls. We can infer only from the play's title the kind of implication for British history that Armistead and Davis claim: there is no explicit reference in the text to the future Christian reign of Lucius and Rosalinda.

Within the play, however, Rosalinda exercises agency in a very important action ignored by Armistead and Davis. Although a recent widow to the rebel king of Aquitaine, she obtains her freedom from Honorius, the Gallic king, defies conventional mourning, chooses Lucius as her new consort, and marries him clandestinely. Moreover, she doubly defies convention by marrying the son of Vortimer, the man who murdered her father, the king of Albany, and then waged war against her first husband. Vortimer now desires her as the victor's spoils. Rosalinda lives to triumph with her new husband over that lawless renegade and over her scheming cousin, Arminius, who is also willing to violate all codes of honor to possess her and thus possess double power as the new king of Albany married to its heir presumptive.

Such successful agency is rare indeed in English tragedy. Witness what happens to the duchess of Malfi or Almeyda in Dryden's *Don Sebastian* or to Almanzor's mother or Felicia in Catharine Trotter's *Fatal Friendship* (see below) when they attempt clandestine marriages to men of their choosing. Witness the painful resistance to such a marriage by Dryden's Maiden Queen in the play of that subtitle. Even in comedy, where feisty women often marry behind the backs of male protectors, those protectors are almost invariably brought to bless the marriages at the end. No real (class) rebellion takes place. Rosalinda needs and gets no one's blessing. At the end she is queen of Albany, married to the king of Britain—an ending we may view as more an emblem of England's current union with Scotland than any Tory myth of historical origins. Note, however, the implicit superiority, despite Rosalinda's agency, of Lucius over her, England over a feminized Scotland.

More probable than reading the play as a myth of origins is reading it as Jacobite allegory.[8] But if *Lucius* is Jacobite propaganda written during The Fifteen, there are problems with its Tory ideology. First, the trope of kingship. Vortimer sounds like Bajazet when he characterizes Honorius as an inept king, hamstrung by his people despite his desire to void the death sentences of Lucius and Rosalinda:

> The Coward *Gaul,* durst not release the *Christians,*
> Durst not command, ev'n in his Capital,
> Lest his good People shou'd, forsooth, grow angry.
> We laugh'd to see the Royal Dastard's Fears;
> Whilst, by our seeming Zeal, and Gold well-plac'd,
> We gain'd a Sentence hateful to their King. [V.i, 49]

Vortimer is vile, and we are invited to see the Gallic people, through their institutions of religion and justice, as corrupt or corruptible—like an English Parliament that twice in one century would remove a legitimate king from his throne. But Vortimer is wrong about Honorius, for he sends troops, under Lucius's uncle, prince of Cambria (Wales), to rescue the condemned despite his people's decree. Obviously, though no explicit mention of it is made, the decree is set at nought at the end, and Lucius and Rosalinda are free to return to England to be the co-sovereigns of a united Great Britain.

Does Manley here offer the image of a king not fettered by Parliament, one who could act independently and forcefully for the good of his people? If so, how would such a ruler escape the Whig accusation of *arbitrary,* especially when Honorius appears to have suspended the laws and institutions of his country, particularly its religion? Moreover, Honorius's intentions are contaminated by his manipulation throughout the play by his sister, Emmelin, who is activated by no higher motive than her desire to have Lucius for herself. If Manley intended to provide a positive Tory alternative image of kingship, she failed.

Second, the trope of restored king. Even though Lucius does not know the rapist executioner is his father, even though he constantly defers to his father in filial piety and refuses to fight him in rivalry for Rosalinda, and even though we discover after he kills him that Vortimer is not his real father and that Lucius has avenged his real father's death at Vortimer's hands, nevertheless the play portrays Oedipal parricide. The audience is forced to experience—and to secretly applaud—the killing *as* parricide, discovering the truth only afterward. Whatever her intention, it is as if Manley is not allowed refuge in myth but is forced to acknowledge history: whether she and the Tories like it or not, succession in England had often been parricidal, and not even a return to the Stuarts could expunge the blot on the escutcheon.

Moreover, the approving experience of parricide in the play works to legitimate de facto succession. It is as if the audience is invited to say, "All our theorizing about legitimate succession notwithstanding, whether aristocratic or bourgeois, this is our history; we are heirs of the success of its usurpations and regicides. Behind any ideology of legitimacy lurks naked power." Unlike Nat Lee in *Lucius Junius Brutus,* then, or Congreve in *The Mourning Bride,* Manley attempts not to finesse the Oedipal crisis inherent in monarchy but to confront and absorb it.

Romantic Tragedy

After the Revolution, romantic tragedy continued to pit Machiavels against the innocent, but the trope is appropriated now to the service of the new order. Most noteworthy perhaps is Rowe's *Ambitious Step-Mother* (LIF 1700), where the legitimate heir to the throne is finally no match for the evil unleashed by the title character and commits suicide in despair, leaving the throne to the stepbrother after all, a man of *virtù* as well as virtue, thus underwriting if not William III's claim to the throne at least the Miltonic ethos of rule by merit.

More interesting is the variation on the trope of incest in two remarkable romantic tragedies, both dating from 1698 (one performed, one written then): Robert Gould's *Innocence Distress'd; or, The Royal Penitents* and the anonymous *Fatal Discovery; or, Love in Ruines.*[9] Both confront not the parricide of the Oedipal crisis but the maternal incest. They are themselves anticipated by Dryden and Lee's *Oedipus,* first performed in 1678, and apparently successfully revived in 1692 and 1696 (Dryden, *Works* 13:446-47). The California editors point out that Gould thought highly of that play (449). It is not surprising that Dryden and Lee's play would have appealed to the authors of the Mysterious Mother plays of 1698, for unlike its predecessor versions in Sophocles, Seneca, and Corneille, it gives expression to erotic incestuous desire. Though blinded, Dryden and Lee's Oedipus hubristically maintains innocence and steals into the arms of a shattered Jocasta, who not only receives her son's advances (until the ghost of Laius frightens the incestuous pair apart), but earlier, more surprisingly expresses continuing erotic desire even though she suspects and tries to stifle the emerging truth:

> Once more, by the Gods,
> I beg, my *Oedipus,* my Lord, my Life,
> My love, my all, my only utmost hope,
> I beg you banish *Phorbas* [the Theban shepherd who knows the truth].
> [IV.i.401-4]

Innocence Distress'd and *The Fatal Discovery* both greatly embellish this erotic desire, but that *Oedipus* influenced both is probable, especially the latter in the duchess's madness and the appearance of the ghost of her husband to forbid valedictory embraces.

Today the best known of the many versions of this story, as it probably was in the late seventeenth century, thanks to a 1654 English translation, is Marguerite de Navarre's thirtieth tale of her *Heptaméron* (1559), in which a prudish widow substitutes herself for her son's paramour and conceives a child, whom the son later marries. What is especially interesting about the late-medieval story is its cryptic expression of feminine desire. Consciously intending to teach her sixteen-year-old son a lesson about sexual restraint, which has been part of his rigorous upbringing, the mother waits so long to be sure of her son's intention, supposedly with her maid of honor, that, as the accurate 1654 translation puts it,

> her patience was so strong, and her Nature so frail, that forgetting the Name of a Mother, she converted her choler into an abominable pleasure. And as the water by force retained, doth run with a greater impetuousnesse when way is made for it, than when it runneth in its ordinary course, so this poor Lady did forfeit her glory by the restraint which she did give unto her self: For when she began to descend from the first degree of her honesty, she found herself suddenly transported to the last, and she herself was great with child by him whom she watched to keep another from running into the same enormity with him.[10]

This would appear to be an Oedipal story with the emphasis on a Jocasta conscious of the incest and coming to desire it. But the Christian ending, where the mother's confessor, the papal legate of Avignon himself, advises her to let the father-daughter / brother-sister couple live in blissful ignorance, is radically different from the Greek: in the one the incest exists and effects a terrible curse on the land until acknowledged; in the other the second incest does not exist because it is unintentional and therefore no sin.

In *Rape and Writing in the Heptaméron of Marguerite de Navarre,* Patricia Francis Cholakian has deftly argued how complicated is this portrayal of desire, for it is refracted through a male narrator who wants to justify his own Oedipal impulses by making the initiative for mother-son incest originate with the mother. Cholakian sees the Christian ending of the story as evidence of a shift from the male narrator's voice to that of the female writer, who is therefore seen as underwriting the agency and power of (what Kristeva would call) a phallic mother (144-57). That is, despite her penitence, the mother is seen as enabling an Edenic existence for the young couple in the absence of the Law of the Father. Ignorant incest is blest, and, unlike the Classical world of Sophocles and Seneca, Marguerite's Christian world needs no violent purgation.[11]

I shall return to Kristeva and the phallic mother in a moment. Let me in the meantime survey the treatment of this story in the Revolutionary romantic tragedies under discussion. The first thing to note is that in neither of them is incest blest. In both the young couple is not allowed to live in blissful ignorance but is killed, and the mother makes a horrifying public manifestation of her crime. In *Innocence Distress'd* she poisons the youngsters and herself to expurgate the world of this terrible double incest. In *The Fatal Discovery,* having gone mad, she stabs the bride. In both the mother apparently descends into hell. I should like to read Gould's play against Cholakian's reading of Marguerite de Navarre's tale. Like Hircan, Marguerite's male narrator, Gould is a misogynist who is preoccupied with the threat of feminine desire. I should like to read both plays in the light of Kristeva's theory of the persistent reemergence of the figure of mother as other. Because we do not know with certainty who wrote it, or therefore the gender of the author, *The Fatal Discovery*'s portrayal of feminine desire is more problematic and thus more interesting, finally, than that of *Innocence Distress'd.*

The action of Gould's play focuses for four acts on the mother's attempts to avert the double incest of the marriage of her children. The setting has been moved from France to Moscow, and she is now the dowager duchess, her son having reached maturity and assumed the dukedom. When her efforts fail and the couple are clandestinely married, the duchess administers poison to them in a desperate attempt to preclude consummation. Only when informed that the newlyweds have been laid in bed does the duchess confess her story to Seraphana, the maid of honor whose place she took with her son. To the young duke's uncle, Berino (the Creon of the play), Seraphana repeats the duchess's narrative, a narrative that reveals feminine desire as her unintentional but conscious motivation:

> The fatal Hour arriv'd: The Dutchess plac'd
> Her self there to receive him, with Intent
> To reprimand him sharply on Conviction,
> For such licentious Courses. Thus, expecting
> His coming long, (as she but now inform'd me)
> Light Fancies touch'd her Breast, a Warmth succeeded,
> Which, by insensible Degrees, at last
> Ripen'd into Desire.—Here the Duke
> Ent'ring, and taking her for me, seiz'd on her,
> With many an eager Kiss; while she, unable
> To speak, or to resist,
> Permitted him to ruin her for ever! [V, 57]

Such conscious desire of a mother for a son has seemed so horrible in ancient and modern Western culture as rarely to be portrayed (the Middle Ages apparently are an exception[12]). But as we can tell from what one critic calls his "she-satires" (Sloane 92-98), Gould was preoccupied with conscious feminine desire. Gould's preoccupation with female depravity, as Felicity Nussbaum has best shown in *The Brink of All We Hate,* reveals male inferiority in the face of female reproductive power.

In *Powers of Horror* Julia Kristeva writes, "Fear of the archaic mother turns out to be essentially fear of her generative power" (77). Within patriarchal cultures, Kristeva explains, rituals and taboos reveal

> everywhere the importance, both social and symbolic, of women and particularly the mother. In societies where it occurs, ritualization of defilement is accompanied by a strong concern for separating the sexes, and this means giving men rights over women. The latter, apparently put in the position of passive objects, are none the less felt to be wily powers, "baleful schemers" from whom rightful beneficiaries must protect themselves. It is as if, lacking a central authoritarian power that would settle the definitive supremacy of one sex—or lacking a legal establishment that would balance the prerogatives of both sexes—two powers attempted to share out society. One of them, the masculine, apparently victorious, confesses through its very relentlessness against the other, the feminine, that it is threatened by an asymmetrical, irrational, wily, uncontrollable power. . . . That other sex, the feminine, becomes synonymous with a radical evil that is to be suppressed. [70]

The ultimate figure for this threat is the phallic mother, the mother who assumes power outside the Law of the Father, such as the duchess in the *Heptaméron* who reappears in Gould's play.

Unlike Hircan's, Gould's misogyny is not tempered by any other, feminine voice in his play. The import of the ending is that the young couple, their *innocence distressed,* will mix in heaven without sin, but the daughter-sister-bride is properly fearful and *dangereuse* when the duke approaches her for a parting kiss (63). Moreover, the play closes focusing on the duchess's sin, as Berino announces the moral:

> This Night we'll give to Grief.—And may this be
> A Warning to us, sink into our Minds,
> And have its full Effect, in bringing forth
> A strong Abhorrence of all foul Desires;
> That vicious Actions never may take Root;
> For if we so will plant,—behold the Fruit!
> [*The Curtain falls*] [V, 65]

Unlike Marguerite de Navarre's novella, Gould's play vigorously reinforces patriarchal suppression of mother as other, for her desires turn so readily "foul" and plant evil "Fruit" that threatens to supplant family trees. The portrait of female desire in Gould's play never escapes being written by a man, a renowned misogynist.

The Fatal Discovery is less misogynistic. The initial incest results from the mother's attempt to reclaim her wayward husband, this time an Italian aristocrat, with a bed-trick, only to discover that she accidentally substituted herself for her son's and not her husband's paramour. But while she is penitent and warns other women to suffer their husbands' affairs rather than try to reclaim them, she reveals that it was also her desire that got her into trouble: "I wanted nothing but a wanton Love" (I, 2). She secretly desired the erotic love her husband enjoyed. Did she also secretly desire an erotic incestuous relationship with her son? Such mistakes as hers Freud would characterize as unconsciously intentional.

We soon discover that this mother is in an abject condition, teetering on the border between patriarchal morality and an unconscious state of mind that reveals transgressive desire. When her son returns to court after fifteen years of banishment by his mother to conceal her sin and its resultant pregnancy, she faints at his approach, then wakes to embrace him, saying distractedly,

> [I]t is not sure a fault to Kiss him now, nor to Embrace him is it? speak all, I wou'd not willingly commit a crime, I never did a wilfull one indeed, and hope all I can do that's kind, and all I have done will not meet a Censure. [II, 11]

A little more than kin and less than kind? At this point in the play, only her handmaid, Arapsia, who first suggested the bed-trick, could possibly know what the duchess is talking about.

Meanwhile, the son, Cornaro, falls in love with his sister-daughter, Eromena, who has been raised as her mother's ward, and the mother grows more distracted, wishing to be punished by a god from whom she cannot hope forgiveness (IV, 31). In order to keep the young couple apart, Arapsia tells Cornaro first that Eromena is his sister. In patriarchal defense of his father's memory, Cornaro leaps to the conclusion that she must then be his mother's bastard. Arapsia is forced to reveal the whole truth that Eromena is Cornaro's daughter as well. Cornaro, clandestinely wedded and bedded with Eromena, frantically confronts his mother to demand the truth. Again she faints, convincing him of her infamy, then raves when she awakes, revealing her repressed desire:

> Stand off, I say, I am *Cornaro*'s Wife,
> Let me run to him, how does my dearest Son?
> What Wife and Mother? that was a mistake:
> Give me a draught of poison presently. [V, 43]

Her Freudian slip has exposed her. The desire to poison herself, like Phédre's, is a trope for guilt over runaway passion. Returning to the stage while Cornaro is trying to explain what has happened to the as yet ignorant Eromena, the mother, like Phédre, madly confuses husband and son and protests that what she did that fatal night was for his love. But whose love is the question. Then, growing insanely jealous of Eromena in the arms of her husband/son, the duchess stabs her.

Eromena's suitor, Segerdo, thinks Cornaro has killed her and fights with him, wounding him mortally. His mother reenters and utters lines that reveal how abjectly torn she is:

> What, my Son, art thou a dying too?
> Why, what should we live for, to be the jest
> Of every fool that had a mind to laugh;
> Wou'd it not make the cruel laugh to see this bloody Floor,
> This blood shed, but for one nights mischance?
> Oh! 'twas a Glorious night, Say, was it not!
> Speak, can you repent of it, I am sure I do? [V, 48]

The question mark that ends this line is a kind of stage direction for the actress to make the last statement ambiguous. She has, after all, by another Freudian slip, celebrated instead of deplored the fatal night when she committed incest with her own son.

When bystanders try to get her into bed, the duchess raves again, as she lies on the floor with her son:

> No, no, no more of Beds.———————
> May I not hug him now—Dear, dear *Cornaro,*
> Let me dye in thy Arms———————. [49]

At this point, as in the Dryden-Lee *Oedipus,* the superego, the Law of the Father, reasserts itself in the form of her husband's ghost, who appears before her distracted mind each time she slips into desire:

> Ha! see, see, there's my Husband come
> To blast my Eyes, and curse me for the Birth of *Eromena.*
> What, is she dead; Why, what need we dye then:
> The cause is now removed——————— Why, what are you
> That dare to contradict me, and say I must not live,
> Nor poor *Cornaro!* ha, Husband again!
> Why do you force me to you; had you been kind alive,
> This had not been—Why do you tear me thus,
> You torturing Spirits; I come, I come!—
> Off all, to make my body bare for suffering—
> So, now 'tis well—Pull, pull—Give me
> Thy hand, *Cornaro,* and we will go together,
> Nothing now shall part us—Open thy Sulph'rous
> And Eternal Mansion, receive us both,
> [W]e sink together now———————
> *Lost in a hopeless state, behold we come,*
> *Thou must receive us, for Heaven has no room.* [49]

The duchess's denudification, whatever her conscious intention of preparing herself for punishment (and whatever stage convention would actually allow), is her last, extraordinary expression of naked sexual desire. She even justifies herself before her husband by accusing him of sexual neglect. She envisions herself and her son in a dark, perverse inversion of Milton's Adam and Eve leaving Paradise hand in hand.

Despite the fact that Cornaro blames himself for disobeying his mother and marrying clandestinely, it appears at the end that he will not accompany his mother to hell, for the Fortinbras who establishes order at the end predicts a heavenly reward for Cornaro. Cornaro's escape from eternal punishment, however, does not represent the same kind of feminine intervention as at the end of Marguerite de Navarre's and Bandello's novellae. Not only is the wicked mother sent to hell but the innocent Eromena is not even mentioned. This neglect, this privileging of the son would seem to be a reinsantiation of the Law of the Father—at least with regard to feminine desire: mother punished for all eternity; daughter-wife dead, silent, absent; son blessed.

On the other hand, *The Fatal Discovery* has a farcical subplot in which a wife, Margaretta, teaches her jealous husband, Dandalo, the lesson that she could commit adultery if she wanted, and—shades of *The Wife of Bath's Tale*—he surrenders sovereignty to her. She thus gains the "liberty" she has sought throughout, "an *English* Freedom of the Wives there" (I, 4). Having gained it, she chooses not to exercise it and, like Chaucer's wife with her fifth husband, demonstrates that she wants not sovereignty but mutual respect.

The comic subplot calls attention to its connection with the main plot, for Dandalo dresses up as a woman to substitute himself for Margaretta in her assignation with her supposed lover, Captain Conall. Folk humor mixes with folk justice in a hilarious bedroom scene where Dandalo is tousled to the brink of being raped. Patriarchal dominance is thus subverted, inverted; the male is placed in the position of the female. The subplot thus tempers the misogyny of the main, where male promiscuity, because it operates on a double standard that denies women their own desire by repressing/oppressing it as evil, has disastrous consequences in the incestuous return of the repressed. By invoking the possibility of the wife's conjugal infidelity, the subplot of *The Fatal Discovery* reminds the audience of what Kristeva would call the Authority of the Mother (73)—that is, woman's real power not only to reproduce but to control paternity. That the comic wife, Margaretta, chooses not to exercise that authority perhaps suggests that the play's author is less unstable, less threatened than Gould, less insistent on the triumph of the masculine over the feminine. For the playwright to have portrayed the wife successfully committing adultery would merely have made her another slut of patriarchal ideology. Though Captain Conall enjoys the sauce of resistance, he, like Gould, believes "*no Woman but in time must yield*" (II, 16); his wife, however, does not yield to him. Derek Hughes believes that the wife achieves "[f]emale dominance . . . through the sacrifice of female sexuality" because her dotard husband is not a suitable sexual partner (440). Too often female sexual rebels remain tropes in a patriarchal discourse, a de Sadean rhetoric of desire that sees liberty only in terms of eroticism. This wife eschews that role.[13]

Given the mitigating effect of *The Fatal Discovery*'s subplot on its misogyny, it is tempting to speculate that the play's author may have been a woman imagining a revolutionary form of resistance. If Kristeva is right that, synchronically, cultures with unstable gender differentiation have a need for more vigorous rituals of defilement, could it be that, diachronically, periods in history where such foundational differentiation is threatened might also produce such rituals—or in more developed societies, literature that performs the same cultural function? I leave it to medievalists to speculate whether the High Middle Ages was such a period. As a

Restoration scholar, I am interested in why both these plays were written circa 1698 (Gould's wasn't published for some forty years). If the bourgeois revolution in England removed direct patrilineal descent from the transmission of political power, was it not free to remove such descent from the inheritance of property? Kristeva writes, "It is . . . not surprising to see pollution rituals proliferating in societies where patrilineal power is poorly secured, as if the latter sought, by means of purification, a support against excessive matrilineality" (77). Mary Stuart had replaced her father on the throne. She was dead by 1694, and a nonlineal king sat on the throne, with another woman waiting in the wings. This at the end of the century in which Levellers had wanted to abolish not just hierarchy but inheritance and in which uppity women from Margaret Fell to Mary Astell were agitating for women's rights. Were these plays written to be "a support against excessive matrilineality," most heinously expressed in a mother's erotic desire for her own son? If so, *The Fatal Discovery* represents a compromise in the ritual battle between the sexes Kristeva so provocatively analyzes—a more equitable sharing out of society, a tempering of the misogynistic bugbear. The tempering is ever so slight, however. Ultimately, patriarchy is preserved intact for the emergent bourgeois order through these romantic tragedies of incestuous defilement.

Political Tragedy

In the midst of Royalism's last dramatic stand emerges from Milton's *Samson Agonistes* and Lee's *Lucius Junius Brutus* the figure of the One Just Man at least morally triumphant over his enemies. Both Samson and Brutus promise new orders that are themselves, ironically, restorations. The Hebrews are delivered from an oppressor and returned to the government of the virtuous elect under God's law. Brutus rescues Rome from monarchy and returns it to its republican origins and to the rule of man's law. The trope undergoes signal development in the hands of Revolutionary playwrights especially as the Glorious Revolution approached the counterrevolution known as The Fifteen. In other words, just as political tragedy flourished as England approached the Exclusion Crisis, so it flourished again as England approached another crisis of succession at the imminent death of Anne Stuart. Three excellent plays of this new crisis deploy the trope of stoic resistance—to different ends.

Joseph Addison's *Cato* (1713) was the most popular political tragedy of the eighteenth century and remains the best-known example of the paradigm shift from the feudal master trope of word-as-bond to the bourgeois master trope of self-reliance. It appropriates the aristocratic language of loyalty, though Cato's loyalty is not to an individual but to Rome, to the *patria,* or as Cato puts it throughout, thus transforming a bogeyword of the Royalists into an honorific term, to the *commonwealth.* The older aristocratic loyalty to a person is portrayed as leading all too often not to bonds but to bondage. As in *Tamerlane* the proper form of social organization is fraternal; the proper body to govern, the Senate (read Parliament). And though constancy of lovers is still important, the main constancy the play celebrates is that of mind. Cato remains true to himself and dies the One Just Man. He becomes the prototype for a series of republican patriotic heroes who regret that "we can die but once to serve our country!" (IV.iv.82; see Loftis, *Politics* 44).

In the subplot concerning Cato's children and their lovers, the trope of neostoic constancy of mind is doubled. Cato's passionate son's liabilities would, in Restoration drama, have recommended him. Lucia, beloved of both brothers, describes him to the self-controlled Portius thus:

> Marcus is over-warm: his fond complaints
> Have so much earnestness and passion in them,
> I hear him with a secret kind of dread,
> And tremble at his vehemence of temper. [I.vi.49-52]

But Lucia is not only won by the new man of reason and control. She must also overcome her "own weak sex" (I.vi.22) and imitate Cato's daughter, who in emulation of the great self-reliant hero "tow'rs above her sex" (I.iv.147). She makes a sacred vow not to "mix plighted hands" with Portius until the storm above them—Caesar's impending defeat of Cato, Marcus's rash pursuit of her—clears (III.ii.31-36). Though she feels "the woman breaking in upon" her (48), she successfully resists it, regains stoic composure, and recalls Portius to his self-control as well. Later, she needs to help Marcia rely on her "wonted strength and constancy of mind" when Marcia believes her lover, Juba, prince of Numidia, from whom she has stoically hidden signs of her affection in these troubled times, to be dead (IV.iii.14).

The problem with this portrayal of female as well as male stoic self-control is that, like Rowe's Arpasia, these women must transcend the inherent *weakness* of their gender and become, like Pope's idealized portrait of Martha Blount in *To a Lady,* little men. Behind such a trope of masculinized women lies latent misogyny. Even more striking is how this passive acceptance of gender inferiority parallels Juba's active embrace of racial inferiority and deference to Rome's (read Europe's) racial and cultural superiority. Even when Juba believes he is positively describing the potential African contribution to Cato's cause, he employs metaphors of barbarism and demonic blackness that are the traditional European tropes for African inferiority:

> Did they know Cato, our remotest kings
> Would pour embattled multitudes about him;
> Their swarthy hosts would darken all our plains,
> Doubling the native horror of the war,
> And making death more grim. [II.iv.36-40]

But when he admonishes his old counselor, Syphax, for his views of Numidian martial assets, Juba articulates the rationale for European colonial and cultural imperialism, emerging now from subtext to maintext in this mainstream play:

> These all are virtues of a meaner rank,
> Perfections that are placed in bones and nerves.
> A Roman soul is bent on higher views:
> To civilize the rude, unpolished world,
> And lay it under the restraint of laws;
> To make man mild and sociable to man;
> To cultivate the wild, licentious savage
> With wisdom, discipline, and lib'ral arts—
> Th'embellishments of life; virtues like these
> Make human nature shine, reform the soul,
> And break our fierce barbarians into men. [I.iv.28-38]

In language Frantz Fanon would bitterly understand (*Black Skin, White Masks*), Juba rejoices in his ability to emulate the European patriarch: in order to become worthy of his daughter, Juba pledges to Marcia, "I'll gaze forever on thy godlike father, / Transplanting, one by one, into my life, / His bright perfections, till I shine like him" (I.v.19-21). Unfortunately, no matter what white mask, his skin will always shine black. Addison's political tragedy is tragically unaware of the *liberty,* that Whig keyword touted throughout, it denies to supposedly inferior race and gender in its celebration of the triumph of bourgeois ideology.

Nicholas Rowe's *Tragedy of Jane Shore* (1714) rivaled *Cato* in immediate popularity and surpassed it in endurance on the English stage. Though a play filled with tropes of the new bourgeois order, it had a topical political relevance to the problem of succession and may well have given aid and comfort to the Jacobites. The historical Jane Shore was married to a gold merchant in London when she was espied, courted, and carried off by King Edward IV. She remained at court as Edward's mistress until he died, the point at which Rowe's play takes up the action. Edward's brother, the infamous Richard, duke of Gloucester, wants to usurp the succession from Edward's infant sons, the eldest of whom was Edward V. In order to do so he needs the support of sufficient powerful barons, among them Lord Hastings, a member of his Council. Richard's equally infamous advisers Ratcliffe and Catesby (known popularly as the Rat and the Cat) counsel him to employ Hastings's new mistress, Jane Shore, to manage him, since she is totally dependent now on Richard's bounty.

Jane is Hastings's mistress only in his desire, however. Rowe portrays her as thoroughly penitent for her transgressive behavior, and when Hastings believes he has secured Jane's position at court and comes in the middle of the night to take his reward, she steadfastly refuses him and is rescued from rape by her former husband, disguised as a servant. Jane also resists Richard's tyranny. Betrayed by Hastings's cast mistress, Alicia, she becomes a figure of stoic endurance and is finally reconciled to her husband and her god.

There is a bourgeois component to the figure Jane cuts, obviously. Though she protests that "High-born Beauties of the Court" are far worthier than she (II, 19), the audience witnesses her ability to continue to attract highborn lovers. It also witnesses her heroic dignity and fortitude. All this despite her class, for which Richard and his cohorts demean her. Even more, when Jane's husband stands up to Hastings, and with his sword at that—quite an aristocratic martial art for a goldsmith—Shore boasts, "[N]o gaudy Titles grac'd my Birth, . . . / Yet Heav'n that made me Honest, made me more / Than ever King did, when he made a Lord" (21). After he disarms Hastings, Shore credits his own "inborn Virtue" and triumphantly asks, "[W]here is our difference now? . . . a Lord / Oppos'd against a Man is but a Man" (23).

Yet amidst the drama of Jane's penitent endurance and the bourgeois ethos of the play rises the drama of Hastings's resistance to Richard's tyranny as well. Right in the middle of the play Hastings stands up for the legitimacy of succession, and his action is reported by Catesby to Jane in rhetoric almost Royalist: "[H]e bears a most religious Reverence / To his dead Master *Edward's* Royal Memory" (I.i, 3). Victim of Hastings's near rape the night before, Jane nevertheless exults in his loyalty, and it is her own refusal to "see [Edward's] Children robb'd of Right" (IV, 44) that causes her to be sentenced to public penance in the streets. Jane's and Hastings's defenses of hereditary succession must have seemed, at least to the Jacobites in the audience, as a political warning to those about to ignore the son of their legitimate monarch and seek for "hereditary"

Protestant succession in the ranks of distant cousins in the distant provinces of Germany.

Perhaps trimming after the Hanoverian succession, Rowe in his next play, *Lady Jane Gray* (1715), represents the opposite political position. The play is written during The Fifteen to support the cementing of England's Revolution (see Loftis, *Politics* 79-80). Lady Jane, grandniece to Henry VIII, is as far-fetched an heir to the throne as was George I, but the end—preserving a Protestant succession—justifies the means.

Jane's questions of Northumberland when he offers her the throne contain crucial assumptions of emergent social contract theory:

> Can *Edward*'s Will,
> Or Twenty met in Council, make a Queen?
> . . . [W]here are those . . . who make the Law?
> Where are the Ancient Honours of the Realm,
> The Nobles, with the Mitre'd Fathers join'd?
> The Wealthy Commons solemnly Assembled?
> Where is that Voice of a Consenting People,
> To pledge the Universal Faith with mine,
> And call me justly Queen? [III, 55]

When Northumberland promises Jane that just such Parliamentary approval is forthcoming, she accepts the crown. That no such approval is ever obtained implicitly explains the failure of that particular revolution. But the further implication is that when such approval is obtained (as in 1688 and again in 1715), succession can be altered—and should be in order to avoid the oppressive tyranny of absolute and therefore arbitrary monarchy. The play concludes with prophecies of future heroes (read William III, George I, and his son, the Prince of Wales, to whose wife Rowe dedicated the play) who would finally complete the Protestant Reformation—and the bourgeois revolution—in England.

Of course, one sect's *Book of Martyrs* is another sect's *Book of Heretics,* and while Rowe's play invokes Whig rhetoric of justification—complete with villainous bishops and *Bloody* Mary—obscured is the blood of martyrs on the other side from Thomas More and John Fisher to Charles I to the Irish at the Battle of the Boyne. Once again it is not really a Parliament but an ax that rules.

In addition to its political tropes, the play portrays the bourgeois ethical trope of self-reliance in its manifestations of stoic self-mastery and constancy of mind in adversity, in short, standing firm on the fixed center of one's being, what Lady Jane calls "the settled Quiet of my Soul" (V, 83).

What is remarkable about Rowe's play is that the "Divine Example" (V, 87) is not the typical male (Tamerlane, Cato) but, as in *Jane Shore,* a woman—and in this instance, one in a position of real power. As "A Prologue to *Lady Jane Gray,* sent by an Unknown Hand" (probably Pope's) puts it,

> Nobly to bear the Changes of our State,
> To stand unmov'd against the Storms of Fate,
> A brave Contempt of Life, and Grandeur lost;
> Such glorious Toils a Female Name can boast. [appended, 94]

And the only reference in the text to woman's proverbial weakness is Northumberland's misogynistic complaint, which turns out to be ironic:

> What trivial Influences hold Dominion
> O'er Wise Men's Counsels, and the Fate of Empire?
> The greatest Schemes that human Wit can forge,
> Or bold Ambition dares to put in Practice,
> Depend upon our husbanding a Moment,
> And the light lasting of a Woman's Will. [I, 18]

Stronger than Manley's Rosalinda, Lady Jane manifests the greatest strength of "Will" in the play, constantly teaching others, especially her husband, Guilford, Christian-stoic endurance. Instead of overcoming the woman in her soul (like Arpasia or Lucia or Marcia), Lady Jane boasts that, if she were sure she had legal warrant to be queen, her "Soul . . . could be more than Man, in her [England's] Defence" (III, 54). Appearing at first to accept the crown passively—"Take me, Crown me"—she quickly asserts her own agency, "I take the Lot with Joy" (56). Even the treacherous bishop of Winchester marvels at the "Command" with which Lady Jane awed the court before which she was tried offstage (V, 80). And she finally puts him in his place with two beautifully imperious imperatives: at his self-righteous condemnation of her husband's persistence in his Protestant "heresy" (V, 86), Lady Jane commands, "Cease, thou Raven; / Nor violate, with thy profaner Malice, / My bleeding *Gilford's* Ghost" (V, 89). Finally, when he unctuously attempts to lay the blame for her own death on her stubbornness and proclaims, "Thy Blood be on thy Head," she wonderfully retorts,

> My Blood be where it falls, let the Earth hide it,
> And may it never rise, or call for Vengeance:
> Oh, that it were the last shall fall a Victim
> To Zeal's inhumane Wrath! [V, 90]

Inspired, I believe, especially by John Banks's queens—Elizabeth, Anna Bullen, Mary Queen of Scots—but perhaps also influenced by the first feminists of the preceding century up to Mary Astell in his own time, Rowe would seem to have provided a role model for the new bourgeois woman to emulate and a series of goals for her to aspire to: first education, then the vote, finally prime minister. But Jane's early death seems to underscore the fact that the hour of this new woman had not yet come. It was acceptable for Rowe to portray a strong woman in command because she was only queen for a day. Moreover, unlike Banks's Queen Elizabeth, despite her command presence Lady Jane never gets to really run the country. She actually becomes a figure for the new constitutional monarch in England—Anne or George I—a figurehead behind whom the Northumberlands and Harleys and Walpoles, the male prime ministers, have the real power (backed, of course, by the army and the navy).[14]

Personal Tragedy

As we have seen, Restoration personal tragedy features great-souled protagonists torn apart by conflicting emotions—Lee's Alexander, Dryden's Antony. One need only to contrast that aristocratic magnanimity, that capacity for great passion, with Cato's neostoic coldness or George Lillo's portrayal of an ethic that totally suppresses passion (see below). Juxtaposed to the centrifugality of their passion and to the mutability of their worlds and of their own wills remains generally the aristocratic virtue of constancy to one's word, oath, vow.

Nevertheless, lurking within Dryden's *All for Love* itself are two figures who become prominent in bourgeois personal tragedy, the self-controlled man and the domestic woman. Although satirized in Dryden's play as a Hobbist pragmatist in pursuit only of his "Int'rest" and a bourgeois "Usurer," "fit . . . to buy, not conquer Kingdoms" (III.i.213-15) because he coldly refuses to meet Antony in personal combat to decide their contestation, the unheroic Octavius might, in bourgeois dress, become the heroic Bevil Junior of Sir Richard Steele's *Conscious Lovers* (see below), who refuses to fight a duel. More interesting, perhaps, is the figure of Dryden's Cleopatra, who has fallen off from Shakespeare's outrageously unpredictable enigma to dwindle into a constant lover whom "Nature meant . . . / A Wife, a silly, harmless, houshold Dove" (IV.i.93-94).

The best of the Revolutionary personal tragedies—Southerne's *Fatal Marriage; or, The Innocent Adultery* (1694) and Rowe's *Fair Penitent* (LIF 1703)—developed what Rowe called "She-*Tragedies*" (epilogue to *Jane Shore*) from Otway's and Banks's earlier tragedies and satires. The most classically tragical of these is *The Fair Penitent,* because its protagonist is great-souled and destructively passionate. What is new is that she is a woman, the fiery Calista, who contemns the gay Lothario who seduced her and the patriarchal father who now demands her suicide. Despite her final, penitent kneeling to her dying father, to her forgiving husband, and to Heaven, the audience cannot forget her ringing, feminist soliloquy, "How hard is the Condition of our Sex" (III, 30), a soliloquy that implicitly demands women's inclusion in the emerging bourgeois doctrine of the rights of man:[15]

> How hard is the Condition of our Sex,
> Thro' ev'ry State of Life the Slaves of Man?
> In all the dear delightful Days of Youth
> A rigid Father dictates to our Wills,
> And deals out Pleasure with a scanty Hand;
> To his, the Tyrant Husband's Reign succeeds
> Proud with Opinion of superior Reason,
> He holds Domestick Bus'ness and Devotion
> All we are capable to know, and shuts us,
> Like Cloyster'd Ideots, from the World's Acquaintance,
> And all the Joys of Freedom; wherefore are we
> Born with high Souls, but to assert our selves,
> Shake off this vile Obedience they exact,
> And claim an equal Empire o'er the World?[16]

What is also new is the figure of the husband. Though Altamont leaps to the usual precipitate misogyny when Calista is cold to him on their wedding night and though he kills her libertine seducer, he undergoes a transformation away from patriarchy, stopping Calista's father from killing her and forgiving her himself. To take her back at the end would present a challenge indeed to patriarchy, for their offspring might be polluted. The patriarchal configuration of the ending—with the uppity Calista finally begging forgiveness from her dying father and from the divine Superego, Altamont languishing into death, and his friend, a lesser superego, articulating a typical male moral—allows no such heresy. Does the play not, however, plant the seeds of feminist inclusion as well as the softening of patriarchy itself, potentials of the bourgeois revolution not yet fulfilled?[17]

It remains a critical commonplace that she-tragedies produced mainly the figure of the domestic woman as generally passive, pathetic, suffering, innocent.[18] And it was long a theatrical commonplace to juxtapose against this essentially submissive woman a termagant antagonist, from Lee's rival queens in the play of that name to Cleopatra and Octavia in Dryden's play to the contrast between Jane Shore and Alicia in Rowe's *Jane Shore*. Playwrights created such contrasting pairs to take advantage of talented actresses, no pair more famous than Elizabeth Barry and Anne Bracegirdle. If we turn to a lesser known she-tragedy—and one written by a woman—we can see the exploitation of this pairing for the shaping of the figure of the perfect bourgeois wife—and the complicity of a woman author in such a creation.

Catharine Trotter's *Fatal Friendship* (LIF 1698) contrasts the fiery, passionate Lamira with the patient, submissive Felicia. The former is a wealthy widow whose jealous husband's will enjoins her from marrying again at the risk of forfeiture of her fortune to his sister. She is in love with the penurious younger brother, Gramont, who marries her hastily (and secretly, to avoid the forfeiture) for necessary cash to pay fines unjustly levied against him and his best friend, Castalio, and a ransom to pirates who have kidnapped his infant son from a previous clandestine marriage to Felicia. In a scene that must have been an excellent vehicle for Barry, Lamira, left alone on her wedding night by the conscience-stricken Gramont, gradually surmises the presence of a rival in his affections and grows furiously vengeful in splendidly written dialogue. In contrast, Felicia is astounded and hurt by the news her husband has committed bigamy, and she becomes quickly submissive in the face of her patriarchal brother's anger at her for her secret marriage with Gramont:

Bellgard. Ay, trait'ress, weep,
Weep for thy shame, thy sin, thy disobedience,
Rebellious girl, pollution of my blood!
Felicia. Oh I deserve all this, that could deceive
And disobey the best of brothers. [III.ii, 176]

In one of those confrontational scenes between such female antagonists, Trotter brings them together for a gradual unfolding to Lamira of not just Felicia's rivalry but her prior legitimate claim. Both women are strong in this scene, Felicia having determined to "tear" Gramont from Lamira (III.ii, 178). Throughout she asserts her "right" to him, even as Lamira asserts her "right" to vengeance (178-80). But Lamira has contempt for Felicia's meek continued acceptance of Gramont: "Thou art so poorly spirited, / T'accept and yield t'adulterated love" (180). Yet Lamira loses the contest—at least in the ideological intentionality of the play. Her failure to control her rage leads her ignominiously to attempt to prey upon Felicia's poverty and bribe her with her fortune never to see Gramont again. Meanwhile, although she upbraids him for his perjury to their vows, Felicia forgives Gramont and even blames herself for his misery in that she in her "inconsiderate passion" revealed the "fatal secret" of their marriage to her brother:

> it was my duty, as your wife,
> Whate'er I suffered, not to have accused you,
> And as I loved, I should have had no thought
> Of my own misery whilst you were happy. [IV.i, 183]

Moreover, Felicia rejects Lamira's bribe, choosing "the bitterness of poverty" and insisting, "The marriage vows are not conditional" (V.i, 191-92). To Gramont she pledges to "labour for our food, or beg an alms" (V.i, 195). This is standing by your man *without* a vengeance!

When, even in the face of her husband's pleading with her to redeem their son, Felicia calls her refusal of Lamira's bribe "the strongest trial" (V.i, 197), she underscores the real meaning of the play. Throughout *Nicholas Rowe and Christian Tragedy,* I argued that *trial* is a central metaphor in the religious rhetoric of Rowe's theodicean plays. I still think it is, though I am now more interested in the ideological significance of the trope. If passion in aristocratic personal tragedy causes fatal vacillation between objects of desire, with fidelity to one's word the central test or trial, in bourgeois serious drama the trial is of one's constancy of mind (Arpasia, Marcia, Cato, Lady Jane). Let us see how these various shifts play themselves out in Trotter's tragedy.

In *The Fatal Friendship,* word-as-bond remains a central theme: Gramont has perjured his vows to Felicia, yet he is praised—even by Lamira, if only grudgingly (IV.ii, 189)—for his remarkable fidelity to Felicia on the night of his wedding to Lamira by abstaining from consummation despite Lamira's abundant charms. Castalio is finally won over to reconciliation with his rival by his "superior virtue": "By Heaven, I think . . . not all my honour could / Have guarded me against so strong a trial" (V.i, 203). But Felicia's "trial" and Gramont's most serious trial in the play are tests of constancy of mind. More particularly, they are tests of resolve against economic exigencies, and in that sense, under the still familiar guise of an aristocratic domestic tragedy, Trotter's is a specifically bourgeois morality play.

Like the protagonists of more obvious examples of this genre—from George Barnwell (see below) to Hirstwood in Dreiser's *Sister Carrie*—Gramont is besieged by a series of financial woes. His father, the count, because he wants Felicia for himself and wants to eliminate his rival by forcing Gramont into a marriage with Lamira, blackmails Gramont by refusing to pay his or Castalio's fines. Marriage with the rich widow will give Gramont himself the means to do so. When he refuses, his father casts him out penniless. Then Gramont discovers that not only has the king not intervened with the vengeful general who holds them both hostage but the king suspects Castalio of treason. Gramont must act quickly to save his life. Then the coup de grâce: Gramont learns pirates have his son.

If Trotter has modeled her plot at least in part on Otway's *Venice Preserv'd* (1682), one significant difference is that Jaffeir, though bribed by Pierre's money to supply his immediate financial needs, is also prompted to join the rebellion perhaps out of principle, especially as articulated by Pierre, but certainly out of revenge. Gramont describes his motivation as "nature," that is, the natural concern of a husband, father, friend:

> I must, I must prevent at any rate
> This dismal scene of misery and ruin,
> Turn villain, any thing, when she's at stake,
> My child too, and my best friend. I could, by Heav'n,
> Suffer a thousand racking deaths for each,
> And should I sacrifice 'em all, to keep
> A little peace of mind, the pride of never straying?
> Walk on by rules, and calmly let 'em perish,
> Rather than tread one step beyond to save 'em?
> Forbid it nature! [II.ii, 167-68]

When he concludes, "[N]ot I, but fate resolves it," Trotter has made him as much as possible the passive victim of economic necessity.

Nevertheless, the moral of the play plasters over that necessity with an ethic designed to neutralize potential radicals: "[T]here's not a state / So miserable, but may with greater ease / Be suffered than dishonour" (V.i, 194). When Felicia, who as a last resort to save her son has left to plead for mercy with Gramont's father, returns with him, like Otway's Priuli, ready to help, it is too late. Gramont has accidentally killed Castalio trying to break up a duel between him and Bellgard, and he stabs himself. But not only has Felicia succeeded in softening the count; the king has learned the truth and offered satisfaction and preferment to both Castalio and Gramont. Gramont reads the lesson that underwrites the moral:

> Oh, what a wretch was I, that could not wait
> Heaven's time, the providence that never fails
> Those who dare to trust it. Durst I have been honest,
> One day had changed the scene, and made me happy. [V.i, 206]

At one point Gramont compares his behavior with that of the lower classes in a similar situation:

> Better I might have borne the worst of miseries,
> That threatened me; which not the meanest wretch,
> That begs, or toils for bread, but can support,
> And does not truck his honesty for fortune. [IV.i, 183]

In other words, Trotter's play is a warning to lesser members of the middle and lower classes to keep strict, neostoical resolve in the face of financial ruin for, as with Micawber, something will turn up: God's in his heaven and all's right with the system. Both Gramont and Felicia represent the "necessity" (read *social desideratum*) for those without money and power—the lower classes and the lower gender—to endure.

In George Lillo's *London Merchant; or, The History of George Barnwell* (1731), Barnwell and his master, Thorowgood, present class triumph not for the petty bourgeoisie but for the upper middle merchant class, for although Barnwell is apprentice to Thorowgood, he may well come from the same stratum of society; in fact, as the beloved of Thorowgood's daughter, Maria, he probably does.[19] (Who is, then, the London merchant of the title?) David Wallace demonstrates how the new bourgeois ethos interpenetrates public and private realms, socioeconomic theory and ethics. Not only have merchants become respectable, as attests the opening appropriation from the aristocracy of credit for the defeat of the Spanish Armada by the London merchants (who convinced the Genoese to deny Spain a necessary loan); but capitalism is portrayed as natural, "founded in Reason, and the Nature of Things" (III.i.3-4). Because it is natural, it can be universally applied in a system of mercantile expansion that is, in effect, a justification for European, specifically British imperialism.[20] Thorowgood's *good* apprentice, Trueman, merely a bourgeois Juba, articulates colonialism rhapsodically:

> I have observ'd those Countries, where Trade is promoted and encouraged, do not make Discoveries to destroy, but to improve, Mankind,—by Love and Friendship, to tame the fierce, and polish the most savage,—to teach them the Advantages of honest Traffick,—by taking from them, with their own Consent, their useless Superfluities, and giving them, in Return, what, from their Ignorance in manual Arts, their Situation, or some other Accident, they stand in need of. [III.i.9-15]

The same rationalization for the exploitation of Third World peoples and their resources can still be heard today. In words that more nakedly justify the importation of everything from gold to oil to the Elgin marbles, Thorowgood adds, "It is the industrious Merchant's Business to collect the various Blessings of each Soil and Climate, and, with the Product of the whole, to enrich his native Country" (III.i.20-22).

What is less obvious is that the strict bourgeois ethic in the play, complete with metaphysical sanctions, portrays the simple crime of lust leading to theft and ultimately to parricide, not only because of the interpenetration of public and private, as Wallace shows, but because, as the seductress Millwood's maid, Lucy, puts it, "One Vice as naturally begets another, as a Father a Son" (II.xiii.7). That is, this begetting of vices is portrayed as a "natural" progression because the system such vices attack is still a patrilineal system for the transmission of power and property. Barnwell's rebellion against his master and uncle/father (who raised this orphan) is called "Parricide" because it is an Oedipal rebellion against patriarchal control of the access to the inextricably connected money and sex of the play. In a bourgeois political economy, where time is money and reputation is credit, in contradistinction to the celebration of youth in Restoration comedy in particular, Thorowgood and Trueman are right to proclaim, respectively, "The State of Youth is much to be deplored," its "Idleness [the] worst of Snares" (II.iv.17-18; II.ii.77). Thus the play's insistence on absolute self-control—and the disastrous consequences when it is lost, whether that loss is a woman's loss of marketability or a young merchant's loss of credibility—or credit.

Wallace is correct to point out that while ostensibly free to marry whom she chooses, Maria would never dream of violating her father's wishes (133). Moreover, while pretending that a young man's "Merit" recommends him more as a husband for Maria than "high Birth and Titles," nevertheless, "tho' they make not a bad Man good, yet they are a real Advantage to a worthy one, and place his Virtues in the fairest Light." It is no accident that Thorowgood's drawing room is filled with "noble Lords," for Thorowgood seeks a worthy partner in his only child's inheritance of "the Fruits of many Years successful Industry" (I.ii.29-52). And at the end, when she is described as "lost" and "undone" (V.ix.4, 40), the only possible explanation is that Maria has made her love for Barnwell public, thus damaging her trade value in the marriage market. Her melancholy throughout has resulted from knowing that her father would be disappointed if she chose Barnwell instead of one of those lords, marriage with whom, on the part of merchants' daughters, helped build those crucial estates, like the one Hogarth pictures out the window of the opening panel of *Marriage à la Mode*. Finally, even when she confesses her love to Barnwell in prison, she apologizes for *invading* "the Freedom of your Sex's Choice" (V.ix.32-33).

Splitting off his good from his bad girl, in traditional fashion but with a bourgeois twist, Lillo portrays the ultimate threat to the system as an uppity promiscuous woman, a "Sorceress," naturally—a witch (IV.xvi.18). Her misanthropic uppitiness is even more articulate than Calista's. Railing against perjuring Don Juans, she sounds like a typical cast mistress become a termagant. But she puts the case against men with special poignancy:

> It's a general Maxim among the knowing Part of Mankind, that a Woman without Virtue, like a Man without Honour or Honesty, is capable of any Action, tho never so vile: And yet, what Pains will they not take, what Arts not use, to seduce us from our Innocence, and make us contemptible and wicked, even in their own Opinions? Then, is it not just, the Villains to their Cost, should find us so? [I.iii.26-31]

When Thorowgood attempts to enchain her power in religious rhetoric by calling her "Devil," she defiantly responds with a nominalism that strikes at the heart of patriarchal discourse: "That imaginary Being is an Emblem of the cursed Sex collected. A Mirrour, wherein each particular Man may see his own Likeness, and that of all Mankind" (IV.xviii.3-6). Moreover, she sees that man's dominance and woman's consequent plight are based on economics. When Lucy insists that men, not women, are the real slaves, Millwood responds bitterly, "Slaves have no Property—no, not even in themselves" (I.iii.16-18). Her foil, the virtuous Maria, has value in the eyes of her father and her aristocratic suitors because she is the unadulterated vessel of her father's wealth and, potentially, of one of their seeds, the guarantor of genealogical purity. "Robbed" of that virtue and value, Millwood curses the "barbarous Sex" that left her nothing but "Poverty and Reproach" (IV.xviii.10-13). In response she constitutes herself as survivor: "I found it therefore necessary to be rich; and, to that End I summon'd all my Arts" (V.xviii.15-16). And when she says she learned those arts from men, she refers to naked capitalist and imperialist rapacity—and to systematic enslavement of the dispossessed indigenous peoples of the Americas:

> I would have my Conquests compleat, like those of the *Spaniards* in the New World; who first plunder'd the Natives of all the Wealth they had, and then condemn'd the Wretches to the Mines for Life to work for more. [I.iii.20-22]

She exposes the Social Darwinism that underlies the hegemonic rhetoric of bourgeois ideology:

> Men of all Degrees and all Professions I have known, yet found no Difference, but in their several Capacities; all were alike wicked to the utmost of their Power. . . . I know you and I hate you all; I expect no Mercy, and

> I ask for none; I follow'd my Inclinations, and that the best of you does every Day. All actions seem alike natural and indifferent to Man and Beast, who devour, or are devour'd as they meet with others weaker or stronger than themselves. [IV.xviii.29-36]

Yet Lillo attempts to counter Millwood's rhetoric not only by the rhetoric of benevolent Christianity and benevolent imperialism but finally by Millwood's own self-contradiction. Human nature may be rapacious, but at one point she makes an acknowledgment that enmeshes her in not just misanthropy but misogyny. She says of her plan to seduce Barnwell,

> I'll e'en trust to Nature, who does Wonders in these Matters.—If to seem what one is not, in order to be the better liked for what one really is; if to speak one thing and mean the direct contrary, be Art in a Woman, I know nothing of Nature. [I.iv.7-10]

She has constituted no radical selfhood but reinscribed herself into the ideology she sought to escape. Moreover, though she claims not to believe in the devil, she is not so thorough a nominalist as to be an "Atheist" (IV.xviii.41), and she dies defying "Heaven" and its mercy in such a way as to echo Milton's Satan and thus reify, through her Calvinism and/or despair, the very transcendental realm that gives Western patriarchy its final sanction and ultimate threat: "I tell thee, Youth, I am by Heaven devoted a dreadful Instance of its Power to punish" (V.xi.45-46).

Lillo may have thought adding the last scene would contain Millwood's critique of capitalism. As several critics have noted, however, when Thorowgood acknowledges the "Truth" of what she says, he is referring only to religious hypocrisy, not business hypocrisy (IV.xviii.45). And Lillo may have thought that he successfully countered Millwood's negative female image with the positive one of Maria, the contaminated vessel of patriarchal seed versus the pure. Making Millwood a witch may have been the easiest way to discredit her in an essentially misogynistic culture, where power is really shared *between men*—witness the male bonding between Barnwell and Trueman. But like Lyndaraxa and Calista, Millwood is invested with too much energy to be contained, and her critique actually gains power by her being a woman, an oppressed "Slave" because she owns no "Property" (I.iii.18). In an important sense she speaks for the have-nots in capitalism, all those whom poverty drives to murder oppressors. Going beyond Trotter's Gramont, Barnwell seeks to murder his uncle/father/business patriarch for his money. Like Millwood, he has found it "necessary to be rich" in order to survive in a capitalist economy of unlimited acquisition for the few (IV.xviii.15). In short, the bourgeois ideology of the play has generated its own antithesis, which it has charmed back into the lamp of its justifying rhetorical metaphysic, where it appears to remain today.

Tragical Satire

No tragical satire of the Revolutionary period matches in greatness—and in the strident critique of the bourgeois order—John Gay's comical satire, *The Beggar's Opera.*[21] But in the first decade of the Revolutionary period, three of the Restoration's greatest playwrights wrote tragical satires: John Dryden, John Crowne, and Thomas Southerne. As we might expect from these erstwhile defenders of monarchial ideology, their portrayals of the new order are ambivalent at best.

Notwithstanding the protestations of Dryden and his friends, the Lords Falkland and Rochester, as Anne Barbeau Gardiner has argued, Dryden and Southerne's *Cleomenes* (1692) is obviously Jacobite, and Queen Mary was right to suspect and temporarily ban the play.[22] Certain details in Plutarch's original were tailor-made for Dryden's Jacobitism.[23] Yet other details in Plutarch allow Dryden to pursue not so much his specifically personal as his thematic allegory. Dryden transforms Plutarch's Agathoclea, Ptolomy's scheming mistress, into Cassandra, who in the fashion typical of Dryden's own and the Restoration's villainesses, schemes sexually against Cleomenes. Dryden's misogyny in her portrayal might be a veiled attack against Queen Mary: turning her affection to Cleomenes, Cassandra berates Ptolomy as an "easy Wretch," yet "Fools we [women] must have, or else we cannot sway; / For none but Fools will Woman-kind Obey" (IV.i.112-15). But Cassandra's part is extended more for the purposes of Dryden's theme of word-as-bond. She repeatedly refers to Ptolomy's promise to help Cleomenes, a promise she herself conspires to defer in order to keep Cleomenes for her own lascivious purposes. When she tries to seduce him through her commentary on the painting of Paris's rape of Helen, Cleomenes finally condemns "both the Lovers," for they "broke their plighted Vows" (II.ii.343). When Cassandra tempts him to leave his wife and fly with her to Greece to reclaim his kingdom, he refuses to break his own plighted faith, though his action entails his wife's and mother's eventual murder at Cassandra's hands.

Plutarch warrants Dryden's use of the contrasting pair, Coenus and Cleanthes, the former a subject who betrays his king, the latter a foreigner yet a friend who appears to betray Cleomenes but proves more loyal than the subject and does his utmost to redeem his friend. At the end of the play, Cleomenes and Cleanthes's repeated embraces conclude in a death embrace as they close upon each other's sword in an emblem of loyalty in the face of a faithless Fortune. In a description added to Plutarch, Dryden has Coenus deliver the cruelest news of all: that when Antigonus entered Sparta, the people offered no resistance but received their conqueror as if he were their "King," nay, a "Deity" on his progress through the land (I.i.229, 234). Thus once again Dryden satirizes the faithless, fickle populace.

Uncharacteristically, however, Dryden provides the audience with no metaphysical solace. Cleomenes opens the play complaining to the "Gods" that they make him, a great hero, wait for deliverance upon an effeminate court (I.i.17). When Coenus hails him as Cleomenes still, he bitterly replies, "No thanks to Heaven for that: I shou'd have dy'd, / And then I had not been this *Cleomenes*"—that is, one virtually alone and in exile (202-3). When he learns he must leave his mother, wife, and children as hostages in order to return to Greece, he bitterly complains:

> The Propositions are unjust and hard;
> And if I swallow 'em, 'Tis as we take
> The Wrath of Heaven.
> We must have patience, for they will be Gods,
> And give us no account of what we suffer. [III.iii.1-5]

His faithful soldier, Pantheus, has warned Cleomenes against railing at the gods, but that was when he thought that the death of Antigonus provided them with an opportunity for a "new and nobler Fortune" (I.i.288). When by Cassandra's order they are all shut up to starve, Cleomenes concludes, "The Gods are deaf to Pray'rs!" (IV.ii.209). Though at the beginning of his imprisonment, he counsels against suicide out of piety ("[W]e durst not tempt the gods" [265]) and seems to have hope that "Heaven has means to free us" (271), as his family starves around him, his patience ebbs:

> Virtue in Distress, and Vice in Triumph
> Make Atheists of Mankind. . . .
> I am strangely tempted to blaspheme the Gods;
> . . . Devotion
> Will cool in after times, if none but good Men suffer.
> [V.ii.106-7, 18, 46-47]

Cleomenes's most crucial temptation to despair and blasphemy comes in this exchange with his son:

> *Cleomenes.* . . . I am loath
> To say hard things of Heaven!
> *Cleonidas.* But what if Heaven
> Will do hard things, must not hard things be said?
> Y'have often told me, That the Souls of Kings
> Are made above the rest of Humane Race;
> Have they not Fortunes fitted for those Souls?
> Did ever King die Starv'd?
> *Cleomenes.* I know not that:
> Yet still be firm in this: The Gods are good,
> Tho' thou and I may perish.
> *Cleonidas.* Indeed I know not,
> That ever I offended Heaven in thought:
> I always said my Prayers.
> *Cleomenes.* Thou didst thy Duty.
> *Cleonidas.* And yet you lost the Battel when I Pray'd.
> *Cleomenes.* 'Twas in the Fates I should: But hold thee there!
> The rest is all unfathomable depth:
> This we well know, That if there be a Bliss
> Beyond this present Life, 'tis purchas'd here,
> And Virtue is its price. [V.ii.56-72]

This exchange goes beyond typical theodicean complaints to confront the unanswerable problem of evil. And the last statement is no ringing assertion of faith, no consolation of philosophy, but a rather desperate, hypothetical clinging by one's fingernails over the abyss of metaphysical "unfathomable depth"—the last refuge of theodicy, of those who have already lost the debate.

Pantheus enters bringing relief from Cleanthes and the gods, and Cleomenes concludes in the typical theodicean metaphor that they had "try'd" him to the "longest" possible extent (91-92). But the play does not end here, and the relief is not enduring. As Cleomenes and Pantheus venture upon their attempted rebellion against the Egyptians, Cleomenes challenges the gods once again: "And if I fall their shame, / Let 'em ne'er think of making Heroes more, / If Cowards must prevail" (259-61). It can be argued that Cleomenes and his party do not finally fall the "shame" of the gods, for Cleonidas and Pantheus die praying, and Cleanthes asserts, "The Gods at last are kind" in providing his sword for Cleomenes to die honorably upon (V.v.67).

Yet the other half of Cleomenes's challenge goes unanswered: cowards prevail. And Dryden must have received some criticism for the lack of poetical justice, which he answers in his preface by insisting that

Cassandra and company got theirs in the subsequent history (*Works* 16:81). But the fact that the play does not end with such a prophecy leaves us short of religious consolation, and Cleomenes's complaints keep haunting us: such a lack of poetical justice may indeed cool devotion and make atheists.[24]

The most telling consolation in the play comes in the closing tag of Act III: when his mother, Cratisiclea, thinking Cleomenes has a shot at regaining his kingdom, counsels him to be cheerful, fight well, and leave the rest "to the Gods and Fortune," Cleomenes replies defiantly, "If they fail me, / *Theirs be the Fault, For Fate is theirs alone: / My Virtue, Fame, and Honour are my own*" (III.iii.137-39). After 1688, Dryden portrays a new theme of stoic resignation based upon the centered self, a theme that receives its best treatment in "To My Honour'd Kinsman."[25] Cleomenes begins the play with a grand stoic boast:

> Dejected! no, it never shall be said,
> That Fate had power upon a *Spartan* Soul:
> My mind on its own Centre stands unmov'd,
> And Stable as the Fabrick of the World
> Propt on it self; still I am *Cleomenes*. [I.i.1-5]

Perhaps Dryden was beginning to resign himself to that world ironically described by the disappointed Milton before him:

> so shall the World go on,
> To good malignant, to bad men benign,
> Under her own weight groaning, till the day
> Appear of respiration to the just,
> And vengeance to the wicked. [*Paradise Lost* XII.537-41]

Unlike Milton, however, Dryden concludes with no celebration of the Second Coming. Instead, he can offer at best the consolation of history, at worst that of mere resignation and satire. In *Don Sebastian* the tragic ending is ultimately caused by an original breach of faith by Sebastian's father. But in *Cleomenes* (and *Amphitryon* as well; see *Tricksters and Estates* 241-48) Dryden portrays a world where the ultimate betrayal is the "Fault" of Heaven itself. Frustrated at Heaven's tardy vengeance, one can only adopt the stance of the One Just Man and rail at a faithless world.

So as not to take himself too seriously, however, Dryden seems to offer something of a self-portrait as stoic satirist more given to raillery than railing, more Momus than Juvenal. When at the beginning of the play Cleomenes asks Pantheus where he has been "this long long Year of

Hours," there follows this exchange:

> *Pantheus.* Where I have past a merry Mornings Walk,
> With the best Company.
> *Cleomenes.* With whom?
> *Pantheus.* Why with my self, in laughing at the World,
> Making a Farce of Life, where Knaves and Fools,
> And Mad-men, that's all Human-kind were Actors.
> *Cleomenes.* And what part Acted you?
> *Pantheus.* As little as I could: And daily would have less,
> So please the Gods, for that's a Wise Man's part. [I.i.103-12]

Pantheus's posture is that of Dryden's Momus in *The Secular Masque,* which he wrote for Sir John Vanbrugh's adaptation of John Fletcher's *Pilgrim* (1700). Momus summarizes the seventeenth century thus. Pointing to Diana, who presided over the reigns of the early Stuarts, Momus mocks, "Thy Chase had a Beast in View" [a beheaded king]; pointing to Mars, who presided over the Interregnum, "Thy Wars brought nothing about"; pointing to Venus, who presided over the reigns of the later Stuarts, "Thy Lovers were all untrue." Concludes the fin-de-siècle weary Momus—and one can hear the voice of the ex-laureate himself in the year of his death, "'Tis well an Old Age is out, / And time to begin a New" (*Works* 16:273). The consolation of satire allowed Dryden at once to mark and to mock the ideological shift to a Mad Max world of a voice crying in the wilderness.

Crowne's *Regulus* (1692) and *Caligula* (1698) both portray just men amidst faithlessness. The ideology in the first play is not quite clear, but it clarifies in the second. *Regulus* begins with a prologue full of jingoistic, anti-French sentiment in apparent support of William III's war policy. And the epilogue concludes thus: "The *French,* ay and some *English* I'm afraid, / Have cause to wish Heroes had ne're been made" (italics reversed). Ostensibly the couplet again praises King Billy and his war. But why are there some English who need dread heroes? Are these nonjuring Jacobites? Derek Hughes has offered a corrective to my earlier reading that, on the contrary, the play has Jacobite sympathies (*English Drama* 361n), and he may be right.

Regulus is set in the First Punic War but is full of anachronisms. The character Regulus remains the historical heroic general who wreaked havoc on Carthage until he was finally captured by Carthage's mercenary Spartan commander, Xantippus. But Crowne portrays Carthage as a "Commonwealth" torn by a power struggle between Hamilcar and Asdrubal, important figures from the Second Punic War. Asdrubal is an effete, luxurious, self-interested prince of ancient royal blood (of specious value in a republic), who would impose himself as "absolute Head" upon the Senate (II, 11-12), a fickle parliament, powerless to protect itself against Machiavellian politicians, merchants, and priests. Throughout, Asdrubal is the consummate hypocrite, whose real ethic, despite his oaths and protestations, is sheer power: "He is not fit to rule, whom Vertue reigns, / He's fit to rule, who has at his Command / Vertue or Vice, as needs of State require" (13). By excusing treasonous talk as mere "matter of discourse" (IV, 36), he reveals his essential nominalism.

The noble and valiant Hamilcar, prince of the Senate, and Xantippus appear to triumph over the cowardly Asdrubal and his corrupt court minions, who in prison reveal not only their thoroughly double-crossing natures but their impiety as well—they cannot pray because they have no friends in heaven (IV, 36). But the Senate, fearing the true aristocratic nobility of Hamilcar and Xantippus, rejects them and invites Asdrubal to be "Protector o' the Commonwealth" (42).

Crowne may be suggesting that if England rejects its new oligarchy, where the king is *primus inter pares,* in favor of a king with pretensions to hereditary and absolute right, it is doomed to the anarchy that results in the play. Asdrubal betrays his conspirators, the Senate condemns them to death, but they rouse the rabble against Asdrubal, who departs, cursing the Senate and insisting that a commonwealth is fundamentally flawed, for it is incapable of keeping faith with a leader and cannot tolerate heroes, a judgment with which the Senate concurs in both word and deed. After Asdrubal is gone, they baldly admit, "A Commonwealth bears no imparity" (V, 58), and they proceed to break their faith with Regulus and torture him ignominiously. Although it is ironic for Asdrubal to level these charges, faithless as he is, Crowne may be underwriting the ideology not of bourgeois democracy but of bourgeois oligarchy. Hamilcar himself has earlier lectured the meddling sans-culottes:

> Now, Sirs, I hope you will learn modesty.
> And no more censure things above your reach.
> We do not know the mysteries of your Trades,
> Because we never were instructed in 'em.
> Pray who taught you the mysteries o' State?
> What strange conceits Men have of governing?
> Men must serve Years to know a Handicraft;
> Yet all pretend to skill in Government,
> By natural light and instinct, as Birds build.
> Men will pretend to't who want common Sense,
> Yet are not laugh'd at neither; every Man

> Willingly lets the Frolick go about,
> So he has leave to take it in his turn. [III, 28]

Thus Crowne drives a wedge between monarchism and democracy, staking out the ground for the new ruling class.

The stoic hero, Regulus, is a rebuke to the faithlessness of Carthage. Captured by the Carthaginians, he agrees to act as an ambassador to Rome to carry Carthage's terms for peace. He plights his word to return no matter what Rome's response and, knowing his probable fate, actually urges Rome to resist despite his loss. But he must return to face certain death, for "my word and oath are past, / And nothing do I fear, like breach o' faith":

> By keeping faith, o're *Carthage* I triumph,
> A *Roman* Ghost will triumph over her.
> Not by short pomp which blazes but some hours;
> My triumph shall go on, from age to age,
> While *Rome* shall stand, which shall the longer stand
> For my example of unshaken Faith,
> For what Foundation to a State like Faith? [IV, 44]

The play ends with Regulus ignominiously tortured to death and Hamilcar accompanying Xantippus into exile in Sparta, where one can live a life of stoic "Vertue," whose "joys no fortune can oppress," and leaving the faithless Carthage to the "Vengeance" of not just Rome but "Heaven" (V, 63). Crowne's message seems clear: whatever the new government of England, it still must rely on faith, loyalty to whoever is "Prince of the Senate." Yet could not nonjurors as well as jurors take aid and comfort from this play and its central theme of faith?[26] Howbeit, no one can take much comfort from a play that ends so apocalyptically.

In *Caligula,* Crowne wrote a fin-de-siècle rhymed tragical satire. The play opens with noble Romans lamenting the tyranny of the mad, effeminate emperor, who has no legitimate reasons for his wars, is paranoid about his prisoners, and in an act revealing his failure as father to his people, destroys the harvest intended to feed Rome. Ironically, it is he who inveighs against the "Luxury" of the court (I.i, 10). Violating all trust himself, he projects outward the vision of the malcontent:

> How false are Men, both in their Heads and Hearts;
> And there is falshood in all Trades and Arts.
> Lawyers deceive their Clients by false Law;

Priests, by false Gods, keep all the World in awe.
By their false tongues such flatt'ring Knaves are rais'd;
For their false wit, Scriblers by fools are prais'd.
Whores, by false beauty, *Venusses* appear;
Hect'ring *Faux*—braves o'er Cowards, domineer:
Look round the World, what shall we find sincere? [II, 14-15]

Yet right before him stands the One Just Man who gives Caligula's diatribe the counterexample if not the lie: Valerius Asiaticus, who vows to be "faithful to my trust," even to the point of reserving the right to chastise Caligula "if I think you err" (II, 14).

Caligula's other counselors are fawning flatterers, not least of whom is his empress, Cesonia. They feed his delusions of divinity. In his delusions he sees the Senate (read *Parliament*) as seeking power and attempting to reduce him to its slave. He warns the senators and consuls to fear him or die. At this moment, the priests bring him a golden image of himself.

When one of the nobles talks sedition, Valerius has him arrested, insisting,

On Faith and Honour I have fixt my foot. . . .
But I'll to him [Caligula], and all mankind be just,
Protect his Person and oppose his Lust.
I'll try by Counsel first to stop his course;
That failing, I'll to fair and open force. [III, 21]

But when Caligula rapes Valerius's wife, Julia, though she preaches "patience" (IV, 39), he complains against the gods for their impotent justice:

New Giants have bound *Jove,* so he lies still,
And lets this filthy Tyrant take his fill
Of Whoredom, Blood, Rapes, Incest, what he will.

Julia wills to die a martyr, but Valerius vows revenge.

Like Hamlet, Valerius procrastinates, and Julia kills herself. In seeming contradiction to his earlier stance, he predicts of Caligula, "[I]f there be Gods, thy fall is near" (V, 42). When others employ the palace guards to rebel, Valerius condemns such a path as that of the coward, yet he interprets and generalizes the judgment on Caligula:

A debauch'd vitious Prince does often find
'Tis very dangerous to corrupt mankind.

'Tis odds, he by his own corruption dies,
And crimes by crimes justly the Gods chastize. [V, 50]

Yet Valerius refuses the imperial throne himself:

I'd rather be an honest slave, I swear,
Than buy the Empire of the world so dear.
I never yet in crimes employ'd my Sword. [51-52]

Instead, he will avenge this Caesar against Cassius, turn over power to the Senate, and retire to mourn Julia's martyrdom.

In Caligula, Crowne has created a parody of the megalomaniac absolute monarch. His sexual debauches are most signal. Was Crowne glancing at William and his catamites? The play has a strange Royalist feeling in the trope of the hero refusing to participate in parricide. Yet Valerius's gesture at the end frees him from Oedipal guilt and allows the power to devolve onto the Senate. This is certainly a Revolutionary trope.

Southerne's *Fate of Capua* (LIF 1700) is also a satire on faithlessness. Set after the victory of Hannibal at Cannae, the play's conflict is over whether Capua should remain faithful to Rome, who has defended her countless times and is now in her hour of need against Carthage. Decius Magius, a lone voice for honor, friendship, loyalty, goes unheeded. Employing the rhetoric of social contract theory, the rabble marches on the Senate, which, they maintain, but holds "the Government in trust / For them . . . they can recall it when they please" (I.i.191-93). They wish to form a "Common-wealth" (I.ii.14). Meanwhile, the Senate makes Pacuvius, a Hannibal sympathizer on good terms with the crowd, their dictator. He immediately exits, has the Senate house locked, and warns the guards that if but one escapes, "You answer with your lives / To our great Lords the People" (3-4).[27] Pacuvius cynically manipulates both crowd and Senate, and the city is turned over to Hannibal.

Gradually Capua reaps the whirlwind of its radical infidelity. Roman families and then Roman sympathizers within the city are butchered. But more and more citizens are killed by outsiders as the protective Roman umbrella collapses. Hannibal proves a tyrant and places his own garrison in control of Capua. With signal self-awareness, Pacuvius says in soliloquy,

I cannot be surpriz'd, that *Hannibal*
Should leave a Garison, should not trust me
With full command, which I had just before
Abus'd, betray'd, and given up to him. [III.iii.58-61]

Perhaps most telling about the play is the way in which the Machiavellian Pacuvius appropriates rhetoric: first, republican rhetoric to manipulate the mob; second, the rhetoric of word-as-bond to demand allegiance from his son to the licentious Hannibal; finally, a hollow-sounding rhetoric of transcendence as Capua falls. While a vengeful Rome approaches, those who betrayed their trust with her all commit suicide, even Decius Magius, released from captivity under Hannibal but like Socrates loyal to his city to the last.

In a subplot, Favonia, the matron who secretly loves her husband's best friend, Junius, whom she thought dead when she married Virginius, tragically gives him her hand to kiss in the middle of the night even as he departs to commit suicide over his fate. They are espied and, of course, she must kill herself to purge her pollution. Junius lives after all, only to kill Virginius, who kills him in return. The subplot is lugubrious, but on the symbolic level, Favonia is a figure for the unfaithful land that cannot determine its loyalties (much less its political theory) and must suffer the consequences. Its fate is annihilation (see Hughes, *English Drama* 434-35).

These Revolutionary tragical satires are all corrective in the sense that the audience can perceive the standard of faith and loyalty that is violated with disastrous results. That loyalty has been a master-trope of feudal aristocracy. Yet significantly, these satires are all set in the Classical world, a setting that militates against monarchial theory and suggests instead a new, more republican world order—not democratic, still aristocratic, but a more fraternal than paternal order, where the leader is *primus inter pares*. Whatever the ambivalence of these authors, they have suggested a figuration that mythifies the Revolutionary ruling oligarchy. And they have woven into it the trope of the One Just Man in a world of faithlessness. In that sense all three contribute to the development of the bourgeois master trope of self-reliance.

Tragicomic Romance

If Restoration tragicomedy in the main also reaffirms aristocratic ideology, I have nevertheless cited McKeon's dialectical reading of *Marriage A-la-Mode,* a reading that highlights emergent bourgeois tropes like the self-made man and freedom of marital choice (156-62). Sounding like Almanzor, Leonidas at one point exclaims, "Though meanly born, I have a Kingly Soul yet" (IV.i.22), and he and Palmyra insist on their right to choose marital partners (though not to the point of her defying her father). I would add to McKeon's tropes Doralice's threatening the male double standard as another example of the uppity women claiming equal sexual rights—in this case, to adultery.

Aristocratic tragicomedy as a dramatic form persists into the Revolutionary period. *Timoleon; or, The Revolution* (1697? but perhaps unperformed) mixes the serious with the comic in a play where the hero saves the state from a tyrant, then retires to private life with the daughter of the tyrant, leaving a full-scale republic behind him and arguing for an egalitarian society where nobles and plebes alike shall partake "each [in] a just share of Government" and the rich shall not oppress the poor (V, 79). The anonymous author sounds like a proto-Rousseau: "Let not one Man grow greater than the rest."

Nevertheless, aristocratic tragicomedy no longer had the energy of its Restoration examples. Instead, in the paradigm shift from aristocratic to bourgeois ideology, tragicomic form gets appropriated not only by the novel (*Pamela, Evelina*) but also by that dramatic form critics have always found so off-putting, sentimental comedy—the bourgeois family romance par excellence. In this hybrid of somber high-plot cum comic low-plot similar to tragicomedy, we find as early as Shadwell's comedies of the 1680s some of those emergent bourgeois tropes already triumphing over aristocratic tropes. *The Squire of Alsatia* (1688) has long held a secure place in the history of the emergence of sentimental drama. And coming as it does at the virtual moment of revolution, it seems to me to signal a dramatic shift in ideological paradigm. Even earlier, Shadwell's *Lancashire Witches, and Tegue o Divelly the Irish-Priest* (1681) strikes me as a more interesting play for purposes of analyzing these ideological shifts. In it Shadwell first develops the trope of the benevolent *fratriarch* (if I may coin the term), Sir Edward Hartfort. Shadwell describes him in the dramatis personae as a "worthy Hospitable true English Gentleman, of good understanding, and honest Principles." Sir Edward merits his position in society because of his essential worthiness. Marks of this worth are his "good understanding," which consistently manifests itself in his enlightened, unsuperstitious reasonableness; his impatience with insinuating clerics; his warm affection for his daughter and the memory of his departed wife; his "honest Principles" of both domestic and national order, especially his neostoical morality and his patriotism: *"I am a true English-man, I love the Princes Rights and Peoples Liberties, and will defend 'em both with the last penny in my purse, and the last drop in my veins, and dare defy the witless Plots of Papists."* For such sentiments, he is called "a Noble Patriot," a Whig keyword, and instead of familial loyalty to a father-king, he articulates a loyalty to the English "Constitution" as "the Noblest in the World." Ashamed of a decadent, Frenchified aristocracy, he agrees that "the Genius of *England*" has devolved upon the "Yeomanry" (III.47-59). But his care for building his estate through marriages between his and his neighbor's children marks him as a "true English Gentleman," one of the new country gentry upon which England will build its fame and strength (in union with its merchants).

Shadwell's young male lovers are also members of this enlightened country gentry as opposed to Restoration comedy's Town Wits. Unlike his earlier rakish pairs in *Epsom Wells* (1672) and *The Virtuoso* (1676), these lovers are already converted to true love, and while they display a faith in the new science similar to Sir Edward's, they display no wit. That is left to their female counterparts, and here Shadwell's play is most revolutionary. Yet here it is also conservative, marking the emergence of a bourgeois order but marking also its political and patriarchal limits.

The major conflict in the play is the familiar one of enforced marriage, this one to unite Sir Edward's estate with that of his neighbor, Sir Jeffrey Shackelhead, through a double marriage of their sons and daughters. The problem is that witty women are to be matched with two different kinds of fool. Sir Jeffrey is married to a status-conscious wife who would not only take on airs but impose Town airs on their son, whom she has turned into the fop Sir Timothy. And Sir Edward's own son, like so many country bumpkins in later eighteenth-century drama, loves his hunting, horses, and dogs more than women. So the arranged marriages are doomed, and the women properly rebel:

> *Isabella* [Sir Edward's daughter]. Well, we are resolved never to Marry where we are designed, that's certain. For my part I am a free English woman, and will stand up for my Liberty, and Property of Choice.
>
> *Theodosia* [Sir Jeffrey's daughter]. And Faith, Girl, I'le be a mutineer on thy side; I hate the imposition of a Husband, 'tis as bad as Popery. [I.272-76]

The reference to popery is not gratuitous, for the very subtitle of the play announces the presence of the delightful Tegue o Divelly, the infamous Catholic Father Kelly of the Popish Plot, but both fathers who arrange forced marriages (Sir Edward's progressiveness is herein qualified) and the pope are traditional patriarchs who inhibit liberty.

Shadwell had been developing the figure of this resourceful English woman in *A True Widow* (1678) and *The Woman-Captain* (1679), and Isabella, played by the irrepressible Elizabeth Barry, boldly proclaims, "I warrant thee, a Womans wit will naturally work about these matters" (II.429-30). She is generally the witty one, outrageously teasing Sir Timothy and even throwing stones at him, then covering up in front of the parents. At one point, their wit induces these female rebels to put on the disguises of the Lancashire witches of the title.

Michael Alssid has done an excellent job of detailing "the implicit parallels between feminine mischief and true sorcery" in the play (90-95). But because he sees the real witches' behavior as simply chaotic, as opposed to the rational order of Sir Edward, he seems to me to miss the profound implications of the revolutionary agency of all the witches in the play, that is, all the uppity women who would challenge patriarchal control. The ultimate liberating act of wit on the part of the heroines is to disguise themselves as witches, for in the chaotic night before their forced marriages they thus escape the reappearing representatives of patriarchal order—especially Sir Jeffrey, who is looking for his own rebellious wife, herself seeking an adulterous liaison with one of the young men. And, like Manley's Rosalinda and Trotter's Felicia, they proceed to marry their lovers clandestinely without patriarchal approval and at the risk of losing their portions and rupturing the familial warmth at least between Isabella and her father.

Agency is complicated in this night scene. Often characters attribute human agency to witches, for example, when Sir Jeffrey trips over a servant upon entering the men's chamber, where hide the two young women and his lady (IV, 158). But it is important to note that the real witches abet the women's rebellion, providing, in the words of Alssid, "a figurative smoke screen for the harassed couples" (93). Moreover, as Alssid also notes, the real witches provide the storm that brings the young men mistakenly to the very estate which houses the women who bewitched them at the spa just in the nick of time to prevent their enforced marriage and to get the women for themselves despite "the laws of Sir Edward and Sir Jeffrey" (93).

What Alssid does not see is that the witches represent both female agency—in this case, the freedom of women to choose sexual partners—and the limitations of that agency—the partners chosen do not finally rupture the patriarchal bonds, for the young men are themselves well bred, from good estates, and can provide superior portions for their brides. Thus Sir Edward accepts them and offers to reconcile Doubty and Theodosia to the Shackleheads. Sir Edward considers Doubty to "have most Injur'd me" (V.654). The reason is that Doubty has supplanted his son with Theodosia, thus denying him the male heir he so desperately wants to carry on his name (V.663). Instead, he accepts Bellfort as his son-in-law.

Through the repeated references to their hidden teats, whereby they suckle all manner of beast and imp, and to their constant involvement in infant mortality (see the ends of Acts II and III), the real witches are associated with the powers of fertility and impotence or barrenness, of womb and tomb. They represent the ultimate uppity women, matriarchs who threaten patriarchal control of female reproduction, the archetype of the Great Mother (see Neumann):

> *Men and Beasts are in thy Power,*
> *Thou canst Save, and canst Devour,*
> *Thou canst Bless, and Curse the Earth,*
> *And cause Plenty, or a Dearth.* [III.642-45]

Their *"Power"* is so great that *"Heaven it self can have no more"* (II.518-19). They threaten the Western male deity, the superego of Western law. Thus they must finally be subjected to that law at the end of the play, when they are sent to jail. Moreover, Shadwell tempers their threat by subjecting them to a "Master" throughout, the Devil: uppity whores must be controlled by a patriarchal superpimp.

It is no accident that one of the witches, Mother Dickenson, copulates with Tegue o Divelly in the chaotic night scene. As Alssid notes, she thus "prevents Tegue's rape of Lady Shacklehead" (93). More important, she prevents her adultery with Doubty as well: women's freedom in the play does not extend to adultery either (shades of Doralice). But most important, the copulation represents the essential similarity between witchcraft and popery,[28] not just because both are superstitious but because both threaten the emergent bourgeois order. From Marlowe's *Dr. Faustus* to Marx's interpretations of the failure of the revolutions in France, the emergent middle class gains power by driving a wedge between right and left, between the ancien régime and any real democratic revolution. Tegue is associated not just with popery but with a clergy, a court, and a class too sympathetic with Rome and France and late European feudal aristocracy. And the witches are associated with not just female but class uppitiness. Thus through the servant Susan's potion, they help bring the Anglican chaplain Smerk down, as Alssid notes without seeing the sociopolitical significance, from his "social climbing" (93) and limit him to a more proper status. Thus the human witches bring Sir Timothy—and by implication his mother—down from their unmerited status aspirations. By the end of the play, not only is the country bumpkin Clod back on top of his witch and in control with *her* bridle; the benevolent fratriarch is back on top, threats to his new order banished to jail (the witches and Tegue) or put in their place. Sir Edward has earlier rationalized his disbelief in the power of witches as anti-Manichaean: "'[T]is such as you [Smerk] are Atheistical, that would equal the Devils power with that of Heaven its self" (I.356-57). Yet he does not attribute the dynamic of the dénouement to Heaven, as in the typical ending of Restoration and Revolutionary drama, but instead to

"Fate" (V.701). Nevertheless, the real dynamic is the incipient shift in power relations between one dominant class and another.

Loftis has briefly analyzed Mr. Sealand in Steele's *Conscious Lovers* (1722) as a figure for not only the equality of the emergent (upper) middle class but (implicit in Loftis's treatment) its superiority. He notes that the play satirizes aristocratic pretensions to class superiority (*Comedy and Society* 84-85). Loftis quotes this key statement by Sealand to Sir John Bevil, one of those who assumes class privilege, in this instance by excusing his son's putative sowing of wild oats:

> Sir, as much a Cit as you take me for—I know the Town, and the World—and give me leave to say, that we Merchants are a Species of Gentry, that have grown into the World this last Century, and are as honourable, and almost as useful, as you landed Folks, that have always thought your selves so much above us; For your trading, forsooth! is extended no farther, than a Load of Hay, or a fat Ox—You are pleasant People, indeed; because you are generally bred up to be lazy, therefore, I warrant you, Industry is dishonourable. [IV.ii.49-57]

The sneeringly sarcastic dichotomy between aristocratic laziness and bourgeois industry and utility connotes not just equality but superiority.

Brown astutely analyzes the play's inherent contradiction between bourgeois value based on merit and the marriage that concludes the action (170-73). While Sealand and Bevil Junior may both protest that virtue is their only concern in a marriage, as in the typical tragicomic romance each of the nubile characters turns out to be in the right class anyway, so any real challenge to the traffic in women to improve estates proves moot. If she had not been preoccupied with matters of generic form, Brown might have availed herself of more of Loftis's analysis of shifts in society to make the point that, despite Sealand's protestations, he is participating in the building of that gentry-merchant middle class Hogarth depicts as *Marriage à la Mode.* As Sealand says in a conciliatory tone to the elder Bevil, "Look you, Sir *John,* Comparisons [between our classes] are odious, and more particularly so, on Occasions of this Kind, when we are projecting Races, that are to be made out of both Sides of the Comparisons" (IV.ii.61-64).

In "'Sure I Have Seen That Face Before,'" James Thompson astutely analyzes the relationship between sign and value especially, for my purposes here, as it relates to Indiana, the perdita of *The Conscious Lovers.* Supposedly, she represents inherent value to which nothing need be added. Of course, as Thompson notes of the irony of the ending, the superaddition of Sealand's vast wealth makes moot the question whether she is such a value or not. In short, the play wants to have it both ways: the bourgeois doctrine of inherent worth cum aristocratic inherited wealth, still signified by both money *and* land. And is it not interesting that Cimberton's ostensibly satirized point turns out to be well taken: "Sir, since it is a Girl that they have, I am, for the Honour of my Family, willing to take it in again; and to sink her into our Name, and no harm done" (V.i.16-18)? That is, since Lucinda Sealand's mother is herself a Cimberton cousin and since, after all, she is a "Girl" and not a male, Cimberton's marriage to her he can justify to the family patriarch, Sir Geoffry, for she will not represent any real threat to patrilinearity. As in most of the plays that deal with miscegenation between gentry and merchant class, the male comes from the former and the female from the latter. Less contamination, you know. It is no accident that Indiana is the scion of a merchant, Bevil Junior that of a landed squire.

What my old friends and colleagues have omitted from their analyses, however, is, to me at least, potentially more interesting in terms of the tropes of both class and gender. Just as in *The Lancashire Witches* Shadwell drives a wedge between discredited ancien régime and excluded radical potential, so does Steele here. Cimberton is a displaced version of the Restoration rake. Beneath the veneer of his supposedly superior breeding, he is unable to control his sexual passion for Lucinda, leers and paws at her, and fears he "shan't, for many Years, have Discretion enough to give her one fallow Season"; "I must depend upon my own Reflection, and Philosophy, not to overstock my Family" (III.i.290-92, 320-22). Instead, Bevil Junior is the one who exhibits the new bourgeois concept of "breeding" (an important metaphor from the prologue on): morals, manners, taste, decorum. He reads moral authors every morning; he treats artists with magnanimity and Indiana with incredible generosity; and he exercises neostoical self-control in the face of insufferable provocation from his friend Myrtle. The point of this last display is the triumph of bourgeois ethics, sanctioned by law rather than force, over what the new dominant class portrays as the aristocratic "vice" of dueling—as if its ethics represented not just the *virtù* of the winning side, as Nietzsche would express it, but natural law.

On the other side of the wedge are the very entertaining scenes between Tom and Phillis, servants to Bevil Junior and Lucinda, respectively. The two of them hilariously ape aristocratic manners of courtship and decorum. But we are never allowed to view them as the threat of any real democracy. The older, more decorous servant, Humphrey, makes fun of Tom's pretensions: "I hope the Fashion of being lewd and extravagant, despising of Decency and Order, is almost at an End, since it is arrived at Persons of your Quality." When at another of Tom's extravagances he exclaims, "What will this World come to!" or when Tom himself laments, "The Devil's in my Master! he has always more Wit than I have," we are invited to disapprove of further social mobility than the play allows the upper middle merchant class (I.i.166-68, 228-29; I.ii.21-22). Upstairs and Downstairs must remain firmly situated. Indeed, Tom has really only modest aspirations for himself and Phillis: "[O]ne Acre, with Phillis, wou'd be worth a whole County without her" (III.78-79). Note that, despite all of their pretensions, it is this lower-class couple that is satisfied with (and ends up with, we must assume) the modest little love nest—not either of the middle-class couples, who end up with money *and* status, as bourgeois gentlemen heroes with estates.

The play also keeps women in their place. However much she indignantly responds to Cimberton, Lucinda is really a passive object of exchange. Phillis shows more wit and agency in forestalling Mrs. Sealand and Cimberton by suggesting to Myrtle that he disguise himself as Sir Geoffry. Indiana is as helpless as Clarissa, just luckier—that her aunt's reading of Bevil Junior as Lovelace proves to be not true. Indiana may love Bevil, but she is completely dependent on events, rationalized at the end as "Providence," for fulfillment of her desires. As Lucinda pouts to Phillis, nubile women in the system of exchange designed to build estates "must have no Desires" (III.171-72).

Yet the play somewhat surprisingly reveals the animal desires, the real breeding that underlies male-female relationships and that must be contained by social code. Not only can Cimberton not control his lust; Tom can't keep his lips off Phillis. When she complains, "Lard, we have been Fooling and Toying, and not consider'd the main Business of our Masters and Mistresses," Tom archly responds, "Why, their Business is to be Fooling and Toying, as soon as the Parchments are ready" (III.96-99). In other words, the business of planning marriages is an elaborate system of control over the real biological business of coupling. People with money can afford such elaboration, as Phillis archly reminds Lucinda, who wonders why Phillis suffers Tom to kiss her thus: "Why, Madam, we Vulgar take it to be a Sign of Love; we Servants, we poor People, that have nothing but our Persons to bestow, or treat for, are forc'd to deal, and bargain by way of Sample; and therefore, as we have no Parchments, or Wax necessary in our Agreements, we squeeze with our Hands, and seal with our Lips, to ratifie Vows and Promises" (III.126-31).

But even the lower classes are controlled by the patriarchal sexual system, enforced by religious sanction. And though the play shows middle-class impatience with a double standard in this system that is an undesirable aristocratic residual component in the new bourgeois compromise—

Sealand preaches against it to Sir John, who foolishly defends it—it is not a male who suffers the play's disapprobation for sexual transgression. After all, Bevil Junior is not really guilty of keeping a mistress. It is Mrs. Sealand who comes in for the harshest treatment as transgressor. We learn in Act V that her precipitancy in getting her daughter married results from typical mother's jealousy of a daughter who now puts her candle under a bushel. Mrs. Sealand is another Lady Wishfort, the type of superannuated woman who would continue sexual activity beyond her patriarchally allotted time. Yet Mrs. Sealand is Sealand's second wife and is probably not that old. Ah, but the generational law, at least in Western comedy and tragicomedy, is cruel.

Mrs. Sealand is even more transgressive, however. In the funny scene between her and Cimberton when he indecorously begins talking about married couples in bed and she hides her blushes with her fan, under the guise of advocacy for decent silence about such matters, Cimberton absurdly recounts the sexual practices of the Spartans: "*Lycurgus,* Madam, instituted otherwise; among the *Lacedemonians,* the whole Female World was pregnant, but none, but the Mothers themselves, knew by whom; their Meetings were secret, and the Amorous Congress always by Stealth; and no such professed Doings between the Sexes, as are tolerated among us, under the audacious Word, Marriage." Mrs. Sealand breaks out in a rapture of wish fulfillment: "Oh! had I liv'd, in those Days, and been a Matron of *Sparta,* one might, with less Indecency, have had ten Children, according to that modest Institution, than one, under the Confusion of our modern, barefac'd manner" (III.237-46). Whatever they think they are saying, they are revealing the threat to patriarchy of uncontrolled female sexuality and therefore the need for the Western system of absolute control. If none but the mothers know, then the male ego and the patriarchal control of property are both destroyed. At the end of the play there is no sentimental absorption of Mrs. Sealand into the concluding euphoria. She continues to be satirized as rejoicing only at no longer having her daughter around the soirées. This sentimental comedy par excellence marks the shift to a new trope of class, but it leaves much to be desired for a truly "democratic romance"—in terms of not only class but gender.

Thomas Southerne's *Oroonoko* (1695) was one of the most popular tragedies on the English stage in the eighteenth century.[29] Well before *Cato, The Conscious Lovers,* and *The London Merchant,* it marks the full movement into maintext of Britain's romance of empire—and the dreadful "Commodity" upon which it was based (I.i.245), at least in part, slavery.

Unlike the Widdow Ranter's negroes, Southerne's are given speaking parts, and they cry out for "liberty" from oppression (III.ii.220),

> the heavy Grievances,
> The Toyls, the Labours, weary Drudgeries
> . . . Burdens more fit for Beasts,
> For senseless Beasts to bear, than thinking Men.
> Then if you saw the bloody Cruelties
> They execute on every slight offense;
> Nay sometimes in their proud, insulting sport:
> How worse than Dogs they lash their fellow Creatures:
> Your heart wou'd bleed for 'em. [121-29]

This is Aboan, faithful servant, slave even, of Oroonoko, to whom he appeals in terms of noblesse oblige:

> O Royal Sir, remember who you are,
> A Prince, born for the good of other Men,
> Whose God-like Office is to draw the Sword
> Against Oppression and set free Mankind. [134-37]

Like Behn's Oroonoko (and Abdelazer as well), Southerne's Oroonoko is an African prince of royal blood. Here transnational aristocracy is put in service of bourgeois revolutionary ideals. Oroonoko is a black Tamerlane.

Oroonoko wills his revolution to be bloodless. First, he proposes that the freed African slaves should live like maroons, farming their own plantation, where "in our native innocence, we shall live Free" (III.iv.26-27). Then he suggests they appropriate a ship to return to their homeland in Africa—adumbrations of Liberia. Like a black Patrick Henry, he proclaims,

> There is no mean, but Death or Liberty.
> . . . But if we fall
> In our attempt, 'tis nobler still to dye
> Then drag the galling yoke of slavery. [51, 118-20]

As Maximillian Novak and David Rodes point out, Southerne's is not an abolitionist play (xxviii-xxxii). Oroonoko himself justifies slavery as a time-honored practice among Africans themselves, as a form of property, and he portrays rebellion, ironically, as "black Ingratitude" (III.ii.104). Perhaps most disappointing to our modern sensibilities is Oroonoko's condemnation of his fellow slave revolutionaries, most of whom desert him: "To think I cou'd design to make those free, / Who were by Nature

Slaves" (IV.ii.60-61). Why would he then lead a rebellion? Like Otway's Jaffeir, he finally capitulates to Aboan out of concern that he and his white wife, Imoinda, will breed not a race of free mulattoes but slaves.

Southerne treats the conflict in the play as if it were primarily over the old aristocratic ethos of word-as-bond. It is another Southerne play about faithlessness, from the captain of the slave ship's treachery in luring Oroonoko aboard to the lieutenant governor's breaking of his word with him when he surrenders. When the captain defends himself as a "better Christian" than to keep his word "with a heathen" (I.ii.176-77), Oroonoko responds with contempt:

> You are a Christian, be a Christian still:
> If you have any God that teaches you
> To break your Word, I need not curse you more:
> Let him cheat you, as you are false to me.
> . . . Nature abhors,
> And drives thee out from the Society
> And Commerce of Mankind, for Breach of Faith.
> Men live and prosper but in Mutual Trust,
> A Confidence of one another's Truth. [I.ii.178-99]

The noble Blanford, agent of the absent governor's plantation and friend to Oroonoko, warns the treacherous lieutenant governor of Heaven's wrath, which will transmute him to a "Monument of Faithless Infamy" (V.ii.10) for breaking his word. His speech, along with that just quoted from Oroonoko, constitutes a swan song to the feudal era:

> Remember, sir, he yielded on your word;
> Your Word! which honest Men will think should be
> The last resort of Truth, and trust on Earth:
> There's no Appeal beyond it, but to Heaven:
> An Oath is a recognisance to Heaven:
> Binding us over, in the Courts above,
> To plead to the Indictment of our Crimes
> That those who 'scape this World should suffer there.
> But in the common Intercourse of Men,
> (Where the dread Majesty is not Invok'd,
> His Honour not immediately concern'd,
> Not made a Party in our Interests),
> Our Word is all to be rely'd upon. [40-52]

Blanford knows the lieutenant governor swore no oath. We move in this passage from aristocratic to bourgeois world, where increasing skepticism about the deity leaves humans dependent upon a system of honor enforced by men alone.

Oroonoko begins and ends the play a man alone. To his enslavers he declares, "[T]here's another, Nobler Part of Me, / Out of your reach, which you can never tame" (I.ii.234-35). He cares not what Western name they give him: "I am my self; but call me what you please" (242). At the end, convinced that "The Gods themselves conspire with faithless Men / To our destruction" (V.v.132-33), Oroonoko kills first his pregnant wife, then the lieutenant governor in vengeance, then himself. Aboan's words prove ironically true: "When you put off the hopes of other men [that is, no longer rely on them to keep their words], / You will rely upon your God-like self: / And then you may be sure of liberty" (III.ii.58-60). Oroonoko can find liberty only in death, where he is confident he will be reunited in "Happiness" with Imoinda, as the lieutenant governor looks on with (satanic) envy (V.v.302-4). Oroonoko is finally a figure for stoic self-reliance.

Oroonoko and Imoinda must die because the cultural equality embodied in transnational aristocracy and imaged in their onstage, in-your-face miscegenation must finally be denied.[30] Britain needs another ending, and Southerne supplies it in his comic plot. There a couple of women tricksters, driven out of England because of their dwindling supply of currency both literal and metaphoric, seek husbands in the New World. They manipulate words and promises to obtain security in their own form of commodity exchange. As Novak and Rodes argue, "[T]here is . . . a clear parallel between the institution of slavery and the institution of marriage" (xxii). Witty and resourceful as particularly Charlotte Welldon is, however, just as when, disguised as her brother, she leaves all her wealth in the hands of the Stanmore she both trusts and woos, so when she marries him must she repose in him all her independence. The Widow Lackitt, upon whom Charlotte works a delicious bed-trick, complete with titillating discourse of performance, of course, surrenders her wealth and independence at the end to Charlotte's brother-in-law, Jack.

Charlotte is not quite as outrageous as Southerne's Sir Anthony Love, in his play of that title, for she, like Farquhar's Dorinda in *The Beaux' Stratagem,* "cou'd not consent to cheat" the object of her desire, Stanmore (V.i.63), though there's nothing sentimental in her sister Lucy's marriage to the widow's booby son. But the ending of this tragicomedy does not work to reaffirm the code of word-as-bond in both heroic and comic plots, the one on idealistic, the other on pragmatic grounds. In fact, Southerne's play may be better described, like *The Princess of Cleve,* as tragicomical satire. The heroic plot ends more like a corrective satire than a personal tragedy, for Oroonoko seems guilty of no unbridled passion that destroys him. Instead, the play ends in an indictment of colonial society, the audience being aware of the standard of faith that was violated.[31]

The death of the lieutenant governor is certainly poetical justice. And the stage is filled at the end with sympathetic, apparently gentry characters. But what is out of sight is of great importance. The planters who demand Oroonoko's death, who are portrayed as nothing better than rabble, are absent, secure on their plantations, their hegemony not significantly challenged. Since their noble, heroic revolutionary leaders are dead, those slaves by nature are back on the plantations where even Oroonoko would say they belong. There is still "no danger of the White Slaves," like Imoinda and the Irish, the transported and the dispossessed, for "they'll not stir," as the lieutenant governor says cynically (II.iv.43).[32] The Indians, against whom, like Bacon, Oroonoko has led a successful expedition in self-defense against their raids on the colony, are back in the woods awaiting further colonial expansion. And the Stanmores and Lackitts are part of the creolizing colonials, ready to have children to inherit this little corner of the New World—until the Dutch take it away from them. With parting patronism—"Pagan or unbeliever," Blanford says over Oroonoko's dead body, "yet he liv'd [virtuously] / To all he knew: And if he went astray, / There's Mercy still above to set him right" (V.v.308-10)—they leave to inhabit such estates as Stanmore has earlier described:

> Enquire into the great Estates, and you will find most of 'em depend upon the same Title of Honesty [as the slaver captain]: The men who raise 'em first are much of the Captain's Principles. [I.ii.262-64]

The ending of Southerne's play implicitly predicts with prescience that the new heroes, imperial tricksters, who still break words and treaties, will inherit the earth and disseminate throughout it their states and estates.

In another, unfortunately not mainstream tragicomical satire, John Gay's *Polly* (written 1728 but not performed until 1777, even then only as revised), Gay extends his leveling satire in *The Beggar's Opera* (1728) in such a way that the pirates of the play represent all Europeans. Their leader, Macheath, who has disguised himself from his former wives in blackface and masquerades as the maroon Morano, has an opportunity, if like Antony he can only tear himself away from his Cleopatra-like wife, Jenny Diver, in order to pursue his glory, to conquer all the Indies.[33] When his men discuss who will get Peru (probably Morano as chief will get this treasure trove of gold), Mexico, Cuba, or Cartagena, the audience gets a parodic image of the Old World dividing up the New. As Gay portrays them, all Europeans are morally bankrupt. Gay's model of rectitude and probity is an Indian, the prince Cawwawkee, who has come to distrust all Europeans as cowards, especially word-breakers: "You have cancell'd faith. How can I believe you?" (II.xi.12).

Gay outrageously grants his Indians sole propriety over Old World notions of honor and honesty. Morano complains, "Meer downright Barbarians, you see lieutenant. They have our notional honour still in practice among 'em" (II.viii.36-37). In a parody of the justifying rhetoric of colonization, Lieutenant Vanderbluffe replies, "We must beat civilizing into 'em, to make 'em capable of common society, and common conversation" (38-39). "Common" society and conversation are, of course, hypocritical. The pirates say Cawwawkee would make a spectacle in England, but that old trope (going back at least to Shakespeare's *Tempest*) is changed here: "[T]hey would only take him for a fool" (64) not because Cawwawkee, like Caliban, is an ignorant savage but because he is noble, honorable.

Gay appropriates to Cawwawkee the figure of the stoic hero. Faced with torture, he proclaims, "[M]y virtue is in my own [power]" (II.viii.42). And he delightfully sings stoic resolution:

> *The body of the brave may be taken,*
> *If chance bring on our adverse hour;*
> *But the noble soul is unshaken,*
> *For that still is in our power:*
> *'Tis a rock whose firm foundation*
> *Mocks the waves of perturbation;*
> *'Tis a never-dying ray,*
> *Brighter in our evil day.* [28-35][34]

To the cross-dressed Polly, figure of sexual fidelity who has come seeking her husband, Macheath, Gay appropriates the additional figure of the One Just Man. Cawwawkee's father, the Indian king Pohetohee, is so impressed by Polly's virtue and constancy that he reluctantly allows at least one European honest. Cawwawkee and Polly sing a paean to that old Roman value of friendship.

The inevitable marriage of Polly and Cawwawkee, however, does not serve to negotiate a discursive peace between Old World and New. Instead, Gay gives us another of his patented romance endings that is patently absurd. Indeed, Gay warns us ahead of time. In his introduction, the poet calls sequels "a kind of Absurdity" (1-2), and the first player opines, "I hope, Sir, in the Catastrophe you have not run into the absurdity of your last Piece. . . . I am indeed afraid too that your Satyr here and there is too free" (29-36). Gay's wish-fulfillment ending is thoroughly satirical. Like

Dryden's Guyomar and Alibech, Cawwawkee and Polly retreat from the stage. After her period of mourning for Macheath, she will obviously marry Cawwawkee. Symbolically, then, honor is forced to retire from the civilized world to the state of nature, where, as Maja-Lisa von Sneidern argues (227-28), it has no meaning. Such a state is a vacuum. Cawwawkee and Polly actually represent at the end a dying culture, not just that of the Indians, who will eventually be conquered, but of the Europeans themselves. Gay's ending is nothing more than a ludic dance on the grave of the feudal ethos. The rapacious bourgeoisie has no credible code with which to replace it. Its money ethic has totally prevailed, and will prevail, as we say these days with so much pride in advanced capitalism, *globally.*

Conclusion

By definition, ruling-class ideology obfuscates. Recall the words of d'Aubignac with which I began, that seventeenth-century tragedy features "the Agitations and sudden turns of the fortune of great people." For French and English state-sponsored theater in at least the second half of this century in general, and for Restoration tragedy in particular, then, tragedy is a large but exceedingly class-based tent. What is remarkable about such tragedy is the way in which conflict is portrayed as almost exclusively intraclass, obscuring most power relations beyond the dynastic. The common people are a trope, the stereotype of the *mobile:* unfixed, capricious, mindless. The bourgeoisie hardly make an appearance. Yet in the subtext of the romance of empire, the audience is vouchsafed a glimpse of the exploited backs upon whom the empire is being built.

The cultural work that Restoration tragedy performs is primarily to legitimate the aristocracy's natural right to rule states through the heroes that its genealogy guarantees. To preserve both hierarchy and the genealogy that produces it, subjects, friends, wives, and even mistresses must remain loyal, constant—a system of *affiance* cemented by oaths and sanctioned by a divine enforcer. Transgressors are portrayed within the system as troth-breakers, traitors. Retributive if not distributive justice, portrayed as emanating from a divine providence, reinforces the system. Real oppositional ideology—for example, republican or even democratic theory; Levellers and Diggers; matriarchalism as a more logical genealogical system—are at best wildly caricatured, at worst totally absent.

Occasionally, contradiction inherent to the system breaks through, as in the return of the Oedipal repressed in political tragedy, the problem of the glorification of adulterous love in personal tragedy, the triumph of hypocrisy and absurdity in tragical satire, the need for pragmatic supplementary ideology in tragicomic romance. It seems no accident that these breakthroughs are most often engineered by Dryden, Lee, and Otway. Perhaps their conventional excellence can now be predicated more on their ability to construct what Eagleton calls second-power ideological works that both reveal and constitute the complexities of power relations in Restoration history.

I hope to have shown, by representative sampling, shifting tropes of ideology in Revolutionary tragedy. What I find most interesting is the way bourgeois ideology freezes out radical potentialities: real equality and power for women or for classes lower than the upper middle class. Bourgeois meritocracy, though dominant rhetorically, actually translates in these plays into a plutocratic oligarchy, whose rapacious exploitation both at home and abroad is justified as the natural, civilizing order of things. Some of the women in these plays may be hopeful signs for the future—Manley's Rosalinda; Rowe's Calista, Jane Shore, and Lady Jane Gray; Trotter's Lamira; Lillo's Millwood. And some of the lower-class characters shine out a resilient, irrepressible spirit—*Fatal Discovery*'s Margaretta, Shadwell's Clod, Steele's Tom and Phillis. But for the historical nonce these truly revolutionary genies are all contained in their lamps as the curtains fall.

Obviously, I flaunt the word *revolutionary* because I believe, in contrast to the revisionist historians, that a revolution did take place in 1688—a revolution in ideology. Through its imaging of possibilities lost as well as possibilities achieved, that revolution may have enabled the more thorough social and political revolution the revisionists believe occurred in the reform laws of 1832. The theater is a powerful state apparatus for the production of hegemonic ideology. But it is also a site where the critical subject, resisting the interpellation Althusser insists makes us into subjects in an ideological fiction, can constitute as playwright or discover as spectator the fissures in such ideology as well as the hint of radical possibilities.

I believe it is the job of cultural critique to appreciate the ordering function of the wallpaper while running our fingers over the crevices beneath, musing on the meaning of their silences and absences. Do I have my own ideology? You bet. I believe in the possibility of a world that finally achieves instead of betrays the bourgeois ideals of democracy, human rights, and social justice—hints of which we get, if only negatively, in English Revolutionary drama: in Calista's complaints about female inequality or Altamont's gentleness, for example, or Dumont-Shore's class leveling in my beloved Nicholas Rowe's *Fair Penitent* and *Jane Shore,* respectively; or Millwood's fiery exposé of the rapacious Social Darwinism inherent in capitalism in *The London Merchant;* or Aboan's diatribe against the horrid injustices of slavery or Oroonoko's defiance of European, Christian (inherently racist) cultural imperialism in the play that carries the latter's name like a river that runs through it.

Notes

Introduction

1. Late twentieth-century Marxists, New Historicists, and cultural materialists have interpreted dramatic conflict (I'm thinking especially of work done on English Renaissance drama) in terms of struggles for dominance related to the culture at large. I come down on the side of critics who see this (state-sponsored) drama as generally conservative, proceeding by strategies of containment and reaffirmation of ruling-class ideology. Not that there are not powerful, subversive exceptions. Though he comes down on the side of those who see Renaissance tragedy as subverting rather than containing (albeit he concentrates on the more subversive Jacobean period), I found a kindred spirit indeed when I finally read Dollimore's *Radical Tragedy* in its second edition, published the same year as *Word as Bond.* The introduction to that edition plus the book's opening section on contexts situates our kind of analysis splendidly. Also published virtually simultaneously was Markley's *Two-Edg'd Weapons,* which, although it deals primarily with comedy, nevertheless has a fine analysis of "the dialogics of style" and its relationship with ideology (see chaps. 1 and 2). Markley's analysis reminds us of the slippage of language—as seen through not just the twentieth-century lenses of Bakhtin but also the seventeenth-century lenses of contemporary theorists of language—even as it attempts to portray a dominant class's ideology as natural.

2. For this use of the vexed term *absolutism,* consult McKeon, *Origins,* chap. 5.

1. Heroes and States

1. Dates are of first performances insofar as we know them (as in *The London Stage,* corrected by the scholarship of Hume and Milhous over the years). References to plays are by act.scene.line or by act.scene, page. Sometimes scene numbering is absent or superfluous, as in Clark's edition of Orrery and Todd's edition of Behn, where they have numbered lines continuously throughout acts without clear scene divisions.

2. For a provocative and persuasive reading of these two plays by Orrery as reaffirming Stuart ideology even as they negotiate class heterogeneity, see Flores, "Orrery's *The Generall* and *Henry the Fifth.*"

3. There are rhymed heroic romances I have not mentioned: Sir Robert Howard, *The Vestal Virgin* (1665); Orrery, *The Black Prince* (1667); John Crowne, *The History of Charles the Eighth of France* (1671); Settle, *Ibrahim the Illustrious Bassa* (1676); Banks, *The Rival Kings* (1677). Note their dates as well.

4. *Works* 11:23 (part 1, act I, scene i, line 10, hereafter abbreviated as 1.I.i.10).

5. For the concept of the *unheimlich,* see Freud's classic essay, translated as "The Uncanny."

6. John Wallace brilliantly analyzed the theme of ingratitude in "John Dryden's Plays and the Conception of an Heroic Society."

7. Quinsey argues that Almahide's subjectivity is thus suppressed. It is important to remember that she is merely a trope in a patriarchal paradigm, the trope of the faithful Penelope, guardian of her chastity. True, she wishes to be free of both Boabdelin *and* Almanzor after they doubt her faith. But like Isabella in Shakespeare's *Measure for Measure,* her function is not to sequester her reproductive role but to play it out.

8. For a complementary interpretation, see Barbeau, *The Intellectual Design of John Dryden's Heroic Plays* 105-26.

9. See my *Word as Bond,* esp. chap. 6; see also Boehrer, esp. 5-11, and Tumir, 415.

10. The California editors in their notes to this word when it occurs in the play fail to see that it has the specific meaning of seizing a throne by both regicide and patricide.

11. For a good contrast between Nourmahal and Racine's Phèdre, see McCabe 264-72, although he seriously misreads Aureng-Zebe's metaphor of virtue centering on itself; moreover, to quote with approval his father's sarcastic misrepresentation of Aureng-Zebe's piety as "'self-denying cant'" is disingenuous. For the philosophical implications of the metaphor of circle and center, especially as used by Dryden, see my "Image of the Circle in Dryden's 'To My Honour'd Kinsman.'"

12. She may also, as Bhattacharya suggests, be a figure for the feminized exotic, needing the conquest of dominant British masculinity. The "emasculated" Aureng-Zebe that Bhattacharya sees may, on the other hand, be not so much a feminized exotic other ripe for dominance as a potential Oedipal rebel weak from the return of the repressed. For Dryden's appropriation of the Indian other into Britain's own self-image with incipient imperial consequences, see Choudhury, chap. 5.

13. Thompson, "Dryden's *Conquest of Granada* and the Dutch Wars": "The religious victory of the distant empire in historical Granada promotes the immediate, commercial ends of the immediate empire, as Dryden's play celebrates both the origin and the extension of European hegemony over the third world. . . . The aged Empire [of Ferdinand's remarks at the opening of the play] is not Moorish, but the Moorish conquerors, Portugal, Spain, and by extension, France, whose hegemony will shortly be overrun by 'some petty State,' the maritime nation and future commercial giant, England" (219). Brown's title of her watershed article on Behn's *Oroonoko,* first published in 1987, was "The Romance of Empire: *Oroonoko*

and the Trade in Slaves," which now, in an expanded, further theorized version, constitutes chap. 2 of *Ends of Empire.*

See also Barthelemy, *Black Face Maligned Race* 186-97, for a reading of the distortion of Moorish culture in both *The Conquest of Granada* and *Don Sebastian* for purposes of cultural imperialism. Seeing the connection between the political and the sexual in these plays, Barthelemy notes quite rightly, "Fathering children through the women of the enemy represents the ultimate symbol of political and cultural conquest" (197).

14. Another prediction of *Rule, Britannia,* amazing in its anachronicity, occurs in Orrery's *History of Henry the Fifth.* The war with France is won as much at sea as at land! Henry, whose brother, of course, commanded the fleet, predicts English imperial hegemony:

> That Prince, whose Flags are bow'd to on the Seas,
> Of all Kings shores keeps in his hand the Keys:
> No King can him, he may all Kings invade;
> And on his Will depends their Peace and Trade.
> Trade, which does Kings and Subjects wealth increase;
> Trade, which more necessary is than Peace. [V.i.57-62]

2. Villains and States

1. Queen Fredigond in *Love and Revenge* (1674), the Machiavel Pyrgus in *Fatal Love* (1680), and the Machiavel Meroin in *The Heir of Morocco* (1682).

2. Plays like Orrery's *Herod the Great* (1672) and, if he had anything to do with it, as I doubt, *Zoroastres* (not acted; written in mid-1670s); Thomas Shipman's *Henry the Third of France* (possibly acted 1672); Tate's *Brutus of Alba* (1678); Sir Francis Fane's *Sacrifice* (1686).

3. It is worth noting that Zanger and Mustapha, as they debate like Palamon and Arcite over the priority of love, employ the metaphor of the discovery of the "new World" (III.iii.59). Such a casual metaphor reminds us that Western Europe's wars with Turkey were about not only cultural hegemony in Europe but trade routes to the East.

4. For the best treatment of Behn's play so far, see von Sneidern 165-82, a reading with which I disagree even as I honor it. For a reading that attempts to deracialize Abdelazer, see Thomas. I think Thomas seriously miscalculates the significance of fewer references to race (quantity vs. quality) and also misreads Behn's rather competent ability to create a character similar to Iago and Edmund in his hypocritical posturing.

5. Barthelemy, 115-16, also sees Abdelazer's "execution" as "a communal activity," with the white community expunging the threatening blackamoor (abetted by the good Moor, Osmin—as if to prove some blacks are salvageable, assimilable to the European, Christian community).

6. See headnote to Dryden's *Works* 9:317 and n. 98, which refers to Loftis's own *Politics of Drama in Augustan England.*

7. Cf. Thompson, "Dryden's *Conquest of Granada* and the Dutch Wars," on Ferdinand's opening historical prophecy in *The Conquest of Granada.*

3. Fathers and Sons

1. For similar readings of these Shakespearean adaptations, see Wikander.

2. For the connection with Shaftesbury, see Rachel Miller, "Political Satire in the Malicorne-Melanax Scenes of *The Duke of Guise.*"

3. For a study of the play's topicality, see Moore; see also Ehrenpreis 47-50 and, more recently, Bywaters 34-56 and Erskine-Hill, chap. 7.

4. As I fear is California editor Earl Miner, who in his headnote to the play (*Works* 15:403-8) sees the energy of Mustafa and the rabble as the redemptive force in the play. But then, Miner's reading of the political implications of the play seems to me in general short-sighted in claiming the play's transcendence of politics toward a Christian moral vision of the universe. The metaphysical rhetoric of the play, however, is inextricably entwined with the political and the ethical: all three are strands of the durable rope that was aristocratic ideology.

5. King 171-73. King's remains the best treatment of the play; for his analysis of the political implications, a reading similar to mine, see 187-89.

6. As has been most recently argued by MacCallum.

7. *Paradise Lost* IX.6. For a reading of the religious meaning of the play, see King 166-79.

8. See my *Nicholas Rowe and Christian Tragedy,* chap. 1.

9. See Crowne's *Ambitious Statesman* (1679), Tate's *Loyal General* (1679), Lee's *Massacre of Paris* (not acted, but composed ca. 1679), Crowne's *Henry the Sixth* (1681), Settle's *Heir of Morocco,* where the mute sacrifice is indeed the son of the emperor (1682), and William Mountfort's *Injur'd Lovers* (1688). Owen reads the earlier of these plays not tropically but topically (that is, as partisan political gestures); nevertheless, what she calls "Tory quietism" calls attention to the silence of this sacrificial figure. Johnson makes a brilliant point about the return of the repressed, beheaded King Charles anent Tate's *King Lear.*

10. See my "Thomas Otway" (150-52); see also Munns's similar reading, which she develops handsomely (*Restoration Politics and Drama* 36-49).

11. Flores shrewdly relates Mithridates's fate to pressures endemic to patriarchal monarchy ("Patriarchal Politics under Cultural Stress" 11-14). Flores comes very close to describing those pressures as Oedipal: "Despite his virtue, Ziphares occupies a place beside his father and his brother within a system that produces not simply deep resentment at the father's authority, but rivalry over the distribution of power and women, which confer, in turn, one's heroic and masculine identity" (13).

12. McCabe writes, "Dryden was intent upon a tragedy of fate, still regarded as the essence of the Oedipus myth, Lee upon a tragedy of desire" (276). Given his Christianity and given his treatment of incestuous desire elsewhere in his canon, Dryden is no classical fatalist; moreover, he obviously approved Lee's treatment. So

McCabe's dichotomy would appear to be false. Dryden's theme of *the sins of the fathers being visited upon the sons* is the analogue and answer to classical fate. Nevertheless, McCabe is right to call attention to the role of desire in the play.

13. McCabe reads this line as a reference to the regicide of Charles I (275). As in his reading of *Aureng-Zebe,* McCabe concentrates on the incestuous side of the Oedipal triangle, not the side of parricidal conflict.

14. Banks probably took the mythological figuration from Francis Bacon's analogy between Essex and Icarus (quoted in Lacey xi). Bacon, Essex's protégé, turned against him in the end, throwing for the main chance.

15. Cf. Braverman, *Plots and Counterplots* 165-67. Vieth sees Titus's death by Valerius as signifying "a healing and a reintegration into the ongoing processes of society" (75 n. 86). For the importance of the concept "between men," see Sedgwick. See also Boehrer, who argues that Republican theory did not escape the Oedipal inherent in the patriarchal: "The phallus is dead; long live the phallus" (11; see 132-37).

16. For the most recent biography of Essex see Lacey; for Elizabeth's complaint, see p. 238. At the meeting, Tyrone and Essex negotiated a truce. He had been sent not to negotiate but to conquer.

17. Lacey perpetuates the rhetoric: "The rebel was . . . so civilized and reasonable. Not at all the uncouth savage Essex had expected" (236).

4. States of Mind

1. Lesser attempts at stringing this bow include Orrery, *King Saul* (acted, if at all, between 1676 and 1679); Crowne, *The Destruction of Jerusalem by Titus Vespasian* (1677); Banks, *The Destruction of Troy* (1678); Dryden, *Troilus and Cressida; or, The Truth Found Too Late* (1679); Lee, *Theodosius; or, The Force of Love* (1680).

2. It is fascinating to speculate, as I have with Derek Hughes in private correspondence, whether there was a tradition of playing Cleopatra as tawny (to use Shakespeare's term), darkened against history (she was a descendant of Macedonian Greeks) into a figure for the erotic, exotic other that threatens Roman cultural superiority. One of Hughes's consultants thinks it possible. Nyquist raises the same possibility of a racially exotic Cleopatra in the Renaissance but argues that Dryden's Cleopatra is explicitly white (those "white arms" as the site of Antony's conquering fantasy in III.i.1), her very whiteness, like her submissiveness, making her a figure for the nonthreatening, nonbarbaric object of a new, bourgeois masculinity's right to dominate. But Dryden may have had it both ways: Cleopatra's whiteness makes her an acceptable exotic.

3. See Flores's fine treatment of the relationship between passion and ideology in this play ("Patriarchal Politics under Cultural Stress" 3-10). Flores writes with insight, "Alexander's apparently pathological need for passion—heterosexual and homosocial—is produced both by his political identity and by the social relations he draws upon to justify his political status" (7). Alexander, according to Flores, is a victim of the "star-system" of monarchial government (6).

4. Repeated by the California editors without citation (*Works* 13:423n), this point was originally mine and published in "The Jewel of Great Price" in 1975.

5. Suppressed from the play are Cleopatra's other liaisons, both historical (her marriages to her brothers) and putative (her affair with Gnaius Pompey). Shakespeare's Cleopatra claims this last to have been with Pompey the Great (I.5.31), but Antony later corrects her (III.xiii.118).

6. Dryden seems simply to nod here, perhaps under the influence of Shakespeare's lines (V.ii.227-29), which he is clearly imitating. Earlier, he has Antony say not only that he first met Cleopatra in Egypt but that he beheld her in Cilicia "after" her affair with Caesar (II.i.272)—that is, after Caesar's assassination and close to the battle at Philippi (42 B.C.). Dryden also has Antony describe Cleopatra on the Cydnos as the "first" time not *he* but *Dolabella* saw her (III.i.155 ff). But Dryden may have nodded a second time when he has Alexas say he "first" saw Ventidius at Cilicia "When *Cleopatra* there met *Antony*" (I.i.97-98), although perhaps Alexas could well have seen Ventidius there for the "first" time when Cleopatra *met* Antony in the sense of rendezvous. One final complication: despite his marriage to Octavia, Antony *did* marry Cleopatra in Alexandria in ca. 36 B.C., as Dryden would have known from Plutarch. If that is what Cleopatra is referring to, Dryden has backdated the marriage as far as he logically could, to a time when Caesar was dead and Cleopatra was eligible for marriage. Even then, Dryden blinks the fact that Antony was married to Fulvia at the time. And if this is the meaning he wanted to suggest, he should have made more of it in the play, and he should not have called the meeting at Tarsus Antony and Cleopatra's "first." Of course, it is absurd for anyone to call this meeting their first, since Cleopatra was Caesar's mistress in Rome from 47 to 44 B.C., when Marc Antony was one of his closest associates.

7. One is reminded of Dryden's subsequent rendering of *Troilus and Cressida* (1679), wherein he reverses tradition and makes Cressida true and Troilus deceived; the subtitle of Dryden's play is *Truth Found Too Late.*

8. The California Edition has the italics reversed.

9. The best treatment of this imagery remains that of Hughes, "Significance." My "Jewel of Great Price" was written in response and sparked a lively debate between us (see Hughes, "Aphrodite Katadyomene" and "Art and Life in *All for Love*"). "Jewel" traces the theme of mutability versus constancy in all the extant Renaissance dramatic treatments of the story of Antony and Cleopatra. I respectfully disagree with Hughes about the tradition and about Dryden's play. Nevertheless, I am impressed and moved by Hughes's most recent treatment of the play, especially Cleopatra's being forced to be a trope in a patriarchal discourse (*English Drama* 254).

10. It would seem that Hughes in his various treatments of the play, as well as Fisher, however provocative their readings, both try to turn Dryden's play into Shakespeare's. For my reading of *Antony and Cleopatra,* see *Word as Bond* 291-300.

11. See *The Ready and Easy Way to Establish a Free Commonwealth* and the selections from *Second Defence of the English People,* both included in Merritt Hughes's edition. For a recent political (though more topical than tropical) reading of *Sampson Agonistes* see Erskine-Hill, chap. 7.

12. Von Sneidern's dissertation, which I had the honor to direct, caused me to think about these matters in Milton.

5. Apocalypse Now

1. Of course, Lee would have had access to the many other versions of the legend of Don Juan, including the two great classic treatments of the seventeenth century, Tirso de Molina's *El Burlador de Sevilla y Convidado de Piedra* (1623) and Molière's *Dom Juan; ou, Le festin de pierre* (1665). For my treatment of these two plays, plus Mozart and da Ponte's *Don Giovanni,* and the cultural work they perform, see "The Classic Treatment of Don Juan."

2. For the best readings of the play and its satire, see Hume, "Satiric Design"; Weber, *Restoration Rake-Hero* 69-78; Hughes, *English Drama* 313-14.

3. See the title page of the first edition, reproduced in Stroup and Cooke's modern edition, and the dedication (*Works* 2:147, 153).

4. Other tragical satires by Lee include *The Tragedy of Nero* (1675) and *Caesar Borgia; Son of Pope Alexander the Sixth* (1680?), both satires on thoroughly corrupt rulers and regimes (the latter featuring Machiavelli himself). I would also classify as tragical satires Henry Neville Payne's *Siege of Constantinople* (1674), Ravenscroft's adaptation of *Titus Andronicus; or, The Rape of Lavinia* (1678?), Settle's propagandistic and vitriolic *The Female Prelate: Being the History of the Life and Death of Pope Joan* (1680), and the anonymous *Farce of Sodom; or, The Quintessence of Debauchery* (if acted, only privately), a satire on libertinism where the author (in my opinion, just on grounds of style, surely not Rochester) is guilty of satire's endemic problem of the fallacy of imitative form—in these cases excesses that are hardly palatable. *Sodom* is clearly a corrective satire, for in the midst of the sodomy, even though their love is incestuous, the sex between the prince and the princess is presented as positive, for it is heterosexual. *Sodom* is thus a satire on the bisexuality of court libertinism (another reason it is probably not by Rochester, who celebrates bisexualism in his poetry). For a good reading of the political implications of *Sodom,* see Weber, "Carolinean Sexuality and the Restoration Stage."

5. Edmunds calls Shadwell's play a "tragic satire" (506).

6.For the best recent treatment of Shakespeare's Restoration adaptations, see Marsden, *The Re-Imagined Text.*

7. For an appreciation of this link, as well as of the play's relationship to Restoration comedy, see Vernon.

8. For different readings, cf. Sorelius 238; Edmunds 505 n. 1; Marsden, *The Re-Imagined Text* 44; Hughes, *English Drama* 256.

9. At the same time as Otway's initial offerings, Durfey wrote an absurdist rhymed heroic play, *The Siege of Memphis* (1676), where the language of official discourse collapses upon itself. Given Durfey's signal contributions to comical satire (see *Tricksters and Estates,* chaps. 11 and 12), it should not come as a surprise that this neglected playwright was, as usual, experimenting at the margins.

10. For *Don Carlos* (1676) see above, chap. 3; for the other early tragedies through *Caius Marius* (1679), see my "Thomas Otway" 149-60.

11. For corroborative though more radically feminist readings of Otway's two last tragedies, see Munns, *Restoration Politics and Drama,* who also deploys Girard, as I had done in 1989 in both "Thomas Otway" and *Word as Bond.*

12. Tumir has argued very persuasively that the patriarchy Otway satirizes is "exacerbated by the pressures of an absolutist regime" (422).

13. Previous readings closest to mine are those of Stroup, Hughes, "A New Look at *Venice Preserv'd,*" and DePorte.

14. Other critics, seeking New Critical ambiguity or poststructuralist self-deconstruction, would find such absurdity everywhere, or at least in every "great work," which in order to be great, they contend, cannot be naive and affirm an order. *Respondeo:* If all works laid bare the meaninglessness of social codes, then all literature and all criticism would be tautological; there would be no *official discourse* against which others could be marginal or subversive. We should not diminish Otway's achievement: no other playwright in his time stared so relentlessly, so disconsolately into Nietzsche's tragic abyss.

15. Markley, "Violence and Profits on the Restoration Stage," has brilliantly analyzed the fissures in the ideology of the play, the way it suppresses contradictions in England's national self-image and in the competetive, even violent nature of trade.

6. States and Estates

1. I treat Porter's play in *Tricksters and Estates* 200-202.

2. Alexander Greene, *The Politician Cheated* (probably not acted); Abraham Bailey, *The Spightful Sister* (probably not acted); John Corye, *The Generous Enemies; or, The Ridiculous Lovers* (1671); Thomas Duffet, *The Spanish Rogue* (1673); Edward Ravenscroft, *The English Lawyer* (1677); John Leanerd, *The Counterfeits* (1678).

3. John Tutchin's *Unfortunate Shepherd* is called a "Pastoral" on its title page but ends tragically.

4. The plays in this larger group include Richard Flecknoe's *Erminia; or, The Fair and Vertuous Lady* (not acted; later revised as *Emilia,* also not acted; see Canfield, "Authorship"); Thomas Shadwell's *Royal Shepherdesse* (1669; an improved version of John Fountaine's *Rewards of Virtue,* itself probably not acted); Thomas Durfey's *Injured Princess* (1682; adapted from Shakespeare's *Cymbeline* in a manner to stress constancy even more); Thomas Southerne's *Disappointment* (1684); Anne Finch, the countess of Winchelsea's *Triumphs of Love and Innocence* (written ca. 1688); and James Harris's *Mistakes; or, The False Report* (1690).

5. I treat both these comic plots in the section on subversive comedy in *Tricksters and Estates.*

6. For analysis of the ideological implications of this kind of punitive action in Restoration comedy, see my *Tricksters and Estates,* chap. 6, "Satiric Butts Get Disciplined."

7. Cf. Hughes's sensitive reading of this play, *English Drama* 64-66. Cf. also Flores, "Negotiating Cultural Prerogatives."

8. I briefly allude to this play's tricksters in *Tricksters and Estates* 53, where I also treat comic plots from several other split-plot tragicomedies in which both plots come to complementary closure: Abraham Cowley, *The Cutter of Coleman-Street* (1661); Thomas Duffet, *The Amorous Old-Woman; or, 'Tis Well If It Take* (1674); anon., *The Counterfeit Bridegroom; or, The Defeated Widow* (1677); Behn, *The Revenge; or, A Match in Newgate* (1680); and John Lacy, *Sir Hercules Buffoon; or, The Poetical Squire* (1684).

9. See also Frances Boothby's *Marcelia; or, The Treacherous Friend* (1669) and Aphra Behn's *Forc'd Marriage; or, The Jealous Bridegroom* (1670).

10. Hughes, *English Drama* 63, sees Lucy as really turning into "'a virtuous well-bred Lady'"; I see her as continuing the gulling of this cully into the cuckoldom that is his inevitable fate.

11. Braverman, "Rake's Progress" 149, notes the significance of the name.

12. See also Davenant's adaptation of Shakespeare's *Measure for Measure* cum the Beatrice/Benedick subplot of *Much Ado about Nothing, The Law against Lovers* (1662); Lewis Maidwell's *Loving Enemies* (1680); and William Mountfort's *Successfull Straingers* (1690).

13. Cf. McKeon, "Marxist Criticism and *Marriage à la Mode,*" whose argument is provocative.

14. For the concepts being employed here, see not only *Of Grammatology,* but also and especially Derrida, "The Pharmacy of Plato," pt. 1 of *Dissemination.*

15. See Hughes, "The Unity of Dryden's *Marriage A-la-Mode*" 131, 141; Braverman, *Plots and Counterplots* 100-101.

16. See esp. *Violence and the Sacred,* chap. 7, and also his earlier *Deceit, Desire, and the Novel.*

17. In readings subsequent to my first publication of this argument, Braverman, *Plots and Counterplots* 96-113, and Kroll, "Instituting Empiricism: Hobbes's *Leviathan* and Dryden's *Marriage à la Mode*" 55-63, emphasize the pragmatics of Dryden's language as negotiation of his moment in time. We have several moments of agreement. I differ in still seeing Dryden as attempting to revivify the idealistic as well as indulging the pragmatic rhetorics of order, and I see him as bringing them together in a dialogic union of *vouloir-dire.*

18. "Let *Caesar* take the World,— / An Empty Circle, since the Jewel's gone / Which made it worth my strife" (*All for Love* V.i.273-75).

19. See Ferguson and Hendricks for excellent analyses of the figure of this queen and its revelation of the incompatibility underlying England's colonial enterprise in this play. They, along with Todd, "Spectacular Deaths," have carefully analyzed the relationship between Behn's play and the historical record of Bacon's Rebellion. For a perceptive reading of the political ideology of the play, see Todd, *The Secret Life of Aphra Behn* 412-17.

7. Dramatic Shifts

1. The work of Loftis pointed the way to the interpretation of this shift, and work by Staves and Brown two decades ago began to blaze a trail. But Loftis

inferred change more in terms of topical than ideological politics, that is, more in terms of topical allusion than tropic transformation. And Staves and Brown employ an evolutionary model that posits early Restoration forms unproblematically representing Royalist ideology followed by forms emptied of any ideological content before they are filled with bourgeois ideology. Moreover, Staves focuses on transformations of portraits of authority ostensibly leading to more democracy in both political and domestic realms, and Brown (references in this chapter are to *English Dramatic Form* unless otherwise noted) on transformations of generic form leading to the "moral action" of drama and the novel in the new era—the former failing and the latter succeeding in embodying a supposedly exemplary morality.

Recent work by revisionist historians calls this entire paradigm shift into question (see J.C.D. Clark's review of this recent historiography). My own research seems to justify it.

2. I shall note in this chapter the plays produced by this Revolutionary company as LIF.

3. Brown sees the complexity of Almanzor's character as effecting a "juxtaposition of radical challenge and royalist resolution." But because she sees the ending as completely arbitrary and insists on "the inherent weakness of our concern for the ending of a heroic action" (14-19), she does not see the same legitimating sense of an ending as do I.

4. Staves notes the similarity between Almanzor and Lyndaraxa and says that "because she exists and because her view is fully expressed, the play is an agon where the view ultimately rejected is sufficiently interesting and persuasive to be considered" (69-70).

5. See Thompson, "Dryden"; McKeon, *Politics,* esp. 164-77.

6. See my *Nicholas Rowe and Christian Tragedy* 74 n. 2.

7. In the 1720 Rowe edition, the plays have separate pagination. *Tamerlane* is found in the first volume.

8. Vortimer is a usurper, who pursues in Gallia "loyal Chiefs, / Who ill cou'd bear the Murther of their King" (V.i, 53) and who is killed by the son of the man whose throne he usurped. Moreover, Lucius's ascendancy is enabled by the timely intervention of the Gallic king, Honorius. Could not a contemporary audience, especially one familiar with Manley's Tory sentiments, read Vortimer as George I, displaced avatar of William III and perhaps even Cromwell; Lucius as James Stuart, son of James II, known as the Old Pretender, the King across the Water; and Honorius as the French king (Louis XIV had died in 1715 and was succeeded by the five-year-old Louis XV)? Would not such an interpretation be especially accessible during the later stages of the Jacobite revolution known as "The Fifteen"?

9. Hughes says George Powell "brought" *The Fatal Discovery* on the stage for the Patent Company (*English Drama* 440). Since he was a notorious plagiarizer, might he have purloined the play from Gould, who, because of his problems with Barry and Betterton and their breakaway company, perhaps could not get this play performed? (Sloane, 111, discusses Gould's conflict especially with Barry, as Gould himself records it in "The Play-House: A Satyr" [*Works* 2:227-62], but Sloane, 209, also thinks *Fatal Discovery* predates *Innocence Distress'd.* About Powell,

Sloane says only that he may have written *Fatal Discovery*. Milhous and Hume discuss the evidence for authorship and decide to leave the play unattributed [16].) Whether Powell purloined the play or not, might he have had a ghost writer alter it for the stage? Might the writer, ghost or not, have been a woman?

McCabe concludes *Incest, Drama, and Nature's Law* by asserting that after Dryden's plays "the temper of English drama was not favourable" to further analysis of incest in order to probe either psychological or political depths the way that it had been throughout the seventeenth century (290). By his own admission, the breadth of McCabe's study made him perforce selective. But it is disappointing that McCabe overlooks two shocking plays of mother-son incest in the very year of Collier's *Short View of the Immorality and Profaneness of the English Stage*—1698—a diatribe McCabe sees as lying "like a dead weight" on subsequent English drama (290). Ironically, when McCabe writes that "it was not until the Gothic and Romantic periods that [incest] again emerged as a major focus for the examination of human nature" (291), his footnote calls our attention to—and misattributes to "Robert Walpole" (352 n. 106)—*Horace* Walpole's play, *The Mysterious Mother* (1768), for the mother-son incest plot that now takes its name from Walpole's play is the very plot of these two late Restoration tragedies.

10. *Heptameron* 265-66. The French reads,

> [M]ais sa patience fut si longue et sa nature si fragille, qu'elle convertit sa collere en ung plaisir trop abominable, obliant le nom de mere. Et, tout ainsy que l'eaue par force retenue court avecq plus d'impetuosité quant on la laisse aller, que celle qui court ordinairement, ainsy ceste pauvre dame tourna sa gloire à la contraincte qu'elle donnoit à son corps. Quant elle vint à descendre le premier degré de son honnesteté, se trouva soubdainement portée jusques au dernier. Et, en ceste nuict là, engrossa de celluy, lequel elle vouloit garder d'engrossir les autres. [1943 edn., 230-31]

In a version of the same story, published contemporaneously (1554) and perhaps derived from Marguerite, perhaps not, Matteo Bandello indulged in speculation about the widow's motive:

> La vedova, o ch'ella fosse disonestamente del vietato amor del figliuolo accesa, o che pure in effetto gli volesse far un gran romore in capo per fargliene una gran vergogna, o che che se ne fosse cagione, . . . si corcò nel letto. . . . Era la vedova assai giovane ancora, di trentuno in trentadui anni, e sentendosi il figliuolo appresso, e in lei destatosi il concupiscibile appetito, quello non como figliuolo ma come caro amante ne le braccia ricevendo, del suo corpo impiamente gli compiacque. [Bandello 1:1020]

> [The widow, whether she had unchastely acceded to a forbidden love of her dear son, or whether in effect she wanted to give him a vertiginous rebuke by administering to him through her action so great a shame—or

> whatever may have been the reason—laid herself in the bed. The widow was still young, in her early thirties, and feeling her son near and carnal desire having arisen in her, receiving him into her arms not as a son but as a cherished lover, she impiously pleasured him with her body.] (My translation)

Note that Bandello shies away from naming her motivation explicitly, but the rest of the passage insists on her desire.

Cazauran has argued persuasively that the incestuous mother was long a trope of sermons about the efficacy of repentance; that perhaps following Luther, Marguerite centered her narrative on the lesson of the need for grace; and that her incestuous mother has nothing of the wicked woman of the pre-Bandello Italian novellae about her. But even as Cazauran argues for the essentially religious message of the text, she underscores its "romanesque" treatment of the story. Marguerite and Bandello would seem to have begun the process of psychologizing religious figures into the three-dimensional characters of Renaissance humanism.

11. Bandello has the widow's confessor, after she has died, tell the queen of Navarre, at whose court the daughter was a lady in waiting, the truth of the incest. The queen insists that they silently allow the young couple, "il marito e moglie, padre e figliuola, fratello e sorella, in buona fede si lasciassero" (1:1022). By giving the decision to a woman, Bandello's story perhaps achieves the same effect Cholakian argues: a woman's allowing this couple to live "in buona fede" marks a feminine intervention, not present in the medieval sermons and satires, that puts them beyond the Law of the Father.

12. Fabrizio's article on "Incest" in *Dictionary of Literary Themes and Motifs* notes several medieval versions of the Oedipus story that emphasize "the love between child-parent and husband-wife" (655). In some Jocasta becomes conscious of incest not through oracles but through the scars on Oedipus's ankles. Cazauran shows how widespread the trope of the incestuous mother is in the homiletic literature of the Middle Ages and how it manifested itself in an unpsychologized version in at least two early Italian novellae. This unpsychologized, two-dimensional figure is thoroughly misogynized. She exhibits conscious, intentional, incestuous lust and thus represents male fears of uncontrolled feminine erotic desire. Since the Renaissance, such conscious desire of a mother for her son has been mostly displaced onto stepmothers, although Cazauran notes a few later versions of the Mysterious Mother story through Horace Walpole's (625) and there are apparently one or two others (see the notes to the 1880 edition of *L'Heptaméron,* 4:283); Rank is aware of some but not all of these (298). Racine's *Phèdre* is, of course, the classic example of stepmother incest during the baroque age, featuring full-blown eroticism just ever so slightly displaced from mother-son incest: even when the mortified Phèdre wants Hippolyte to punish her, she begs that he drive his sword up into her.

13. Hughes himself toward the end of *English Drama* takes good note of similar heroines in satirical plays by Shadwell and Durfey. What interests me about

such figures is not the psychology of their private sex lives but the ideology of their resistance to patriarchy.

14. Clark and the revisionists would have us believe that the Hanoverian monarchs still retained the real power (see Clark, chap. 5). Rowe would not have known that. The point is that he portrays his monarch as limited, constitutional.

15. I have argued in "Female Rebels" that Rowe contrasts Calista with the perfect domestic wife, Lavinia (156-57); nevertheless, it is Calista whom we remember.

16. For a stylistic analysis, see my *Nicholas Rowe and Christian Tragedy* 139.

17. Tumir again provocatively argues for a difference between Otway's absolutist patriarchy and Rowe's more shared version. She sees the form of tragedy itself as containing Calista's "insubordination" (425). But she does not see the potential in the figures of Calista and Altamont that I see, the possibility that Calista—or the figure of liberated woman she adumbrates—may not remain forever "dispossessed," that Altamont—or the figure of enlightened husband he adumbrates—may not remain forever unrealized.

18. In her recent *Ends of Empire,* Brown repeats her earlier characterization of she-tragedies as essentially vehicles for emoting over the victimization of women. She extends her argument to Rowe, whom she sees as adding to the emptiness of Otway, Banks, and Southerne bourgeois moralizing and especially the motif of commodification. Brown thereby sets up a provocative homology between the figures of women in these plays and the social history of middle- to upper-class women, emptied of significance in both material (domestic industry) and symbolic terms and made figures for the acquisitiveness of mercantile capitalist imperialism (chap. 3). While again I admire her project, I am convinced that a great deal can be learned, including much about the ideology of patriarchy and its misogyny, by interpreting the cognitive and not just the affective aspects of these plays.

19. See David Wallace 132 n. 22. Wallace's sociopolitical reading of Lillo's play is the most sophisticated to date, improving vastly on Loftis, *Politics* 125-27, and Brown 157-63, if only because Loftis concentrates solely on the portrayal of the merchant and Brown on the development of form. Wallace avails himself of recent work in social history as well as Marxist and Frankfurt School methodology.

20. Wallace slights the imperialism here, since his concerns, like Brown's, are ultimately generic as well. But Flores, "Mastering the Self," adeptly analyzes the play's ability to displace onto various scapegoats the contradictions within bourgeois ideology, including the rapacity of "England's own colonial exploitation" (94). In *Ends of Empire* (86-88), Brown places *The London Merchant* in the context of her argument that generic transition from heroic play through she-tragedy to bourgeois morality plays is homologous to the transition from a land-based feudal economy to a trade-based bourgeois imperialist economy.

21. See my "Critique of Capitalism and the Retreat into Art in Gay's *Beggar's Opera* and Fielding's *Author's Farce.*"

22. "Dryden's *Cleomenes* (1692) and Contemporary Jacobite Verse." Barbeau-Gardiner reads different subtexts in the play than I. For Falkland and

Rochester's intervention, see the headnote to the California edition. See also Winn 453.

23. Dryden published Creech's translation of Plutarch's *Life of Cleomenes* along with the play (appendix B in the California edition), portraying Cleomenes's precipitate fall from power and his exile in a decadent, luxuriant foreign court (France was often portrayed as Egypt in political poetry and pamphlets of the period), waiting for promised aid to return to his kingdom and to wrest it from the usurper Antigonus. Plutarch portrays a son of Cleomenes so brave he throws himself off the battlements, a detail that allows Dryden the excuse for the portrait of the ideal royal son, Cleonidas, who stands as an explicit model for any such son and an implicit model for the Prince of Wales. Plutarch's narrative also allows Dryden to portray Cleomenes leading a battle (a counterrevolution?) to liberate the oppressed Egyptians and thus have the power to escape, reenter Sparta, and regain his throne. The implications come clearest when the Alexandrians are too timid to join him but stay to see who has the advantage before joining the corrupt statesman, Sosybius. How disappointed Dryden and the Jacobites must have been when all England did not rise along with Ireland to throw off William. Other details of Cleomenes's losing his coregent brother in the war and his being asked to join in a conspiracy against Ptolomy's loyal and popular brother allow Dryden to build into his play a reminder of another king's brother against whom many of them had conspired.

Dryden invents other details for obvious purposes. He has given Cleomenes a "*second Wife*," as he admits in the preface, claiming a slim warrant in Plutarch, the mention of a "*Free-born Woman of* Megalopolis," who greeted Cleomenes in his house upon his return from defeat and well after the death of his first wife (*Works* 16:80). But Cleora, portrayed as a faithful wife, pathetically starved in exile, has great propaganda value, suggesting another queen horribly mistreated by a deceiving Fortune and a disloyal people. Dryden has added the further detail of a newborn infant (one closer in age to the infant James) who cannot get nourishment from his starving mother. Such rhetoric is positively inflammatory, and Dryden—or perhaps William—is lucky that the play did not result in a riot.

24. Vinton Dearing implicitly (and sanctimoniously) responds to this reading as published earlier: "Reaction to plays like *Cleomenes* or to real-life occasions 'when bad things happen to good people' may take two opposite directions. Some persons experience only despair when confronted with a picture of ineluctable evil, whereas others resolve to prevent any further such injustice as much as in them lies" (*Works* 16:357). This is an ethical response to a metaphysical challenge, which Dearing ignores—just as he explicitly ignores my article. Both acts of ignorance are irresponsible.

25. The best treatment of the politics of the late Dryden remains Fujimura. For the theme of the centered self in "To My Honour'd Kinsman" see my "Image of the Circle." And for an elaboration of the argument here see *Word as Bond*, afterword.

26. One detail sticks in my craw: Crowne's Asdrubal tries to marry Hamilcar's daughter (as indeed he did historically). Doesn't this make the villain of the piece a would-be son-in-law, foiled only because the rightful king's daughter ac-

companies him into exile? Might not a Jacobite read something into this detail? Could Crowne, despite his explicit protestations, have remained a crypto-loyalist?

27. The phrase may allude to Dryden's scathingly sarcastic appellation in *Absalom and Achitophel:* "Yet, grant our Lords the People Kings can make" (795).

28. Brown says of the witches, "They and the characters who believe in them are explicitly associated with Toryism, Popery, and the Popish Plot in particular" (107). Staves dismisses them as "merely part of an entertaining operatic and comic spectacle" (309). Neither performs an ideological analysis. Munns, on the other hand, has a fine political reading of the witches and of the play in general in "'The Golden Days of Queen Elizabeth.'" See also Marsden, "Ideology, Sex, and Satire."

29. See Novak and Rodes xvi n. 16.

30. Cf. Ferguson's acute reading of race and miscegenation in Behn (with reference to Southerne).

31. Barthelemy senses the satire: "What better way is there to point out the moral failing of a superior people than to have that group surpassed by a uniquely virtuous member of a supposedly inferior race? This surely is the moral of the closing lines of the play" (178).

32. Von Sneidern, citing Winthrop Jordan, argues that "Imoinda's enslavement is patently absurd" (215 and n. 24), for the enslavement of white women was a great rarity in the West Indies. Yet von Sneidern provides a provocative reading of the way the white body of Imoinda links with the bodies of the Welldons as "priceless possessions" whose exchange needs to be negotiated in a manner to avoid the contamination of the planters (204-19). I do not believe such negotiation is successful.

33. For a reading of *Polly* as a parody of *All for Love,* as a divesting of the old heroic code of love and glory (expressed even in female warrior ballads), and as a deconstruction of European imperialism, see Dugaw, chap. 8.

34. For the way in which Gay's ballad opera simply "dissembles" any *reality* about Indians, see R. Canfield, chap. 1.

Bibliography

Primary Sources

Addison, Joseph. *Cato.* In *British Dramatists from Dryden to Sheridan,* 473-99. Ed. George H. Nettleton and Arthur E. Case. Rev. George Winchester Stone Jr. Boston: Houghton, 1969.

Ashton, Robert. *The Battle of Aughrim; or, The Fall of Monsieur St. Ruth.* Dublin, 1728.

Bailey, Abraham. *The Spightful Sister.* London, 1667.

Bancroft, John. *The Tragedy of Sertorius.* London, 1679.

Bandello, Matteo. *Tutte le opere di Matteo Bandello.* Ed. Francesco Flora. 3d ed. 2 vols. I Classici Mondadori. Verona: Arnoldo Mondadori, 1952.

Banks, John. *Cyrus the Great.* London, 1696.

———. *The Destruction of Troy.* London, 1679.

———. *The Innocent Usurper; or, The Death of the Lady Jane Gray.* London, 1694.

———. *The Island Queens; or, The Death of Mary Queen of Scotland.* London, 1684.

———. *The Rival Kings; or, The Loves of Oroondates and Statira.* London, 1677.

———. *The Unhappy Favourite; or, The Earl of Essex.* London, 1682.

———. *Vertue Betray'd; or, Anna Bullen.* London, 1682.

Behn, Aphra. *The Works of Aphra Behn.* Ed. Janet Todd. 7 vols. Columbus: Ohio State Univ. Press, 1992-96.

Boothby, Frances. *Marcelia; or, The Treacherous Friend.* London, 1670.

Boyle, Roger, earl of Orrery. *The Dramatic Works of Roger Boyle, Earl of Orrery.* Ed. William Smith Clark II. 2 vols. Cambridge: Harvard Univ. Press, 1937.

Cartwright, George. *The Heroick-Lover; or, The Infanta of Spain.* London, 1661.

Cary, Henry, Viscount Faulkland. *The Marriage Night.* London, 1664.

Caryll, John. *The English Princess; or, The Death of Richard the III.* London, 1669.

Chamberlayne, William. *Wits Led by the Nose; or, A Poet's Revenge.* London, 1678.

Clark, William. *Marciano; or, The Discovery.* London, 1663.

Congreve, William. *The Mourning Bride.* In *The Complete Plays of William Congreve,* 317-85. Ed. Herbert Davis. Chicago: Univ. of Chicago Press, 1967.

The Constant Nymph; or, The Rambling Shepherd. London, 1678.

Cooke, Edward. *Love's Triumph; or, The Royal Union.* London, 1678.

Corye, John. *The Generous Enemies; or, The Ridiculous Lovers.* London, 1672.

The Counterfeit Bridegroom; or, The Defeated Widow. London, 1677.

Cowley, Abraham. *A Critical Edition of Abraham Cowley's "Cutter of Coleman Street."* Ed. Darlene Johnson Gravett. New York: Garland, 1987.
Crowne, John. *The Ambitious Statesman.* London, 1679.
———. *Caligula.* London, 1698.
———. *Darius, King of Persia.* London, 1688.
———. *The Destruction of Jerusalem by Titus Vespasian.* London, 1677.
———. *Henry the Sixth; The First Part, with the Murder of Humphrey, Duke of Gloucester.* London, 1681.
———. *The History of Charles the Eighth of France; or, The Invasion of Naples by the French.* London, 1672.
———. *Juliana; or, The Princess of Poland.* London, 1671.
———. *The Misery of Civil-War.* London, 1680.
———. *Regulus.* London, 1694.
Davenant, Sir William. *The Works of Sir William Davenant, Kt.* London, 1673. [Separate pagination for plays.]
[———]. *The Rivals.* London, 1668.
Dryden, John. *Of Dramatic Poesy and Other Critical Essays.* Ed. George Watson. 2 vols. London: Dutton, 1962.
———. *The Works of John Dryden.* Gen. eds. H. T. Swedenberg Jr. and Alan Roper. California Edition. 20 vols. Berkeley: Univ. of California Press, 1956-.
[Duffet, Thomas]. *The Amorous Old-Woman; or, 'Tis Well If It Take.* London 1674.
———. *The Spanish Rogue.* London, 1674.
Durfey, Thomas. *The Banditti; or, A Ladies Distress.* London, 1686.
———. *A Common-Wealth of Women.* London, 1686.
———. *The Injured Princess.* London, 1682.
———. *The Siege of Memphis; or, The Ambitious Queen.* London, 1676.
Etherege, Sir George. *The Comical Revenge; or, Love in a Tub.* In *The Dramatic Works of Sir George Etherege,* 1:1-88. Ed. H. F. B. Brett-Smith. 2 vols. 1927. St. Clair Shores, Mich.: Scholarly Press, 1971.
Fane, Sir Francis. *The Sacrifice.* London, 1686.
The Farce of Sodom; or, The Quintessence of Debauchery. In *Rochester: Complete Poems and Plays,* 125-54. Ed. Paddy Lyons. Everyman's Library. London: J. M. Dent, 1993.
The Fatal Discovery; or, Love in Ruines. London, 1698.
Finch, Anne, countess of Winchilsea. *The Triumphs of Love and Innocence.* In *The Poems of Anne Countess of Winchilsea,* 271-336. Ed. Myra Reynolds. Chicago: Univ. of Chicago Press, 1903.
[Flecknoe, Richard]. *Emilia.* London, 1672.
———. *Erminia; or, The Fair and Vertuous Lady.* London, 1661.
———. *Love's Dominion.* London, 1654.
———. *Love's Kingdom.* London, 1664.
Forde, Thomas. *Love's Labyrinth; or, The Royal Shepherdess.* London, 1660.
[Fountaine, John]. *The Rewards of Virtue.* London, 1661.
Gay, John. *Polly: An Opera. Being the Second Part of the Beggar's Opera.* In *Dramatic Works,* 2:67-146. Ed. John Fuller. 2 vols. Oxford: Clarendon, 1983.

Gould, [Robert]. *Innocence Distress'd; or, The Royal Penitents.* London, 1737.
Greene, Alexander. *The Politician Cheated.* London, 1663.
Harris, James [and William Mountfort]. *The Mistakes; or, The False Report.* London, 1691.
Howard, Edward. *The Change of Crownes.* Ed. Frederick S. Boas. London: Oxford Univ. Press, 1949.
———. *The Women's Conquest.* London, 1671.
Howard, James. *All Mistaken; or, The Mad Couple.* London, 1672.
Howard, Sir Robert. *The Blind Lady.* In *Poems.* London, 1660.
———. *Five New Plays.* London, 1692.
Irena. London, 1664.
Killigrew, Sir William. *Four New Playes.* Oxford, 1666. [Separate pagination.]
Lacy, John. *Sir Hercules Buffoon; or, The Poetical Squire.* London, 1684.
[Leanerd, John]. *The Counterfeits.* London, 1679.
———. *The Country Innocence; or, The Chamber-Maid Turn'd Quaker.* London, 1677.
Lee, Nathaniel. *The Works of Nathaniel Lee.* Ed. Thomas B. Stroup and Arthur L. Cooke. 2 vols. 1954-55. Metuchen, N.J.: Scarecrow, 1968.
Lillo, George. *The London Merchant; or, The History of George Barnwell.* In *The Dramatic Works of George Lillo,* 113-209. Ed. James L. Steffensen. Oxford: Clarendon, 1993.
Maidwell, Lewis. *The Loving Enemies.* London, 1680.
Manley, Delariviere [*sic*]. *Lucius, the First Christian King of Britain.* 1717. Intro. Jack M. Armistead and Debbie K. Davis. Augustan Reprint Society, 253-54. Los Angeles: Clark Library, 1989.
Milton, John. *Complete Poems and Major Prose.* Ed. Merritt Y. Hughes. New York: Odyssey, 1957.
Mountfort, William. *The Injur'd Lovers; or, The Ambitious Father.* London, 1688.
———. *The Successfull Straingers.* London, 1690.
Navarre, Marguerite de [a.k.a. Marguerite de Valois, Marguerite d'Angoulême]. *L'Heptaméron.* Ed. Michel François. Paris: Garnier, 1943.
———. *L'Heptaméron des nouvelles.* Ed. Le Roux de Lincy and Anatole de Montaiglon. 4 vols. Paris, 1880.
———. *Heptameron; or, The History of the Fortunate Lovers.* Trans. Robert Codrington. London, 1654.
Otway, Thomas. *The Works of Thomas Otway: Plays, Poems, and Love Letters.* Ed. J. C. Ghosh. 2 vols. 1932. Oxford: Clarendon, 1968.
[Payne, Henry Neville]. *The Fatal Jealousy.* London, 1672.
———. *The Siege of Constantinople.* London, 1675.
Pordage, Samuel. *The Siege of Babylon.* London, 1678.
Porter, Thomas. *The Villain.* London, 1663.
Ravenscroft, Edward. *The English Lawyer.* London, 1678.
———. *King Edgar and Alfreda.* London, 1677.
———. *Titus Andronicus; or, The Rape of Lavinia.* London, 1687.
Romulus and Hersilia; or, The Sabine War. London, 1683.
Rowe, Nicholas. *The Dramatick Works of Nicholas Rowe, Esq.* 2 vols. 1720. Westmead, Eng.: Gregg, 1971. [Separate pagination.]

Rymer, Thomas. *Edgar; or, The English Monarch.* London, 1678.
Saunders, Charles. *Tamerlane the Great.* London, 1681.
Sedley, Sir Charles. *The Mulberry Garden.* In *The Poetical and Dramatic Works of Sir Charles Sedley,* 1:99-186. Ed. V. de Sola Pinto. 2 vols. London: Constable, 1928.
Settle, Elkanah. *Cambyses King of Persia.* London, 1671.
———. *The Conquest of China by the Tartars.* London, 1676.
———. *The Empress of Morocco.* London, 1673.
———. *Fatal Love; or, The Forc'd Inconstancy.* London, 1680.
———. *The Female Prelate: Being the History of the Life and Death of Pope Joan.* London, 1680.
———. *The Heir of Morocco, with the Death of Gayland.* London, 1682.
———. *Ibrahim the Illustrious Bassa.* London, 1677.
———. *Love and Revenge.* London, 1675.
Shadwell, Thomas. *The Complete Works of Thomas Shadwell.* Ed. Montague Summers. 5 vols. 1927. New York: Benjamin Blom, 1968.
———. *Thomas Shadwell's The Lancashire Witches, and Tegue o Divelly the Irish-Priest: A Critical Old-Spelling Edition.* Ed. Judith Bailey Slagle. New York: Garland, 1991.
Shakespeare, William. *The Complete Works.* Gen. ed. Alfred Harbage. Pelican Text Revised. Baltimore: Penguin, 1969.
Shipman, Thomas. *Henry the Third of France, Stabb'd by a Fryer. With the Fall of the Guise.* London, 1678.
Southerne, Thomas. *The Works of Thomas Southerne.* Ed. Robert Jordan and Harold Love. 2 vols. Oxford: Clarendon, 1988.
[Stapylton, Sir Robert]. *The Step-Mother.* London, 1664.
Steele, Richard. *The Conscious Lovers.* In *The Plays of Richard Steele,* 275-382. Ed. Shirley Strum Kenny. Oxford: Clarendon, 1971.
Tate, Nahum. *Brutus of Alba.* London, 1678.
———. *The History of King Lear.* London, 1681.
———. *The History of King Richard the Second.* London, 1681.
———. *The Ingratitude of a Common-Wealth; or, The Fall of Caius Martius Coriolanus.* London, 1682.
———. *The Loyal General.* London, 1680.
T[hompson], T[homas]. *The English Rogue.* London, 1668.
Timoleon; or, The Revolution. London, 1697.
Trotter, Catherine. *The Fatal Friendship.* In *The Female Wits: Women Playwrights on the London Stage, 1660-1720,* 145-207. Ed. Fidelis Morgan. London: Virago, 1981.
Tuke, Sir Samuel. *The Adventures of Five Hours.* London, 1663.
[Tutchin, John]. *The Unfortunate Shepherd.* London, 1685.
Villiers, George, duke of Buckingham. *The Chances.* London, 1682.
Weston, John. *The Amazon Queen; or, The Amours of Thalestris to Alexander the Great.* London, 1677.
Whitaker, William. *The Conspiracy; or, The Change of Government.* London, 1680.
Wilmot, John, earl of Rochester. *Valentinian.* London, 1685.

Wilson, John. *Andronicus Comnenius.* In *A Critical Old-Spelling Edition of the Plays of John Wilson (1626-1695?),* 405-510. Ed. Kathleen Menzie Lesko. Ph.D. diss., George Washington Univ., 1980.

Secondary Sources

Alssid, Michael W. *Thomas Shadwell.* Twayne's English Authors Series 50. New York: Twayne, 1967.

Althusser, Louis. "Ideology and Ideological State Apparatuses (Notes towards an Investigation)." In *Lenin and Philosophy and Other Essays.* Trans. Ben Brewster. New York: Monthly Review Press, 1971.

Bakhtin, Mikhail M. *The Dialogic Imagination: Four Essays by M. M. Bakhtin.* Ed. Michael Holquist. Trans. Caryl Emerson and Michael Holquist. Austin: Univ. of Texas Press, 1981.

Barbeau, Anne T. (Gardiner). "Dryden's *Cleomenes* (1692) and Contemporary Jacobite Verse." *Restoration: Studies in English Literary Culture, 1660-1700* 12 (Fall 1988): 87-95.

———. *The Intellectual Design of John Dryden's Heroic Plays.* New Haven: Yale Univ. Press, 1970.

Barthelemy, Anthony Gerard. *Black Face Maligned Race: The Representation of Blacks in English Drama from Shakespeare to Southerne.* Baton Rouge: Louisiana State Univ. Press, 1987.

Bhattacharya, Nandini. "Ethnopolitical Dynamics and the Language of Gendering in Dryden's *Aureng-Zebe.*" *Cultural Critique* 25 (1993): 153-76.

Boehrer, Bruce Thomas. *Monarchy and Incest in Renaissance England: Literature, Culture, Kinship, and Kingship.* Philadelphia: Univ. of Pennsylvania Press, 1992.

Braverman, Richard. *Plots and Counterplots: Sexual Politics and the Body Politic in English Literature, 1660-1730.* Cambridge Studies in Eighteenth-Century English Literature and Thought 18. Cambridge: Cambridge Univ. Press, 1993.

———. "The Rake's Progress Revisited: Politics and Comedy in the Restoration." In *Cultural Readings of Restoration and Eighteenth-Century English Theater,* 141-68. Ed. J. Douglas Canfield and Deborah C. Payne. Athens: Univ. of Georgia Press, 1995.

Brown, Laura S. "The Divided Plot: Tragicomic Form in the Restoration." *ELH: A Journal of English Literary History* 47 (1980): 67-79.

———. *Ends of Empire: Women and Ideology in Early Eighteenth-Century English Literature.* Ithaca: Cornell Univ. Press, 1993.

———. *English Dramatic Form, 1660-1760: An Essay in Generic History.* New Haven: Yale Univ. Press, 1981.

Brown, Richard E. "Heroics Satirized by 'Mad Nat. Lee.'" *Papers on Language and Literature* 19 (1983): 385-401.

Bywaters, David. *Dryden in Revolutionary England.* Berkeley: Univ. of California Press, 1991.

Canfield, J. Douglas. "The Authorship of *Emilia:* Richard Flecknoe's Revision of *Erminia.*" *Restoration: Studies in English Literary Culture, 1660-1700* 3 (1979): 3-7.

———. "The Classic Treatment of Don Juan in Tirso, Molière, and Mozart: What Cultural Work Does It Perform?" In *Drama and Opera of the Enlightenment.* Ed. Luis Gámez. Special issue of *Comparative Drama* 31 (Spring 1997): 42-64.

———. "The Critique of Capitalism and the Retreat into Art in Gay's *Beggar's Opera* and Fielding's *Author's Farce.*" In *Cutting Edges: Postmodern Studies in Eighteenth-Century Satire,* 320-34. Ed. James E. Gill. Special issue of *Tennessee Studies in Literature* 37. Knoxville: Univ. of Tennessee Press, 1995.

———. "Female Rebels and Patriarchal Paradigms in Some Neoclassical Works." *Studies in Eighteenth-Century Culture* 18 (1988): 153-66.

———. "The Ideology of Restoration Tragicomedy." *ELH: A Journal of English Literary History* 51 (1984): 447-64.

———. "The Image of the Circle in Dryden's 'To My Honour'd Kinsman.'" *Papers on Language and Literature* 11 (1975): 168-76.

———. "The Jewel of Great Price: Mutability and Constancy in Dryden's *All for Love.*" *ELH: A Journal of English Literary History* 42 (1975): 38-61.

———. "Mother as Other: The Eruption of Feminine Desire in Some Late Restoration Incest Plays." *The Eighteenth Century: Theory and Interpretation.* Special Issue. Ed. Ellen Pollak. 39.3 (1998): 209-19.

———. *Nicholas Rowe and Christian Tragedy.* Gainesville: Univ. Press of Florida, 1977.

———. "Poetical Injustice in Some Neglected Masterpieces of Restoration Drama." In *Rhetorics of Order/Ordering Rhetorics,* 23-45. Ed. Canfield and J. Paul Hunter. Newark: Univ. of Delaware Press, 1989.

———. "*Regulus* and *Cleomenes* and 1688: From Royalism to Self-Reliance." In *English Culture at the End of the Seventeenth Century.* Ed. Robert P. Maccubbin and David F. Morrill. Special issue of *Eighteenth-Century Life* 12, n.s., 3 (November 1988): 67-75.

———. "Royalism's Last Dramatic Stand: English Political Tragedy, 1679-89." *Studies in Philology* 82 (1985): 234-63.

———. "Shifting Tropes of Ideology in English Serious Drama, Late Stuart to Early Georgian." In *Cultural Readings of Restoration and Eighteenth-Century English Theater,* 195-227. Ed. Canfield and Deborah C. Payne. Athens: Univ. of Georgia Press, 1995.

———. "The Significance of the Restoration Rhymed Heroic Play." *Eighteenth-Century Studies* 13 (1979): 49-62.

———. "Thomas Otway." *Dictionary of Literary Biography.* Vol. 80: *Restoration and Eighteenth-Century Dramatists, First Series,* 146-71. Ed. Paula Backscheider. Detroit: Bruccoli Clark Layman/Gale, 1989.

———. *Tricksters and Estates: On the Ideology of Restoration Comedy.* Lexington: Univ. Press of Kentucky, 1979.

———. *Word as Bond in English Literature from the Middle Ages to the Restoration.* Philadelphia: Univ. of Pennsylvania Press, 1989.

Canfield, J. Douglas, and Alfred W. Hesse. "Nicholas Rowe." In *Dictionary of Literary Biography.* Vol. 84: *Restoration and Eighteenth-Century Dramatists, Second Series,* 262-89. Ed. Paula Backscheider. Detroit: Bruccoli Clark Layman/Gale, 1989.

Canfield, Robert Alan. "Renaming the Rituals: Theatralizations of the Caribbean in the 1980s." Ph.D. diss., Univ. of Arizona, 1998.

Cazauran, Nicole. "La Trentième nouvelle de L'*Heptaméron*, ou la méditation d'un 'exemple.'" In *Mélanges de littérature du moyen age au XXe siècle*, 617-52. Collection de l'Ecole Normale Supériuere de Jeunes Filles, no. 10. Paris, 1978.

Cholakian, Patricia Francis. *Rape and Writing in the Heptaméron of Marguerite de Navarre*. Carbondale: Southern Illinois Univ. Press, 1991.

Choudhury, Mita. *Interculturalism and Resistance in the London Theater, 1660-1800: Identity, Performance, Empire*. Lewisburg, Pa.: Bucknell Univ. Press, forthcoming.

Clark, J. C. D. *Revolution and Rebellion: State and Society in England in the Seventeenth and Eighteenth Centuries*. Cambridge: Cambridge Univ. Press, 1986.

DePorte, Michael. "Otway and the Straits of Venice." *Papers on Language and Literature* 18 (1982): 245-57.

Derrida, Jacques. *Dissemination*. Trans. Barbara Johnson. Chicago: Univ. of Chicago Press, 1981.

———. *Of Grammatology*. Trans. Gayatri Chakravorty Spivak. Baltimore: Johns Hopkins Univ. Press, 1976.

Dollimore, Jonathan. *Radical Tragedy: Religion, Ideology, and Power in the Drama of Shakespeare and His Contemporaries*. 2d ed. New York: Harvester Wheatsheaf, 1989.

Dugaw, Dianne. *Warrior Women and Popular Balladry, 1650-1850*. 1989. 2d ed. Chicago: Univ. of Chicago Press, 1996.

Eagleton, Terry. *Criticism and Ideology: A Study in Marxist Literary Theory*. 1976. London: Verso, 1978.

Edmunds, John. "'Timon of Athens' Blended with 'Le Misanthrope': Shadwell's Recipe for Satirical Tragedy." *Modern Language Review* 64 (1969): 500-507.

Ehrenpreis, Irvin. *Acts of Implication: Suggestion and Covert Meaning in the Works of Dryden, Swift, Pope, and Austen*. Berkeley: Univ. of California Press, 1980.

Erskine-Hill, Howard. *Poetry and the Realm of Politics: Shakespeare to Dryden*. Oxford: Clarendon, 1996.

Fabrizio, Richard. "Incest." In *Dictionary of Literary Themes and Motifs, A-J*, 649-55. Ed. Jean-Charles Seigneuret. Westport, Conn.: Greenwood Press, 1988.

Fanon, Frantz. *Black Skin, White Masks*. Trans. Charles Lam Markmann. New York: Grove Weidenfeld, 1967.

Ferguson, Margaret. "News from the New World: Miscegenous Romance in Aphra Behn's *Oroonoko* and *The Widow Ranter*." In *The Production of English Renaissance Culture*, 150-89. Ed. David Lee Miller, Sharon O'Dair, and Harold Weber. Ithaca: Cornell Univ. Press, 1994.

Fisher, Alan S. "Necessity and Winter: The Tragedy of *All for Love*." *Philological Quarterly* 56 (1977): 183-203.

Flores, Stephan P. "Mastering the Self: The Ideological Incorporation of Desire in Lillo's 'The London Merchant.'" *Essays in Theater* 5 (1987): 91-102.

———. "Negotiating Cultural Prerogatives in Dryden's *Secret Love* and *Sir Martin Marall.*" *Papers on Language and Literature* 29 (1993): 170-96.

———. "Orrery's *The Generall* and *Henry the Fifth.*" *Eighteenth Century: Theory and Interpretation* 37 (1996): 56-74.

———. "Patriarchal Politics under Cultural Stress: Nathaniel Lee's Passion Plays." *Restoration and 18th Century Theatre Research* 2d ser. 8 (Winter 1993): 1-28.

Foucault, Michel. *The Order of Things: An Archaeology of the Human Sciences.* 1970. New York: Vintage, 1973.

Freud, Sigmund. "The Uncanny." In *On Creativity and the Unconscious: Papers on the Psychology of Art, Literature, Love, Religion,* 122-61. Ed. Benjamin Nelson. New York: Harper and Row, 1958.

Frye, Northrop. *Anatomy of Criticism: Four Essays.* Princeton: Princeton Univ. Press, 1957.

———. *The Secular Scripture: A Study of the Structure of Romance.* Charles Eliot Norton Lectures, 1974-75. Cambridge: Harvard Univ. Press, 1976.

Fujimura, Thomas J. "Dryden's Changing Political Views." *Restoration: Studies in English Literary Culture, 1660-1700* 10 (1986): 93-104.

Girard, René. *Deceit, Desire, and the Novel: Self and Other in Literary Structure.* Trans. Yvonne Freccero. Baltimore: Johns Hopkins Univ. Press, 1965.

———. *Violence and the Sacred.* Trans. Patrick Gregory. Baltimore: Johns Hopkins Univ. Press, 1977.

Hartsock, Mildred E. "Dryden's Plays: A Study in Ideas." In *Seventeenth Century Studies,* 69-176. 2d ser. Ed. Robert Shafer. Princeton: Princeton Univ. Press, 1937.

Hendricks, Margo. "Civility, Barbarism, and Aphra Behn's *The Widow Ranter.*" In *Women, "Race," and Writing in the Early Modern Period,* 225-39. Ed. Margo Hendricks and Patricia Parker. London: Routledge, 1994.

Hughes, Derek. "Aphrodite Katadyomene: Dryden's Cleopatra on the Cydnos." *Comparative Drama* 14 (1980): 35-45.

———. "Art and Life in *All for Love.*" *Studies in Philology* 80 (1983): 84-107.

———. *Dryden's Heroic Plays.* Lincoln: Univ. of Nebraska Press, 1981.

———. *English Drama, 1660-1700.* Oxford: Clarendon, 1996.

———. "A New Look at *Venice Preserv'd.*" *Studies in English Literature* 11 (1971): 437-57.

———. "The Significance of *All for Love.*" *ELH: A Journal of English Literary History* 37 (1970): 540-63.

———. "The Unity of Dryden's *Marriage A-la-Mode.*" *Philological Quarterly* 61 (1982): 125-42.

Hume, Robert D. *The Development of English Drama in the Late Seventeenth Century.* Oxford: Clarendon, 1976.

———. "The Satiric Design of Nat. Lee's *The Princess of Cleve.*" *Journal of English and Germanic Philology* 75 (1976): 117-38.

Jameson, Fredric. *The Political Unconscious.* Ithaca: Cornell Univ. Press, 1981.

Johnson, Odai. "Rehearsing the Revolution: Radical Theater, Radical Politics in the English Restoration." Newark: Univ. of Delaware Press, forthcoming.

King, Bruce. *Dryden's Major Plays.* Edinburgh: Oliver and Boyd, 1966.
Kristeva, Julia. *Powers of Horror: An Essay on Abjection.* Trans. Leon S. Roudiez. New York: Columbia Univ. Press, 1982.
Kroll, Richard. "Instituting Empiricism: Hobbes's *Leviathan* and Dryden's *Marriage à la Mode.*" In *Cultural Readings of Restoration and Eighteenth-Century English Theater,* 39-66. Ed. J. Douglas Canfield and Deborah C. Payne. Athens: Univ. of Georgia Press, 1995.
Kuhn, Thomas. *The Structure of Scientific Revolutions.* 2d ed. enlarged. *International Encyclopedia of Unified Sciences* 2.2 (1970).
Lacey, Robert. *Robert, Earl of Essex.* New York: Atheneum, 1971.
Loftis, John. *Comedy and Society from Congreve to Fielding.* Stanford Studies in Language and Literature, 19. Stanford: Stanford Univ. Press, 1959.
———. *The Politics of Drama in Augustan England.* Oxford: Clarendon, 1963.
MacCallum, Hugh. "'A Track of Glory': Dryden's *Don Sebastian* and the Tragedy of Heroic Leadership." *Restoration: Studies in English Literary Culture, 1660-1700* 19 (1995): 43-54.
Mack, Maynard. *King Lear in Our Time.* Berkeley: Univ. of California Press, 1965.
McCabe, Richard A. *Incest, Drama, and Nature's Law, 1550-1700.* Cambridge: Cambridge Univ. Press, 1993.
McKeon, Michael. "Marxist Criticism and *Marriage à la Mode.*" *Eighteenth Century: Theory and Interpretation* 24 (1983): 141-62.
———. *The Origins of the English Novel, 1600-1740.* Baltimore: Johns Hopkins Univ. Press, 1987.
———. *Politics and Poetry in Restoration England: The Case of Dryden's "Annus Mirabilis."* Cambridge: Harvard Univ. Press, 1975.
Maguire, Nancy Klein. "Factionary Politics: John Crowne's *Henry VI.*" In *Culture and Society in the Stuart Restoration: Literature, Drama, History,* 70-92. Ed. Gerald Maclean. Cambridge: Cambridge Univ. Press, 1995.
———. *Regicide and Restoration: English Tragicomedy, 1660-1671.* Cambridge: Cambridge Univ. Press, 1992.
Markley, Robert. *Two-Edg'd Weapons: Style and Ideology in the Comedies of Etherege, Wycherley, and Congreve.* Oxford, Clarendon, 1988.
———. "Violence and Profits on the Restoration Stage: Trade, Nationalism, and Insecurity in Dryden's *Amboyna.*" *Eighteenth-Century Life* 22.1 (1998): 2-17.
Marsden, Jean I. "Ideology, Sex, and Satire: The Case of Thomas Shadwell." In *The Cutting Edge: Postmodern Studies in Eighteenth-Century Satire,* 43-58. Ed. James E. Gill. Special issue of *Tennessee Studies in Literature* 37. Knoxville: Univ. of Tennessee Press, 1995.
———. *The Re-Imagined Text: Shakespeare, Adaptation, and Eighteenth-Century Literary Theory.* Lexington: Univ. Press of Kentucky, 1995.
Milhous, Judith, and Robert D. Hume. "Attribution Problems in English Drama, 1660-1700." *Harvard Library Bulletin* 31 (1983): 5-39.
Miller, Nancy K. "Emphasis Added: Plots and Plausibilities in Women's Fiction." *PMLA* 96 (1981): 36-48.
Miller, Rachel A. "Political Satire in the Malicorne-Melanax Scenes of *The Duke of Guise.*" *English Language Notes* 16 (1979): 212-18.

Moore, John R. "Political Allusions in Dryden's Later Plays." *PMLA* 73 (1958): 36-42.

Morrow, Laurie P. "Chastity and Castration in Otway's *The Orphan*." *South Central Review* 2, no. 4 (1985): 31-38.

Munns, Jessica. "'The Golden Days of Queen Elizabeth': Thomas Shadwell's *The Lancashire-Witches* and the Politics of Nostalgia." In *Thomas Shadwell Reconsider'd: Essays in Criticism.* Ed. Judith Bailey Slagle. Special issue of *Restoration: Studies in English Literary Culture, 1660-1700* 20 (Fall 1996): 195-216.

———. *Restoration Politics and Drama: The Plays of Thomas Otway, 1675-1683.* Newark: Univ. of Delaware Press, 1995.

Neumann, Erich. *The Great Mother: An Analysis of the Archetype.* Trans. Ralph Manheim. 2d ed. Princeton: Princeton Univ. Press, 1963.

Nietzsche, Friedrich. *The Birth of Tragedy and the Genealogy of Morals.* Trans. Francis Golffing. Garden City, N.J.: Anchor-Doubleday, 1956.

Novak, Maximillian E., and David Stuart Rodes, eds. *Oroonoko,* by Thomas Southerne. Regents Restoration Drama Series. Lincoln: Univ. of Nebraska Press, 1976.

Nussbaum, Felicity. *The Brink of All We Hate: English Satires on Women, 1660-1750.* Lexington: Univ. Press of Kentucky, 1984.

Nyquist, Mary. "'Profuse, Proud Cleopatra': 'Barbarism,' and Female Rule in Early Modern English Republicanism." *Women's Studies* 24.1-2 (1994): 85-130.

Owen, Susan J. "Interpreting the Politics of Restoration Drama." In *Forms of Authority in the Restoration.* Ed. Paul Hammond. Special issue of *Seventeenth Century* 8.1 (Spring 1993): 67-97.

———. *Restoration Theatre and Crisis.* Oxford: Clarendon, 1996.

Payne, Deborah C. "Patronage and the Dramatic Marketplace under Charles I and II." *Yearbook of English Studies* 21 (1991): 137-52.

Quinsey, Katherine M. "Almahide Still Lives: Feminine Will and Identity in Dryden's *Conquest of Granada.*" In *Broken Boundaries: Women and Feminism in Restoration Drama,* 129-49. Ed. Katherine M. Quinsey. Lexington: Univ. Press of Kentucky, 1996.

Rank, Otto. *The Incest Theme in Literature and Legend.* Baltimore: Johns Hopkins Univ. Press, 1992.

Rothstein, Eric. *Restoration Tragedy: Form and the Process of Change.* Madison: Univ. of Wisconsin Press, 1967.

Sedgwick, Eve Kosofsky. *Between Men: English Literature and Male Homosocial Desire.* New York: Columbia Univ. Press, 1985.

Sloane, Eugene Hulse. *Robert Gould: Seventeenth Century Satirist.* Ph.D. diss., Univ. of Pennsylvania, 1940.

Sorelius, Gunnar. "Shadwell Deviating into Sense: *Timon of Athens* and the Duke of Buckingham." *Studia Neophilologica* 36 (1964): 232-44.

Staves, Susan. *Players' Scepters: Fictions of Authority in the Restoration.* Lincoln: Univ. of Nebraska Press, 1979.

Stroup, Thomas B. "Otway's Bitter Pessimism." In *Essays in English Literature of the Classical Period Presented to Dougald MacMillan.* Ed. Daniel W. Patterson and Albrecht B. Strauss. *Studies in Philology,* extra ser., no. 4 (Jan. 1967): 54-75.

Tanner, Tony. *Adultery in the Novel: Contract and Transgression.* Baltimore: Johns Hopkins Univ. Press, 1979.

Thomas, Susie. "This Thing of Darkness I Acknowledge Mine: Aphra Behn's *Abdelazer; or, The Moor's Revenge.*" *Restoration: Studies in English Literary Culture, 1660-1700* 22 (1998): 18-39.

Thompson, James. "Dryden's *Conquest of Granada* and the Dutch Wars." *Eighteenth Century: Theory and Interpretation* 31 (1990): 211-26.

———. "'Sure I Have Seen That Face Before': Representation and Value in Eighteenth-Century Drama." In *Cultural Readings of Restoration and Eighteenth-Century English Theater,* 281-308. Ed. J. Douglas Canfield and Deborah C. Payne. Athens: Univ. of Georgia Press, 1995.

Todd, Janet. *The Secret Life of Aphra Behn.* 1996. New Brunswick, N.J.: Rutgers Univ. Press, 1997.

———. "Spectacular Deaths: History and Story in Aphra Behn's *Love Letters, Oroonoko,* and *The Widow Ranter.*" In *Gender, Art, and Death.* Cambridge: Polity Press, 1993.

Tumir, Vaska. "She-tragedy and Its Men: Conflict and Form in *The Orphan* and *The Fair Penitent.*" *Studies in English Literature* 30 (1990): 411-28.

Vance, John A. "Antony Bound: Fragmentation and Insecurity in *All for Love.*" *Studies in English Literature* 26 (1986): 421-38.

Vernon, P. F. "Social Satire in Shadwell's *Timon.*" *Studia Neophilologica* 35 (1963): 221-26.

Vieth, David M. "Psychological Myth as Tragedy: Nathaniel Lee's *Lucius Junius Brutus.*" *Huntington Library Quarterly* 39 (1975): 57-76.

von Sneidern, Maja-Lisa. "Figures of Appetite and Slavery from Milton to Swift." Ph.D. diss., Univ. of Arizona, 1997.

Waith, Eugene M. *The Pattern of Tragicomedy in Beaumont and Fletcher.* Yale Studies in English 120. 1952. New Haven: Archon, 1969.

Wallace, David. "Bourgeois Tragedy or Sentimental Melodrama? The Significance of George Lillo's *The London Merchant.*" *Eighteenth-Century Studies* 25 (Winter 1991-92): 123-43.

Wallace, John M. "John Dryden's Plays and the Conception of an Heroic Society." In *Culture and Politics from Puritanism to the Enlightenment,* 113-34. Ed. Perez Zagorin. Berkeley: Univ. of California Press, 1980.

———. "*Timon of Athens* and the Three Graces: Shakespeare's Senecan Study." *Modern Philology* 83 (1986): 349-63.

Weber, Harold. "Carolinean Sexuality and the Restoration Stage: Reconstructing the Royal Phallus in *Sodom.*" In *Cultural Readings of Restoration and Eighteenth-Century English Theater,* 67-88. Ed. J. Douglas Canfield and Deborah C. Payne. Athens: Univ. of Georgia Press, 1995.

———. *The Restoration Rake-Hero: Transformations in Sexual Understanding in Seventeenth-Century England.* Madison: Univ. of Wisconsin Press, 1986.

Wikander, Matthew H. "The Spitted Infant: Scenic Emblem and Exclusionist Politics in Restoration Adaptations of Shakespeare." *Shakespeare Quarterly* 37 (1986): 340-58.

Williams, Aubrey. "The Decking of Ruins: Dryden's *All for Love.*" *South Atlantic Review* 49.2 (1984): 6-18.
Williams, Raymond. *Marxism and Literature.* Oxford: Oxford Univ. Press, 1977.
Winn, James Anderson. *John Dryden and His World.* New Haven: Yale Univ. Press, 1987.

Index

Note: Bold indicates substantive treatement of plays.

abjection. *See under* Kristeva, Julia
absolutism. *See* monarchy, absolute
Addison, Joseph: *Cato,* **160–62,** 165, 166, 169, 171, 192
adulterous father (trope of), 64, 66, 68, 75
aesthetics, x, 4–5
African blacks (blackamoors), 141, 144, 192–96. *See also under* racism; slavery, of Moors; slavery, of sub-Saharan Africans
Althusser, Louis, xv, 2; ideological state apparatuses, xv, 2, 3, 5, 200; interpellation, 200
Alva, duke of, 110
Amazons. *See under* women, tropes of
ambitious queen. *See under* women, tropes of
Anne (Stuart queen of England), 160, 166
Aphrodite. *See under* women, tropes of
Appian of Alexandria, 69
Aristotle, 4, 53, 60, 82
Armistead, Jack M., 150
Arnold, Matthew, x
Ashton, Robert: *Battle of Aughrim, The,* 59
Astell, Mary, 160, 166
atheist (character type), xii, 1, 26, 53, 110, 115, 174, 178
Authority of the Mother. *See under* Kristeva, Julia

Bacon, Francis, 205 n 14
Bailey, Abraham: *Spightful Sister, The,* 208 n 2
Bakhtin, Mikhail M., x, 2, 114, 201 n 1 (introduction); carnival(esque), 133; official discourse, x, xiii, 3, 5, 101, 121, 139, 208 n 14
Bancroft, John: *Tragedy of Sertorius, The,* 54
Bandello, Matteo, 158, 211-12 n 10, 212 n 11
Banks, John, 62, 166, 213 n 18; *Cyrus the Great,* 9; *Destruction of Troy, The,* 205 n 1; *Innocent Usurper, The,* **46-47;** *Island Queens, The,* 27, 166; *Rival Kings, The,* 202 n 3; *Unhappy Favourite, The* (aka *Earl of Essex, The*), 4, **56-57, 58-59,** 142, 166; *Vertue Betray'd,* 27, 166
Barbeau, Anne. *See* Gardiner, Anne Barbeau
Barry, Elizabeth, 168, 186, 210 n 9
Barthelemy, Anthony Gerard, 203 n 13, 203 n 5, 215 n 31
Beaumont, Francis, 114
Behn, Aphra, 93, 110; *Abdelazer,* x, 4, **33-39,** 193; *Dutch Lover, The,* 116; *False Count, The,* 110; *Forc'd Marriage, The,* 209 n 9; *Oroonoko,* 144, 193; *Revenge, The,* 209 n 8; *Rover, The,* 82, 93; *Second Part of the Rover, The,* 93; *Sir Patient Fancy,* 85; *Town-Fopp, The,* **116;** *Widdow Ranter, The,* **141-44;** *Young King, The,* 120
Betterton, Thomas, 145, 210 n 9
between men. *See* Sedwick, Eve Kosofsky
Bhattacharya, Nandini, 202 n 12
Boccaccio, Giovanni: *Il Teseida,* 118
Boehrer, Bruce Thomas, 202 n 9, 205 n 15
Boothby, Frances: *Marcelia,* 209 n 9
Boyne, Battle of, 1, 164
Bracegirdle, Anne, 168
Braverman, Richard, xiv-xv, 20, 57, 125-26, 205 n 15, 209 n 11, 209 n 15, 209 n 17
breeding, 190, 191
Brook, Peter, 90
Brown, Laura, xii, xiii, xiv, xv, 24, 114, 120, 148, 189, 202-3 n 13, 209-10 n 1, 210 n 3, 213 n 18, 213 n 19, 213 n 20, 215 n 28. *See also* empire, romance of
Brown, Richard, 88
Buckingham, George Villiers, duke of, 98; *Chances, The,* 121
Burghers of Calais, 96
Bywaters, David, 204 n 3

Canfield, Robert Alan, 215 n 34
capitalism, 171, 173, 174, 198, 213 n 18
carnival(esque). *See under* Bakhtin, Mikhail M.
Cartwright, George: *Heroick-Lover, The,* 8
Cary, Anthony, Viscount Falkland, 175
Cary, Henry, Viscount Faulkland: *Marriage Night, The,* 9

Caryll, John: *English Princess, The,* 8
Cazauran, Nicole, 212 n 10, 212 n 12
centered being. *See under* stoicism
Chamberlayne, William: *Wits Led by the Nose,* **121**
charity. *See under* Christian values
Charles I (Stuart king of England), 147, 164, 205 n 13
Charles II (Stuart king of England), 2, 6, 9, 33, 43, 76, 112, 117, 118, 124, 127
Chaucer, Geoffrey: *Knight's Tale, The,* 118, 203 n 3; *Wife of Bath's Tale, The,* 159
Chingada, La. *See* Malinche, La
Cholakian, Patricia Francis, 154, 212 n 11
Choudhury, Mita, 202 n 12
Christian values: charity, 19; forgiveness, 22, 24-25, 30, 44, 52, 56, 77, 121, 167; pity, 19; sacrifice, 19, 58, 137
Circe. *See under* women, tropes of
City on the Hill. *See under* Puritans
Civil War (English), 1, 9, 12, 96
Clark, J.C.D., 210 n 1, 213 n 14
Clark, William: *Marciano,* 123-24
Collier, Jeremy: *Short View of the Immorality and Profaneness of the English Stage, A,* 211 n 9
commonwealth (form of government), 12, 32, 41, 54, 96, 118-19, 161, 179-80, 183
Commonwealth period, ix, 59, 125-26, 126-28, 141
Congreve, William: *Mourning Bride, The,* **147,** 152; *Way of the World, The,* 192
"Conqu'ring Crosses" (Christian imperialism), 19, 20, 24, 40, 77, 146
constancy of mind. *See under* stoicism
Constant Nymph, The, 117
contemptus mundi. See under stoicism
Cooke, Edward: *Love's Triumph,* 7, 9
Corey, Katherine, 64
Corneille, Pierre (*also* Cornelian), 6, 20, 22, 71, 152; *Cid, Le,* 20; *gloire,* 22; *Oedipe,* 152
Corye, John: *Generous Enemies, The,* 208 n 2
Counterfeit Bridegroom, The, 209 n 8
Cowley, Abraham: *Cutter of Coleman-Street, The,* 209 n 8
Creech, Thomas, 214 n 23
creoles (plantation class), 143-44, 196
Criseyde. *See under* women, tropes of
Cromwell, Oliver, 76, 77, 125
Crowne, John, 41, 175; *The Ambitious Statesman,* **54,** 204 n 9; *Caligula,* 179, **181-83;** *Darius,* 4, **47-48;** *Destruction of Jerusalem, The,* 205 n 1; *Henry the Sixth,* **42-44,** 54, 204 n 9; *History of Charles the Eighth of France, The,* 202 n 3; *Juliana,* 119; *Misery of Civil-War, The,* **42-44;** *Regulus,* xvi, **179-81**
cultural studies. *See under* theory

dangerous supplement. *See* Derrida, Jacques, supplementing/supplanting
dark woman. *See under* women, tropes of
d'Aubignac, François Hédelin, l'abbé, 2, 199
Davenant, Sir William: *Cruelty of the Spaniards in Peru, The,* 24-25; *History of Sir Francis Drake, The,* 24-25; *Law against Lovers, The,* 209 n 12; *Play-house to Be Let, The,* 24; *Rivals, The,* **118;** *Siege of Rhodes, The,* 6, 7. *See also* Dryden, John, *The Tempest*
Davis, Debbie, 150
Dearing, Vinton, 214 n 24
deconstruction. *See under* theory
de facto government, 6, 12, 23, 46, 152
defiance (also *défiance*), 27, 52, 54, 58, 81, 82-83, 89, 178
defilement, rituals of. *See under* Kristeva, Julia
deism, 40
de jure government, 6, 12
democracy (*also* democratic, undemocratic), xii, xiv, 32, 58, 76, 98, 118, 146, 148-49, 180, 181, 184, 188, 190, 192, 199, 200, 210 n 1
DePorte, Michael, 208 n 13
Derrida, Jacques, x, xiii, xv, 85, 135; *différance,* x, 135; logocentric, the, xiii, 135; *pharmakon,* 99; supplementing/supplanting (dangerous supplement), 1, 20, 24, 54, 58, 78, 82, 85-88, 90, 135-39, 199; *vouloir-dire* (will-to-meaning), 136, 138, 139, 209 n 17
de Sade, Marquis, 159
diamond in the rough, 8, 17. *See also* noble savage
Dickens, Charles: *David Copperfield,* 171
différance. See under Derrida, Jacques

Diggers, 199
discipline and punishment (through farce), 121, 125, 126
Dollimore, Jonathan, 201 n 1 (introduction)
Don Juan (character type). *See under* rake
double standard, 132, 159, 185, 191
Dread Maternal Anarch. *See under* women, tropes of
Dreiser, Theodore, *Sister Carrie,* 169
droit du seigneur, 116
Dryden, John, xii, xiii, 2, 4, 6, 8, 9, 37, 60, 83, 175, 199; *Absalom and Achitophel,* 215 n 27; *All for Love,* xii, xvi, 4, 21, 63-64, **66-75,** 76, 93-94, 101, 142, 166, 167, 196, 209 n 18; *Amboyna,* **110-13;** *Amphitryon,* 178; *Annus Mirabilis,* 147; *Aureng-Zebe,* xv, 4, 7, 8, 9, **20-24,** 30, 39, 54, 105; *Cleomenes,* xvi, **175-79;** *Conquest of Granada, The,* xiv, xv, 4, 7, 8, **10-20,** 24, 30, 37, 52, 130, 136, 146-47, 149, 150, 174, 184, 203 n 13; *Don Sebastian,* 4, **49-53,** 150, 178, 202 n 13; *Duke of Guise, The* (with Nathaniel Lee), **44-46;** *Indian Emperour, The,* 39-40, 77, 198; *Indian Queen, The* (with Sir Robert Howard), 7, 8, 24, 39, 77; *Maiden Queen, The* (*see* Dryden, John, *Secret Love*); *Marriage A-la-Mode,* xiv, xvi, 4, **128-39,** 140, 146, 184-85, 188; *Oedipus,* **55-56,** 105, 152-53, 158; *Rival Ladies, The,* **115-16;** *Secret Love,* 4, **122-23,** 150; *Secular Masque, The,* 179; *Spanish Fryar, The,* **121-22;** *Tempest, The* (with Sir William Davenant), 120, **139-41;** "To My Honour'd Kinsman," 178, 214 n 25; *Troilus and Cressida,* 205 n 1, 206 n 7; *Tyrannick Love,* 27; *Vindication of the Duke of Guise, The,* 46
Duffet, Thomas: *Amorous Old-Woman, The,* 209 n 8; *Spanish Rogue, The,* 208 n 2
Dugaw, Dianne, 215 n 33
Durfey, Thomas, 83, 212 n 13; *Banditti, The,* **117;** *Common-Wealth of Women, A,* **118-19;** *Injured Princess, The,* 120, 208 n 4; *Siege of Memphis, The,* 207 n 9
Dutch republicanism. *See* republicanism, Dutch
Dutch War, Third, 110

Eagleton, Terry, x, xi, xv, 2, 5, 200
East Indies. *See under* Indies
Edmunds, John, 207 n 5, 207 n 8
Edward III (Plantagenet king of England), 96
Edward IV (Yorkist king of England), 163
effeminacy, 52, 61, 64, 76, 100, 106, 176, 181, 202 n 12
egalitarianism, 129-30, 163, 185
Ehrenpreis, Irvin, 204 n 3
Elgin marbles, 171
empire, romance of, xv, 5, 24, 39, 144, 192, 199
ending(s), sense of, 3, passim
Epicurean deities, 51
epistemic shift. *See under* Foucault, Michel
Erskine-Hill, Howard, 204 n 3, 206 n 11
Etherege, Sir George: *Comical Revenge, The,* **125-26;** *Man of Mode, The,* 44, 82, 84, 90, 91-92, 95
Eve. *See under* women, tropes of
Evelina (Frances Burney), 185
Examiner, 150
Exclusion Crisis, xiv, 9, 41, 44, 54, 160
extramarital fidelity, 68-71, 93-95

Fabrizio, Richard, 212 n 12
faithful wife/lover. *See under* women, tropes of
Falkland, Anthony Cary, Viscount. *See* Cary, Anthony, Viscount Falkland
Fall, the, 53
Fane, Sir Francis: *Sacrifice, The,* 203 n 2
Fanon, Frantz, 162
Farce of Sodom, The, 207 n 4
Farquhar, George: *Beaux' Stratagem, The,* 195
Fatal Discovery, The, **152-60,** 200
Fell, Margaret (Fox), 160
Ferguson, Margaret, 209 n 19, 215 n 30
fidelity, extramarital, 68-71, 93-95
Fifteen, The. *See under* Jacobite
Finch, Anne. *See* Winchelsea
Fisher, Alan S., 206 n 10
Fisher, Bishop John, 164
Flecknoe, Richard: *Emilia,* 208 n 4; *Erminia,* 120, 208 n 4; *Love's Dominion,* 121; *Love's Kingdom,* 121-22
Fletcher, John, 114, 117, 118; *Chances, The,* 121; *Pilgrim, The,* 179; *Two Noble Kins-*

men (with Shakespeare?), 118. *See also* Vanbrugh, Sir John
Flores, Stephan, 201 n 2 (chap. 1), 204 n 11, 205 n 3, 208 n 7, 213 n 20
Forde, Thomas: *Love's Labyrinth,* **117-18**
Fortune (goddess Fortuna), 13-14, 28, 62, 66-67, 70, 72, 74, 80, 100, 101, 119, 127, 176, 178
Foucault, Michel, xi, xiii, xv; epistemic shift, 145; power relations, x, xv, 2, 5, 139, 189, 199, 200
Fowles, John: *The French Lieutenant's Woman,* 78
Frankfurt School. *See under* theory
fraternal society, 148, 161, 184; *primus inter pares,* 148, 180, 184
fratriarch, benevolent (trope of), 185, 188
fratricide. *See* parricide
French drama, 6. *See also* Corneille, Pierre; Molière; Racine, Jean
Freud, Sigmund, xi; Oedipus (Oedipal) crisis/rebellion, xi, 4, 20-24, 30-31, 39, 41, 54-58, 62, 65-66, 88, 99, 116, 121, 122, 130, 136, 140, 147, 152, 172, 183, 199, 202 n 12, 204 n 11, 205 n 13, 205 n 15 (*see also* parricide); return of the repressed, xv, 54-58, 140-41, 159, 199, 202 n 12; sado-masochism, 104-10 passim; slips and errors, 156, 157; superego, 20, 88, 124, 158, 167, 188; *unheimlich,* 10, 33-39, 90. *See also* misogyny
friendship, 7, 17, 30, 31, 51, 68, 72, 85, 88, 131-34, 138, 175-76, 183, 197
Frye, Northrop, xi, 3, 114-15
Fujimura, Thomas J., 214 n 25

Gardiner, Anne Barbeau, 175, 202 n 8
Gay, John: *Beggar's Opera, The,* 175, 196; *Polly,* x, **196-98**
gay couple, 123, 125, 127, 128
genocide, 77
George I (Hanoverian king of England), 164, 166
Girard, René, x, xiii, xv, 10, 17, 20, 59, 85, 99, 136, 150; mimetic desire, 54, 138, 150; monstrous double, 10, 19; Oedipus complex, reinterpretation of, 20; rivalry, deadly, xiii, 10-24 passim, 52, 85, 99, 116, 118, 133, 138, 140, 142, 150, 151; sacrificial crisis, 10, 136, 140; twins, 99-101; violence, endless reciprocal, x, 24
Gould, Robert: *Innocence Distress'd,* **152-60**
Greene, Alexander: *Politician Cheated, The,* 208 n 2
Guarini, Battista, 117

Hanover, House of, 164
Harley, Robert, earl of Oxford, 166
Harris, James: *Mistakes, The,* 120, 208 n 4
Hartsock, Mildred E., xiv
Hemingway, Ernest, 53
Hendricks, Margo, 290 n 19
Henry, Patrick, 193
Henry VI (Lancastrian king of England), 42
Henry VIII (Tudor king of England), 164
Hercules: distaff, 100; Herculean hero, 7, 148; poisoned shirt of, 61
heroic romance: rhymed, 6-9, 10-24; unrhymed, 9-10
Hesse, Alfred W., xvi
history, as manifest destiny, 40
history of ideas. *See under* theory
Hobbes, Thomas (*also* Hobbist thought), xiii, xiv, 6, 16, 26, 44, 46, 50, 53, 82, 98, 119, 122; *Leviathan, The,* 6. *See also* de facto government
Hogarth, William: *Marriage à la Mode,* 172, 189
homosocial bonding, 99-110 passim. *See also* Sedgwick, Eve Kosofsky
Howard, Edward: *Change of Crownes, The,* 119; *Women's Conquest, The,* **124-25**
Howard, James: *All Mistaken,* 120-21
Howard, Sir Robert, 6, 83; *Blind Lady, The,* 120-21; *Duke of Lerma, The,* 4, **78-82,** 8; *Vestal Virgin, The,* 26, 78, 202 n 3. *See also* Dryden, John, *The Indian Queen*
Hughes, Derek, xiii, xiv, xv, 3-4, 144, 159, 179, 184, 205 n 2, 206 n 9, 206 n 10, 207 n 2, 207 n 8, 208 n 13, 208 n 7, 209 n 10, 209 n 15, 210 n 9, 212 n 13
human rights, 167, 200
Hume, Robert D., 2, 201 n 1 (chap. 1), 207 n 2, 211 n 9
Hundred Years' War, 96

ideological state apparatuses. *See under* Althusser, Louis

imperialism, 147, 173-74; British, x, xvi, 5, 24-25, 40, 58-59, 110-13, 140-44, 149, 171-72, 196, 199, 202 n 12, 203 n 14, 213 n 18; cultural, 25, 77, 162, 197, 200, 203 n 13, 213 n 20. *See also* genocide; racism
incest, 49, 53, 55, 99, 116, 117, 121-22, 140-41, 152-60, 182, 207 n 4
inconstant woman. *See under* women, tropes of
Indians: American, 24-25, 39-40, 141-44, 173, 196-98 (*see also* racism, against American Indians; slavery, of American Indians); Asian, 25, 111-13
Indies: East, x, 110-13; West, x, 25, 40, 59, 140, 192-98, 215 n 32
individualism, bourgeois, 146, 147
Ireland, x, 58-59, 214 n 23
Irena, 9
Irish, 59, 140, 164. *See also* racism, against Irish; slavery, of Irish
iron law of oligarchy. *See under* oligarchy

Jacobite (adj. as well as noun), 48-49, 151, 162, 163, 175, 179; Fifteen, The, 151, 160, 164, 210 n 8, 214 n 23, 215 n 26
James, duke of York. *See* James II
James II (Stuart king of England), 2, 118, 214 n 23
Jameson, Fredric, xi, xv, 145; ideologemes, 145
jewelry/treasure (trope of transcendent love), 63, 72-74, 101-2, 209 n 18
Job, Book of, 108
Johnson, Odai, 204 n 9
Jonson, Ben, 64, 83
Jordan, Winthrop, 215 n 32
jugement de dieu. See trial by combat
Juvenal, 178

Keats, John, 137
Kelly, Father Edward, 186
Killigrew, Sir William, 6; *Ormasdes,* 8, 114; *Seege of Urbin, The,* 119-20; *Selindra,* 119-20
King, Bruce, 52, 204 n 5, 204 n 7 (chap. 3)
King Billy. *See* William III
Kristeva, Julia, xi, xv, 154; abjection, xi, 156-57; archaic mother, 155; Authority of the Mother, 159; defilement, rituals of, xi, 155, 159-60; phallic mother, 154, 155. *See also* Lacan, Jacques, Law of the Father
Kroll, Richard, 209 n 17
Kuhn, Thomas: paradigm shift, 145, 185, 210 n 1

Lacan, Jacques, x, xv; Law of the Father, 154, 155, 158, 212 n 11; the other (in the context of the Other), x-xi, 33-36, 58-59, 141, 152-60
Lacey, Robert, 205 n 14, 205 n 16, 205 n 17
Lacy, John: *Sir Hercules Buffoon,* 209 n 8
Lady of the Lake. *See under* women, tropes of
Lafayette, Madame de (Marie-Madeleine, comtesse de), 85
land itself, woman as the, 184; England, 7; English colonies, 112, 141, 142; Scotland, 151
Law of the Father. *See under* Lacan, Jacques
Leanerd, John: *Counterfeits, The,* 208 n 2; *Country Innocence, The,* **116-17**
Lee, Nathaniel, 60, 199; *Caesar Borgia,* 207 n 4; *Gloriana,* **60-61;** *Lucius Junius Brutus,* 4, **57-58,** 88, 152, 160; *Massacre at Paris, The,* 204 n 9; *Mithridates,* 4, **55,** 88, 105; *Princess of Cleve, The,* 4, **82-90,** 195; *Rival Queens, The,* 4, **63-66,** 72, 75, 76, 166, 167; *Sophonisba,* 4, 60, **61-63;** *Theodosius,* 205 n 1; *Tragedy of Nero, The,* 207 n 4. *See also* Dryden, John, *The Duke of Guise, Oedipus*
Leigh, Anthony, 109-10
Levellers, 160, 199
Liberia, 193
libertine (character type). *See* rake
libertinism, xii, 13, 50, 82-101 passim, 131-34, 137, 138, 207 n 4
Lillo, George, 166; *The London Merchant,* 169, **171-75,** 192, 200
Lincoln's Inn Fields, 145, 147, 152, 166, 183
Locke, John, 98, 148
Loftis, John, 39, 148, 161, 164, 189, 209-10 n 1, 213 n 19
logocentric, the. *See under* Derrida, Jacques
Logos, xiii, 8, 45, 83, 108, 110, 135-36
London Stage, The, 201 n 1 (chap. 1)
Louis XIV (king of France), 33, 47, 148

love, ennobling power of, 8, 17-18, 32 (*see also* savage ennobled); Platonic 26, 88; transcendent, 16, 21, 37, 62-63, 70-72, 74-75, 88, 140. *See also* jewelry/treasure
loyal general (trope of), xiv, 7, 20, 26, 52, 53, 56, 57, 65, 102, 121, 147
Luther, Martin, 212 n 10

MacCallum, Hugh, 204 n 6
Machiavel (character type), 1, 6, 7, 10, 20, 26-39, 42, 50, 55, 56, 78, 119, 152, 180, 184. *See also* women, tropes of, female Machiavel
Machiavelli, Niccolò, 6, 28, 207 n 4; end justifies the means, 6, 39, 164; *Prince, The,* 6. *See also virtù*
Mack, Maynard, 82
Mad Max and the Thunderdome. See under Road Warrior
Magdalene. *See under* women, tropes of
Maguire, Nancy Klein, xiii-xiv, xv
Maidwell, Lewis: *Loving Enemies, The,* 209 n 12
malcontent (character type), 38, 90, 181
Malinche, La, 77
Malory, Sir Thomas: *Le Morte Darthur,* 36, 37, 139
Manley, Delarivier: *Lucius,* **149-52,** 165, 187, 200
Marguerite de Navarre (queen of), *l'Heptaméron,* 153-56, 158
Markley, Robert, 201 n 1 (introduction), 208 n 15
Marlborough, John Churchill, duke of, 98, 149
Marlowe, Christopher: *Doctor Faustus,* 188
maroon, 25, 193, 196
marriage market, 93-94, 172, 191
Marsden, Jean I., 207 n 6, 207 n 8, 215 n 28
Marshall, Rebecca, 64
martyr plays, 27, 46
Marx, Karl, xi, xiii, 188
Marxism. *See under* theory
Mary I ("Bloody Mary," Tudor queen of England), 164
Mary II (Stuart queen of England), 160, 175
masculinized woman. *See under* women, tropes of
matriarchal(ism), 119, 140, 188, 192, 199
matrilineality, 160, 192
McCabe, Richard A., 202 n 11, 204-5 n 12, 205 n 13, 211 n 9
McKeon, Michael, xiv, 146, 184-85, 201 n 2 (introduction), 209 n 13, 210 n 5
Medea. *See under* women, tropes of
Mediterranean, economic battle over, 38-39
mercenariness, 90-99 passim
meritocracy (*also* merit, meritocratic), 22, 76, 97-98, 146, 148, 152, 172, 185, 189, 200
Milhous, Judith, 201 n 1 (chap. 1), 211 n 9
Miller, Nancy K., 84
Miller, Rachel A., 204 n 2
Milton, John, 52-53, 75-77, 98, 152, 178; *Paradise Lost,* 53, 77, 158, 174, 178; *Ready and Easy Way to Establish a Free Commonwealth, The,* 206 n 11; *Samson Agonistes,* 4, **75-77,** 92, 160; *Second Defence of the English People, The,* 206 n 11
Miner, Earl, 204 n 4
misanthrope, 90-99
miscegenation: between races, 40, 77, 111-12, 141, 144, 194; between classes, 172, 190
misogyny, 15-16, 67, 83, 99-101, 106-7, 110, 161, 164, 167, 174, 175, 212 n 12, 213 n 18
mob. *See* rabble
mobile. *See* rabble
Molière: *Dom Juan,* 89, 90, 207 n 1
Momus, 178-79
monarchy: absolute, 2, 6, 33, 98, 148, 164, 180, 183, 208 n 12; constitutional, 147, 148, 166, 213 n 14; late feudal, Stuart, passim
Monck, General George, 128
Monmouth, James Scott, duke of, 20, 41, 45
Moore, John R., 204 n 3
More, Sir Thomas, 164
Morrow, Laurie P., 99
Mountfort, William: *Injur'd Lovers, The,* 204 n 9; *Successful Straingers, The,* 209 n 12
Mozart, Wolfgang Amodeus, and Lorenzo da Ponte: *Don Giovanni,* 207 n 1
Munns, Jessica, 204 n 10, 208 n 11, 215 n 28
Mysterious Mother (trope of). *See under* women, tropes of

Navarre, Marguerite de. *See* Marguerite de Navarre

Nelson, Admiral Horatio, 149
neoclassicism. *See under* theory
neostoicism. *See under* stoicism
New Criticism. *See under* theory
New Historicism. *See under* theory
New World, 20, 24, 141, 144, 173, 195, 196, 197, 203 n 3
Nietzsche, Friedrich, 82; Will to Power, 17, 20, 82, 90, 190, 208 n 14. *See also virtù*
noble savage, 14, 17, 120, 129, 146. *See also* diamond in the rough; savage ennobled
nominalism, 1, 14, 16, 18, 26, 30, 43, 47, 49, 50, 86-87, 107-10, 115, 119, 120, 130, 134-35, 173, 174, 179, 197
Novak, Maximillian E., 193, 195, 215 n 29
Nussbaum, Felicity, 155
Nyquist, Mary, 205 n 2

obligation, 1, 7, 87
Odysseus (character type), 120
Oedipus (Oedipal) crisis/rebellion. *See under* Freud
official discourse. *See under* Bakhtin, Mikhail M.
Old World, 24, 143, 196, 197
oligarchy, 96, 180, 184; iron law of, 103-4; plutocratic, 200
O'Neill, Hugh (The Tyrone), 58-59, 205 n 16
One Just Man. *See under* stoicism
Original Sin, 53
original sin (of distrust), 12, 53, 122, 178
Orrery, Roger Boyle, earl of, xiii, 6, 7-8; *Black Prince, The,* 202 n 3; *Generall, The,* xiv, 7, 8, 20, 54; *Herod the Great,* 203 n 2; *History of Henry the Fifth, The,* 7-8, 203 n 14; *King Saul,* 205 n 1; *Mustapha,* 4, **29-33,** 105; *Tryphon,* 8; *Zoroastres,* 203 n 2
other (Other). *See under* Lacan, Jacques
Otway, Thomas, xii, xvi, 82, 84, 166, 199, 213 n 17, 213 n 18; *Don Carlos,* 4, **54-55,** 105, 207 n 10; *Fall of Caius Marius, The,* 207 n 10; *Friendship in Fashion,* 82, 85; *Orphan, The,* 4, **99-101;** *Venice Preserv'd,* xvi, **101-10,** 170, 194
Overreacher (character type), 78, 81, 82, 141-42
Owen, Susan J., xiv, xv, 204 n 9

Pamela (Samuel Richardson), 185
paradigm shift. *See under* Kuhn, Thomas
parricide, 1, 20, 22, 24, 30, 39, 55, 72, 105, 121-22, 133, 152, 172, 183, 202 n 10, 205 n 13
parvenu (character type), xii, 83, chap. 6 passim, 141-44
patricide. *See* parricide
patrilinearity (patrilineality), 7, 18, 19, 20, 24, 37, 39, 54, 56, 62, 95, 99, 115, 120, 138, 146, 160, 172, 189
patriot(ism), 185
Payne, Deborah C., 3
Payne, Henry Neville: *Fatal Jealousy, The,* 27; *Siege of Constantinople, The,* 207 n 4
Phaedra, 21. *See also* Racine, *Phèdre*
phallic mother. *See under* Kristeva, Julia
pharmakon. See under Derrida, Jacques
piety, filial, 21-23, 31, 37, 80, 151
pity. *See under* Christian values
Platonic love. *See under* love
Plutarch(an), 74, 95, 175-76, 214 n 23
poetical justice, 3, 53, 78, 178, passim; distributive, 3, 26, 78, 199; folk (communal), 35, 83, 159; retributive, 3, 26, 78, 199
political economy, bourgeois, 172
Pope, Alexander, 150; "A Prologue to *Lady Jane Gray,*" 165; *To a Lady,* 161
Popish Plot, 41, 42, 186
Pordage, Samuel: *Siege of Babylon, The,* 7, 9
Porter, Thomas: *Villain, The,* 27; *Witty Combat, The,* 114
postcolonial. *See under* theory
poststructuralism. *See under* theory
Powell, George, 210-11 n 9
power relations. *See under* Foucault, Michel
pragmatics (*also* pragmatic, pragmatist), x, xii, 5, 72, 115, 121, 123, 125, 137, 138, 140, 166, 195, 199, 209 n 17
primogeniture, 13, 23, 24, 99
primus inter pares. See under fraternal society
Prince of Wales: George, future George II, 164; James Stuart, the Old Pretender, 214 n 23
private (bourgeois fantasy of), 75

Puritans (Saints), ix, 6, 45, 76-77, 126; City on the Hill, 77; Good Old Cause, 96, 141

Quinsey, Katherine M., 202 n 7

rabble, 6, 12, 29, 41, 42-44, 50, 55, 98, 104, 176, 183, 196, 199, 204 n 4
Racine, Jean, 60, 75; *Phèdre,* 21, 157, 202 n 11, 212 n 12
racism: against African blacks (blackamoors), 33-35, 141, 161-62; against American Indians, 24-25, 140-41, 144; against Irish, 58-59, 141, 205 n 17
rake: Don Juan (character type), 82, 89, 90, 91, 99, 120, 173; libertine, xii, 18, 53, 82-90, 91-92, 112, 115-16, 122, 123, 124, 125, 127, 133, 140, 186, 190; reformed, 53, 89, 116, 120, 123, 124, 125, 127, 138
Rank, Otto, 212 n 12
Ravenscroft, Edward: *English Lawyer, The,* 208 n 2; *King Edgar and Alfreda,* 9; *London Cuckolds, The,* 110; *Titus Andronicus,* 297 n 4
Reconquista, La (the Reconquest of Spain from the Moors), 24, 39
Reeves, Anne, 75
regicide. *See* parricide
religious language: parody/perversion of, 50, 87, 88, 133-34
republican(ism), 41, 47, 58, 98, 110, 148, 160, 161, 184, 185, 199, 205 n 15; Dutch, 110
return of the repressed. *See under* Freud
revisionist historians, 5, 200
revolution, right of, 39, 44-45, 103
Richard III (Yorkist king of England), 8, 43
Richardson, Samuel: *Clarissa,* 191
rights of man. *See* human rights
rivalry, deadly. *See under* Girard
Road Warrior, 179
Rochester, John Wilmot, earl of, 84, 89, 207 n 4; "Letter from Artemisa to Chloe," 84; *Valentinian,* **57,** 86
Rochester, Lawrence Hyde, earl of, 175
Rodes, David Stuart, 193, 195, 215 n 29
Rodin, Auguste, 96
Romulus and Hersilia, 9
Rothstein, Eric, 3
Rousseau, Jean Jacques, 185
Rowe, Nicholas, xvi, 213 n 18; *Ambitious Step-Mother, The,* 152; *Fair Penitent, The,* 166, **167,** 173, 174, 200; *Lady Jane Gray,* **164-66,** 169, 200; *Tamerlane,* **147-49,** 161, 165, 169, 193; *Tragedy of Jane Shore, The,* **162-64,** 165, 166, 167, 200
Royalist (*also* Royalists, Royalism), xii, xiv, xv, chap. 3 passim, 125-28, 146, 160, 163, 183, 210 n 1
Rudolph, Archduke (crown prince of Austria), 75
Rymer, Thomas: *Edgar,* 9

sacrifice. *See under* Christian values
sado-masochism. *See under* Freud
Saints, The. *See* Puritans
Saunders, Charles: *Tamerlane the Great,* 9
savage ennobled, 17, 22, 120, 140
Sedgwick, Eve Kosofsky, 149; between men, 58, 99, 110, 148, 174, 205 n 15. *See also* homosocial bonding
Sedley, Sir Charles: *Mulberry Garden, The,* 4, **126-28**
self-control. *See under* stoicism
self-made man. *See under* stoicism
self-made woman. *See under* stoicism
self-reliance. *See under* stoicism
self-sacrifice, 19, 21, 22, 52
Seneca(n), 61, 90, 95, 152, 154; *Oedipus,* 152
Settle, Elkanah, 83; *Cambyses,* 8; *Conquest of China, The,* 8-9; *Empress of Morocco, The,* 26-27; *Fatal Love,* 203 n 1; *Female Prelate, The,* 207 n 4; *Heir of Morocco, The,* 203 n 1, 204 n 9; *Ibrahim,* 202 n 3; *Love and Revenge,* 203 n 1
Shadwell, Thomas, 212 n 13; *Epsom Wells,* 83, 186; *History of Timon of Athens, Man-Hater, The,* xvi, 4, **90-99;** *Lancashire Witches, The,* **185-89,** 190, 200; *Libertine, The,* 82-83, 89, 90, 91; *Royal Shepherdesse, The,* 120, 208 n 4; *Squire of Alsatia, The,* 185; *True Widow, A,* 186; *Virtuoso, The,* 186; *Woman-Captain, The,* 91, 95, 186
Shakespeare, William, xiv, 41-44, 54, 63, 68, 70, 74, 90-99, 101, 117, 118, 207 n 6; *Antony and Cleopatra,* 74, 166, 206 n 6, 206 n 10; *Coriolanus,* 54, 96;

Cymbeline, 118, 208 n 4; *Hamlet,* 37, 108, 118, 182; *2 Henry VI,* 42-43; *3 Henry VI,* 42-43; *King Lear,* 9, 61, 82, 90, 203 n 4; *Macbeth,* 29, 35; *Measure for Measure,* 202 n 7, 209 n 12; *Much Ado about Nothing,* 209 n 12; *Othello,* 27, 34, 73, 203 n 4; *Richard II,* 41; *Richard III,* 28; *Romeo and Juliet,* 10; *Tempest, The,* 120, 139-41, 197; *Timon of Athens,* 90-99 passim; *Titus Andronicus,* 207 n 4. *See also* Fletcher, John, *Two Noble Kinsmen*

she-tragedies, 166, 167, 168, 213 n 18

Shipman, Thomas: *Henry the Third of France,* 203 n 2

Shore, Jane, 44, 162-63. *See also* Rowe, Nicholas, *The Tragedy of Jane Shore*

sic transit gloria mundi (*see* stoicism, tropes of)

Sidney, Sir Philip, 53, 62

sins of the fathers (visited upon the sons), 53, 55, 205 n 12

slavery, 200; of Indians, 25, 140; of Irish, 59, 196; of Moors, 33-39 passim; of sub-Saharan Africans, 144, 192-96; of women, 143, 173, 196, 215 n 32

Sloane, Eugene Hulse, 155, 210-11 n 9

social contract theory, 98, 146, 164, 183

Social Darwinism, 173-74

social justice, 200

Socrates, 184

Sodom. See Farce of Sodom, The

Sophia (Wisdom), 24

Sophocles, 152, 154; *Oedipus Rex,* 101, 152

Sorelius, Gunnar, 98, 207 n 8

Southerne, Thomas, 175, 213 n 18; *Disappointment, The,* 208 n 4; *Fatal Marriage, The,* 166; *Fate of Capua, The,* **183-84;** *Loyal Brother, The,* 9-10; *Oroonoko,* x, **192-96,** 200; *Sir Anthony Love,* 85, 195; *Spartan Dame, The,* **48-49**

Spanish Succession, War of, 148

Spenser, Edmund, 22, 53

Stapylton, Sir Robert: *Step-Mother, The,* 119

Staves, Susan, xii, xiii, xiv, xv, 148, 209-10 n 1, 210 n 4, 215 n 28

Steele, Sir Richard: *Conscious Lovers, The,* 166, **189-92,** 200

stoicism: Christian, 80, 113, 165; Classical, 58, 64-65, 80, 90, 101; neostoicism, 146, 149, 166, 171, 185. *See also* Seneca(n)

—, tropes of: centered being, 149, 164, 178, 202 n 11, 214 n 25; constancy of mind, 101, 149, 161, 164, 169; *contemptus mundi,* 41, 42, 53, 61, 73, 101; endurance, 163, 165, 171; One Just Man (*also* couple), 58, 99, 160, 161, 178, 182, 184, 197; resignation, 178, 197; self-control, 149, 161, 166, 172; self-made man, xiv, 147, 184; self-made woman, 147; self-mastery, 164; self-reliance, 149, 161, 164, 184, 195; *sic transit gloria mundi,* 55, 61, 63

Stroup, Thomas B., 208 n 13

structuralism. *See under* theory

sublation, 8, 16, 19, 137, 139

superego. *See under* Freud

supplementing/supplanting. *See under* Derrida, Jacques

Swift, Jonathan, 150; *Gulliver's Travels,* 97

Tanner, Tony: *Adultery in the Novel,* 139

Tasso, Torquato, 117

Tate, Nahum: *Brutus of Alba,* 203 n 2; *History of King Lear, The,* 9; *History of King Richard the Second, The* (aka *The Sicilian Usurper*), **41-42;** *Ingratitude of a Common-Wealth, The,* 54, 96; *Loyal General, The,* 204 n 9

Terence, 126

theodicy, 169, 177

theory: cultural studies (*also* culturalist criticism, cultural materialism), xv, 201 n 1 (introduction); deconstruction, xiii, 208 n 14; Frankfurt School, xv, 213 n 19; history of ideas, xv; Marxism, 20l n 1 (introduction), 213 n 19; neoclassicism, 2, 60; New Criticism, xiii, xv, 208 n 14; New Historicism, xi, xv, 201 n 1 (introduction); postcolonial, xv, 59; poststructuralism, xv, 208 n 14; structuralism, xv. *See also* Althusser, Louis; Arnold, Matthew; Bakhtin, Mikhail M.; d'Aubignac, François Hédelin, l'abbé; Derrida, Jacques; Eagleton, Terry; Foucault, Michel; Freud, Sigmund; Frye, Northrop; Girard, René; Jameson, Fredric; Kristeva, Julia; Lacan, Jacques; Marx, Karl; McKeon, Michael; Nietzsche, Friedrich; Sedgwick, Eve Kosofsky; Williams, Raymond

Third World, 171, 202 n 13
Thomas, Susie, 203 n 4
Thompson, James, 24, 110, 189-90, 202 n 13, 204 n 7 (chap. 2), 210 n 5
Thompson, Thomas: *The English Rogue,* **124**
Timoleon, 185
Tirso de Molina: *El Burlador de Sevilla,* 89, 90, 207 n 1
Todd, Janet, 209 n 19
Tory(ies), xiv, 150, 151, 152, 204 n 9
trade, 38-39, 57, 96, 110, 111-13, 147, 171, 203 n 14, 203 n 3, 208 n 15, 213 n 20
transnational aristocracy, 40, 48, 111, 193, 195
Trent, Council of, 93
trial (trope), 15, 114, 123, 127, 129, 169-70, 177
trial by combat, 7, 16
Trotter (Cockburn), Catherine: *The Fatal Friendship,* 150, **168-71,** 187, 200
Tukes, Sir Samuel: *Adventures of Five Hours, The,* **115-16**
Tumir, Vaska, 99, 202 n 9, 208 n 12, 213 n 17
Tutchin, John: *Unfortunate Shepherd, The,* 208 n 3
Tyrone, the. *See* O'Neill, Hugh

unheimlich. See under Freud

Vanbrugh, Sir John: *Pilgrim, The,* 179
Vance, John, 72
verbum dei. See Word (of God)
Vernon, P.F., 207 n 7
Vieth, David M., 205 n 15
violence, endless reciprocal. *See under* Girard, René
virtù (concept central to Machiavelli and Nietzsche), 28, 29, 82, 152, 190
von Sneidern, Maja-Lisa, 198, 203 n 4, 207 n 12, 215 n 32
vouloir-dire. See under Derrida, Jacques
vox populi, 48, 50

Waith, Eugene, 114
Wallace, David, 171, 172, 213 n 19, 213 n 20
Wallace, John, 90, 98, 202 n 6
Walpole, Horace: *Mysterious Mother, The,* 211 n 9, 212 n 12
Walpole, Sir Robert, 166, 211 n 9
Weber, Harold, 89, 207 n 2, 207 n 4
Webster, John: *Duchess of Malfi, The,* 150
Wellington, Arthur Wellesley, duke of, 149
West Indies. *See under* Indies
Weston, John: *Amazon Queen, The,* 7, 114
Whig(s), xiv, 96, 118, 148, 149, 151, 162, 164, 185
Whitaker, William: *Conspiracy, The,* 7, 9
white slavery. *See* slavery, of Irish; of women
Wikander, Matthew H., 204 n 1
William III (king of England), 49, **148,** 149, 152, 164, 179, 183, 214 n 23
Williams, Aubrey, 70
Williams, Raymond, xi, xv, 5, 145; dominant tropes, 146, 147; emergent tropes, 146, 147, 185; residual tropes, 191
will-to-meaning. *See* Derrida, Jacques, *vouloir-dire*
Will to Power. *See under* Nietzsche
Wilson, John: *Andronicus Comnenius,* **27-29**
Winchelsea, Anne Finch, countess of: *Triumphs of Love and Innocence, The,* 120, 208 n 4
Winn, James A., 75, 213 n 22
women: feminine desire of, 152-60; traffic in, 93-94, 189 (*see also* marriage market). *See also* extramarital fidelity; land itself, woman as the; matriarch; matrilineality; misogyny; slavery, of women
—, tropes of: Amazons, 118-19, 124-25, 144; ambitious queen, 1, 21, 29-30, 152; Aphrodite, 71; bourgeois wife, 168; cast mistress, 91, 125, 163, 173; Circe, 13, 14; conduit (for succession), 60, 95; (*see also* vessel, *below*); Criseyde, 67; dark woman, 68, 119; domestic woman, 166, 167-69; Dread Maternal Anarch, 13 (*see also* Great Mother, *below*); empowered agent, 165-66, 187-88, 195; Eve, 67; exotic mistress, 64, 72; faithful (constant, etc.) woman, 7, 8, 14-15, 21, 27, 37, 42, 45, 52, 53, chap. 4 passim, 93-95, chap. 6 passim (*see also* Penelope, *below*); female Machiavel (villainess), 7, 8, 26, 39, 56, 175; frontier woman, 143-44; gold digger, 92-93; Great Mother, 188 (*see also* Dread Maternal Anarch, *above*); hypocrite, 83; inconstant woman, 13, 67, 100; incubator, 149; Lady of the Lake

women, tropes of (*cont.*)
(progenitive goddess), 139 (*see also* Malory, Sir Thomas); Magdalene, 27; masculinized woman, 149, 161; matron, 64; Medea, 55, 64, 66; mother as (monstrous, mysterious) other, 21, 35-36, 39-40, 152-60, 212 n 12; Penelope, 14, 21, 120, 202 n 7 (*see also* faithful wife/lover, *above*); phallic mother (*see under* Kristeva, Julia); seductress/temptress (pervertor of genealogy), passim; sign of societal stability, 60; superannuated woman, 192; termagant, 109, 167-69, 173-75; uppity woman, 7, 37, 92, 124, 147, 173, 185, 187-88; vessel, 21, 27, 95, 120, 138, 173, 174; weak woman, 165; Whore with the Golden Heart, 69; wicked stepmother, 21, 29-30, 119, 152; witch, 27, 140, 173, 174, 187-88, 215 n 28
Word (of God), xiii, 42, 49, 52, 110, 115. *See also* Logos
Wycherley, William: *Country Wife, The,* 82

Younger Brother (trope of), xv

Index of Characters

Abdalla (Dryden, *The Conquest of Granada*), 10-19, 147
Abdelazer (Behn, *Abdelazer*), 33-39, 193, 203 nn 4, 5
Abdelmelech (Dryden, *The Conquest of Granada*), 10-19, 147
Abenamar (Dryden, *The Conquest of Granada*), 10-19
Aboan (Southerne, *Oroonoko*), 193-95, 200
Acasto (Otway, *The Orphan*), 99-101
Adam (Milton, *Paradise Lost*), 52, 158
Adorissa. *See* duchess, young
Aecius (Rochester, *Valentinian*), 57
Aelius (Shadwell, *The History of Timon of Athens*), 96
Aeneas (Virgil, *The Aeneid*), 22
Alcara, marquess of. *See* counselor
Alcibiades (Shakespeare, *Timon of Athens*), 91
Alcibides (Shadwell, *The History of Timon of Athens,* 92-99
Alexander the Great (Crowne, *Darius*), 48
Alexander the Great (Lee, *The Rival Queens*), 64-66, 75, 76, 166, 205 n 3
Alexas (Dryden, *All for Love*), 67-72, 206 n 6
Alibech (Dryden, *The Indian Emperour*), 39-40, 198
Alicia (Rowe, *The Tragedy of Jane Shore*), 163, 168
Alithea (Wycherley, *The Country Wife*), 82
Almahide (Dryden, *The Conquest of Granada*), 10-20, 37, 130, 202 n 7
Almanzor (Dryden, *The Conquest of Granada*), xiv, 8, 10-20, 130, 146-47, 150, 184, 202 n 7, 210 nn 3, 4
Almeria (Congreve, *The Mourning Bride*). *See* daughter to King Manuel
Almeria (Dryden, *The Indian Emperour*), 39-40
Almeyda (Dryden, *Don Sebastian*), 49-53, 150
Alonzo (Behn, *Abdelazer*), 37
Alonzo (Dryden, *Don Sebastian*). *See* Dorax
Alphonso (Davenant, *The Siege of Rhodes*), 7
Altamont (Rowe, *The Fair Penitent*), 167, 200, 213 n 17
Altemira (Orrery, *The Generall*), 7
Althea (Sedley, *The Mulberry Garden*), 126-28
Alva, duke of (Robert Howard, *The Duke of Lerma*), 80
Amalthea (Dryden, *Marriage A-la-Mode*), 128-39
ambitious statesman [Constable of France] (Crowne, *Ambitious Statesman*), 54
Andronicus Comnenius (Wilson, *Andronicus Comnenius*), 27-29
Antigonus (Dryden, *Cleomenes*), 176
Antonio (Dryden, *Don Sebastian*), 50, 53
Antonio (Otway, *Venice Preserv'd*), 102-10
Antonio (Payne, *The Fatal Jealousy*), 27
Antony [Marc] (Dryden, *All for Love*), 63, 64, 66-75, 76, 94, 142, 166, 196, 205 n 2, 206 n 6
Antony, Marc (Shakespeare, *Antony and Cleopatra*), 206 n 5
Apemantus (Shadwell, *The History of Timon of Athens*), 97-98
Apemantus (Shakespeare, *Timon of Athens*), 90, 95
Aquilina (Otway, *Venice Preserv'd*), 102-9
Arapsia (*The Fatal Discovery*), 157-58
Arcite (Chaucer, *The Knight's Tale*), 203 n 3
Arcon, prince of Arcadia. *See* prince [Arcon]
Arcos, duke of (Dryden, *The Conquest of Granada*), 10, 12, 18, 146
Aretus (Orrery, *Tryphon*), 8
Argaleon (Dryden, *Marriage A-la-Mode*), 128-39
Ariel (Dryden and Davenant, *The Tempest*), 140
Ariell, Don (Durfey, *The Banditti*), 117
Arminius (Manley, *Lucius*), 150
Arpasia (Rowe, *Tamerlane*), 149, 161, 165, 169
Artabasus (Crowne, *Darius*), 47-48
Asdrubal (Crowne, *Regulus*), 179-80, 214 n 26

Augustus Caesar (Lee, *Gloriana*), 60-61
aunt [Isabella Sealand] (Steele, *The Conscious Lovers*), 191
Aurelia (Etherege, *The Comical Revenge*), 125
Aureng-Zebe (Dryden, *Aureng-Zebe*), 8, 21-24, 31, 202 nn 11, 12
Avaritius (Thompson, *The English Rogue*), 124
Axalla (Rowe, *Tamerlane*), 148-49
Aztec spirits (Dryden, *The Indian Emperour*), 40

Bacon (Behn, *The Widdow Ranter*), 141-43, 196
Bajazet (Rowe, *Tamerlane*), 148-49
Barnwell. *See* uncle
Barnwell, George (Lillo, *The London Merchant*), 169, 171-74
Beatrice (Shakespeare, *Much Ado about Nothing*), 209 n 12
Beaufort (Etherege, *The Comical Revenge*), 125
Beaufort, Cardinal (Crowne, *Henry the Sixth*), 42
Beaumont (Dryden, *Amboyna*), 110-12
Bedamore (Otway, *Venice Preserv'd*), 103
Bedford, duke of. *See* brother to Henry V
Bellamore (Lee, *The Princess of Cleve*), 87-90
Bellfort (Shadwell, *The Lancashire Witches*), 187
Bellgard (Trotter, *The Fatal Friendship*), 168, 170
Bellmour (Behn, *The Town-Fopp*), 116
Belvidera (Otway, *Venice Preserv'd*), 101-8
Benducar (Dryden, *Don Sebastian*), 50-51
Benedick (Shakespeare, *Much Ado about Nothing*), 209 n 12
Benzayda (Dryden, *The Conquest of Granada*), 10, 18, 19, 136
Berengaria. *See* mother
Berino (Gould, *Innocence Distress'd*), 154-56
Bertram (Dryden, *The Spanish Fryar*), 122
Bevil, Sir John (Steele, *The Conscious Lovers*), 189-92
Bevil Junior (Steele, *The Conscious Lovers*), 166, 189-92
Bevill, Lord (Etherege, *The Comical Revenge*), 125
Blanford (Southerne, *Oroonoko*), 193-96
Blount, Martha (Pope, *To a Lady*), 161
Boabdelin (Dryden, *The Conquest of Granada*), 10-19, 202 n 7
Boozer. *See* parvenu councilors
Brightstone, Widow (Sedley, *The Mulberry Garden*), 126-27
brother to Felicia. *See* Bellgard
brother to Henry V [duke of Bedford] (Orrery, *The History of King Henry the Fifth*), 203 n 14
Bruce, Colonel (Etherege, *The Comical Revenge*), 125-26
Brutus, Lucius Junius (Lee, *Lucius Junius Brutus*), 57-58, 88, 160
Bullen, Anna (Banks, *Vertue Betray'd*), 166
Bullingbrook (Tate, *The History of Richard the Second*), 41-42
Bussy (Dryden and Lee, *The Duke of Guise*), 45
butcher (Crowne, *The Misery of Civil-War*), 43
Butler, Lady Elianor (Crowne, *The Misery of Civil-War*), 43-44

Cade, Jack (Crowne, *The Misery of Civil-War*), 43
Cade, Jack (Shakespeare, *2 Henry VI*), 43
Caelia (Payne, *The Fatal Jealousy*), 27
Caesario (Lee, *Gloriana*), 60-61
Caldroon (Robert Howard, *The Duke of Lerma*), 80
Caliban (Dryden and Davenant, *The Tempest*), 140-41
Caliban (Shakespeare, *The Tempest*), 140-41, 197
Caligula (Crowne, *Caligula*), 181-83
Calista (Rowe, *The Fair Penitent*), 167, 173, 174, 200, 213 nn 15, 16
Cambria, prince of (Manley, *Lucius),* 151
Camilla (Otway, *Friendship in Fashion*), 82
Candiope (Dryden, *Secret Love*), 122-23
captain [Driver] (Southerne, *Oroonoko*), 193-96
cardinal [governor of Poland] (Crowne, *Juliana*), 119
Carlos, Don (Otway, *Don Carlos*), 54-55
Cassandra (Dryden, *Cleomenes*), 175-78
Cassius (Crowne, *Regulus*), 181
Castalio (Otway, *The Orphan*), 99-101
Castalio (Trotter, *The Fatal Friendship*), 168-70

Catesby (Rowe, *The Tragedy of Jane Shore*), 163
Cato (Addison, *Cato*), 161-62, 165, 166, 169
Cavarnio. *See* Indian king
Cawwawkee (Gay, *Polly*), 197-98
Celadon (Dryden, *Secret Love*), 123
Celania (Davenant, *The Rivals*), 118
Celia (Lee, *The Princess of Cleve*), 82-84
Celinda (Behn, *The Town-Fopp*), 116
Celona (Southerne, *The Spartan Dame*), 48-49
Cesonia (Crowne, *Regulus*), 180-81
Chamont (Otway, *The Orphan*), 100
Charleloys (Orrery, *The History of King Henry the Fifth*), 7
children to Antony (Dryden, *All for Love*), 64, 68
Cid, Le (Corneille, *Le Cid*), 20
Cimberton (Steele, *The Conscious Lovers*), 190-92
Cimberton, Sir Geoffrey (Steele, *The Conscious Lovers*), 190-91
Clarissa (Richardson, *Clarissa*), 191
Cleandra, Queen (Killigrew, *Ormasdes*), 8
Cleanthes (Dryden, *Cleomenes*), 175-78
Cleombrotus (Southerne, *The Spartan Dame*), 48-49
Cleomenes (Dryden, *Cleomenes*), 175-79
Cleon (Shadwell, *The History of Timon of Athens*), 96
Cleonidas (Dryden, *Cleomenes*), 177-78
Cleopatra (Dryden, *All for Love*), 64, 66-75, 93, 94, 166, 167, 196, 205 n 2, 206 nn 6, 9
Cleopatra (Shakespeare, *Antony and Cleopatra*), 68, 70, 166, 205 n 2, 206 n 5
Cleora (Dryden, *Cleomenes*), 214 n 23
Cleve, prince of (Lee, *The Princess of Cleve*), 83-90
Cleve, princess of (Lee, *The Princess of Cleve*), 85-90
Clèves, la princesse de (La Fayette, *La princesse de Clèves*), 85
Clod (Shadwell, *The Lancashire Witches*), 188, 200
Clorimun (Orrery, *The Generall*), 7, 8
Clytus (Lee, *The Rival Queens*), 64-66
cobbler (Crowne, *The Misery of Civil-War*), 43
Coenus (Dryden, *Cleomenes*), 175-76
Conall, Captain (*The Fatal Discovery*), 159
confessor (Bandello, *Novelle*), 212 n 11
confessor (Robert Howard, *The Duke of Lerma*), 79-80
Constable of France. *See* ambitious statesman
Constantinus (Wilson, *Andronicus Comnenius*), 29
Cordelia (Shakespeare, *King Lear*), 95
Cordelia (Tate, *The History of King Lear*), 9
Cornaro (*The Fatal Discovery*), 157-58
Cornwall, duchess of (Malory, *Le Morte Darthur*), 36
Corso, Alphonso (Dryden and Lee, *The Duke of Guise*), 46
Cortez (Dryden, *The Indian Emperour*), 40, 77
counselor [marquess of Alcara] (Robert Howard, *The Duke of Lerma*), 81
count [Roquelare] (Trotter, *The Fatal Friendship*), 169-70
courtier (Robert Howard, *The Duke of Lerma*), 79
Cozen (Thompson, *The English Rogue*), 124
Cratisiclea (Dryden, *Cleomenes*), 178
Creon (Dryden and Lee, *Oedipus*), 55
Cressida (Dryden, *Troilus and Cressida*), 206 n 7
Crimalhaz (Settle, *The Empress of Morocco*), 26
Cully, Sir Nicholas (Etherege, *The Comical Revenge*), 125
Cydaria (Dryden, *The Indian Emperour*), 40, 77

Dalila (Milton, *Samson Agonistes*), 76-77, 92
Dandalo (*The Fatal Discovery*), 159
Dareing (Behn, *The Widdow Ranter*), 143
Darius (Crowne, *Darius*), 47-48
Darius (Settle *Cambyses*), 8
daughter to Bajazet [Selima] (Rowe, *Tamerlane*), 149
daughter to Hamilcar [Elisa] (Crowne, *Regulus*), 214 n 16
daughter to King Manuel [Almeria] (Congreve, *The Mourning Bride*), 147
dauphin (Crowne, *Ambitious Statesman*), 54
dauphine (Crowne, *Ambitious Statesman*), 54
Decius Magius (Southerne, *The Fate of Capua*), 183-84

Desdemona (Shakespeare, *Othello*), 15
Despayre (Spenser, *The Faerie Queene,* Bk 1), 53
Devil, the (Shadwell, *The Lancashire Witches*), 188
Diana (Sedley, *The Mulberry Garden*), 126-28
Diana, goddess of the hunt (Dryden, *The Secular Masque*), 179
Diana, Lady (Behn, *The Town-Fopp*), 116
Dianet (Dryden, *Aureng-Zebe*), 22
Dickenson, Mother (Shadwell, *The Lancashire Witches*), 188
Diego, Don (Durfey, *The Banditti*), 117
Diver, Jenny (Gay, *Polly*), 196
Dolabella (Dryden, *All for Love*), 67-73, 206 n 6
Dominic. *See* friar
Dom Juan (Molière, *Dom Juan*), 89, 90, 91, 207 n 1
Don ______. *See under second name*
Doralice (Dryden, *Marriage A-la-Mode*), 131-39, 185, 188
Dorax (Dryden, *Don Sebastian*), 50-53
Dorimant (Etherege, *The Man of Mode*), 44, 82, 90, 92
Dorinda (Dryden and Davenant, *The Tempest*), 140
Dorinda (Farquhar, *The Beaux' Stratagem*), 195
Doubty (Shadwell, *The Lancashire Witches*), 187
Driver, Captain. *See* captain
duchess [dowager] (Gould, *Innocence Distress'd*), 154-56
duchess, young [Adorissa] (Gould, *Innocence Distress'd*), 154-56
duke, young [Theodorus] (Gould, *Innocence Distress'd*), 154-56
Dullman (Behn, *The Widdow Ranter*), 144
Dumont. *See* Shore
Du Piere (Durfey, *A Common-Wealth of Women*), 119-20
Dutch governor [Harmon Senior] (Dryden, *Amboyna*), 110-12

Edgar (Ravenscroft, *King Edgar and Alfreda*), 9
Edgar (Tate, *The History of King Lear*), 9
Edmund (Shakespeare, *King Lear*), 203 n 4
Edward of York [future Edward IV] (Crowne, *Henry the Sixth*), 42
Edward of York [future Edvard IV] (Crowne, *The Misery of Civil-War*), 43
Elianor (Lee, *The Princess of Cleve*), 82-84
Elianor, Lady. *See* Butler, Lady Elianor
Elisa. *See* daughter to Hamilcar
Elizabeth, Queen (Banks, *The Unhappy Favourite*), 56, 59, 166
Elvira (Dryden, *The Spanish Fryar*), 122
Emmelin (Manley, *Lucius*), 151
emperor [Shah Jahan] (Dryden, *Aureng-Zebe*), 20-23, 202 n 11
empress [Laula] (Settle, *The Empress of Morocco*), 26
English sailors (Davenant, *The History of Sir Francis Drake*), 24-25
Enriquez (Dryden, *Don Sebastian*), 52
Ephesus, widow of (Petronius, *Satyricon*), 88
Erminia (Thompson, *The English Rogue*), 124
Eromena (*The Fatal Discovery*), 157-58
Esperanza (Dryden, *The Conquest of Granada*), 16
Essex, earl of (Banks, *The Unhappy Favourite*), 56-57, 58-59, 142
Estridge, Ned (Sedley, *The Mulberry Garden*), 127
Eubulus (Dryden, *Marriage A-la-Mode*), 128-39
Eugenia (Payne, *The Fatal Jealousy*), 27
Eugenio (Sedley, *The Mulberry Garden*), 126-28
eunuch [Lycias] (Rochester, *Valentinian*), 57
Eusames (Thompson, *The English Rogue*), 124
Evander (Shadwell, *The History of Timon of Athens),* 91-99
Eve (Milton, *Paradise Lost*), 158
Everyoung, Sir John (Sedley, *The Mulberry Garden*), 126-28

Fancy, Lady (Behn, *Sir Patient Fancy*), 85
father-daughter/brother-sister couple (Marguerite, *L'Heptaméron*), 153-54
father to Calista [Sciolto] (Rowe, *The Fair Penitent*), 167
Favonia (Southerne, *The Fate of Capua*), 184

Felicia (Trotter, *The Fatal Friendship*), 150, 168-70, 187
Ferdinand (Dryden and Davenant, *The Tempest*), 140
Ferdinand, King (Behn, *Abdelazer*), 33-38
Ferdinand, King (Dryden, *The Conquest of Granada*), 12, 19, 24
Fernand, Don (Durfey, *The Banditti*), 117
first player (Gay, *Polly*), 197
Flauntit, Betty (Behn, *The Town-Fopp*), 116
Flavius. *See* steward
Florella (Behn, *Abdelazer*), 33, 37
Florentio (Thompson, *The English Rogue*), 124
Florimel (Dryden, *Secret Love*), 123
Forecast, Sir Samuel (Sedley, *The Mulberry Garden*), 126-28
Frederick, Sir [Frollick] (Etherege, *The Comical Revenge*), 125-26
Fredigond, Queen (Settle, *Love and Revenge*), 203 n 1
friar [Dominic] (Dryden, *The Spanish Fryar*), 122
Friendly (Behn, *The Widdow Ranter*), 141-43

Garcia (Congreve, *The Mourning Bride*), 147
Garcia, Don (Durfey, *The Banditti*), 117
Gertrude, Queen (Shakespeare, *Hamlet*), 37
ghost of Almanzor's mother (Dryden, *The Conquest of Granada*), 18
ghost of husband (*The Fatal Discovery*), 158
ghost of Richard II (Crowne, *The Misery of Civil-War*), 42
Gilford (Banks, *The Innocent Usurper*), 46-47
Giovanni, Don (Mozart and da Ponte, *Don Giovanni*), 207 n 1
Glocester, duchess of (Crowne, *Henry the Sixth*), 42
Glocester, Humphrey, duke of (Crowne, *Henry the Sixth*), 42, 54
Glocester, Humphrey, duke of (Shakespeare, *2 Henry VI*), 42
Gloriana (Lee, *Gloriana*), 60-61
Gloucester, earl of (Shakespeare, *King Lear*), 90
Gonsalez (Congreve, *The Mourning Bride*), 147
Goodvile, Mrs. (Otway, *Friendship in Fashion*), 85
Graciana (Etherege, *The Comical Revenge*), 125
Gramont (Trotter, *The Fatal Friendship*), 168-70, 174
Gray, Lady (Crowne, *The Misery of Civil-War*), 44
Gray, Lady Jane (Banks, *The Innocent Usurper*), 46-47
Gray, Lady Jane (Rowe, *Lady Jane Gray*), 164-66, 169, 200
Grillon (Dryden and Lee, *The Duke of Guise*), 45-46
Guilford (Rowe, *Lady Jane Gray*), 165
Guinivere, Queen (Malory, *Le Morte Darthur*), 37
Guise, duke of (Dryden and Lee, *The Duke of Guise*), 45-46
Guyomar (Dryden, *The Indian Emperour*), 39-40, 198

Haemon (Dryden and Lee, *Oedipus*), 55-56
Hamet (Dryden, *The Conquest of Granada*), 15
Hametalhaz (Settle, *The Empress of Morocco*), 26
Hamilcar (Crowne, *Regulus*), 179-81, 214 n 26
Hamlet (Shakespeare, *Hamlet*), 37, 118, 180
Hannibal (Lee, *Sophonisba*), 61-63
Hannibal (Southerne, *The Fate of Capua*), 183-84
Harapha (Milton, *Samson Agonistes*), 76
Harcourt (Wycherley, *The Country Wife*), 82
Harmon Junior. *See* son to Dutch governor
Harmon Senior. *See* Dutch governor
Harpacus (Davenant, *The Rivals*), 118
Harriet (Etherege, *The Man of Mode*), 92, 95
Hartfort, Sir Edward (Shadwell, *The Lancashire Witches*), 185-89
Hastings, Lord (Rowe, *The Tragedy of Jane Shore*), 163
Hazard (Behn, *The Widdow Ranter*), 143-44
Henry III [of France] (Dryden and Lee, *The Duke of Guise*), 45-46
Henry V (Orrery, *The History of King Henry the Fifth*), 7, 203 n 14

Henry VI (Crowne, *Henry the Sixth*), 42
Henry VI (Crowne, *The Misery of Civil-War*), 42-44
Henry VI (Shakespeare, *2 Henry VI*), 42
Henry VI (Shakespeare, *3 Henry VI*), 42-43
Hephestion (Lee, *The Rival Queens*), 65
Heraclia (Davenant, *The Rivals*), 118
Hermogenes (Dryden, *Marriage A-la-Mode*), 129
Hersilia (*Romulus and Hersilia*), 9
Hippolito (Dryden and Davenant, *The Tempest*), 140
Hippolyte (Racine, *Phèdre*), 212 n 12
Hircan (Marguerite, *L'Heptaméron*), 154, 155
Hirstwood (Dreiser, *Sister Carrie*), 169
Honorius (Manley, *Lucius*), 150-51, 210 n 8
Horatio (Sedley, *The Mulberry Garden*), 127-28
Horatio (Shakespeare, *Hamlet*), 108
Horner (Wycherley, *The Country Wife*), 82
Humphrey (Steele, *The Conscious Lovers*), 190-91

Iago (Shakespeare, *Othello*), 27, 203 n 4
Ianthe (Davenant, *The Siege of Rhodes*), 7
Imogen (Shakespeare, *Cymbeline*), 118
Imoinda (Southerne, *Oroonoko*), 194-96, 215 n 32
Indamora (Dryden, *Aureng-Zebe*), 8, 20-24
Indiana (Steele, *The Conscious Lovers*), 189-92
Indian boy (Dryden and Robert Howard, *The Indian Queen*), 24
Indian chorus (Davenant, *The History of Sir Francis Drake*), 25
Indian girl (Dryden and Robert Howard, *The Indian Queen*), 24
Indian king [Cavarnio] (Behn, *The Widdow Ranter*), 142-44
Indian queen [Semernia] (Behn, *The Widdow Ranter*), 142-44
Indians (Gay, *Polly*), 196-98
Indians (Southerne, *Oroonoko*), 196
infant son (Dryden, *Cleomenes*), 214 n 23
Isabella [Hartfort] (Shadwell, *The Lancashire Witches*), 186-88
Isabella (Shakespeare, *Measure for Measure*), 202 n 7
Isabella, queen of Spain (Behn, *Abdelazer*). *See* queen of Spain [Isabella]
Isabella, queen of Spain (Dryden, *The Conquest of Granada*), 16, 19
Isander (Shadwell, *The History of Timon of Athens*), 96
Isidore (Shadwell, *The History of Timon of Athens*), 96

Jack [Stanmore] (Southerne, *Oroonoko*), 195-96
Jaffeir (Otway, *Venice Preserv'd*), 101-10, 170, 194
Jaspar (Payne, *The Fatal Jealousy*), 27
Job (Book of Job), 108
Job's wife (Book of Job), 108
Jocasta (Dryden and Lee, *Oedipus*), 55, 105, 153
Jocasta (medieval legend), 212 n 12
Johayma (Dryden, *Don Sebastian*), 50
John, Don (Shadwell, *The Libertine*), 82-83, 89, 90, 91
Juan, Don (Tirso, *El Burlador de Sevilla*), 89, 90, 91, 207 n 1
Juba (Addison, *Cato*), 161-62, 171
Julia (Crowne, *Regulus*), 180-81
Julia (Dryden, *Amboyna*), 112
Julia (Dryden, *The Rival Ladies*), 115
Julia (Lee, *Gloriana*), 60-61
Juliet (Shakespeare, *Romeo and Juliet*), 10
Junius (Southerne, *The Fate of Capua*), 184

Katherine, Princess (Orrery, *The History of King Henry the Fifth*), 7
Kent (Shakespeare, *King Lear*), 95
king [Charles VI of France] (Crowne, *Ambitious Statesman*), 54
king [of France] (Trotter, *The Fatal Friendship*), 170
king of Spain [Philip II] (Otway, *Don Carlos*), 54-55
king of Spain [Sancho] (Dryden, *The Spanish Fryar*), 122

Lackitt (Southerne, *Oroonoko*), 195-96
Lackitt, Widow (Southerne, *Oroonoko*), 195-96
Lady of the Lake (Malory, *Le Morte Darthur*), 139
Laertes (Shakespeare, *Hamlet*), 37
Laius (Dryden and Lee, *Oedipus*), 55, 153

Lamira (Trotter, *The Fatal Friendship*), 168-69, 200
Lancashire witches (Shadwell, *The Lancashire Witches*), 187-88, 215 n 28
Laula. *See* empress
Lavinia (Rowe, *The Fair Penitent*), 213 n 15
Lear, King (Shakespeare, *King Lear*), 90
Lear, King (Tate, *The History of King Lear*), 9
legate, papal, of Avignon (Marguerite, *L'Heptaméron*), 153
Leon (Durfey, *The Banditti*), 117
Leonidas (Dryden, *Marriage A-la-Mode*), xiv, 128-39, 146, 184
Leonidas (Southerne, *The Spartan Dame*), 48-49
Leonora, Princess (Behn, *Abdelazer*), 33-38
Leonora, queen of Arragon. *See* queen of Arragon
Lerma, duke of (Robert Howard, *The Duke of Lerma*), 78-82, 86-87
lieutenant goveror [of Surinam] (Southerne, *Oroonoko*), 193-96
Lorenzo (Dryden, *The Spanish Fryar*), 122
Lothario (Rowe, *The Fair Penitent*), 167
Love, Sir Anthony (Southerne, *Sir Anthony Love*), 85, 195
Loveit, Mrs. (Etherege, *The Man of Mode*), 84, 91
Lovis (Etherege, *The Comical Revenge*), 125
loyal general [duke of Vendosme] (Crowne, *Ambitious Statesman*), 54
Lucia (Addison, *Cato*), 161, 165
Lucina (Rochester, *Valentinian*), 57
Lucius (Manley, *Lucius*), 150-52, 210 n 8
Lucy (Etherege, *The Comical Revenge*), 125, 209 n 10
Lucy (Lillo, *The London Merchant*), 172-73
Lycias. *See* eunuch
Lycungus (Settle, *The Conquest of China*), 8
Lyndaraxa (Dryden, *The Conquest of Granada*), 7, 10-19, 146-47, 174, 210 n 4
Lysimachus (Lee, *The Rival Queens*), 66

Macbeth (Shakespeare, *Macbeth*), 29
Macbeth, Lady (Shakespeare, *Macbeth*), 36
Macheath (Gay, *Polly*), 196-98
Machiavelli (Lee, *Caesar Borgia*), 207 n 4
Mad Max (*Road Warrior, Mad Max and the Thunderdome*), 179
maiden queen [of Sicily] (Dryden, *Secret Love*), 122-23, 150
Malfi, duchess of (Webster, *The Duchess of Malfi*), 150
Malicorn (Dryden and Lee, *The Duke of Guise*), 45
Malignii (Porter, *The Villain*), 27
Mamalus (Wilson, *Andronicus Comnenius*), 27-28
Manuel (Wilson, *Andronicus Comnenius*), 28-29
Manuel, King (Congreve, *The Mourning Bride*), 147
Marcellus (Lee, *Gloriana*), 60-61
Marcia (Addison, *Cato*), 161-62, 165, 169
Marcus (Addison, *Cato*), 161
Margaretta (*The Fatal Discovery*), 159, 200
Marguerite (Lee, *The Princess of Cleve*), 84-90
Maria (Lillo, *The London Merchant*), 171-74
Maria (Robert Howard, *The Duke of Lerma*), 78-82
marito, il, e moglie, padre e figliuola, fratello e sorella (Bandello, *Novelle*), 211-12 nn 10, 11
Marmoutiere (Dryden and Lee, *The Duke of Guise*), 45-46
maroon (Davenant, *The History of Sir Francis Drake*), 25
Mars, god of war (Dryden, *The Secular Masque*), 179
Mary, Queen of Scots (Banks, *The Island Queens*), 166
Massina (Lee, *Sophonisba*), 61-63
Massinissa (Lee, *Sophonisba*), 61-63
Maximin (Dryden, *Tyrannick Love*), 27
Maximus (Rochester, *Valentinian*), 57
Medina, duke of (Robert Howard, *The Duke of Lerma*), 79-82
Melantha (Dryden, *Marriage A-la-Mode*), 132-39
Melesinda (Dryden, *Aureng-Zebe*), 21-22
Melissa (Shadwell, *The History of Timon of Athens*, 92-95
Mendozo. *See* prince cardinal
Meroin (Settle, *The Heir of Morocco*), 203 n 1
Micawber (Dickens, *David Copperfield*), 171
Millwood (Lillo, *The London Merchant*), 172-74, 200

Miranda (Dryden and Davenant, *The Tempest*), 139-40
Mithridates (Lee, *Mithridates*), 55, 88, 204 n 11
Modish, Henry (Sedley, *The Mulberry Garden*), 127
Momus (Dryden, *The Secular Masque*), 179
Moneses (Rowe, *Tamerlane*), 149
Monimia (Otway, *The Orphan*), 99-101
Montezuma (Dryden, *The Indian Emperour*), 39-40
Montezuma (Dryden and Robert Howard, *The Indian Queen*), 8
Morano. *See* Macheath
Morat (Dryden, *Aureng-Zebe*), 8, 20-23, 39
Morayma (Dryden, *Don Sebastian*), 50
mother [Berengaria] (*The Fatal Discovery*), 156-58
mufti (Dryden, *Don Sebastian*), 49-51
Muley-Moluch, Emperor (Dryden, *Don Sebastian*), 49-51
Muley-Zeydan (Dryden, *Don Sebastian*), 53
Mustafa (Dryden, *Don Sebastian*), 50
Mustapha (Orrery, *Mustapha*), 29-33, 203 n 3
Myrtle (Steele, *The Conscious Lovers*), 190-91

Navarre, queen of (Bandello, *Novelle*), 212 n 11
negroes (Behn, *The Widdow Ranter*), 144, 193
negroes (Southerne, *Oroonoko*), 193-95
Nemours, duke of (Lee, *The Princess of Cleve*), 82-90
Nicias (Shadwell, *The History of Timon of Athens*), 96
Northumberland, earl of (Banks, *The Innocent Usurper*), 46-47
Northumberland, earl of (Rowe, *Lady Jane Gray*), 164-66
Nottingham, countess of (Banks, *The Unhappy Favourite*), 56-57
Nourmahal (Dryden, *Aureng-Zebe*), 7, 21, 202 n 11

Octavia (Dryden, *All for Love*), 64, 67-71, 94, 167
Octavius (Dryden, *All for Love*), 166
Odmar (Dryden, *The Indian Emperour*), 39-40
Oedipus (Dryden and Lee, *Oedipus*), 55, 152-53
Oedipus (medieval legend), 212 n 12
officer (Otway, *Venice Preserv'd*), 108
Olivia (Sedley, *The Mulberry Garden*), 127-28
Ophelia (Shakespeare, *Hamlet*), 118
Oroonoko (Behn, *Oroonoko*), 193
Oroonoko (Southerne, *Oroonoko*), x, 193-96, 200, 215 n 31
Osmin (Behn, *Abdelazer*), 34-38, 203 n 5
Osmyn. *See* prince of Valencia
Othello (Shakespeare, *Othello*), 27
Ozymn (Dryden, *The Conquest of Granada*), 10, 14, 16, 18, 19, 136

Pacuvius (Southerne, *The Fate of Capua*), 183-84
Palamede (Dryden, *Marriage A-la-Mode*), 131-39, 140
Palamon (Chaucer, *The Knight's Tale*), 203 n 3
Palmer (Etherege, *The Comical Revenge*), 125
Palmyra (Dryden, *Marriage A-la-Mode*), 128-39, 184
Pantheus (Dryden, *Cleomenes*), 176-79
paramour [lady in waiting] (Marguerite, *L'Heptaméron*), 153
parvenu councilors [Whimsey, Whiff, and Boozer] (Behn, *The Widdow Ranter*), 141-44
Perez (Dryden, *Amboyna*), 111-12
Perolla. *See* son of Pacuvius
Peruvians (Davenant, *The Cruelty of the Spaniards in Peru*), 25
Phaeax (Shadwell, *The History of Timon of Athens*), 96
Pharnaces (Lee, *Mithridates*), 55, 88
Phèdre (Racine, *Phèdre*), 157, 202 n 11; (Bandello, *Novelle*), 211-12 n 10, 212 n 12
Philander (Davenant, *The Rivals*), 118
Philander (Sedley, *The Mulberry Garden*), 126-28
Philip, King (Robert Howard, *The Duke of Lerma*), 78-81
Philip, Prince (Behn, *Abdelazer*), 33-39
Phillis (Steele, *The Conscious Lovers*), 190-91, 200

Philo (Wilson, *Andronicus Comnenius*), 28-29
Philocles (Dryden, *Secret Love*), 122-23
Philotis (Dryden, *Marriage A-la-Mode*), 134
Pierre (Otway, *Venice Preserv'd*), 101-10, 170
pirates (Gay, *Polly*), 196-97
Pizarro (Dryden, *The Indian Emperour*), 40
planters (Southerne, *Oroonoko*), 196, 215 n 31
Plot-thrift (Thompson, *The English Rogue*), 124
Plotwell, Lord (Behn, *The Town-Fopp*), 116
poet (Gay, *Polly*), 197
Pohetohee (Gay, *Polly*), 197
Polly (Gay, *Polly*), x, 197-98
Poltrot (Lee, *The Princess of Cleve*), 83-84
Polydamas (Dryden, *Marriage A-la-Mode*), 128-39
Polydore (Otway, *The Orphan*), 99-101
Pontia, Queen (Stapylton, *The Step-Mother*), 119
Portius (Addison, *Cato*), 161
prince [Arcon, prince of Arcadia] (Davenant, *The Rivals*), 118
prince (*The Farce of Sodom*), 207 n 4
prince cardinal [Mendozo] (Behn, *Abdelazer*), 33-38
prince of Cambria (Manley, *Lucius*), 151
prince of Valencia [Osmyn] (Congreve, *The Mourning Bride*), 147
princess (*The Farce of Sodom*), 207 n 4
Priuli (Otway, *Venice Preserv'd*), 101-8, 170
Prospero (Dryden and Davenant, *The Tempest*), 139-40
Ptolomy (Dryden, *Cleomenes*), 175
provost (Davenant, *The Rivals*), 118
Pyrgus (Settle, *Fatal Love*), 203 n 1

Queen Mother (Robert Howard, *The Duke of Lerma*), 78
queen of Arragon [Leonora] (Dryden, *The Spanish Fryar*), 122
queen of England [Margaret] (Crowne, *Henry the Sixth*), 42
queen of England [Margaret] (Crowne, *The Misery of Civil-War*), 44
queen of England (Tate, *The History of Richard the Second*), 42
queen of Hungary (Orrery, *Mustapha*), 30-33
queen of Spain [Isabella] (Behn, *Abdelazer*), 33-38
queen of Spain (Otway, *Don Carlos*), 54-55
Quitazo (Settle, *The Conquest of China*), 9

rabble (Southerne, *The Fate of Capua*), 183-84
Ranter, Widdow (Behn, *The Widdow Ranter*), 143-44
Ratcliffe (Rowe, *The Tragedy of Jane Shore*), 163
rebels (Crowne, *Darius*), 47-48
rebels (Dryden and Lee, *Oedipus*), 55
Regulus (Crowne, *Regulus*), 179-81
Renault (Otway, *Venice Preserv'd*), 103-8
Rhodophil (Dryden, *Marriage A-la-Mode*), 131-39, 140
Rich, Widow (Etherege, *The Comical Revenge*), 125-26
Richard, duke of Gloucester [future Richard III] (Rowe, *The Tragedy of Jane Shore*), 163
Richard II (Tate, *The History of Richard the Second*), 41-42
Richard III (Shakespeare, *Richard III*), 28
Richard of York [duke of Gloucester, future Richard III] (Crowne, *The Misery of Civil-War*), 43-44
Richmond (Caryll, *The English Princess*), 8
Robert, Sir (Leanerd, *Country Innocence*), 116-17
Romeo (Shakespeare, *Romeo and Juliet*), 10
Romulus (*Romulus and Hersilia*), 9
Roquelare, Count. *See* count
Rosalinda (Lee, *Sophonisba*), 61-63
Rosalinda (Manley, *Lucius*), 150-51, 165, 187, 200
Roselia (Durfey, *A Common-Wealth of Women*), 119-20
Rosidore, Count (Lee, *The Princess of Cleve*), 86-87
Roxalana (Davenant, *The Siege of Rhodes*), 7
Roxana (Cooke, *Love's Triumph*), 7
Roxana (Lee, *The Rival Queens*), 64-66
Roxana (Pordage, *The Siege of Babylon*), 7, 9
Roxana (Weston, *The Amazon Queen*), 7
Roxolana (Orrery, *Mustapha*), 29-32
Rustan (Orrery, *Mustapha*), 29-32

Samson (Milton, *Samson Agonistes*), 76-77, 92, 160
Sancho. *See* king of Spain [Sancho]

Satan (Milton, *Paradise Lost*), 52, 174
Sciolto. *See* father to Calista
Scipio (Lee, *Sophonisba*), 61-63
Sealand, Isabella. *See* aunt
Sealand, Lucinda (Steele, *The Conscious Lovers*), 190-92
Sealand, Mr. (Steele, *The Conscious Lovers*), 189-92, 213 n 19
Sealand, Mrs. (Steele, *The Conscious Lovers*), 190-92
Sebastian, Don (Dryden, *Don Sebastian*), 49-53, 178
Sebastian, Don (Durfey, *A Common-Wealth of Women*), 120
Segerdo (*The Fatal Discovery*), 157-58
Selima. *See* daughter to Bajazet
Seliman (Southern, *The Loyal Brother*), 9
Selin (Dryden, *The Conquest of Granada*), 10, 13, 19
Semandra (Lee, *Mithridates*), 55
Semernia. *See* Indian queen
Seraphana (Gould, *Innocence Distress'd*), 154-55
Serapion (Dryden, *All for Love*), 67, 74-75
Serina (Otway, *The Orphan*), 100
Sertorius (Bancroft, *The Tragedy of Sertorius*), 54
Shacklehead, Sir Jeffrey (Shadwell, *The Lancashire Witches*), 186-88
Shacklehead, Lady (Shadwell, *The Lancashire Witches*), 185-88
Shacklehead, Sir Timothy (Shadwell, *The Lancashire Witches*), 185-88
Shah Jahan. *See* emperor
Shore (Rowe, *The Tragedy of Jane Shore*), 163, 200
Shore, Jane (Rowe, *The Tragedy of Jane Shore*), 163, 168, 200
Smerk (Shadwell, *The Lancashire Witches*), 188
soldiers (Crowne, *The Misery of Civil-War*), 43
Solyman (Davenant, *The Siege of Rhodes*), 7
Solyman (Orrery, *Mustapha*), 29-33
son of Dutch governor [Harmon Junior] (Dryden, *Amboyna*), 112
son of Pacuvius [Perolla] (Southerne, *The Fate of Capua*), 184
son of Sir Edward Hartfort. *See* Clod
Sophonisba (Lee, *Sophonisba*), 61-63
Spanish priest (Dryden, *The Indian Emperour*), 40
Spirit (Crowne, *The Misery of Civil-War*), 42-43
St. Andre (Lee, *The Princess of Cleve*), 83-84
Stanmore (Southerne, *Oroonoko*), 195-96
Stanmore, Jack. *See* Jack
Statira (Lee, *The Rival Queens*), 64-66
Statira (Pordage, *The Siege of Babylon*), 9
Stephano (Dryden and Davenant, *The Tempest*), 140
St. Eustace, curate of (Dryden and Lee, *The Duke of Guise*), 45
steward [Flavius] (Shakespeare, *Timon of Athens*), 94-95
Suffolk, duchess of (Banks, *The Innocent Usurper*), 47
Sulla (Bancroft, *The Tragedy of Sertorius*), 54
Susan (Shadwell, *The Lancashire Witches*), 188
Sycorax (Dryden and Davenant, *The Tempest*), 140-41
Syphax (Addison, *Cato*), 162

tailor (Crowne, *The Misery of Civil-War*), 43
Tamerlane (Rowe, *Tamerlane*), 148-49, 165, 193
Tamerlane (Saunders, *Tamerlane the Great*), 9
Tarifa (Dryden, *The Conquest of Granada*), 10, 19
Tarquin (Lee, *Lucius Junius Brutus*), 58
Tawdrey, Sir Timothy (Behn, *The Town-Fopp*), 116
Tegue o Divelly (Shadwell, *The Lancashire Witches*), 186-88
Theagenes [*fils*] (Dryden, *Marriage A-la-Mode*), 129-39
Theagenes [*père*] (Dryden, *Marriage A-la-Mode*), 128-39
Thelamia (Southerne, *The Spartan Dame*), 49
Theocles (Davenant, *The Rivals*), 118
Theodorus. *See* duke, young
Theodosia [Shackelhead] (Shadwell, *The Lancashire Witches*), 186-88
Thorowgood (Lillo, *The London Merchant*), 171-74
Thrasilius (Shadwell, *The History of Timon of Athens*), 96

Tiberius (Lee, *Lucius Junius Brutus*), 58, 88
Timoleon (*Timoleon*), 185
Timon (Shadwell, *The History of Timon of Athens*), 91-99
Timon (Shakespeare, *Timon of Athens*), 90, 95
Titus (Lee, *Lucius Junius Brutus*), 58
Tom (Steele, *The Conscious Lovers*), 190-91, 200
Torrismond (Dryden, *The Spanish Fryar*), 122
Tournon (Lee, *The Princess of Cleve*), 83-90
Towerson (Dryden, *Amboyna*), 110-13, 141
Trincalo (Dryden and Davenant, *The Tempest*), 140-41
Troilus (Dryden, *Troilus and Cressida*), 206 n 7
Trueman (Lillo, *The London Merchant*), 171-74
Truman (Otway, *Friendship in Fashion*), 82
Tryphon (Orrery, *Tryphon*), 8
Tudor, Owen (Orrery, *The History of King Henry the Fifth*), 7

uncle [Barnwell] (Lillo, *The London Merchant*), 172-74

Valencia, prince of. *See* prince of Valencia
Valentine (Otway, *Friendship in Fashion*), 82
Valentinian (Rochester, *Valentinian*), 57
Valerius Asiaticus (Crowne, *Regulus*), 180-81
Vanderbluffe, Lieutenant (Gay, *Polly*), 197
vedova, la (Bandello, *Novelle*), 211-12 nn 10, 11
Vendosme, duke of. *See* loyal general
Ventidius (Dryden, *All for Love*), 66-75, 206 n 6
Venus, goddess of love (Dryden, *The Secular Masque*), 179
Victoria (Sedley, *The Mulberry Garden*), 127-28
vidam [of Chartres] (Lee, *The Princess of Cleve*), 86-90
Villerius (Davenant, *The Siege of Rhodes*), 7
Violante (Dryden, *Don Sebastian*), 52
Virginius (Southerne, *The Fate of Capua*), 184
Vortimer (Manley, *Lucius*), 150-52, 210 n 8

Warwick, earl of (Crowne, *The Misery of Civil-War*), 43-44
Welldon, Charlotte (Southerne, *Oroonoko*), 195-96, 215 n 32
Welldon, Lucy (Southerne, *Oroonoko*), 195-96, 215 n 32
Wellman (Behn, *The Widdow Ranter*), 142-43
Wheadle (Etherege, *The Comical Revenge*), 125
Whiff. *See* parvenu councilors
Whimsey. *See* parvenu councilors
white slaves (Southerne, *Oroonoko*), 196
widow (Marguerite, *L'Heptaméron*), 153-54
Wife of Bath (Chaucer, *The Wife of Bath's Tale*), 159
Wildish, Jack (Sedley, *The Mulberry Garden*), 127-28
Willmore (Behn, *The Rover*), 82
Winchester, bishop of (Rowe, *Lady Jane Gray*), 165
Wishfort, Lady (Congreve, *The Way of the World*, 192
Wolsey (Banks, *Vertue Betray'd*), 27

Xantippus (Crowne, *Regulus*), 179-81

York (Tate, *The History of Richard the Second*), 41-42
Ysabinda (Dryden, *Amboyna*), 111-13

Zanger (Orrery, *Mustapha*), 30-32, 203 n 3
Zarrack (Behn, *Abdelazer*), 34
Zempoalla (Dryden and Robert Howard, *The Indian Queen*), 7, 39
Ziphares (Lee, *Mithridates*), 55, 204 n 11
Zulema (Dryden, *The Conquest of Granada*),

Gramley Library
Salem Academy and College
Winston-Salem, N.C. 27108